T0377234

MARINE POLLUTION CONTROL

LLOYD'S PRACTICAL SHIPPING GUIDES
Series Editor: Peter J. McArthur

LLOYD'S PRACTICAL SHIPPING GUIDES

Series Editor: Peter J. McArthur

Maritime Law

Sixth Edition
Chris Hill

**Risk Management in Port Operations,
Logistics and Supply Chain Security**

*Khalid Bichou, Michel G.H Bell and Andrew
Evans*

Port Management and Operations

Third Edition
Professor Patrick M. Alderton

Port Operations

Planning and Logistics
Khalid Bichou

Steel

Carriage by Sea

Fifth Edition
Arthur Sparks

Introduction to Marine Cargo Management

Second Edition
Mark Rowbotham

ISM Code

*A Practical Guide to the Legal and Insurance
Implications*

Third Edition
Dr Phil Anderson

**Corporate Manslaughter in the Maritime
and Aviation Industries**
Simon Daniels

Shipbroking and Chartering Practice

Eighth Edition
Evi Plomaritou and Anthony Papadopoulos

Marine Pollution Control

Legal and Managerial Frameworks
Iliana Christodoulou-Varotsi

For more information about this series, please visit: www.routledge.com/Lloyds-
Practical-Shipping-Guides/book-series/LPSG

MARINE POLLUTION CONTROL

LEGAL AND MANAGERIAL FRAMEWORKS

ILIANA CHRISTODOULOU-VAROTSI

informa law
from Routledge

First edition published 2018
by Informa Law from Routledge
2 Park Square, Milton Park, Abingdon, Oxon OX14 4RN

and by Informa Law from Routledge
711 Third Avenue, New York, NY 10017

Informa Law from Routledge is an imprint of the Taylor & Francis Group, an Informa business

© 2018 selection and editorial matter, Iliana Christodoulou-Varotsi; individual chapters, the contributors

The right of Iliana Christodoulou-Varotsi to be identified as author of this work has been asserted by her in accordance with sections 77 and 78 of the Copyright, Designs and Patents Act 1988.

All rights reserved. No part of this book may be reprinted or reproduced or utilised in any form or by any electronic, mechanical, or other means, now known or hereafter invented, including photocopying and recording, or in any information storage or retrieval system, without permission in writing from the publishers.

Whilst every effort has been made to ensure that the information contained in this book is correct, neither the author nor Informa Law can accept any responsibility for any errors or omissions or for any consequences arising therefrom.

"Material from the IMO website HYPERLINK "http://www.imo.org" www.imo.org is reproduced with the permission of the International Maritime Organization (IMO), which does not accept responsibility for the correctness of the material as reproduced: in case of doubt, IMO's authentic text shall prevail. Readers should check with their national maritime Administration for any further amendments or latest advice. International Maritime Organization, 4 Albert Embankment, London, SE1 7SR, United Kingdom".

Trademark notice: Product or corporate names may be trademarks or registered trademarks, and are used only for identification and explanation without intent to infringe.

British Library Cataloguing-in-Publication Data
A catalogue record for this book is available from the British Library

Library of Congress Cataloging-in-Publication Data
Names: Christodoulou-Varotsi, Iliana, author, compiler.
Title: Marine pollution control : legal and managerial frameworks / by Iliana Christodoulou-Varotsi.
Description: Abingdon, Oxon [UK] ; New York, NY : Routledge, 2018. | Series: Lloyd's practical shipping guides | Includes index.
Identifiers: LCCN 2017057194 | ISBN 9781138856684 (hbk) | ISBN 9781315709925 (ebk)
Subjects: LCSH: Marine pollution—Law and legislation. | Oil pollution of the sea—Law and legislation. | Waste disposal in the ocean—Law and legislation. | Ships—Waste disposal.
Classification: LCC K3590.4.C49 2018 | DDC 344.04/6343—dc23
LC record available at https://lccn.loc.gov/2017057194

ISBN: 978-1-138-85668-4 hbk
eISBN: 978-1-315-70992-5 ebk

Typeset in Times New Roman
by Apex CoVantage, LLC

CONTENTS

Foreword	xix
Preface	xxi
Author's note and acknowledgements	xxiii
List of figures, graphs and tables	xxvii
Table of cases	xxix
Table of statutes	xxxi
Table of European legislation	xxxiii
Table of conventions and treaties	xxxvii

INTRODUCTORY CHAPTER	MARINE ENVIRONMENT PROTECTION AND SHIPPING REGULATIONS	1
CHAPTER 1	MARINE POLLUTION FROM OIL	31
CHAPTER 2	THE INTERNATIONAL REGULATION, PREVENTION AND MANAGEMENT OF MARINE ENVIRONMENTAL POLLUTION CREATED BY THE OFFSHORE OIL AND GAS INDUSTRY *Wylie Spicer, Q.C. and Peter L'Esperance*	57
CHAPTER 3	MARINE OIL POLLUTION IN THE UNITED STATES OF AMERICA: A FRAMEWORK FOR PREVENTION AND RESPONSE TO MARINE OIL POLLUTION INCIDENTS *Antonio Rodriguez and Jake Rodriguez*	95
CHAPTER 4	MARINE POLLUTION FROM SEWAGE	107
CHAPTER 5	MARINE POLLUTION FROM WASTES	125

CONTENTS

CHAPTER 6   FRAMEWORKS GOVERNING MARINE POLLUTION
FROM THE TRANSPORTATION OF CHEMICALS
BY SEA   155

CHAPTER 7   AIR POLLUTION FROM SHIPPING   179

CHAPTER 8   OTHER SOURCES OF MARINE POLLUTION:
BALLAST WATER, HARMFUL SUBSTANCES
IN ANTI-FOULING SYSTEMS, SHIP-BREAKING
ACTIVITIES AND OTHER   205

CHAPTER 9   PREPAREDNESS, RESPONSE, AND COOPERATION
IN THE CONTEXT OF MARINE POLLUTION   233

CHAPTER 10   THE CONTRIBUTION OF THE HUMAN ELEMENT
TO MARINE POLLUTION CONTROL   261

CHAPTER 11   LEGAL ASPECTS OF MARINE POLLUTION FROM
SHIPS   295

Index   335

DETAILED CONTENTS

Foreword	xix
Preface	xxi
Author's note and acknowledgements	xxiii
List of figures, graphs and tables	xxvii
Table of cases	xxix
Table of statutes	xxxi
Table of European legislation	xxxiii
Table of conventions and treaties	xxxvii

INTRODUCTORY CHAPTER	MARINE ENVIRONMENT PROTECTION AND SHIPPING REGULATIONS	1
Section 1	Shipping, the environment and the international standard-setting process	2
0.1	Setting the scene	2
0.2	The nature of the standard-setting process	3
0.3	The four pillars of shipping legislation	5
0.4	The role of the International Maritime Organisation	5
	0.4.1 Description, including structure	5
	0.4.2 The adoption of conventions	7
	0.4.3 Typology of IMO acts	9
0.5	Overview of marine pollution control regulatory framework	10
Section 2	The United Nations Convention on the Law of the Sea (UNCLOS III) and key stakeholders	11
0.6	The role of flag States, coastal States and port States	11
	0.6.1 The United Nations Convention on the Law of the Sea (UNCLOS III)	11
	0.6.2 UNCLOS III and marine environment protection viewed from the standpoint of flag States, coastal States and port States	13
	0.6.3 How does UNCLOS III reach private operators?	19
0.7	The contribution of classification societies	20
0.8	The contribution of the European Union	21
	0.8.1 How do EU acts reach private operators?	23
	0.8.2 The future of the EU agenda on marine pollution	24

DETAILED CONTENTS

0.9	The contribution of non-governmental organisations	25
	0.9.1 Industry Best practices	26
	0.9.2 International Organisation for Standardisation	26
Section 3	Where are environmental regulations impacting on shipping heading for?	26
0.10	Where do we stand at present?	26
0.11	Identifying possible drivers for the future	27
Bibliography		28

CHAPTER 1   MARINE POLLUTION FROM OIL   31

Section 1	Identifying the subject area	32
1.1	General discussion – challenges relating to marine pollution by oil	32
	1.1.1 Pollution by oil and Port State Control findings	38
1.2	Key terms/definitions	39
Section 2	Main discussion of the regulatory framework (MARPOL Annex I)	41
1.3	Overview of the legal basis	41
1.4	Structure of the Annex I	42
1.5	Key resolutions (non-exhaustive list)	42
1.6	Construction requirements	44
1.7	Protection of fuel oil tanks	44
1.8	Control of operational discharges of oil from machinery spaces	45
1.9	Discharges from the cargo area of oil tankers	46
Section 3	Key management issues, including documentation	46
1.10	Surveys and certification	46
	1.10.1 Shipboard Oil Pollution Emergency Plan	47
	1.10.2 Oil Record Book	47
	1.10.3 International Oil Pollution Prevention Certificate	48
1.11	Relevance of the International Safety Management Code	48
1.12	Industry best practices	49
Section 4	Areas of special interest	50
1.13	Ship-to-ship transfer of crude oil and petroleum products	50
1.14	Recent developments: oil tankers operations in ice-covered waters (the Polar Code)	51
Section 5	Selected aspects concerning implementation and enforcement	52
1.15	Selected highlights on national jurisdictions	52
Bibliography		55

viii

DETAILED CONTENTS

CHAPTER 2   THE INTERNATIONAL REGULATION, PREVENTION AND MANAGEMENT OF MARINE ENVIRONMENTAL POLLUTION CREATED BY THE OFFSHORE OIL AND GAS INDUSTRY   57
Wylie Spicer, Q.C. and Peter L'Esperance

Section 1	The offshore oil and gas industry as a source of marine environmental pollution	58
2.1	The offshore oil and gas industry as a source of marine environmental pollution	59
2.2	Contextualising the problem: the offshore oil and gas industry's relative contribution to marine environmental pollution	60
2.3	Regulating marine environmental pollution from the offshore oil and gas industry	60
Section 2	Specific sources of marine pollution from offshore oil and gas operations	63
2.4	Pollution from seabed activities	64
2.4.1	Oil	64
2.4.2	Drilling fluid	64
2.4.3	Drill cuttings	65
2.4.4	Produced water	65
2.4.5	Chemicals	66
2.4.6	Sound production	66
2.4.7	Other sources	66
2.5	Pollution by dumping	67
2.6	Pollution from vessels	67
2.7	Atmospheric pollution	67
Section 3	International law and policy	68
2.8	International legal framework	68
2.8.1	Customary international law	69
2.8.2	1958 Geneva Conventions	69
2.8.3	*UNCLOS III*	70
2.8.3.1	State obligations to protect and preserve the marine environment	71
2.8.3.2	State obligations to regulate pollution from seabed activities	72
2.8.3.3	State obligations to regulate dumping	72
2.8.3.4	State obligations to regulate pollution from or through the atmosphere	74
2.8.3.5	State obligations to regulate pollution from activities carried out in the area	75

ix

DETAILED CONTENTS

2.9		International instruments addressing specific pollution sources	75
	2.9.1	*MARPOL 73/78*	75
		2.9.1.1 Annex I: regulations for the prevention of pollution by oil	76
		2.9.1.2 Annex V: regulations for the prevention of pollution by garbage from ships	79
		2.9.1.3 Annex VI: regulations for the prevention of air pollution by ships	80
	2.9.2	*London Convention, 1972*	81
	2.9.3	*1996 Protocol to the London Convention, 1972*	82
2.10		International instruments addressing liability, clean-up and compensation for environmental damage	83
	2.10.1	*UNCLOS III*	83
	2.10.2	*The 1974 Offshore Pollution Liability Agreement*	84
	2.10.3	*Convention on Civil Liability for Oil Pollution Damage resulting from Exploration for and Exploitation of Seabed Mineral Resources, 1977*	85
	2.10.4	*1990 International Convention on Oil Pollution Preparedness, Response and Cooperation*	85
2.11		International policy statements	86
	2.11.1	United Nations Conference on the Environment and Development Rio Declaration	86
	2.11.2	United Nations Environment Programme	87
	2.11.3	*Convention on Environmental Impact Assessment in a Transboundary Context*	88
	2.11.4	*2003 Protocol on Strategic Environmental Assessment*	89
2.12		Select regional agreements	89
	2.12.1	*OSPAR Convention*	89
Section 4		Conclusions	90
2.13		Limits of the international legal framework	90
2.14		Future directions	92
Bibliography			93

CHAPTER 3	MARINE OIL POLLUTION IN THE UNITED STATES OF AMERICA: A FRAMEWORK FOR PREVENTION AND RESPONSE TO MARINE OIL POLLUTION INCIDENTS	95
	Antonio Rodriguez and Jake Rodriguez	
Section 1	The Oil Pollution Act of 1990 and the Clean Water Act	95
3.1	Introduction	95
3.2	Civil liability	96
3.3	Financial responsibility	98

DETAILED CONTENTS

Section 2	Prevention of pollution	99
3.4	Vessel response plans	99
3.5	Port State Control	101
3.6	Penalties for failure to comply	102
Section 3	Response	102
3.7	The National Contingency Plan	102
3.8	Spill notification requirements	103
3.9	Civil and criminal penalties	104
Section 4	Conclusions	105
Bibliography		105

CHAPTER 4   MARINE POLLUTION FROM SEWAGE   107

Section 1	Identifying the subject area	107
4.1	The meaning of "sewage" and the challenges for the marine environment	107
4.2	Key terms and definitions	109
Section 2	Overview of the legal basis	110
4.3	Main discussion	110
4.3.1	Control of discharges of sewage into the sea	113
4.3.2	Reception facilities	115
4.3.3	Selected insights on items of regional interest	116
Section 3	Key management issues, including documentation	120
4.4	Surveys and certification	120
4.4.1	International Sewage Pollution Prevention Certificate	120
4.5	Best practice	121
Section 4	Areas of special interest in relation to the legal framework	121
4.6	The IMO Member State Audit Scheme	121
Bibliography		122

CHAPTER 5   MARINE POLLUTION FROM WASTES   125

Section 1	Overview of the challenges raised by marine pollution from wastes	125
5.1	Identifying the problem of marine pollution from wastes: setting the scene	125
5.2	Key terms and definitions	128
Section 2	General (non-shipping specific) regulatory framework	131
5.3	Legislative background and discussion	131
5.3.1	In relation to marine pollution from dumping of wastes	133
5.3.2	In relation to transboundary movements of hazardous wastes and their disposal	138

xi

DETAILED CONTENTS

Section 3	MARPOL Annex V regulations for the prevention of pollution by garbage from ships	140
5.4	General discussion and overview	140
5.5	Key management issues, including documentation	144
	5.5.1 Garbage Management Plan	144
	5.5.2 Placards	145
	5.5.3 Garbage Record Book	146
	5.5.4 Good practices for shipmasters, shipowners and operators	147
5.6	Areas of special interest	151
	5.6.1 Adequacy of port reception facilities	151
	5.6.2 Port State Control findings	152
	5.6.3 The impact of the Polar Code	152
Bibliography		153

CHAPTER 6	FRAMEWORKS GOVERNING MARINE POLLUTION FROM THE TRANSPORTATION OF CHEMICALS BY SEA	155
Section 1	Carriage of chemicals by sea	156
6.1	Introductory remarks	156
6.2	Glossary	160
6.3	Selected systems of classification	161
	6.3.1 Globally Harmonized System of Classification and Labelling of Chemicals	161
	6.3.2 Standard European Behaviour Classification	163
	6.3.3 GESAMP hazard profiles	163
	6.3.4 European Union Regulation 1272/2008	164
6.4	United Nations Recommendations on the Transport of Dangerous Goods – Model Regulations	165
Section 2	Overview of MARPOL Annex II	166
6.5	Material scope of application	167
6.6	Categorisation of Noxious Liquid Substances	167
6.7	Design and construction	168
6.8	Discharge prohibitions	169
6.9	Verification of compliance – recently adopted Chapter IX of MARPOL Annex II	170
6.10	Polar Code – recently adopted Chapter X of MARPOL Annex II	170
Section 3	Overview of MARPOL Annex III	171
6.11	Material scope of application	171
6.12	Substantial requirements (packing, marking, labelling, stowage)	172
6.13	Quantity limitations	172
6.14	Exceptions	172

xii

DETAILED CONTENTS

Section 4	Certification, Port State Control on Operational Requirements and Other Aspects Stemming From MARPOL Annex II and Annex III		173
6.15	In relation to MARPOL Annex II		173
	6.15.1	Surveys and certificates	173
		6.15.1.1 The International Pollution Prevention Certificate for the Carriage of Noxious Liquid Substances in Bulk (NLS certificate)	173
		6.15.1.2 Procedures and Arrangements Manual	174
		6.15.1.3 Cargo Record Book	174
		6.15.1.4 Shipboard Marine Pollution Emergency Plan for Noxious Liquid Substances	174
	6.15.2	Port State Control on operational requirements	174
	6.15.3	Port reception facilities	175
6.16	In relation to MARPOL Annex III		176
	6.16.1	Documentation	176
	6.16.2	Port State Control on operational requirements	177
Bibliography			177

CHAPTER 7	AIR POLLUTION FROM SHIPPING		179
Section 1	Identifying the subject area		180
7.1	What is the problem?		180
	7.1.1	The contribution of shipping to air pollution and climate change	181
7.2	Glossary		182
Section 2	Main discussion of the regulatory framework		183
7.3	The regulatory framework at the international level: MARPOL Annex VI		184
	7.3.1	Setting sulphur caps on the content of marine fuels with a view to reducing SOx and PM	185
	7.3.2	Emission Control Areas	185
	7.3.3	Control of emissions of NOx	186
	7.3.4	Regulation of ozone depleting substances	186
	7.3.5	Measures involving ship energy efficiency	186
		7.3.5.1 Energy Efficiency Design Index	187
	7.3.6	Identifying challenges	187
7.4	The regulatory framework at the EU level		188
	7.4.1	Overview	188
	7.4.2	Monitoring, Reporting and Verification Regulation (Regulation (EU) 2015/757)	190
	7.4.3	The future: is shipping heading towards an EU emission trading scheme?	191

xiii

DETAILED CONTENTS

Section 3	Key management issues, including surveys and certification	192
7.5	Surveys and inspections	192
7.6	Certificates and plans	193
	7.6.1 International Air Pollution Prevention Certificate	193
	7.6.2 International Energy Efficiency Certificate	193
	7.6.3 Ship Energy Efficiency Management Plan	194
7.7	Key management issues stemming from the EU regime	199
	7.7.1 MRV Regulation (EU) – related documentation	199
7.8	Port State Control	200
Section 4	Areas of special interest	201
7.9	Market-based approaches	201
Section 5	Developments underway	202
7.10	IMO's fuel consumption data	202
7.11	Recent development stemming from the European Union	202
7.12	Alternative solutions	202
	7.12.1 Liquefied Natural Gas	202
	7.12.2 Bioenergy/biofuels	203
Bibliography		203

CHAPTER 8	OTHER SOURCES OF MARINE POLLUTION: BALLAST WATER, HARMFUL SUBSTANCES IN ANTI-FOULING SYSTEMS, SHIP-BREAKING ACTIVITIES AND OTHER	205
Section 1	Identifying the subject area	206
8.1	Potential sources of marine pollution outside the scope of MARPOL	206
8.2	Key terms/definitions	207
Section 2	Main discussion of the regulatory framework	207
8.3	Marine pollution from ballast water	207
	8.3.1 International regulations	209
	8.3.2 Key management issues, including documentation	213
	8.3.2.1 Standards	213
	8.3.2.2 Surveys and certification	214
	8.3.2.3 Ballast Water Management Plan	214
	8.3.2.4 Ballast Water Record Book	215
	8.3.3 Port State Control	215
8.4	Harmful substances used in anti-fouling systems	216
	8.4.1 What is the problem?	216
	8.4.1.1 The International Convention on the Control of Harmful Anti-fouling Systems on Ships, 2001	217
	8.4.1.2 Surveys and certification	218

xiv

DETAILED CONTENTS

	8.4.1.3 Best management practices	218
	8.4.1.4 The European Union approach: Regulation 782/2003 of 14 April 2003 and Regulation 536/2008 of 13 June 2008	219
8.5	Ship recycling	220
	8.5.1 What is the problem?	220
	8.5.2 The Hong Kong Convention 2009	220
	8.5.2.1 Documentation	224
	8.5.3 European Union (EU) action	224
Section 3	Areas of special interest, including current developments	226
8.6	Ship strikes with marine mammals	226
8.7	Underwater noise emissions from vessels	227
	8.7.1 On the IMO level	228
	8.7.2 The action undertaken by the European Union	229
	8.7.2.1 Monitoring underwater energy of marine waters	229
	8.7.2.2 Monitoring impacts of individual projects	230
Bibliography		231

CHAPTER 9	PREPAREDNESS, RESPONSE, AND COOPERATION IN THE CONTEXT OF MARINE POLLUTION	233
Section 1	Relevance of a coordinated framework and of intervention rights on the high seas to marine pollution control	234
9.1	The impact of landmark accidents on the legal framework governing cooperation and intervention	234
9.2	The position of the United Nations Convention on the Law of the Sea	235
9.3	The bodies involved	237
	9.3.1 The International Maritime Organisation	237
	9.3.2 The United Nations Environment Programme	238
	9.3.3 The European Maritime Safety Agency	238
	9.3.4 Other	239
9.4	Glossary	239
Section 2	The international framework on marine pollution preparedness, response and cooperation	242
9.5	The OPRC Convention	242
	9.5.1 Selected highlights	242
9.6	The OPRC-HNS Protocol	244
	9.6.1 Selected highlights	245
9.7	Spill response contracts	246
9.8	Challenges for preparedness and response	247

DETAILED CONTENTS

Section 3	Regional framework	248
9.9	Regional framework	248
9.10	Selected highlight: REMPEC (Regional Marine Pollution Emergency Response Centre for the Mediterranean Sea)	249
Section 4	Managerial aspects of response	251
9.11	Breaking down oil spill management	251
9.12	Challenges	254
Bibliography		258

CHAPTER 10   THE CONTRIBUTION OF THE HUMAN ELEMENT
             TO MARINE POLLUTION CONTROL   261

Section 1	The importance of the human element and its relevance to marine pollution control	262
10.1	Identifying the human element: setting the scene	262
10.2	Key terms/definitions	266
Section 2	The regulatory framework and related developments	268
10.3	Legislative background and discussion	268
10.3.1	ILO MLC 2006	268
10.3.2	STCW 2010	274
10.3.2.1	STCW 2010 from the standpoint of its contribution to marine pollution control	279
10.3.3	The International Safety Management Code	279
10.3.3.1	Overview	279
10.3.3.2	Selected highlights	282
10.3.3.3	The ISM Code and the marine environment	284
10.4	Areas of special interest (e.g. amendments underway, interface with other areas, etc.)	285
10.4.1	Fatigue	285
10.4.2	Criminalisation of seafarers	286
Section 3	Key management issues	290
10.5	Procedures/operations and relevant documentation	290
10.5.1	Non-exhaustive list of documents generally required by international regulations which relate to the human element to be carried onboard	290
10.5.2	Selective question: the complaints procedure under ILO MLC 2006	290
Bibliography		293

xvi

DETAILED CONTENTS

CHAPTER 11	LEGAL ASPECTS OF MARINE POLLUTION FROM SHIPS	295

Section 1	The basics governing the legal framework on marine pollution damage	296
11.1	About damages/losses and claims	297
	11.1.1 The involvement of the International Oil Pollution Compensation Funds	298
	11.1.1.1 Handling of claims by the IOPC Funds	299
	11.1.2 The involvement of Protection and Indemnity Clubs	300
	11.1.3 The involvement of salvors	301
11.2	Glossary	303
11.3	Types of liability in a nutshell	305
	11.3.1 Civil liability	305
	11.3.2 Criminal liability	306
	11.3.2.1 EU Directive 2005/35, as amended	309
Section 2	Limitation of liability of the polluter	310
11.4	The concept of limitation of liability in a nutshell	310
11.5	Global limitation of liability for maritime claims: the Convention on Limitation of Liability for Maritime Claims Convention (1976), as amended	311
	11.5.1 European Union Directive 2009/20/EC	313
11.6	Limitation of liability for oil pollution damage: the 1992 Civil Liability Convention, the 1992 Fund Convention and the 2003 Supplementary Fund Protocol	315
	11.6.1 The Small Tanker Oil Pollution Indemnification Agreement 2006 and the Tanker Oil Pollution Indemnification Agreement 2006	325
11.7	Limitation of liability for pollution from bunkers: the 2001 Bunker Pollution Convention	326
11.8	Limitation of liability for pollution from chemicals: the 2010 HNS Convention	327
11.9	Liability of the shipowner in the context of wreck removal: the 2007 Nairobi Convention	329
11.10	Liability stemming from maritime carriage of radioactive substances	330
11.11	Liability and the protection of the Antarctic	332
Bibliography		333
Index		335

xvii

FOREWORD

Early marine casualties, going back to the 'Torrey Canyon' in 1967 and the 'Amoco Cadiz' in 1979, highlighted the necessity for protecting the marine environment for future generations. These early casualties also demonstrated that response to marine pollution events, whether deliberate or accidental, was inadequate and unregulated. They were the triggers for a raft of international regulation to address the causes of marine pollution and mitigate the effects of such pollution.

The development of international regulations was accelerated as the effects of marine pollution on the world's environment was brought into the public domain through the development of modern media vehicles. The days when marine pollution events were reported days, or even weeks afterwards, are long gone and it is not unusual these days to have live pictures broadcast through various social media outlets within minutes of an event.

In this book Dr. Christodoulou-Varotsi recognises the leading role of the International Maritime Organisation (IMO) in the development of international regulations to address marine pollution through conventions and protocols. However, she also recognises the important role of other organisations, both public and private, in the development and implementation of such regulations. These include classification societies and port state control authorities.

The regulatory and managerial frameworks currently in force to prevent, counter and respond to marine pollution are complex and perhaps confusing. In light of her experience as a consultant, trainer and law drafter, Dr. Christodoulou-Varotsi has set out to clearly explain the regulatory and managerial framework and has resisted the temptation to go into complex detail. She provides the reader with an overview and clear directions if further research is required. She has expanded the confines of the book so as to include the vast majority of sources of marine pollution including from the offshore oil and gas sector, hazardous and noxious substances (HNS), and from air pollution caused by shipping.

In addition, in recognition of the correlation between polluting incidents and human error, Dr. Christodoulou-Varotsi has reviewed the human element in marine pollution. I have been involved in the marine salvage industry for 35 years and fully agree with her approach to the human factor. The human element is very important; in the development of rules and regulations you cannot legislate for human error. It is a welcome fact that the human element is now considered early in the development of regulation and not, as previously, as an afterthought.

In summary, I commend Dr. Christodoulou-Varotsi's book to all those who require a detailed overview on the subject of marine pollution from the standpoint of regulations and managerial practice. This will include shipowners, master mariners, liability insurers, shipping lawyers, maritime administrators, maritime students, and my own industry peers, the marine salvors.

Captain Mark Hoddinott FNI
General Manager
International Salvage Union

PREFACE

As a retired master mariner, I can reflect over my working life and acknowledge that during the early years of my career I was totally ignorant of the potential damage our actions were causing to the environment. It seemed to all of us that the world's oceans were so enormous that a little amount of oil from tank-cleaning or a bit of shipboard waste could be safely devoured and diluted by this vast salt water resource. We basked in the comfort of knowing that this type of practice had been going on for centuries with apparently no ill effects.

I have always held the view that historically the maritime industry is rather conservative and would generally react to major incidents rather than take a pro-active approach. For example, the Safety of Life at Sea Convention was the result of the *Titanic* tragedy. Indeed, it was the incident of the tanker *Torrey Canyon* in 1967 which set the wheels in motion for the International Conference on Marine Pollution, which was convened by IMO in 1973. From this, MARPOL was created, but perhaps more importantly in 1974 the IMO formed the Marine Environment Protection Committee (MEPC) to amend and introduce regulations to meet the needs of a rapidly developing world. As pointed out by Dr. Iliana Christodoulou-Varotsi in this publication, the work of MEPC did not just consider the prevention of major oil spills, but has been invaluable to direct the maritime industry in making shipping a greener form of transportation.

We are certainly living in an age where the people at large are becoming more informed about the risks to the environment. Since the United Nations brought the nations together in 1972 to discuss the human environment and sustainable development there was a gradual realisation from many governments that states must work and act together to conserve, protect and restore the integrity of the Earth's ecosystem. This brought about an historic landmark of the two-week Earth Summit in Brazil in 1989, which led to the adoption of Agenda 21, intended to announce the international agreement for a combined effort to support plans to protect the environment and aim for sustainable development.

However, it was not until 1995 that nations started serious negotiations to strengthen the global response to climate change and bind developed countries under international law to meet emission reduction targets. Famously in 1997 a positive agreement was reached and this was named the Kyoto Protocol. In spite of much bickering about the levels that some nations were expected to pay, it was

PREFACE

almost universally accepted, at a political level anyway, that measures had to be taken to save the planet.

The most recent step in implementing the UN climate change regime has been the 2015 Paris Agreement, adopted on 12 December 2015. This set a new tougher course to combat climate change built on the previous work.

Whilst nations were negotiating their commitments to implement these changes, the transport industries came under scrutiny. At present there is a concerted effort in many developed countries to stop the production of petrol and diesel cars. Both the aviation and the maritime industry have been guilty of condemning each other for the damage they do to the environment. Of course, both are polluters in the same way that road transport has much to answer for. However, there is a positive note: as in the transport industry, which is an essential service, all branches are working to make their industry greener.

During my 12 years representing an NGO attending meetings at IMO, I witnessed the strenuous work that was done to create and implement conventions and amendments to make our seas clean and protect the environment. This book examines in a structured manner the development of the work done by IMO and the member states to tackle the challenges faced by the industry to protect the environment.

I think that today the maritime industry is far more pro-active. Consider how MARPOL has developed from the original challenge of dealing with pollution from oil spills, to extensively researching and addressing the potential damage caused by ballast water and anti-fouling systems. Noise pollution both above and below the waterline, air pollution caused by the fuel that ships use, recycling ships and many other issues are being addressed. From an industry response, it is heart-warming to hear that a major shipping company is building their new class of huge cruise ships to be delivered from 2019, and these will be fuelled by natural gas. I have no doubt that other major shipping companies are designing their new fleets to meet greener challenges.

Finally, in defence of shipping, it is worth noting that 80 percent of pollution to the marine environment comes from the land, mostly as a result of runoff. However, we must not be complacent, there is still a lot more work to do, because we cannot ignore the fact the world is, on the one hand, dependent on shipping for international trade, whilst on the other hand our planet needs protection. In this context, the book succeeds in examining with clarity the issues facing the shipping industry in the 21st century and how the industry is trying to deal with them through legal and managerial frameworks.

Captain Rodger MacDonald.
C.E.O. Azimuth Marine Ltd

AUTHOR'S NOTE AND ACKNOWLEDGEMENTS

WHY ANOTHER BOOK ON MARINE POLLUTION?

When I was writing this book, my intent was to contribute to the understanding of the international and, on some points, regional legal and managerial frameworks surrounding marine pollution. My focus was clearly placed on policies, regulations and best practices governing ship-source pollution.

Marine pollution has given rise to thousands of legal provisions, and it is clearly a topic at the crossroads of more than one discipline. In this vein, any intention to exhaust the subject matter would not be realistic, and choices had to be made. Furthermore, I did not seek to engage in areas of marine scientific research. More importantly perhaps, I have done my best to present the topics discussed in a concise and accessible manner with busy maritime professionals in mind.

The book acknowledges that this is an area under constant change both regionally and internationally. In recognition of growing environmental and societal awareness having impacted regulations and management best practice, the book examines the six annexes of the instrument of reference addressing marine pollution prevention and management, which is the IMO MARPOL Convention. Additional insights are provided into key international conventions governing marine environment protection, and industry best practice tools. Key highlights, such as the protection of the marine environment in the offshore oil and gas sector, and the oil pollution regulatory framework in the USA are also described.

Part of the motivation to write this book came from observing that readers interested in marine pollution at large and ship-source pollution in particular could benefit from very detailed resources, or from resources intended for specialists in a particular discipline (e.g. natural scientists, litigation lawyers, etc.). In light of the experiences gained as a consultant, trainer and law drafter and the interaction with various professional groups, I have sought to synthesize and share my insights into marine pollution regulations and managerial frameworks. My approach remains primarily legal (I hope not legalistic!), with discussions involving on numerous points the management sphere. For most part, the book is structured over basic directions which should support the understanding of readers: identifying the subject area, explaining key terms and definitions, overview

AUTHOR'S NOTE AND ACKNOWLEDGEMENTS

of the legal basis, selected aspects presenting a special interest, and key management issues (procedures and/or relevant documentation).

Acknowledging that shipping tends to be a minor contributor to marine pollution but, nevertheless, marine pollution needs to be under control, the book clearly aligns with the current perception of the role of shipping: owners, managers, operators, mariners, flag States, port States, and other stakeholders are called upon by regulators to contribute towards environmental sustainability through effective implementation and enforcement. More than 40 years have passed since the adoption of MARPOL. There are projections on the increase of world population and the growth of international trade, which appear to be good drivers for further development of shipping. There are new standards in well-known areas, as well as in areas that have attracted attention only in recent years. Shipping is heading towards full automation, and regulations will have to be adapted accordingly.

Numerous recent developments have been traced and included up to the time of submission of the manuscript, but well-informed readers should know that this is an area with continued and rapid changes.

I hope the benefits of this work will be visible in a straightforward manner to those interested in a methodical overview of the most important aspects of marine pollution control with the emphasis placed on ship-source pollution. When I was writing the manuscript, I had a multi-disciplinary audience in mind, including master mariners, managers ashore, naval architects, surveyors, seafarers, maritime administrators, jurists, educators, students, etc. I hope I will facilitate the easy identification of key areas deserving closer attention, as well as access to more detailed resources, wherever needed (e.g. legal texts, industry best practices, or detailed academic readings, especially, in the latter case, for scholars, educators or students).

The contributions of the authors who have worked on two specialised topics, i.e. marine oil pollution framework in the USA and the international framework of marine environmental pollution created by the offshore oil and gas sector are appreciatively acknowledged. The topic on USA's regulations was covered by Mr. Antonio J. Rodriguez and Mr. Jake Rodriguez (Fowler Rodriguez, New Orleans, USA). Mr. Wylie Spicer, Q.C. and Mr. Peter L'Esperance (McInnes Cooper, Canada) addressed the contribution on the offshore oil and gas sector. Let me cordially thank my peers for joining me onboard and enriching the book with their experience.

I would also like to gratefully acknowledge Capt. Mark Hoddinott, General Manager of the International Salvage Union, and Capt. Rodger MacDonald, Azimuth Marine Ltd., for sharing views with me and honouring my work with their insights, foreword and preface. Let me also cordially thank my colleagues from the industry who have helped me identify areas of improvements during peer-review, and shared useful insights with me despite their busy schedules: my thanks are addressed to Capt. Aleksander Legowski, Österreichischer Lloyd Seereederei (Cyprus) Ltd., Dr. Malgorzata Nesterowicz, EMSA, Mr. Andreas Chrysostomou,

CLIA Europe, Capt. Ilias Ladas, Danaos, Mr. Naim Nazha, Transport Canada, Ms. Anna Doumeni, The Standard Club Europe Ltd., and Capt. Dariusz Gozdzik.

I would like to address my sincere thanks to my publishers, Taylor & Francis (Informa Law from Routledge). My thanks also go to the United Nations (UN), United Nations Conference on Trade and Development (UNCTAD), International Maritime Organisation (IMO), the International Tanker Owners Pollution Federation (ITOPF), and the International Oil Pollution Compensation Funds (IOPC) Funds for addressing my queries and/or courtesy material.

I am more than happy to express my appreciation to my trainees and students, throughout the years, for sharing knowledge with me, and my immense gratitude to my husband, daughter and parents for supporting my efforts during another laborious undertaking.

Dr. Iliana Christodoulou-Varotsi
Athens, 15 November 2017
christodoulou.i@dsa.gr
ilianachristovar@gmail.com
PO BOX 655 33
N. Psychiko 15 402, Greece

LIST OF FIGURES, GRAPHS AND TABLES

FIGURES

1.1	Marine pollution enforcement powers under UNCLOS III	14
5.1	Regulation of discharges and dumping at sea (non-exhaustive list of related instruments)	132
6.1	Standard hazard symbols (GHS)	162
10.1	ILO MLC 2006 overall presentation	275
10.2	Extract from Table A-II/2 on the specification of minimum standard of competence for masters and chief mates on ships of 500 gross tonnage or more	280
10.3	Extracts from Table A-V/1–1–3 on specification of minimum standard of competence in advanced training for chemical tanker cargo operations	281
10.4	Onboard complaint flow-chart (ILO MLC 2006)	292

GRAPHS

1.1	Operation at time of incident for large oil spills (>700 tonnes, 1970–2016)	34
1.2	Causes of large oil spills (>700 tonnes), 1970–2016	34
4.1	Summarised framework of the prohibitions of discharge of sewage from ships other than passenger ships in all areas and discharge of sewage from passenger ships outside special areas	114
5.1	Key land and ocean-based sources of marine debris	127
5.2	Waste management hierarchy showing priority and less preferred options	127
5.3	Options for shipboard handling and discharge of garbage	142
7.1	Who is working on air pollution and climate change agenda?	184
7.2	Regulatory and non-regulatory approaches to air pollution and GHG from ships aimed at potential reductions	184
8.1	Simplified description of the interphase of transferred ballast water with the marine environment	208

LIST OF FIGURES, GRAPHS AND TABLES

8.2	Applicable requirements under the Ballast Water Management (BWM) Convention	213
8.3	Frequency relationships between marine animal sounds and incidental noise from commercial shipping	228
9.1	Pillars of IMO legislation, including preparedness, response and cooperation	235
9.2	Examples of the four-stage components required for a comprehensive and well-designed contingency plan	253
11.1	Marine pollution damage-related costs generally eligible for compensation	298
11.2	Limitation of liability in a nutshell (maritime sector)	312
11.3	The European Union legal regime on marine pollution and environmental liability	314
11.4	Maximum limits of compensation	317

TABLES

0.1	The four pillars of international shipping legislation	6
0.2	Overview of marine pollution control under MARPOL 73/78	10
5.1	Summary of restrictions to the discharge of garbage into the sea under regulations 4, 5 and 6 of MARPOL Annex V	143
5.2	Sample placard targeting crew and shipboard operations	145
5.3	Sample placard targeting fixed or floating platforms and ships operating within 500 metres of such platforms	146
9.1	Obligations in a nutshell (national and international level) under the OPRC Convention	242
9.2	Tiered response and cooperation system in a nutshell	254
9.3	Summary of the primary techniques available for response to oil floating at sea	255
9.4	Summary of the main techniques available for response to oil near and on the shoreline	256
11.1	Simplified table of the main features of the 1992 CLC, the 1992 Fund Convention and the 2003 Supplementary Fund Protocol	318

TABLE OF CASES

Chalos & Co., P.C. v Marine Managers, Ltd., 2015 U.S. Dist. LEXIS
144199, *4–5 (E.D. La. 23 Oct. 2015) 105
CMA CGM S.A. v Classica Shipping Co. Ltd. [2004] 1 Lloyd's Rep. 460 159
Corfu Channel Case (United Kingdom v Albania) [1949] ICJ Rep 4 69
Dune Energy, Inc. v FROGCO Amphibious Equip., LLC, 2013 U.S.
Dist. LEXIS 61515, *8, (E.D. La. Apr. 29, 2013) 98
H.L. Bolton (Engineering) v T.J. Graham & Sons Limited [1956] 3 All ER 624 308
Hellenic State Council judgments Nos 2706/2006, 1834/1988, 35/1989,
2952/1990, 865/1993 (Greece) 54
HMS Truculent v The Divina [1951] 2 All ER 968 307
Lady Gwendoline, The [1965] 2 All ER 283 307
Marathon Pipe Line Co. v LaRoche Indus., 944 F. Supp. 476, 479 (E.D. La. 1996) 98
Metlife Capital Corp. v M/V EMILY S, 132 F.3d 818, 819 (1st Cir. 1997) 97
Nuclear Test Case (New Zealand v France) [1974] ICJ Rep 253 69
Paris (France) Court of First Instance judgment of 16 January 2008
(Tribunal de Grand Instance de Paris, 11ème Chambre, 4ème
section) Paris (France); Court of Appeal judgment of 30
March 2010 (Cour d'Appel de Paris, Pole 4, Chambre 11E);
and French Supreme Court (Cour de Cassation) decision of 25
September 2012 (Cour de Cassation, arrêt no 3439 (10–82.938) de
la Chambre Criminelle) 54
Piraeus (Greece) Administrative Court of Appeal judgment No.
2149/2011 Administrative Court of Appeal (Greece) judgment No. 2149/2011 53
Piraeus (Greece) Administrative Court of Appeal judgment No. 390/2015 53
Piraeus (Greece) three member Administrative Court of First Instance
Decision No. 4711/2011 54
Salomon v A. Salomon & Co. Ltd. [1897] AC 22 308
Shipowners' Mutual v Containerships Denizclik [2015] 1 Lloyd's Rep 567 300
Tesco Supermarkets Ltd v Nattrass [1972] AC 153 (HL) 308
Trail Smelter Case (United States v Canada) (1938–1941) RIAA vol III,
pp. 1905–1982 69
United States v Abrogar 459 F.3d 430 (3d Cir.2006) 52
United States v Ionia Management, 498 Supp. 2d 477 (D. Conn. 2007) 52
United States v Jho, 534 F.3d 398 (5th Cir. 2008) 53

TABLE OF STATUTES

Act to Prevent Pollution from Ships
(APPS) 33 U.S.C. (U.S.A)...... § 1901 et
seq. 52, 101
§ 1908 (a).. 105
Bribery Act 2010 (UK) ....s. 14
.... 308
Code of Federal Regulations 33 C.F.R
(U.S.A.)...................................... § 27.3
.... 102, 104
§ 138.20... 96
§ 138.40... 99
§ 138.230... 97
§ 151.07.. 102
§ 151.09(a)(1)–(4), (c) 101
§ 151.09(d)(2) 101
§ 151.19(a) 102
§ 151.19(b)..................................... 102
§ 151.23.. 102
§ 151.24.. 102
§ 151.25.. 102
§ 151.26(b)(8) 101
§ 151.27.. 101
§ 151.27(c) 101
§ 155.1025(a) 99
§ 155.1026...................................... 100
§ 155.1030...................................... 100
§ 155.1030(k).................................. 101
§ 155.1035...................................... 100
§ 155.1040...................................... 100
§ 155.1045...................................... 100
§ 155.1050...................................... 100
§ 155.1052...................................... 100
§ 155.1055...................................... 100
§ 155.1065...................................... 100
§ 155.4015...................................... 100
§ 155.4030...................................... 100

§ 155.4040...................................... 101
§ 155.4045...................................... 101
§ 155.4052...................................... 101
§ 155.5021(a).................................. 100
§ 155.5030...................................... 100
§ 155.5030(k).................................. 101
§ 155.5035...................................... 100
§ 155.5065...................................... 100
Code of Federal Regulations 40 C.F.R.
(U.S.A)...................................... § 300.1
.... 103
§ 300.110.. 103
§ 300.125.. 103
§ 300.175(b).................................... 103
§ 300.320.. 103
§ 300.322.. 103
§ 300.5.. 103
§ 300.300.. 103
Coroners and Justice Act 2009 (UK) s. 120
.... 307
Federal Water Pollution Control Act
(Clean Water Act) (U.S.A) 95, 96,
97,102, 103, 104
Law 1269 of 21.7.1982 (A'89)(Greece)54, 55
Law 743/1977 on the Protection of the
Marine Environment (A' 319)
(Greece).. 55
Limitation of Liability Act 46 U.S.C.
(U.S.A.) §30501 *et seq*....................... 97
Merchant Shipping Act 1894 (UK)...... 265
Merchant Shipping Act 1995 (UK)..... 307,
308
s. 85 307
s. 131 307
ss. 132–134..................................... 307
s. 136 307

xxxi

TABLE OF STATUTES

s. 143 307
s. 277 308
Merchant Shipping Maritime Security Act
1997 (UK) .... s. 7
.... 307
Migratory Bird Treaty Act 16 U.S.C.
(U.S.A.) .... § 703 et seq,
.... 105
Oil Pollution Act (OPA 1990) (101 H.R.1465,
P.L. 101–380). 40, 56, 95–98, 105, 297, 303
33 U.S.C. (U.S.A.)
§ 2701(8) 96
§ 2701(21) 96
§ 2701(23) 96
§ 2701(26)(B)(ii) 96
§ 2701(31) 97
§ 2701(32)(A) 96
§ 2701(35) 96
§ 2702(a) 96, 97

§ 2702(b)(1) 97
§ 2702(b)(2) 98
§ 2702(d)(1) 98
§ 2703(a) 98
§ 2703(c) 98
§ 2704(a) 97
§ 2704(c)(1) 97
§ 2704(c)(2) 97
§ 2704(c)(3) 97
§ 2716(a) 99, 98
§ 2716(b) 99
§ 2716(e) 99
§ 2716a(a) 99
§ 2716a(b) 99
Presidential Decree 55/1998 (A' 58)
(Greece) .... s. 12
.... 53
Refuse Act 33 U.S.C. (U.S.A.) .... § 407
.... 104

TABLE OF EUROPEAN LEGISLATION

Commission (EC) Directive 2002/62/
EC of 9 July 2002 adapting to
technical progress for the ninth
time Annex I to Council Directive
76/769/EEC on the approximation
of the laws, regulations and
administrative provisions of
the Member States relating to
restrictions on the marketing and
use of certain dangerous substances
and preparations (organostannic
compounds) (Text with EEA
relevance) [2002] OJ L 183/58 219

Commission (EU) Regulation
536/2008 giving effect to Article
6(3) and Article 7 of Regulation
(EC) 782/2003 on the prohibition of
organotin compounds on ships and
amending that Regulation [2008]
OJ L 156/10...................................... 219
Art. 1 219

Commission (EU) Regulation
788/2014 laying down detailed
rules for the imposition of fines and
period penalty payments and the
withdrawal of recognition of ship
inspection and survey organisations
pursuant to Articles 6 and 7 of
Regulation (EC) 391/2009 of the
European Parliament and of the
Council (Text with EEA relevance)
[2014] OJ L 214/12 21

Council (EC) Directive 1999/32/EC
of 26 April 1999 on the reduction in
the sulphur content of certain liquid
fuels [1999] OJ L 121/13 .... 189, 190

Council (EC) Directive 1999/45/
EC of 31 May 1999 concerning
the approximation of the laws,
regulations and administrative
provisions of the Member States
relating to the classification,
packaging and labelling of
dangerous preparations [1999] OJ L
200/1 164

Council (EC) Directive 2000/59/EC
of the European Parliament and of
the Council of 27 November 2000
on port reception facilities for ship
generated waste and cargo residues
[2000] OJ L 332/81 .... 117, 118

Council (EC) Directive 2000/60 of
23 October 2000 establishing a
framework for Community action
in the field of water policy [2000]
OJ L 327/1..
Art. 1 22
Art. 2 22

Council (EC) Directive 2002/6/EC
of 18 February 2002 on reporting
formalities for ships arriving in
and/or departing from ports of the
Member States of the Community
(Text with EEA relevance) [2010]
OJ L 283/1.. 159

Council (EC) Directive 2002/49
relating to the assessment and
management of environmental
noise-Declaration by the
Commission in the Conciliation
Committee on the Directive relating
to the assessment and management

of environmental noise [2002] OJ
L189/12 229
Council (EC) Directive 2004/35 on
environmental liability with regard
to the prevention and remedying of
environmental damage [2004] OJ L
143/56 314
Council (EC) Directive 2005/33/EC
of 6 July 2005 amending Directive
1999/32/EC 188, 189
Recital 22 189
Recital 4 .... 188, 189
Recital 5 et seq. 189
Recital 7 188
Art. 4b(1) 189
Council (EC) Directive 2005/35
on ship-source pollution and on
the introduction of penalties for
infringements [2005] OJ L 255/11
.... 309, 310, 314
Recital 9 310
Council (EC) Directive 2008/56
establishing a framework for
Community action in the field
of marine environmental policy
(Marine Strategy Framework
Directive) (Text with EEA
relevance), [2008]
OJ L164/19 .... 21, 229
Council (EC) Directive 2008/98 of the
19 November 2008 on waste and
repealing certain Directives (The
2008 Waste Framework Directive)
(Text with EEA relevance) [2008]
OJ L 312/3 .... 128, 226
Council (EC) Directive 2009/15
on common rules and standards
for ship inspection and survey
organizations and for the
relevant activities of maritime
administrations (Recast) (Text with
EEA relevance) [2009]
OJ L 131/47 20
Council (EC) Directive 2009/16/EC of
23 April 2009 on port State control
(Text with EEA relevance)[2009]
OJ L 131/57 190
Council (EC) Directive 2009/20 of
23 April 2009 on the insurance of

shipowners for maritime claims
(Text with EEA relevance) [2009]
OJ L 131/128 .... 313, 314
Art. 3(b) 314
Council (EC) Directive 2009/21/EC of
23 April 2009 on compliance with
flag State requirements (Text with
EEA relevance) [2009]
OJ L 131/132 23
Council (EC) Directive 2009/123
of 21 October 2009 amending
Directive 2005/35/EC on ship-
source pollution and on the
introduction of penalties for
infringements (Text with EEA
relevance) [2009] OJ L 280/52 309
Council (EC) Regulation 1013/2006
of 14 June 2006 on shipments of
waste 225, 226
Council (EC) Regulation 1272/2008
of the European Parliament and of
the Council of 16 December 2008
on classification, labelling and
packaging of substances and
mixtures 162, 164
Recital 10 164
Art. 33 165
Council (EC) Regulation 1907/2006
of the European Parliament and of
the Council of 18 December 2006
concerning the Registration,
Evaluation, Authorisation and
Restriction of Chemicals (REACH),
establishing a European Chemicals
Agency, amending Directive
1999/45/EC and repealing Council
Regulation (EEC) No 793/93 and
Commission Regulation (EC)
No 1488/94 as well as Council
Directive 76/769/EEC and
Commission Directives 91/155/
EEC, 93/67/EEC, 93/105/EC
and 2000/21/EC (Text with EEA
relevance)[2006]
OJ L 396/1 .... 164, 165
Council (EC) Regulation 391/2009
on common rules and standards
for ship inspection and survey
organizations (Recast) (Text with

xxxiv

TABLE OF EUROPEAN LEGISLATION

EEA relevance) [2009] OJ L 131/11 ....20, 21

Council (EC) Regulation 392/2009 on the liability of carriers of passengers by sea in the event of accidents (Text with EEA relevance) [2009] OJ L 131/24 ....
Art. 4(1)..314
Art. 4(2)..314

Council (EEC) Directive 67/548/ EEC of 27 June 1967 on the approximation of laws, regulations and administrative provisions relating to the classification, packaging and labelling of dangerous substances [1967] OJ 196/1 164

Council (EU) Directive 2009/16/EC on Port State Control (Recast) (Text with EEA relevance) [2009] OJ L131/57......................................22, 23

Council (EU) Directive 2010/65 on reporting formalities for ships arriving in and/or departing from ports of the Member States and repealing Directive 2002/6/EC (Text with EEA relevance) [2010] OJ L 283/1.......................................159

Council (EU) Directive 2011/92 on the assessment of the effects of certain public and private projects on the environment (codification) (Text with EEA relevance) [2012] L 26/1 ....230, 231

Council (EU) Directive 2012/33 amending Council Directive 1999/32/EC as regards the sulphur content of marine fuels [2012] OJ L327/1...189

Council (EU) Directive 2014/52 amending Directive 2011/92/EU on the assessment of the effects of certain public and private projects on the environment (Text with EEA relevance) [2014] L 124/1................231

Council (EU) Directive 2016/802 of 11 May 2016 relating to a reduction

in the sulphur content of certain liquid fuels 189, 190

Council (EU) Regulation 1257/2013 on ship recycling amending Regulation (EC) No. 1013/2006 and Directive 2009/16/EC [2013] OJ L 330/1 ....224, 225, 226
Art. 3 para 1(6)...............................226
Art. 5 226
Art. 6(2)(a).......................................226
Art. 12 225
Art. 32 225
Recital 10 226

Council (EU) Regulation 757/2015 of 29 April 2015 on the monitoring, reporting and verification of carbon dioxide emissions from maritime transport, and amending Directive 2009/16/EC (Text with EEA relevance)...........24, 190, 191, 199, 200
Recital 10 190
Recital 13 190
Recital 14 191
Art. 2(2)..191
Art. 6 191
Art. 6(3)..200
Art. 8 191
Art. 11 191
Art. 17 200
Art. 18 200
Art. 21 191

Council (EU) Regulation 782/2003 on the prohibition of organotin compounds on ships [2003] OJ L 115/1...219
Recital 12 219
Recital 14 219
Art. 5 219
Art. 6(3)..219
Art. 7 219

Council Framework Decision 2005/667/JHA of 12 July 2005 to strengthen the criminal-law framework for the enforcement of the law against ship-source pollution [2005] OJ L 255/164 ....309, 314

XXXV

TABLE OF CONVENTIONS AND TREATIES

African Charter on Human and Peoples'
   Rights 1981 289
Antarctic Treaty 1959 332
Protocol on Environmental Protection
   to the Antarctic Treaty 1991
   Annex VI.. 332
   Annex VI Art. 1.............................. 332
   Annex VI Art. 5.............................. 333
   Annex VI Art. 6.............................. 333
   Annex VI Art. 9.............................. 333
Basel Convention on the Control
   of Transboundary Movements of
   Hazardous Wastes and their
   Disposal 1989......................... 128, 130,
   131, 132, 138, 139, 220, 224, 225, 226,
   311
   Art. 1 .... 128, 139
   Art. 2 128
   Art. 4 138
   Annex I..................................... 128, 138
   Annex III................................... 128, 138
   Annex IX... 128
   Annex VIII.. 128
Civil Liability Convention (CLC) 1992
   297,
   299, 301, 303–306, 312, 314, 315,
   317–326, 328
   Art. III para. 2 316
   Art. III para. 4 .... 306, 316
   Art. III para. 4(a)............................. 306
   Art. III para. 4(b)............................. 306
   Art. V para. 2................................... 316
   Art. VII para. 8................................ 297
Civil Liability Convention 1969 299,
   312, 315

Convention for the Protection of the
   Black Sea Against Pollution (Bucharest
   Convention) 1992.................... 132, 249
Convention for the Protection of the
   Natural Resources and Environment
   of the South East Pacific (South
   East Pacific Convention) 1981......... 132
Convention for the Protection of the
   Environment of the North-East
   Atlantic (OSPAR Convention)..... 62,89,
   90, 92, 132, 241
Convention for the Protection of the
   Marine Environment and the Coastal
   Area of the Mediterranean (Barcelona
   Convention) 1995............................ 132,
   248, 250, 251
   Art. 4(1)... 250
   Art. 6 250
   Art.9 250
Convention for the Protection of the
   Natural Resources and Environment
   of the South Pacific Region (South
   Pacific) 1986 132
Convention for the Protection,
   Management and Development
   of the Marine and Coastal
   Environment of the Eastern African
   Region (Nairobi Convention) 132
Convention on Civil Liability for Oil
   Pollution Damage Resulting From
   Exploration for and Exploitation of
   Seabed Mineral Resources (CLEE)
   1977...................................... 62, 85, 92
   Art. 2 85
   Art 1(2)... 85

TABLE OF CONVENTIONS AND TREATIES

Convention on Environmental Impact
Assessment in a Transboundary
Context (ESPOO) 1997..........62, 88, 89
  Art. 2.1 88
  Art. 2.3 App. I 88
  Appendix II 89
  Appendix I-IV 89
Convention on Limitation of
Liability for Maritime Claims
(LLMC) 1976..........................297,303,
311, 312, 313, 314, 327, 330, 333
  Art. 1 ....311, 313
  Art. 2 ....311, 313
  Art. 2(1)..311
  Art. 3 ....312, 313
  Art. 3(b)..312
  Art. 3(c)..331
  Art. 4 313
  Art. 6 313
  Art. 7 313
  Art. 8 313
  Art. 9 313
  Art. 10(1)..313
  Art. 11 313
  Art. 12 313
Convention on Supplementary
Compensation for Nuclear Damage
1997..331
Convention on the Control of Harmful
Anti-fouling Systems on Ships
(AFS) 2001...........3, 207, 217, 218, 219
  Art. 2 217
Convention on the Prevention of
Pollution by Dumping of Wastes
and other Matter (London
Convention) 1972..............................62,
74, 81, 82, 83, 91, 129, 130, 132, 133,
134
  Art. 1(a)..82
  Art. I...128, 134
  Art. III 82, 135
  Art. III(1)(c) 82
  Art. IV 134
  Art. X 135
  Art. XI 135
  Annex I.......................................82, 130
  Annex II 82, 134
  Annex III.....................................82, 134
  Annex III(C)...82

Protocol to the London Convention
1972, 1996...................................62,74,
82, 83, 91, 128, 129, 130, 131, 135,
136, 137, 314
  Art. 1 (4.3)..91
  Art. 1 para. 8 128
  Art. 3.3 136
  Art. 4 ....83, 135
  Art. 5 136
  Art. 6 ....136, 137
  Art. 7 137
  Art. 9 ....136, 137
  Art. 10 136
  Art. 11 136
  Art. 13 136
  Art. 16 136
  Art. 16(3)..136
  Annex 1 ....83, 135, 137
  Annex 1 para. 1.8..............................137
  Annex 1 para. 4..................................137
  Annex II 83, 136
  Annex II, para. 17 83
  Annex II, paras 2, 5, 11, 12................83
  Annex 3 137
Convention on the Protection of the
Marine Environment of the Baltic
Sea Area (Helsinki Convention)
1992.................................. 134, 240, 248
Convention on the Protection of the
Underwater Cultural Heritage
2001..330
Convention Relating to Civil Liability
in the Field of Maritime Carriage of
Nuclear Material 1971 331
European Convention on Human
Rights 1950 ....288, 289
  Art. 6(1)..289
  Art. 6(3)..289
Fund Convention 1971.........................315
Fund Convention 1992........................299,
301, 303, 305, 315, 316, 317–326, 328
Geneva Convention on the
Continental Shelf 1958 ....61, 69
  Art. 5(1)..70
  Art. 5(7)..70
  Art. 24 70
Hong Kong International Convention
for the Safe and Environmentally
Sound Recycling of Ships (Hong Kong

xxxviii

TABLE OF CONVENTIONS AND TREATIES

Convention) 2009 .... 27, 206, 220, 221, 225
- Art. 3 para. 2 221
- Art. 3 para. 3 221
- Art. 3 para. 4 221
- Art. 4 221
- Art. 17 221
- Annex reg. 4 222
- Annex reg. 5 222
- Annex reg. 5 para. 2 222
- Annex reg. 8 222
- Annex reg. 9 222
- Annex reg. 10 224
- Annex reg. 11 224
- Annex reg. 11 para. 12 224
- Annex reg. 14, para. 2 224
- Annex reg. 14, para. 3 224
- Annex reg. 16 223
- Annex reg. 18 223
- Annex reg. 21, para. 1 223
- Annex reg. 25 224

ILO Maritime Labour Convention (MLC) 2006 .... 6, 261, 266–274, 275, 278, 285, 286, 290, 291, 293, 294
- Art. I, para. 2 277
- Art. II para. 3 272
- Art. II para. 5 272
- Art. VI 272
- Standard 5.1.5. para. 2 291
- Standard 5.1.5 para. 3 291
- reg. 1.1 .... 270, 271, 275
- reg. 1.2 275
- reg. 1.3 .... 268, 275
- reg. 1.4 276
- reg. 2.1 275
- reg. 2.2 275
- reg. 2.3 275
- reg. 2.4 276
- reg. 2.5 .... 269, 274, 276
- reg. 2.6 276
- reg. 2.7 276
- reg. 2.8 276
- reg. 3.1 275
- reg. 3.2 275
- reg. 4.1 275
- reg. 4.2 .... 269, 274, 275
- reg. 4.3 275
- reg. 4.4 276

- reg. 4.5 276
- reg. 5.1 275
- reg. 5.1.1 para. 4 273
- reg. 5.1.5 291
- reg. 5.2 275
- reg. 5.2.2 291
- reg. 5.3 275

International Code for Ships Operating in Polar Waters (Polar Code), 2017 .... 9, 51, 110, 118, 119, 125, 152, 153, 154, 167, 170, 171, 332
- para. 5.2.2 153
- para. 5.2.3 153

International Convention for the Control and Management of Ships' Ballast Water and Sediments (Ballast Water Management Convention) 2004 .... 3, 8, 207, 209, 210, 211–215
- Reg. A-3 215
- Reg. A-4 215
- Reg. B-1 214
- Reg. B-2 par. 2 215
- Reg. B-2 par. 3 215
- Reg. B-2 par. 5 215
- Reg. B-3, par. 7 209
- Art. 2(4) 213
- Art. 2(7) 212
- Art. 2(8) 212
- Art. 3(1) 212
- Art. 3(2) 212
- Art. 3(3) 212
- Art. 5 213
- Art. 6 213
- Art. 7 214
- Art. 8 213
- Art. 9 .... 215, 216

International Convention for the Prevention of Pollution from Ships, 1973 as modified by the Protocol of 1978 (MARPOL 73/78) 3, 5, 6, 8, 10, 11, 15, 25, 32, 40, 41, 43, 47, 48–55, 61, 75, 76, 77, 78, 79, 80, 81, 82, 91, 95, 101, 117, 121, 128, 131, 140, 145, 146, 157, 176, 206, 234, 235, 270, 274, 281, 288, 309, 310
- Art. 1(1) 75
- Art. 2(3)(b)(ii) 76, 78, 81

xxxix

TABLE OF CONVENTIONS AND TREATIES

Art. 2(4).. 75
Art. 2.2 158
Art. 4 .... 175, 288, 309, 310
Art. 4(4).. 54
Art. 5 175
Art. 5(2)... 175
Art. 5(2)... 102
Art. 6 234
Art. 6(2)... 175
Art. 9 41
Art. 14 .... 109, 140
Annex I.. 39, 40,
   41, 43, 44, 47, 52, 81, 95, 109, 117,
   152, 153, 158, 166, 167, 171, 177
Annex I reg. 1 32
Annex I reg. 1.5 41
Annex I reg. 4 .... 53, 54, 78
Annex I reg. 6.3.1 20
Annex I reg. 6.3.4 20
Annex I reg. 7 48
Annex I reg. 9 48
Annex I reg. 10 48
Annex I reg. 11................................... 38
Annex I reg. 12 77
Annex I reg. 12A................................ 45
Annex I reg. 14 .... 77, 78
Annex I reg. 14.7 45
Annex I reg. 15 .... 45, 78
Annex I reg. 16.2 78
Annex I reg. 17 .... 47, 48
Annex I reg. 17.3 48
Annex I reg. 17.6 48
Annex I reg. 20 53
Annex I reg. 29 46
Annex I reg. 31 .... 41, 46
Annex I reg. 33 41
Annex I reg. 34 .... 46, 78
Annex I reg. 36 48
Annex I reg. 37 .... 42, 47
Annex I reg. 38 .... 41, 116
Annex I reg. 39 .... 76, 77, 78
Annex I reg. 39 par. 1......................... 77
Annex I reg. 39 par. 2......................... 77
Annex I reg. 39 par. 2.1...................... 77
Annex I reg. 39 par. 2.3...................... 78
Annex I reg. 41(3)............................... 51
Annex II 32,
   42, 44, 81, 95, 153, 158, 161, 163,
   166–176, 240

Annex II reg. 1.10 161
Annex II reg. 3 169
Annex II reg. 8.1 173
Annex II reg. 8.2.1 173
Annex II reg. 8.2.6 173
Annex II reg. 9.1 173
Annex II reg. 10 173
Annex II reg. 10.1 173
Annex II reg. 11 169
Annex II reg. 12 169
Annex II reg. 13.1.1 169
Annex II reg. 13.8 170
Annex II reg. 14 174
Annex II reg. 15.1 174
Annex II reg. 17 174
Annex II reg. 18 .... 116, 175
Annex II reg. 19 170
Annex II reg. 19.9.3 175
Annex II reg. 20 170
Annex II Appendix III..................... 173
Annex II Appendix IV..................... 174
Annex III................................... 10,44,
   80, 81, 95, 101, 109, 155, 156, 158,
   171–173, 176, 177
Annex III reg. 1.1.1 158
Annex III reg. 2................................ 172
Annex III reg. 3.1............................. 172
Annex III reg. 3.2............................. 172
Annex III reg. 4.1............................. 176
Annex III reg. 4.2............................. 177
Annex III reg. 5................................ 172
Annex III reg. 6................................ 172
Annex III reg. 7................................ 172
Annex III reg. 7.1............................. 172
Annex III reg. 8................................ 177
Annex III reg. 8.2............................. 177
Annex IV................................... 10,44,
   81, 107, 108, 109, 110, 111, 113, 114,
   115, 116, 117, 119, 120, 121, 122,
   123, 129, 152, 153, 171
Annex IV reg. 1.3............................. 110
Annex IV reg. 2................................ 111
Annex IV reg. 2.1............................. 167
Annex IV reg. 2.2............................. 167
Annex IV reg. 3...................... 111, 113
Annex IV reg. 4...................... 120, 167
Annex IV reg. 4.5............................. 120
Annex IV reg. 4.6............................. 120
Annex IV reg. 4.7............................. 120

TABLE OF CONVENTIONS AND TREATIES

Annex IV reg. 4.9............................ 120
Annex IV reg. 5............................... 167
Annex IV reg. 8.1............................ 120
Annex IV reg. 9............................... 110
Annex IV reg. 9.1.1.................. 113, 119
Annex IV reg. 9.2.1.................. 113, 119
Annex IV reg. 11............................. 113
Annex IV reg. 11.1.................. 114, ~~119~~
Annex IV reg. 11.1.1........................ 119
Annex IV reg. 11.3.................. 113, 114
Annex IV reg. 12...................... 115, 116
Annex IV reg. 12bis.................. 115, 116
Annex V 9, 10,
    44, 76, 79, 80, 81, 95, 107–109,
    116, 117, 125, 128–133, 138, 140,
    141, 143, 144, 145, 146, 148, 149,
    151–153, 154, 171
Annex V reg. 1(12) 79
Annex V reg. 1(9) 79
Annex V reg. 2................................. 141
Annex V reg. 3................................. 141
Annex V reg. 4................................. 143
Annex V reg. 4.3.............................. 140
Annex V reg. 5.......................... 80, 143
Annex V reg. 6................ 143, 151, 153
Annex V reg. 6.4.............................. 140
Annex V reg. 8.......................... 116, 151
Annex V reg. 8 para. 3(2) 151
Annex V reg. 10 145
Annex V reg. 10.2 144
Annex V reg. 10.3 .... 146, 147
Annex VI.................................... 10, 39,
    58, 76, 80, 81, 95, 101, 116, 179,
    180, 182, 184, 185, 187, 190, 192,
    193, 200, 201, 202, 204
Annex VI reg. 2.9............................ 183
Annex VI reg. 3.1...................... 81, 185
Annex VI reg. 3.1.4............................81
Annex VI reg. 4...................... 183, ~~184~~
Annex VI reg. 5..................................80
Annex VI reg. 5.1...................... 80, 192
Annex VI reg. 5.2............................ 192
Annex VI reg. 5.3.3......................... 192
Annex VI reg. 5.3.4......................... 192
Annex VI reg. 5.4............................ 193
Annex VI reg. 5.4.4......................... 192
Annex VI reg. 5.6............................ 192
Annex VI reg. 6............................... 193

Annex VI reg. 6.3............................ 193
Annex VI reg. 6.4............................ 193
Annex VI reg. 7............................... 193
Annex VI reg. 9.1............................ 193
Annex VI reg. 9.10.......................... 193
Annex VI reg. 9.11.................. 193, 194
Annex VI reg. 11.2.......................... 201
Annex VI reg. 11.5.......................... 201
Annex VI reg. 12...................... 81, 185
Annex VI reg. 12.2.......................... 186
Annex VI reg. 12.6.......................... 186
Annex VI reg. 13........81, 183, 185, 186
Annex VI reg. 14...................... 81, 185
Annex VI reg. 15............................. 185
Annex VI reg. 16............................. 185
Annex VI reg. 17............................. 116
Annex VI reg. 20............................. 193
Annex VI reg. 21...................... 185, 193
Annex VI reg. 22............................. 193
Annex VI reg. 22A........................... 202
Protocol 1978 ....9, 40, 43, 44,
    61, 110, 119, 122, 123, 129, 153, 154,
    170, 176
International Convention for the
    Prevention of Pollution of the Sea
    by Oil (OILPOL) 1954...........32, 40, 41
    Art. I...41
International Convention
    for the Safety of Life at Sea (SOLAS)
    1974..4, 5,
    6, 9, 11, 40, 49, 51, 110, 118, 122, 152,
    157, 160, 166, 171, 176, 228, 267, 270,
    274, 279, 290
    reg. 1.2 157
    reg. 3.20 40
    Protocol 1988 ....6, 9
International Convention on Civil
    Liability for Bunker Oil Pollution
    Damage (Bunker Pollution
    Convention) 2001...............................297,
    303, 306, 312, 314, 326, 327
    Art. 1(1).. 327
    Art. 1(3).. 327
    Art. 1(5).. 326
    Art. 1(9).. 326
    Art. 2 326
    Art. 3(1).. 306
    Art. 3(2).. 306

xli

TABLE OF CONVENTIONS AND TREATIES

Art. 3(3)..................................... 327
Art. 3(4)..................................... 327
Art. 4 327
Art. 7 327
Art. 7(10).............................. 297, 327
International Convention on Liability
and Compensation for Damage in
Connection with the Carriage of
Hazardous and Noxious Substances
by Sea (HNS Convention 2010) 158,
245, 297, 303, 314, 327, 328, 329
Art. 3 .... 328, 329
Art. 12(8)................................... 297
International Convention on Load
Lines, 1966.................................. 280
International Convention on Oil
Pollution Preparedness, Response and
Cooperation (OPRC) 1990........... 62,85,
86, 87, 91, 92, 235, 237, 240–242, 243,
244, 245, 246, 249, 250
Art. 2(4)................................... 85, 91
Art. 3 242
Art. 3(2).................................. 86, 92
Art. 4 243
Art. 4(1)(a)(ii) 86, 92
Art. 6 .... 86, 244
Art. 7 86
Art. 10 249
Art. 12(1)................................... 237
Protocol on Preparedness, Response
and Cooperation to Pollution
Incidents by Hazardous and
Noxious Substances (OPRC-HNS
Protocol) 2000.............................. 158,
235, 237, 240, 241, 244, 245, 246, 248,
249
Art. 3 245
Art. 4 .... 245, 246
Art. 8 249
Art. 10(1)................................... 237
International Convention on Salvage
1989...................... 301, 302, 303, 304
Art. 13 302–304
Art. 13(1)(b)................................ 302
Art. 14 .... 302, 303, 304
International Convention on Standards
of Training, Certification and
Watchkeeping for Seafarers
(STCW) 2010............................... 6,11,

152, 266, 267, 268, 270, 274, 277–279,
285, 290
Art. I.. 277
Annex reg. I/6 277
International Convention on the
Control of Harmful Anti-Fouling
Systems on Ships 2001 3,207,
216, 217, 218, 219
Art. 2 217
Art. 3 217
Art. 3, para. 3 217
Art. 6 217
Art. 10 218
International Convention Relating to
Intervention on the High Seas in
Cases of Oil Pollution Casualties,
1969............................. 234, 235, 330
International Convention Relating to
the Limitation of the Liability of
Owners of Seagoing Ships 1957...... 311
Kyoto Protocol to the United Nations
Framework Convention on Climate
Change 1997 .... 182, 201
Minimum Age (Trimmers and
Stockers) Convention, 1921............. 269
Nairobi International Convention
on the Removal of Wrecks 2007...... 297,
305, 314, 329, 330
Art. 12(10)................................... 297
Offshore Pollution Liability Agreement
(OPOL) 1974 .... 62, 84, 85, 91,
92, 304
Paris Convention on Third Party
Liability in the Field of Nuclear
Energy 1960 331
Protocol concerning Co-operation
in Preventing Pollution from
Ships and, in Cases of Emergency
Combating Pollution of the
Mediterranean Sea, 2002 .... 250, 251
Art. 12 250
Protocol Concerning Marine Pollution
Resulting From Exploration and
Exploitation of the Continental
Shelf, 1989.................................... 87
Protocol for the Protection of the
Mediterranean Sea Against
Pollution Resulting From
Exploration and Exploitation of the

xlii

TABLE OF CONVENTIONS AND TREATIES

Continental Shelf and the Seabed and its Subsoil, 1994 .... 87, 88
Protocol for the Protection of the Mediterranean Sea Against Pollution Resulting From Exploration and Exploitation of the Continental Shelf and the Seabed and its Subsoil, 1995 88
Protocol on Strategic Environmental Assessment 2003 .... 62, 89
Regional Convention for the Conservation of the Red Sea and Gulf of Aden (Jeddah Convention) 1982 .... 131, 133
Rotterdam Convention on the Prior Informed Consent Procedure for Certain Hazardous Chemicals and Pesticides in International Trade, and the Stockholm Convention on Persistent Organic Pollutants 1998 .. 138
Seafarers' Identity Document Convention 1958 269
Seafarers' Identity Document Convention 2003 269
Seafarers' Pensions Convention, 1946. 269
Small Tanker Oil Pollution Indemnification Agreement (STOPIA) 2006 .... 300, 304, 324, 325
Stockholm Declaration on the Human Environment 1972 .... 69, 71, 238
Tanker Oil Pollution Indemnification Agreement (TOPIA) 2006 .... 300,304, 324, 325
United Nations Convention on the Environment and Development Rio Declaration (Rio Declaration) 62,86, 87, 208, 216
United Nations Convention on the Law of the Sea (UNCLOS) 1982 .... 3, 11, 12, 13, 14, 15, 16, 17, 18, 19, 61, 63, 64, 68, 70, 71, 72, 73, 74, 75, 83, 84, 86, 90, 133, 136, 206, 208, 227, 235, 236, 237, 287, 288, 296
 Art. 1 71
 Art. 1(1)(4) 63, 227
 Art. 1(1)(5)(a) 72
 Art. 1(1)(5)(b) 73
 Art. 1.1 2
 Art. 2 68

Art. 3 16
Art. 4 16
Art. 21 11
Art. 56 .... 68, 71
Art. 56(1)(b)(iii) 72
Art. 58 16
Art. 60 72
Art. 76 16
Art. 77 68
Art. 80 .... 71, 72
Art. 90 72
Art. 91 .... 13, 14
Art. 94 .... 13, 14
Art. 94(5) 15
Art. 94(7) 15
Art. 111 16
Art. 123 236
Art. 145(a) 71, 75
Art. 192 .... 2, 70, 71
Art. 193 .... 70, 71
Art. 194 .... 70, 71, 235, ~~237~~
Art. 194(1) 2
Art. 194(3)(c) 71
Art. 195 .... 70, 71, 236
Art. 196 .... 70, 71
Art. 197 236
Art. 198 236
Art. 199 236
Art. 200 236
Art. 201 236
Art. 202 236
Art. 203 236
Art. 207 64
Art. 208 .... 13, 16, 64, 70, 72
Art. 208(1) 72, 90
Art. 209 64
Art. 209(2) 71, 75
Art. 210 .... 13, 16, 64, 71, 72, 73, 133
Art. 211 .... 15, 16, 64
Art. 211(4) 17
Art. 211(5) 17
Art. 211(6) 17
Art. 212 .... 71, 74
Art. 214 .... 70, 71, 72
Art. 216 .... 18, 74
Art. 217 .... 13, 14, 15
Art. 217(4) 15
Art. 218 .... 13, 14, 18, 19, 288
Art. 218(1) 18

xliii

TABLE OF CONVENTIONS AND TREATIES

Art. 218(2).................................... 18
Art. 219 .... 13, 14, 18
Art. 220 .... 13, 14, 16, 17, 18, 20
Art. 220(1).................................... 17
Art. 220(3).................................... 17
Art. 220(5).................................... 17
Art. 220(6).................................... 18
Art. 221 13
Art. 221(1).................................... 237
Art. 221(2).................................... 237
Art. 223 13
Art. 224 13
Art. 225 13
Art. 226 .... 13, 18
Art. 226(1)(a) 19
Art. 226(1)(b)................................. 19
Art. 226(1)(c) 19
Art. 226(2).................................... 18
Art. 227 13
Art. 228 13

Art. 229 13
Art. 230 .... 13, 19, 288
Art. 231 13
Art. 232 13
Art. 233 13
Art. 234 13
Art. 235 .... 13, 83, 84
Art. 235(1).................................... 83
Art. 235(2)................................. 84, 296
Art. 235(3).................................... 84
Art. 236 13
Art. 237 13
Art. 287(1).................................... 136
Art. 311 70
Annex V 136
United Nations Framework
Convention on Climate Change
1992.. 182, 183
Vienna Convention on Civil Liability
for Nuclear Damage 1963 331

INTRODUCTORY CHAPTER

Marine environment protection and shipping regulations

TABLE OF CONTENTS

Section 1	Shipping, the environment and the international standard-setting Process	2
0.1	Setting the scene	2
0.2	The nature of the standard-setting process	3
0.3	The four pillars of shipping legislation	5
0.4	The role of the International Maritime Organisation	5
	0.4.1 Description, including structure	5
	0.4.2 The adoption of conventions	7
	0.4.3 Typology of IMO acts	9
0.5	Overview of marine pollution control regulatory framework	10
Section 2	The United Nations Convention on the Law of the Sea (UNCLOS III) and key stakeholders	11
0.6	The role of flag States, coastal States and port States	11
	0.6.1 The United Nations Convention on the Law of the Sea (UNCLOS III)	11
	0.6.2 UNCLOS III and marine environment protection viewed from the standpoint of flag States, coastal States and port States	13
	0.6.3 How does UNCLOS III reach private operators?	19
0.7	The contribution of classification societies	20
0.8	The contribution of the European Union	21
	0.8.1 How do EU acts reach private operators?	23
	0.8.2 The future of the EU agenda on marine pollution	24
0.9	The contribution of non-governmental organisations	25
	0.9.1 Industry Best practices	26
	0.9.2 International Organisation for Standardisation	26
Section 3	Where are environmental regulations impacting on shipping heading for?	26
0.10	Where do we stand at present?	26
0.11	Identifying possible drivers for the future	27

SECTION 1: SHIPPING, THE ENVIRONMENT AND THE INTERNATIONAL STANDARD-SETTING PROCESS

0.1 Setting the scene

Shipping has traditionally been considered as the most environmentally friendly means of transportation. Comprising approximately 89,500 vessels,[1] a significant part of the world commercial fleet contributes to 90% of world trade.[2] Vessels are required by applicable regulations to be compliant. Environmental compliance in the shipping industry is only one facet of the regulatory compliance package that shipping companies are committed to. Maritime safety and standards on seafarers (labour standards, training, certification and watchkeeping-related standards) are additional pillars. Environmental compliance costs are generally considered significant.[3] While non-compliance with maritime regulations in the shipping industry may be viewed as having the potential to generate some cost savings in the short run, such a strategy impairs the industry as a whole, and presents risks for the marine environment. Furthermore, it is in conflict with societal expectations; ultimately, at the individual level, it may lead to an increase of legal costs and insurance premiums, contribute to negative publicity, and distort access of the polluter to viable contracts.

According to international instruments, pollution of the marine environment means "the introduction by man, directly or indirectly, of substances or energy into the marine environment, including estuaries, which results or is likely to result in such deleterious effects as harm to living resources and marine life, hazards to human health, hindrance to marine activities, including fishing and other legitimate uses of the sea, impairment of quality for use of sea water and reduction of amenities".[4] The general obligation of States to protect and preserve the marine environment has been expressly set out by the international legislator.[5] States are consequently held to take all measures in line with international law to prevent, reduce and control pollution of the marine environment from any source.[6]

---

1 United Nations Conference on Trade and Development (UNCTAD), *Revue of Maritime Transport* (2015, p. X). The report states 89,464 vessels.

2 See the website of the International Chamber of Shipping, <www.ics-shipping.org/shipping-facts/shipping-and-world-trade> accessed 5 May 2017.

3 According to the estimates of the Organisation for Economic Cooperation and Development (OECD), environmental compliance costs are approximately at 3.5–6.5% of the daily operating costs of a vessel. See OECD, *Cost Savings Stemming from Non-Compliance with International Environmental Regulations in the Maritime Sector* (Maritime Transport Committee, 2003) p. 5. The report examines unfair commercial advantage afforded to substandard shipowners who fail to comply with international environmental regulations that apply to their ships. Also note OECD, *Economic Aspects of Environmental Compliance Assurance* (Proceedings from the OECD Global Forum on Sustainable Development, Paris, 2–3 December 2004).

4 Article 1(1)(4) of UNCLOS III.

5 Article 192 of UNCLOS III.

6 Article 194(1) of UNCLOS III.

The protection of the marine environment is a key priority nowadays for regulators, institutional stakeholders, private operators in the shipping, oil and gas industries, and civil society at large. Protection of the marine environment is a basic area in legal instruments of reference such as the United Nations Convention on the Law of the Sea (commonly referred to as UNCLOS III), which was adopted in 1982 by the international community. The instrument sets out a framework with the rights and obligations of States in relation to the use of the sea, including navigational freedoms and the management of ocean resources. The International Convention for the Prevention of Pollution from Ships (MARPOL, also referred to as MARPOL 73/78), the international legal instrument of reference governing marine pollution from shipping, addresses the protection of the marine environment through a firm prohibition of illegal discharges at sea, and a number of exceptions under well-defined conditions. Distinct legal texts adopted by the International Maritime Organisation (IMO) govern specific aspects of the protection of the marine environment from varied sources of pollutants. They range from the Convention on the Control of Harmful Anti-fouling Systems on Ships (AFS 2001), to the so-called Hong Kong International Convention for the Safe and Environmentally Sound Recycling of Ships (2009) or the Ballast Water Management Convention (2004), which, incidentally, demanded about 25 years for its negotiation, drafting and entry into force.

Regional agreements signed by countries around a particular sea area with a view to addressing marine environment items presenting a common interest complement the picture.[7] Some of these agreements or conventions that present a regional interest will be touched upon in subsequent chapters.

Let us now place the focus on the nature of the standard-setting process.

0.2 The nature of the standard-setting process

To a large extent, maritime regulations governing marine pollution were adopted in response to maritime accidents which had caused large-scale pollution. In other terms, the international legislator has to a certain extent been reactive rather than proactive. This approach in the standard-setting process has not been confined to the protection of the marine environment, it is also observed in relation to maritime safety. The sinking of the *Titanic* in 1912 prompted the adoption of the first version of the SOLAS Convention on safety of life at sea in 1914; the *Torrey Canyon* (1967) accident in the English Channel, the accident involving the *Exxon Valdez* (1989) in Alaskan waters, the sinking of the *Erika* off the coast of France in 1999, the sinking of the *Prestige*, off the coast of Galicia, Spain, in 2002, and other casualties acted as catalysts for the advent of regulations.[8]

Nowadays, regulations are not limited to the prescriptive approach, which is probably the most straightforward way to spell out standards. A prescriptive approach means that there is a prohibition to do or refrain from doing a certain

---

7 An overview of this aspect can be found in European Maritime Safety Agency (EMSA), *Addressing Illegal Discharges in the Marine Environment* (document date unavailable), p. 20 *et seq.*

8 Some of these accidents will be dealt with in more detail in subsequent chapters.

action, generally in light of known risk factors. In addition to the prescriptive approach, a goal-based approach to the standard-setting process has contributed to better regulations in the area of safety, including ship design, and appears to have a potential in new areas such as regulations applicable in polar waters (Polar Code). The standard-based rationale required, amongst others, that the standards be clear, long standing, verifiable and specific.[9] Adopted on 20 May 2010, IMO Resolution MSC.287(87) pertains to the adoption of the international goal-based ship construction standards for bulk carriers and oil tankers. The Resolution adheres to the idea of ship construction standards that would permit innovation in design, while ensuring that ships constructed in such a manner, if properly maintained, remain safe and environmentally friendly throughout their life. In other words, the standards describe the goals and set out the functional requirements that the rules for the design and construction of bulk carriers and oil tankers shall conform to.

Furthermore, the Formal Safety Assessment (FSA) approach is a proactive tool used by the IMO in the standard-setting process. It constitutes an evaluation methodology that seeks to enhance safety, including marine environment protection, through risk analysis and cost/benefit assessment. According to the IMO it is "a rational and systematic process for assessing the risks associated with shipping activity and for evaluating the costs and benefits of IMO's options for reducing these risks".[10] The FSA is geared towards new regulations or existing regulations considered for amendments; it should normally result in a clear justification of new or amended regulatory measures.

On top of detailed technical prescriptions or goal-based principles, shipping regulations may also make good use of the concept of self-regulation. A representative illustration is the International Safety Management Code (ISM). The latter was adopted in 1993 by IMO Resolution A.741(18); in 1994, it became a chapter within the SOLAS Convention (entry into force of the Code 1 July 1998). The adoption of the Code followed the accident involving the *Herald of Free Enterprise* (1987) where there was a general acknowledgement of the need to take action against poor management standards of ships. Self-regulation entails a self-assessment approach. The latter means that private operators are held to integrate the goals set out by a legal instrument through actions designed and implemented by them, after taking into account relevant risks; the ultimate goal of a self-assessment approach would be the full integration of the goals of the legal instrument into the safety and environmental culture that should be embedded in the crews, managers ashore, senior management, etc. That being said, the above may be complemented by voluntary self-regulation. For example, policies voluntarily adopted by charterers aiming at avoiding the use of inefficient ships on the basis of their greenhouse gas (GHG) emissions performance.[11]

---

9 See the website of the IMO <www.imo.org> ("IMO Goal-based standards – What are goal-based standards?") accessed 5 May 2017.

10 See the website of the IMO <www.imo.org/en/OurWork/Safety/SafetyTopics/Pages/Formal-SafetyAssessment.aspx> accessed 5 May 2017.

11 See International Transport Journal, *Charterers to Exclude Inefficient Vessels* (29 May 2015), cited in *Review of Maritime Transport, supra* note 1, p. 22. The said charterers are reported to represent 20% of global shipped tonnage.

At present, it can be said that shipping legislation is centered on four basic directions. While the protection of the marine environment stems from a specific international convention (MARPOL), as it will be seen below and in the process, the four pillars of shipping legislation interphase between them, and do not function in an isolated manner in relation to the overall goals sought by them.

0.3 The four pillars of shipping legislation

Safe, secure, environmentally sound shipping conducted under decent working and living conditions

As already pointed out, while the four pillars of shipping legislation cover distinct areas, in practice they interphase in a dynamic manner. Viewed from the standpoint of the protection of marine environment, even though MARPOL is the principal instrument on the matter, there cannot be any doubt as to the direct or indirect contribution of the other conventions to the marine environment. One may consider, for example, the correlation between carriage of dangerous goods under SOLAS with marine pollution prevention or the synergies that exist between qualified and certificated crews that are properly trained or who enjoy decent working and living conditions aboard with their ability to prevent and/ or control marine pollution. This approach is moreover strengthened by current trends which view the position of the ship and the company as a system (for example, under the ISM Code). Another illustration of the interphase between the environment and other areas would be the Polar Code (which will be discussed in the chapters that will follow).

Having identified the rationale that guides the adoption of international standards, let us now have a closer look at the IMO, as the body *par excellence* that adopts international regulations in shipping.

0.4 The role of the International Maritime Organisation

The instruments adopted by the International Maritime Organisation (IMO) have been mentioned a number of times so far. On this point a few words on the role of the IMO and the standard-setting process would be useful.

0.4.1 Description, including structure

The IMO, a specialised agency of the United Nations headquartered in London with well-established technical expertise on maritime matters, is considered to be the international regulator of shipping. Its action is intended to be global in order to achieve uniformity. IMO's work is geared towards maritime safety, maritime security, marine pollution prevention and management, liability and other key areas. Within the IMO, member States discuss, deliberate and adopt international regulations. The IMO currently comprises 173 member States and three associate members. Founded following the Second World War, the IMO came into existence in 1958, and was initially named Inter-Governmental Maritime

Table 0.1 The four pillars of international shipping legislation

SOLAS	MARPOL	STCW 2010	ILO MLC 2006
(International Convention for the Safety of Life at Sea, 1974; Protocol of 1988)	**(International Convention for the Prevention of Pollution from Ships)**	**(Standards of Training, Certification and Watchkeeping for Seafarers)**	**(International Labour Organisation Maritime Labour Convention)**
Promotion of safety of life at sea through requirements governing construction, design and operation of ships.	Protection of the marine environment from deliberate, negligent or accidental release of oil and other harmful substances from ships; protection of the environment from air pollution generated by ships.	Enhanced and uniform standards of competence of seafarers – regulation of certification, training, manning, and other related areas.	Enhanced social protection of seafarers through decent living and working conditions aboard.
The SOLAS Convention currently in force was adopted on 1 November 1974 (entry into force on 25 May 1980). It has since been amended twice through protocols (1978 and 1988), and by means of IMO resolutions. Through its 14 chapters, the Convention is the basis for the conduct of surveys, issue of appropriate certification, and addressing of specific matters that are vital for the safety of ships. Such requirements range from construction to life-saving appliances and from radiocommunications to carriage of dangerous goods, safety of navigation, international safety management, security, operation in polar waters, etc.	The MARPOL Convention was adopted in 1973. It was amended by a Protocol adopted in 1978, and was further amended by a number of IMO resolutions. It governs the prevention and control of marine pollution through six technical annexes dealing respectively with the prevention of pollution by oil, noxious liquid substances in bulk, harmful substances carried by sea in packaged form, sewage, garbage, and air emissions from shipping.	The STCW Convention was originally adopted by the IMO in 1978; since then, it was amended a number of times, including in 1995 and in 2010 (in the last case by the so-called Manila amendments, which constitute the reference nowadays). The Convention sets out requirements which involve shipping companies and maritime administrations in relation to seafarers in areas such as certification, standards of competence, manning, hours of work and hours of rest, watch-keeping arrangements, etc.	Adopted in 2006 by the International Labour Organisation. Amended. It replaces (with a few exceptions) and reshapes the "old" maritime labour conventions and recommendations adopted by the same organisation (about 60 instruments). The Convention entered into force internationally on 13 August 2013. It deals with the social protection of seafarers by setting out minimum standards for decent working and living conditions onboard; it enhances the contribution of port State control to the verification of proper implementation of relevant standards, and sets out the maritime labour certificate (MLC) and the declaration of maritime labour compliance (DMLC).

Consultative Organization (IMCO). In 1982 the Organization was renamed IMO. The IMO provides machinery for cooperation among States with a view to promoting safe, secure, efficient and environmentally friendly shipping. The main tools of its mission consist of the instruments adopted by the Organization through its bodies; the Organisation is involved with the review of existing conventions in light of technological and other developments as well as with the adoption of new ones. Through its conventions, IMO aims at enhanced and uniform standards in the shipping industry on the global level. Technical cooperation is also an important platform of action via the involvement of member States. Against the above background, it is noted that the Organisation is not entrusted with the mission of enforcement of standards, as this aspect is in the hands of member States in their capacity as flag States. This also includes the adoption and enforcement of appropriate sanctions in case of non-compliance. This aspect is not changed by the recently adopted IMO Member State Audit Scheme, which is a mandatory self-evaluation tool, and which will be discussed in other chapters.

A number of entities follow the work of the IMO as observers[12] or are associated with it through consultative status.[13]

The structure of the IMO consists of the following bodies:

- Assembly;
- Council;
- Secretariat, and
- a number of technical committees (and sub-committees), namely:
  - Maritime Safety Committee (MSC);
  - Marine Environment Protection Committee (MEPC);
  - Facilitation Committee (FAL);[14]
  - Legal Committee (LEG);
  - Technical Cooperation Committee (TC).[15]

0.4.2 The adoption of conventions

The adoption of conventions may be a lenghty process, it ususaly requires a number of years.

---

12 E.g. Paris Memorandum of Understanding on Port State Control (Paris MOU), OSPAR Commission for the Protection of the Marine Environment of the North-East Atlantic, etc.

13 An example, would be the International Salvage Union (ISU), International Chamber of Shipping (ICS), Baltic and International Maritime Council (BIMCO), International Association of Independent Tanker Owners (INTERTANKO), International Tanker Owners Pollution Federation (ITOPF), International Petroleum Industry Environmental Conservation Association (IPIECA), Oil Companies International Marine Forum (OCIMF), World Fund for Nature (WWF), etc.

14 It works on the simplification of maritime traffic, through, for example, the standardisation of ships' papers.

15 It deals with development aid.

A draft IMO instrument is prepared by an IMO committee/sub-committee following approval from of the Assembly or the Council. The draft is then communicated to IMO member States for examination. The draft is reviewed on the level of the MSC or MEPC, and constitutes the basis for the work of a diplomatic conference, which may adopt the text. The Convention comes into force following specified conditions being met and a time period. The criteria to be met for the entry into force of an IMO convention are set out by the instruments themselves (for example, acceptance by a specified number of member States representing a specific percentage of the world's gross tonnage). A practical illustration would be the Ballast Water Management Convention (International Convention for the Control and Management of Ships' Ballast Water and Sediments), which demanded about 14 years of negotiations. The Convention was adopted on 13 February 2004. The formal conditions for its entry into force were the ratification by 30 States representing a fleet of 35% of world tonnage. The Convention entered into force on 8 September 2017.

That said, it is essential for the Organization to build the consensus needed in the industry for the smooth application of the instruments that are underway. For example, a convention not supported by maritime States is likely to have a more limited effect than a convention massively ahdered to by such States.

On this point, it would be useful perhaps to clarify the terms signature, ratification, acceptance, approval and accession, which represent some of the methods used by States in expressing their consent in being bound by an international convention. Consent may be expressed by signature where, in broad terms, it is provided that signature will have that effect. A State may also sign a treaty subject to ratification, acceptance or approval. When an international instrument stops being open for signature, a State that seeks to become party to it does so through another method, which is called 'accession'.

The action of the international legislature is not limited to the adoption of instruments. Amending existing instruments, thus keeping applicable instruments in line with developments in the industry (e.g. lessons learnt developments following incidents, technological advances, etc.), is an equally important task. Amendments through diplomatic conferences were the rule in the past. However, for institutional reasons, more time could be needed for amendments than for adoption, which was frustrating for the effectiveness of the standar-setting process; it was also possible for an amendment not to enter into force at all. This situation was to a large extent remedied through the so-called "tacit acceptance procedure", a device that is integrated in most IMO's conventions, including MARPOL, for the amendment of technical annexes. The initial practice would be for the amendment to enter into force after being accepted by, for example, one third of the Parties. With the tacit acceptance procedure, no further act of ratification or acceptance is needed, an amendment shall enter into force at a particular time (e.g. in two years) unless, before that date, objections to the amendment are received from a specific number of Parties. In practice, it is observed that objections are rare. This device presents the advantage of flexibility, and speeds up IMO amendments.

INTRODUCTORY CHAPTER

IMO conventions underpin the current system governing ship certification – the latter being central to the conduct of shipping. In conjunction with the type and size of a vessel, an important number of certificates set out in international conventions are required to be carried on board (or, in some cases, be kept ashore). Relevant certificates are issued by the flag State or by entities empowered by the flag State for the purpose (referred to as Recognised Organisations). Certificates are issued following appropriate surveys, and are generally considered to provide evidence at first glance that the ship is compliant with the requirements covered by each certificate. However, there may be circumstances, including clear grounds for believing that the condition of the ship and its equipment does not correspond substantially with the particulars of the certificate, justifying more detailed inspections or the prohibition of sailing (detention). Returning to surveys, a survey can be understood as an inspection of ship items in relation to a particular certificate.

0.4.3 Typology of IMO acts

Conventions	IMO conventions are multilateral treaties which, once they enter into force, are mandatory for the countries that have ratified them; for most part, they pertain to maritime safety, security, marine environment protection and limitation of liability.
Protocols	They amend existing conventions; as a general rule, they have to be ratified separately (e.g. MARPOL Protocol 1978; SOLAS Protocol 1988).
Codes	In areas where the adoption of an international convention is not considered a good solution, Codes can be adopted in the form of binding (e.g. ISM Code, Polar Code, etc.) or recommendatory instruments; for example, certain provisions of the Code on Noise Levels on Board Ships (entry into force 1 July 2014), which is mandatory, remain recommendatory or informative. Codes are commonly integrated into Conventions (e.g. the International Safety Management (ISM) Code and the Noise Code are integrated into SOLAS) through IMO resolutions.
Resolutions	They may be adopted by IMO diplomatic conferences or IMO bodies such as the IMO Assembly (e.g. Assembly Resolution A.1056(27) adopted on 30 November 2011 entitled "Promotion as widely as possible of the application of the 2006 Guidelines on fair treatment of seafarers in the event of a maritime accident"), the Maritime Safety Committee (e.g. MSC.355(92), Amendments to the International Convention for Safe Containers (CSC) 1972), the Marine Environment Protection Committee (e.g. MEPC.239(65) Amendments to the 2012 Guidelines for the Implementation of MARPOL Annex V), etc. Their purpose varies. They may be used to state declarations of intent, interpret existing Conventions, introduce standards or amend existing texts.
Circulars	They provide clarifications, interpretation or other information (e.g. MSC.1/Circ.1503 adopted 24 July 2015 on Electronic Chart Display and Information Systems (ECDIS) Guidance for Good Practice; MSC/Circ.1103, MEPC.6/Circ.9, 31 December 2003, National Contact Points for Safety and Pollution Prevention, etc.).

0.5 Overview of marine pollution control regulatory framework

Table 0.2 Overview of marine pollution control under MARPOL 73/78

Prevention of Pollution by Oil – Regulated in Annex I	Control of Pollution by Noxious Liquid Substances Carried in Bulk by Tankers – Regulated in Annex II	Prevention of Pollution by Harmful Substances Carried by Sea in Packaged Form – Regulated in Annex III	Prevention of Pollution by Sewage from Ships – Regulated in Annex IV	Prevention of Pollution by Garbage from Ships – Regulated in Annex V	Prevention of Air Pollution from Ships – Regulated in Annex VI
Entry into force: 2 October 1983. Amended.	Entry into force: 6 April 1987. Amended.	Entry into force: 1 July 1992. Amended.	Entry into force: 27 September 2003. Amended.	Entry into force: 31 December 1988. Amended.	Entry into force: 19 May 2005. Amended.
Selected highlights: Discharges into the sea of oil or oily mixtures from ships are in principle prohibited. Any discharge into the sea of oil or oily mixtures from the cargo area of an oil tanker shall be prohibited except under strict conditions.	Selected highlights: The discharge into the sea of residues of substances assigned to specified categories (X, Y or Z or of those provisionally assessed as such) are prohibited unless such discharges are made in full compliance with the applicable operational requirements contained in the Annex.	Selected highlights: Prohibition of carriage of harmful substances except when conducted in accordance with the provisions of this Annex.	Selected highlights: The discharge of sewage into the sea is prohibited except under specified conditions. The discharge of sewage from a passenger ship within a special area shall be in principle prohibited.	Selected highlights: Discharge of all garbage into the sea is prohibited, except under specified conditions. Discharge of specified garbage into the sea within special areas shall only be permitted while the ship is en route and under additional conditions.	Selected highlights: The sulphur content of any fuel oil used on board ships shall not exceed specified limits. The operation of a marine diesel engine installed on a ship is subjected to nitrogen oxides' emissions requirements. Any deliberate emissions of ozone-depleting substances are prohibited.
					Emissions directly arising from the exploration, exploitation and associated offshore processing of sea-bed mineral resources are exempt from the provisions of this Annex.

(Source: Dr. Iliana Christodoulou-Varotsi)

INTRODUCTORY CHAPTER

SECTION 2: THE UNITED NATIONS CONVENTION ON THE LAW OF THE SEA (UNCLOS III) AND KEY STAKEHOLDERS

0.6 The role of flag States, coastal States and port States

0.6.1 The United Nations Convention on the Law of the Sea (UNCLOS III)

The international instrument of reference for most States in the area of international law of the sea tackling navigational freedoms and the use of the oceans and their resources, is the United Nations Convention on the Law of the Sea (commonly referred to as UNCLOS III). The Convention was adopted, as its name suggests, by the United Nations in 1982, and has been in force internationally since 16 November 1994. One may notice that the Convention came later than the three IMO quality shipping conventions of reference, i.e. SOLAS, MARPOL and STCW. As UNCLOS III is a framework or umbrella convention, it becomes "operational" via specific regulations in other international instruments.[16] UNCLOS III creates synergies with the pre-existing instruments by taking into account the existence of "generally accepted international rules and standards", "applicable international rules and standards", etc. An illustration of this would be the position of the coastal State,[17] which may legislate over the innocent passage through its territorial sea in respect, amongst others, of the safety of navigation, the preservation of the environment (of the coastal State), and the prevention, reduction and control of pollution thereof; however, "such laws and regulations shall not apply to the design, construction, manning or equipment of foreign ships unless they are giving effect to generally accepted international rules and standards".[18]

The Convention comprises 320 articles and nine annexes. Amongst others, it addresses marine pollution in a lengthy part (see table of contents below), which is Part XII entitled "Protection and preservation of the marine environment". From the standpoint of methodology, Part XII approaches marine pollution to a large extent from the standpoint of the flag State, the coastal State and the port State. This legal analysis that splits State jurisdiction in three parts has given rise to detailed developments in theory/academia and goes beyond the scope of this work. That said, this approach (flag State, coastal State, and port State jurisdiction) has clearly marked the way marine environment has been treated by regulators.

---

16 See Gaetano Librando, 'The International Maritime Organization and the Law of the Sea', in David Joseph Attard (General Ed), *The IMLI Manual on International Maritime Law, Vol. I, The Law of the Sea* (OUP, Oxford, 2014).

17 See *infra* note 19.

18 Article 21.

PART XII OF UNCLOS III

Protection and preservation of the marine environment

SECTION 1 GENERAL PROVISIONS

Article 192. General obligation
Article 193. Sovereign right of States to exploit their natural resources
Article 194. Measures to prevent, reduce and control pollution of the marine environment
Article 195. Duty not to transfer damage or hazards or transform one type of pollution into another
Article 196. Use of technologies or introduction of alien or new species

SECTION 2 GLOBAL AND REGIONAL COOPERATION

Article 197. Cooperation on a global or regional basis
Article 198. Notification of imminent or actual damage
Article 199. Contingency plans against pollution
Article 200. Studies, research programmes and exchange of information and data
Article 201. Scientific criteria for regulations

SECTION 3 TECHNICAL ASSISTANCE

Article 202. Scientific and technical assistance to developing States
Article 203. Preferential treatment for developing States

SECTION 4 MONITORING AND ENVIRONMENTAL ASSESSMENT

Article 204. Monitoring of the risks or effects of pollution
Article 205. Publication of reports
Article 206. Assessment of potential effects of activities

SECTION 5 INTERNATIONAL RULES AND NATIONAL LEGISLATION TO PREVENT, REDUCE AND CONTROL POLLUTION OF THE MARINE ENVIRONMENT

Article 207. Pollution from land-based sources
Article 208. Pollution from seabed activities subject to national jurisdiction
Article 209. Pollution from activities in the Area
Article 210. Pollution by dumping
Article 211. Pollution from vessels
Article 212. Pollution from or through the atmosphere

SECTION 6 ENFORCEMENT

Article 213. Enforcement with respect to pollution from land-based sources
Article 214. Enforcement with respect to pollution from seabed activities
Article 215. Enforcement with respect to pollution from activities in the Area
Article 216. Enforcement with respect to pollution by dumping
Article 217. Enforcement by flag States

INTRODUCTORY CHAPTER

Article 218. Enforcement by port States
Article 219. Measures relating to seaworthiness of vessels to avoid pollution
Article 220. Enforcement by coastal States
Article 221. Measures to avoid pollution arising from or through the atmosphere
Article 222. Enforcement with respect to pollution from or through the atmosphere

SECTION 7 SAFEGUARDS

Article 223. Measures to facilitate proceedings
Article 224. Exercise of powers of enforcement
Article 225. Duty to avoid adverse consequences in the exercise of the powers of enforcement
Article 226. Investigation of foreign vessels
Article 227. Non-discrimination with respect to foreign vessels
Article 228. Suspension and restrictions on institution of proceedings
Article 229. Institution of civil proceedings
Article 230. Monetary penalties and the observance of recognised rights of the accused
Article 231. Notification to the flag State and other States concerned
Article 232. Liability of States arising from enforcement measures
Article 233. Safeguards with respect to straits used for international navigation

SECTION 8 ICE-COVERED AREAS

Article 234. Ice-covered areas

SECTION 9 RESPONSIBILITY AND LIABILITY

Article 235. Responsibility and liability

SECTION 10 SOVEREIGN IMMUNITY

Article 236. Sovereign immunity

SECTION 11 OBLIGATIONS UNDER OTHER CONVENTIONS ON THE PRO-
TECTION AND PRESERVATION OF THE MARINE ENVIRONMENT

Article 237. Obligations under other conventions on the protection and preservation of the marine environment

0.6.2 *UNCLOS III and marine environment protection viewed from the standpoint of flag States, coastal States and port States*

Under UNCLOS III, flag State jurisdiction clearly prevails (Article 91, Article 94, Article 217). The jurisdiction of the coastal State in this area is firm but it follows a gradual diminution of powers the further one moves away from the shore (Article 208, Article 210, Article 220). Last but not least, a separate port State jurisdiction is recognised by the Convention (Article 218, Article 219) despite a partial overlap with the competency of the coastal State – a port State always being a coastal State.[19]

Beginning with the flag State, every registration country has the right, according to Article 91, to determine the conditions for the grant of its nationality to ships, including registration and the right to fly its flag.[20] This is central to the international shipping system and marine pollution control. The same provision also states that "there must exist a genuine link between the State and the ship", without, however, defining the genuine link. It can be said that the nationality of the vessel is the departing point of the exposure of the vessel to regulatory compliance governing marine environment, as a vessel is first of all subject to the laws and regulations of the flag State, including in the area of marine pollution control (the term "marine pollution control" being used here in its broadest sense). Furthermore, every State, according to Article 94 on the duties of the flag State, "shall effectively exercise its jurisdiction and control in administrative, technical and social matters over ships flying its flag". In this context, the flag State is notably held to maintain a register of ships, and assume jurisdiction under its internal law over each ship flying its flag and its master, officers and crew

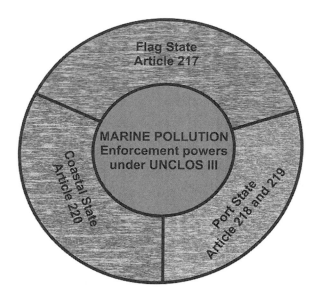

Figure 1.1 Marine pollution enforcement powers under UNCLOS III

---

19 See Maria Gavouneli, 'State Jurisdiction in Relation to the Protection and Preservation of the Marine Environment', pp. 5–29, in David Joseph Attard (General Ed), *The IMLI Manual on International Maritime Law, Vol. III, Marine Environmental Law and Maritime Security Law* (OUP, Oxford, 2016). An overview of the competencies of the flag State, the coastal State and the port State can also be found in G.P. Pamborides, *International Shipping Law* (Kluwer Law International/Ant. N. Sakkoulas Publishers, Athens, 1999).

20 Article 91 is entitled "Nationality of ships".

in respect of the ship's administrative, technical and social matters. Moreover, the flag State has the duty to take measures for its ships that are necessary for safety at sea (e.g. construction, manning, etc.), while conforming to generally accepted international regulations.[21] This is an important legal limitation to unilateral action. Article 94(7) is also relevant to the marine environment as it states that each State "shall cause an inquiry to be held" into every marine casualty or incident of navigation on the high seas involving a ship flying its flag and causing loss of life or serious injury to nationals of another State or serious damage to ships or installations of another State or to the marine environment. A duty of cooperation between the flag State and the other State into the incident is spelled out by the same provision.

In addition to the above, Article 211 should be mentioned. It deals with pollution from vessels and it can be considered as a key provision. The interest of Article 211 is not limited to flag States – flag States being held to adopt laws and regulations for the prevention, reduction and control of pollution of the marine environment from vessels flying their flag or under their registry.

Enforcement powers of the flag State, including in relation to marine pollution, are set out in Article 217, which is entitled "Enforcement by flag States". This is a lengthy provision which can be briefly summarised as follows:

Firstly, flag States have the duty to ensure compliance by the vessels flying their flag with international regulations for the prevention, reduction and control of pollution of the marine environment from vessels. Flag States are also held to provide for the effective enforcement of such rules regardless of where a violation takes place.

Some of the numerous facets of the role of flag States as shaped by this provision, would be the following: flag States must take measures in order to prohibit their vessels from sailing until they can proceed to sea in compliance with existing requirements; furthermore, flag States are held to ensure that their vessels carry on board the certificates required under international conventions. Investigation and, where appropriate, proceedings in respect of alleged violations of international regulations must be provided by the flag State, "irrespective of where the violation occurred or where the pollution caused by such violation has occurred or has been spotted".[22] Additional aspects concerning investigations of violations are provided by the article, including assistance from other States, written requests from other States to the flag State to investigate violations, and information to the requesting State and the competent international organisation of the action taken. It is noteworthy, that in its last paragraph, Article 217 addresses the question of penalties, which is central to the exposure of seafarers to criminalisation. It is provided that penalties set out by national laws for vessels flying their flags must be adequate in severity to discourage violations wherever they take place. The instrument does not define "adequate in severity" and the matter is therefore in the hands of States. At this point it can be noted that the MARPOL Convention, adopted prior

---

21 Article 94(5).
22 Article 217(4).

to UNCLOS III, set out, in Article 4 on violations, that penalties must be adequate in severity to discourage MARPOL violations and shall be equally severe irrespective of where a violation takes place.

Against this background, the jurisdiction of the coastal State is articulated in a firm manner but, as already mentioned, it is subject to a gradual diminution of powers depending on the distance from the shore; this is notably suggested by Article 111 on the right of hot pursuit, Article 208 on pollution from seabed activities subject to national jurisdiction, Article 210 on pollution by dumping, the above-mentioned Article 211 on pollution from vessels, and Article 220 on the enforcement by coastal States.

Among the numerous provisions which are relevant to the position of the coastal State, some of them concern exclusively the coastal State, whereas others present a wider interest.

Returning to Article 111, this provision spells out the right of hot pursuit. The said right may be exercised only by duly authorised warships or military aircraft (or other ships or aircraft on government service), and must be commenced when the foreign ship (or one of its boats) is within sea areas specified by the Convention; this includes the territorial sea of the pursuing State. Article 111 may be relevant to the protection of the marine environment from the standpoint of the coastal State as the coastal State is given the right to undertake the hot pursuit of a foreign vessel when it has "good reason to believe that the ship has violated the laws and regulations of that State". Furthermore, coastal States are held under Article 208 to adopt laws and regulations for the prevention, reduction and control of pollution of the marine environment "arising from or in connection with seabed activities subject to their jurisdiction and from artificial islands, installations and structures under their jurisdiction [...]". The role of the coastal State is also visible in the area of pollution by dumping, where Article 210 provides for the express prior approval of the coastal State in the context of dumping within the territorial sea,[23] the exclusive economic zone[24] or into the continental shelf.[25]

As already mentioned, Article 211, which tackles pollution from vessels, is pivotal to regulatory compliance and to the protection of the marine environment. The article goes beyond the scope of coastal States but it is at the same

---

23 It is noted that under UNCLOS III, the sovereignty of the coastal State extends beyond its land territory and internal waters (and, if relevant, archipelagic waters), to an adjacent belt of sea, referred to as territorial sea. According to Article 3 of UNCLOS III on the breadth of the territorial sea, every State has the right to establish its territorial sea up to a limit not exceeding 12 nautical miles, measured from baselines.

24 The exclusive economic zone (EEZ) is the area beyond and adjacent to the territorial sea where coexist, to different degrees, the rights and jurisdiction of the coastal State (e.g. sovereign rights for the purpose of exploring and exploiting, conserving and managing living and non-living natural resources of the waters superjacent to the seabed and of the seabed and its subsoil), and the rights and freedoms of other States, such as the freedom of navigation, etc. (see Article 58, Part V of UNCLOS III).

25 The continental shelf of a coastal State according to UNCLOS III (Article 76) comprises the seabed and subsoil of the submarine areas that extend beyond its territorial sea, as described by the Convention.

time of particular interest to them. This is because it gives a legal basis to coastal States for legislating on marine pollution agenda. On the one hand, coastal States may, in the exercise of their sovereignty within their territorial sea, adopt laws and regulations for the prevention, reduction and control of marine pollution from foreign vessels, including vessels which exercise their right of innocent passage.[26] The right of innocent passage shall not be hampered, according to the Convention, by such regulatory action. On the other hand, coastal States are entitled under the Convention under conditions, to legislate on marine pollution in relation to their exclusive economic zone. Such action, however, must be in accordance with generally accepted international rules.[27]

Enforcement rights of the coastal State are enshrined in Article 220. This is a rather lengthy provision including eight paragraphs. Amongst others, the right of the coastal State to institute proceedings in respect of any violation of its laws adopted in accordance with international regulations on the prevention, reduction and control of pollution from vessels is set out. This is in the context where a vessel is voluntarily within a port or at an off-shore terminal of the coastal State, and the violation has occurred within the territorial sea or the exclusive economic zone of the coastal State.[28] The Article extends its scope to violations believed to have been committed during a vessel's passage in the territorial sea of a coastal State. More specifically, in case of clear grounds for believing that a vessel navigating in the territorial sea of a State has, during its passage, violated domestic laws adopted in accordance with international rules on the marine environment, the coastal State "may undertake physical inspections of the vessel relating to the violation and may, where the evidence so warrants, institute proceedings, including detention of the vessel, in accordance with its laws, subject to the provisions of section 7". It is noted at this point that section 7 deals with bonding or other appropriate financial security and the release of the vessel. It is not our intention to exhaust Article 220; however, it is noteworthy that where there are clear grounds for believing that a vessel navigating in the exclusive economic zone or in the territorial sea of a State has, in the exclusive economic zone, committed a violation of applicable rules on the marine environment, that State may require the vessel to give information required to establish whether a violation has occurred.[29] In case of clear grounds for believing that the above-mentioned violation committed by a vessel in the EEZ or territorial sea results "in a substantial discharge causing or threatening significant pollution of the marine environment, that State may undertake physical inspection of the vessel for matters relating to the violation if the vessel has refused to give information or if the information supplied by the vessel is manifestly at variance with the evident factual situation and if the circumstances of the case justify such inspection".[30] In the context of "clear objective evidence" about a violation

---

26 Article 211(4).
27 Article 211(5) and (6).
28 Article 220(1).
29 Article 220(3).
30 Article 220(5).

committed in the EEZ "resulting in a discharge causing major damage or threat of major damage to the coastline or related interests of the coastal State, or to any resources of its territorial sea or EEZ, that State may, subject to Section 7, provided that the evidence so warrants, institute proceedings, including detention of the vessel, in accordance with its laws".[31]

Let us shift now the focus from the coastal State to the port State. Port State jurisdiction over the marine environment is enshrined in Article 218 and Article 219. Article 218 is central; it is entitled "enforcement by port States". It is noted that depending on the circumstances touched upon by the provision, the latter shifts from "may" to "shall". In relation to discharges from vessels outside the internal waters, territorial sea or exclusive economic zone that are in violation of applicable international regulations, the port state "may undertake investigations, and where the evidence so warrants, institute proceedings".[32] Against this background, a limitation is set out concerning discharge violations in the internal waters, territorial sea or exclusive economic zone of another State.[33] The same provision deals with State information requests for the investigation of a discharge violation referred to in paragraph 1.[34] Furthermore, mention is made of the treatment of the records of the investigation carried out by a port State.

Port State jurisdiction is further expressed in Article 219 of the Convention, which is entitled "Measures relating to seaworthiness of vessels to avoid pollution". In essence, when a vessel within a (foreign) port or off-shore terminal violates applicable international rules and standards relating to seaworthiness and "thereby threatens damage to the marine environment", States that have ascertained so, "shall, as far as practicable, take measures to prevent the vessel from sailing". In this context, the vessel may be allowed to proceed only to the nearest appropriate repair yard, and upon removal of the causes of the violation, shall be allowed to continue "immediately".

With the above in mind, investigation of foreign vessels is addressed in a specific provision which is Article 226. The provision is of interest to States in all their facets/jurisdictions, i.e. as flag, coastal or port States. States are generally held to cooperate "to develop procedures for the avoidance of unnecessary physical inspection of vessels at sea".[35] More specifically, States have the duty not to delay a foreign vessel longer than is essential for purposes of the investigations set out in Article 216 on enforcement with respect to pollution by dumping, Article 218 on enforcement by port States, and Article 220 on enforcement by coastal States. An important point is the one concerning the nature of inspection of foreign vessels: "Any physical inspection of foreign vessels shall be limited to an examination of such certificates, records or other documents as the vessel is

---

31 Article 220(6).
32 Article 218(1).
33 Article 218(2).
34 Paragraph 1 refers to vessels that are voluntarily within a port or at an off-shore terminal of a State and to evidence suggesting a discharge outside the internal waters, territorial sea or exclusive economic zone of the coastal State in violation of international rules.
35 Article 226(2).

required to carry by generally accepted international rules and standards or of any similar documents which it is carrying [...]". It should be stressed that the further physical inspection of the vessel is placed under strict conditions set out by the same provision.[36] Bonding or other appropriate financial security is also provided for.[37] The release of vessels that would present an unreasonable threat of damage to the marine environment may be refused or made conditional.[38]

0.6.3 How does UNCLOS III reach private operators?

UNCLOS III is clearly addressed to States and reaches private operators through State legislation.

While UNCLOS III has been ratified by more than 150 States (as well as by the European Community), it is noteworthy that the Convention has not been ratified by the USA and some other countries. The Convention was shaped in recognition of well-established principles in the area concerned (e.g. traditional freedoms of navigation); at the same time, it incorporated new legal concepts. UNCLOS III sought to strike the balance between the interests of the institutional players involved with the world's oceans and their use. This approach can be seen in relation to the prevention and control of marine pollution. The Convention provides a general framework on State jurisdiction in relation to marine pollution through, as already described above, a fragmentation of jurisdiction powers. The Convention grasps private stakeholders through the rules and measures adopted by ratifying States for its implementation. The effectiveness of UNCLOS as applied by ratifying States consequently substantially depends on the way ratifying States (or States which adhere otherwise to UNCLOS) bring into action their international commitments. Port State jurisdiction, for example, has developed in recent years in a major complementary tool to the role traditionally assigned to the flag State. Through port State control the commitments of ratifying States as well as the way such commitments are materialised, are subject to the increasing oversight of the port State.

Against the above background, there are, in our opinion, areas where there is room for more clarity or effectiveness. For example, in the area of criminalisation of seafarers, Article 230 on monetary penalties and the observance of recognised rights of the accused, and Article 218, which sets out port State jurisdiction to bring legal proceedings in relation to marine pollution offences committed on the high seas, do not appear to be used smoothly in all instances by States.[39]

Following the overview of the role of the flag State, coastal State and port State, let us now briefly examine the role of classification societies, which appear to provide significant support to States in the exercise of their maritime functions.

---

36 Article 226(1)(a).
37 Article 226(1)(b).
38 Article 226(1)(c).
39 An overview of the challenges relating to the criminalisation of seafarers is given in Chapter X on the human element.

0.7 The contribution of classification societies

Class societies can be viewed as technical supervisory organisations that, in simple terms, undertake to oversee whether a vessel is fit for sailing. Class societies are service providers both to new buildings and to fleets in service; i.e. they are involved during construction as well as during a ship's service life. They contribute to maritime safety and marine environment protection through a multifaceted range of services to the shipping community. More specifically, classification is aimed at verifying "the structural strength and integrity of essential parts of the ship's hull and its appendages, and the reliability and function of the propulsion and steering systems, power generation and those other features and auxiliary systems which have been built into the ship in order to maintain essential services on board".[40] That said, flag States may empower classification societies, through varied delegations, to undertake certain tasks that fall in the remit of registration countries under international instruments.[41] Nevertheless, registration countries cannot, legally speaking, shift the guarantee of their legal duties on classification societies,[42] and the latter are not guarantors of life or property.

The history of class societies dates back to the 19th century: Bureau Veritas was established in Antwerp in 1828; Lloyd's Register of British and Foreign Shipping became a class society in 1834; the American Bureau of Shipping was established in 1862; Det Norske Veritas (DNV) was created in 1864; Germanischer Lloyd (GL) dates back to 1867. Since September 2013, DNV and GL have been merged, forming the world's largest ship classification society. The roots of classification are often correlated with Lloyd's Coffee House in London which, in the second half of the 17th century, had become a maritime hub specialised in the collection of shipping information primarily for marine insurance purposes. Nowadays, the International Association of Classification Societies (IACS) groups 12 classification societies that meet certain standards. This cluster is considered to represent over 90% of the commercial tonnage involved with international shipping.

Classification societies are commonly private and independent. They also tend to be self-regulating and subject to external audits. The oversight of classification societies by the European Commission (European Union level) is noted at this point.[43] At the present stage, out of tens of organisations on the global

---

40 IACS, *Classification Societies – What, Why and How?* (2011, p. 4).

41 On this point, IMO resolution A.739(18), giving guidelines for the authorisation of organisations acting on behalf of the Administration, adopted on 4 November 1993, and amended in 2010 by MSC.208(81), is to be noted.

42 For an illustration of this point, see regulation 6.3.1 of MARPOL Annex I, which sets out that the flag State may entrust the surveys either to surveyors nominated for the purpose or to organizations recognised by it; regulation 6.3.4 sets out that "In every case, the Administration concerned shall fully guarantee the completeness and efficiency of the survey and shall undertake to ensure the necessary arrangements to satisfy this obligation."

43 European Parliament and Council Regulation (EC) 391/2009 on common rules and standards for ship inspection and survey organizations (Recast) (Text with EEA relevance) [2009] OJ L 131/11; European Parliament and Council (EC) Directive 2009/15 on common rules and standards for ship inspection and survey organizations and for the relevant activities of maritime administrations

level that undertake activities which relate to some form of marine classification services, only 12 classification societies have been recognised by the European Commission.

While the classification of a ship may not be strictly speaking a statutory requirement, thus remaining largely voluntary, classification may function as a condition for the insurance of the vessel or for finding a charterer on the market. The effectiveness of classification is largely conditioned by the synergy between the shipowner and the class. Ships may benefit from a series of notations specific to ship types or demonstrating a level higher than the one set out by required standards.

Class surveys are periodical (e.g. annual), non-periodical (e.g. damage and repair survey) and special case-related (e.g. change of class).

An indicator of the performance of classification societies, including in the area of marine environment protection, can be found in the findings of regional memoranda of understanding (MOUs) as published in annual reports.

0.8 The contribution of the European Union

The European Union (EU), which currently comprises 28 member States,[44] and whose part of the legislation is binding on the European Economic Area (EEA),[45] and Switzerland, has strong interests in the maritime sector. In addition to 68,000 km of coastline[46] belonging to EU member States which is exposed to potential shipping incidents, about 25% of world tonnage is registered under an EU flag. Furthermore, about 40% of intra-EU trade and 80% of world trade and EU external trade is conducted by sea.

The EU regulatory framework that impacts on the marine environment can be viewed from more than one standpoint.

Firstly, from the standpoint of the EU coastal and marine policy, which goes into the following directions:

- the Marine Strategy Framework Directive (or Marine Directive)[47] which addresses the protection of the marine environment and natural resources in an integrated (as opposed to sectoral) approach. The Marine Directive relates to the protection of marine biodiversity; it came into force in 2008

(Recast) (Text with EEA relevance) [2009] OJ L 131/47. Also see Commission Regulation (EU) 788/2014 laying down detailed rules for the imposition of fines and period penalty payments and the withdrawal of recognition of ship inspection and survey organisations pursuant to Articles 6 and 7 of Regulation (EC) 391/2009 of the European Parliament and of the Council (Text with EEA relevance) [2014] OJ L 214/12.

44 It is noted at this point that the withdrawal of the United Kingdom from the EU, commonly referred to as Brexit, and currently underway, will impact on the number of EU member States.

45 The EEA comprises the EU and Iceland, Liechtenstein and Norway.

46 The coastline of the EU is more than three times longer than US's coastline, and almost twice that of Russia.

47 European Parliament and Council Directive (EC) 2008/56 establishing a framework for community action in the field of marine environmental policy (Text with EEA relevance) [2008] OJ L164/19.

and EU member States were required to introduce it in their national systems by 15 July 2010. The Directive is aimed at protecting the marine environment across Europe by achieving good environmental status (GES) of the marine waters of the EU by 2020.

- the Integrated Maritime Policy (IMP) takes into account possible inter-connections of industries and human activities; it seeks to achieve the full economic potential of the seas in line with the marine environment by taking into account all the sectors affecting the oceans, thus representing a cross-cutting policy approach. It covers blue growth, marine data and knowledge, maritime spatial planning, integrated maritime surveillance and sea basin strategies.
- the reformed Common Fisheries Policy (CFP), which represents a sectoral approach;
- the Water Framework Directive (WFD), i.e. Directive 2000/60/EC of the European Parliament and of the Council establishing a framework for the Community action in the field of water policy,[48] as amended, sets out water protection objectives, which include and, at the same time, go beyond the protection of coastal waters. More specifically, the Directive aims at establishing a framework for the protection of inland surface waters, transitional waters,[49] coastal waters and groundwater.[50]

Secondly, the EU's regulatory framework is structured over the maritime transport policy, which is applicable to EU fleet and to vessels calling at EU ports. The EU maritime transport policy presents an interest for the marine environment (and for maritime safety). A straightforward illustration of this synergy can be found in the preamble of EU acts in this field. In the introductory part of Directive 2009/16/EC on port state control,[51] for example, it is set out that "safety, pollution prevention and on-board living and working conditions may be effectively enhanced through a drastic reduction of substandard ships from Community waters, by strictly applying Conventions, international codes and resolutions".[52] Among the objectives of the Directive feature the reduction of substandard shipping in waters under member States' jurisdiction through improvement of port State control of seagoing ships and the "development of the means of taking preventive action in the field of pollution of the seas [...]".[53]

The EU has been developing since the 1990s a so-called maritime safety policy. The said policy has been shaped according to the strategic priorities of the

---

48 European Parliament and Council Directive (EC) 2000/60 [2000] OJ L 327/1.

49 They are defined by Directive 2000/60/EC as "the bodies of surface water in the vicinity of river mouths which are partly saline in character as a result of their proximity to coastal waters but which are substantially influenced by freshwater flows" (Article 2 on Definitions).

50 See Article 1 of the Directive.

51 European Parliament and Council Directive (EU) 2009/16/EC on Port State Control (Recast) (Text with EEA relevance) [2009] OJ L131/57.

52 See Recital 4.

53 See Recital 34.

EU, which at times had departed from the IMO agenda.[54] Some aspects of the EU regulatory framework were the result of casualties that had caused major pollution in EU waters; the most well-known are the *Erika* (1999) and the *Prestige* (2002), which contributed to the adoption of important legislation at the EU level (in the form of Directives and Regulations), and constituted the so-called maritime safety packages (Erika I, II and III legislative packages). The first legislative package was adopted in 2001. It pertained to the enhancement of port State control, the enhancement of the rules governing classification societies and the acceleration of the phasing-in of double-hull oil tankers. In 2002, a second legislative package was adopted, often referred to as Erika II. It was geared towards maritime traffic safety and the creation of the European Maritime Safety Agency (EMSA), a technical body that sits in Lisbon and assists the European Commission in a number of tasks relating, amongst others, to the maritime safety/marine environment protection agenda. Following the sinking of the *Prestige* in 2002, the third Maritime Safety Package (commonly referred to as Erika III package) in 2009 aimed at numerous directions, including quality of flags, inspection regimes in EU ports, accident investigation, information collection, passenger protection standards, insurance of shipowners for maritime claims, classification societies and liability of carriers of passengers by sea in the event of an accident. While the above legislative measures do not address environmental issues, through the maritime safety channel, they can be viewed as measures that also benefit the marine environment by preventing marine pollution. An illustration of this would be the enhanced port State control set out by Directive 2009/16/EC or the enhancement of standards of EU flags through Directive 2009/21/EC.

As it will be mentioned below under 0.8.2 the future of EU maritime transport policy is addressed at the long term (10 years) in a strategic document of the European Commission dating to 2009.

0.8.1 *How do EU acts reach private operators?*

Directives adopted by the EU set out objectives that member States are required to achieve through national measures considered fit for the purpose by them, and within specified deadlines. The choice of legislating through the use of directives gives flexibility to member States as they take into consideration the particularities prevailing in a particular field. That said, if member States fail to harmonise their law, they are exposed to the risk of proceedings taken against them by the European Commission, and, ultimately, the sanction of a monetary penalty. In this context, as a matter of principle, private operators are bound by the obligations stemming from directives through national transposition measures. Possible sanctions on account of infringement of a particular provision would also be enshrined in a national act, not in a directive.

---

54 On the challenges of the synergy between the international and regional shipping regulations, see Iliana Christodoulou-Varotsi, *Maritime Safety Law and Policies of the European Union and the United States of America: Antagonism or Synergy* (Springer, Heidelberg, 2009).

As far as EU regulations are concerned, they are directly applicable in the legal systems of member States. Thus, no transposition act introducing the EU instrument within the national legal systems is required, and obligations are generated directly from the EU act itself.

0.8.2 The future of the EU agenda on marine pollution

In its capacity as a regional legislator, the EU has been active over maritime safety and marine environment protection. This has sometimes generated frictions with the international system, but has not prevented the expansion of EU legislative packages. On the other hand, this has also stimulated the international standard-setting process, i.e. in anticipation of EU action, the IMO had to expedite the adoption of certain measures. The eagerness of the EU to adopt legislative action is evidenced at present in areas such as air pollution from shipping. A monitoring, reporting and verification system has been provided for (entry into force of Regulation (EU) 2015/757 on 1 July 2015; the instrument will become fully effective on 1 January 2018).[55] Shipowners and operators are required to monitor, report and verify on annual basis CO_2 emissions for ships above 5,000 gross tonnage (GT) calling at EU ports. The instrument requires data collection on ship's fuel consumption and energy efficiency, which should provide the EU with the information needed so as to proceed to subsequent stages of action on the matter. It should be noted that at present shipping is not included in the EU Emission Trading Scheme (ETS).

In addition to the above, the EU, as the European Commission joint communication on international ocean governance suggests, is strongly interested in the future of the oceans, and seeks to shape its regulatory agenda accordingly.[56] In this strategic document dating to November 2016, the European Commission points out that the oceans "are under threat from over-exploitation, climate change, acidification, pollution and declining biodiversity".[57] Mention is also made of the UN 2030 Agenda for Sustainable Development, which identified conservation and sustainable use of oceans as one of the 17 Sustainable Development Goals (SDG 14). The need for better ocean governance is brought forward by the Commission, in recognition of the weaknesses of the current framework, which "does not ensure the sustainable management of the oceans".[58] It is also recognised that the agreed international rules are not always implemented effectively or enforced uniformly, and that there is inadequate coordination between

---

55 European Parliament and Council Regulation (EU) 2015/757 on the monitoring, reporting and verification of carbon dioxide emissions from maritime transport, and amending Directive 2009/16/EC [2015] OJ L 123/55.

56 European Commission (EU) Joint Communication to the European Parliament, the Council, the European Economic and Social Committee and the Committee of the Regions, *International Ocean Governance: An Agenda for the Future of Our Oceans* (Brussels, 10.11.2016, JOIN (2016)49 final).

57 *Ibid*, p. 2.

58 *Ibid*, p. 3.

international organisations responsible for the oceans. As mentioned in the Communication, the EU considers itself well placed to shape international ocean governance on the basis of its existing policies (which were briefly identified above), and projects into the future through numerous actions, including an action[59] on ensuring the safety and security of seas and oceans; in this context, focus should be placed on better cooperation between national coast guards in order to undertake multipurpose campaigns including, for example, the detection of illegal discharges under MARPOL. Another action will seek to implement the 2015 Paris Climate Conference (COP21) and mitigate the harmful impact of climate change on oceans, coastlines and ecosystems.[60] The fight against marine litter and the "sea of plastic" is also set out.[61]

As already mentioned, in a strategic document of the European Commission where the latter presents recommendations for the EU's maritime transport policy until 2018,[62] key areas for future action are identified. These are areas where EU action will seek to enhance the competitiveness of the sector while boosting its environmental performance. Six areas are tackled in this policy document, namely: shipping trends and business conditions, human resources, quality shipping, international scene, short-sea shipping and research and innovation.

Last, but not least, a new integrated EU policy for the Arctic was adopted in December 2016, focusing on international cooperation, climate change, environmental protection and sustainable development. The said policy will guide EU actions in the Arctic region via 39 actions. It is noted that the EU has three Arctic Council states (Finland, Sweden and Denmark), and that the EU constitutes a major destination for resources and goods from the Arctic region.[63]

0.9 The contribution of non-governmental organisations

Numerous non-governmental organisations (NGOs) develop significant action which impacts on the protection of the marine environment and, indirectly, on regulatory compliance. Some of them are granted the status of consultative organisations at the IMO, thus following more closely the work of the IMO.[64] Their actions vary from awareness campaigns to lobbying for regulatory changes.

---

59 This is referred to as Action 5.

60 This is referred to as Action 6.

61 This is referred to as Action 9.

62 European Commission (EU) Communication to the European Parliament, the Council, the European Economic and Social Committee and the Committee of the Regions, *Strategic Goals and Recommendations for the EU's Maritime Transport Policy Until 2018* (Brussels 21.1.2009, COM(2009)8final).

63 See Magazine Environment for Europeans (https://ec.europa.eu/environment/efe/home> An integrated EU policy for the Arctic, last visit 2 May 2017).

64 The list of NGOs having the status of consultative organisations at the IMO can be found on the website of the IMO.

0.9.1 Industry Best practices

Industry best practices (e.g. through codes of practice) support the goal of proper implementation of international requirements, thus impacting on marine pollution prevention and management.

The International Chamber of Shipping (ICS), the International Shipping Federation (ISF), Oil Companies International Marine Forum (OCIMF), the Baltic and International Maritime Council (BIMCO), the International Association of Independent Tanker Owners (Intertanko), the International Tanker Owners Pollution Federation (ITOPF), and other stakeholders work on standards through guidance and good practice.

0.9.2 International Organisation for Standardisation

The work of the International Organisation for Standardisation (ISO) supports and supplement the contribution of the IMO in many areas, including in relation to the protection of the marine environment. The ISO is a non-governmental organisation with consultative status at the IMO, comprising 163 national standard bodies. It is based in Geneva. The Organisation has been operational since 1947 with a far-reaching scope of action. Over the years more than 21,000 international standards have been developed. ISO standards aim to ensure the safety, reliability and good quality of the products, services and systems concerned, as well as at reducing costs through strategic actions minimising errors.

The generic ISO 14000 series on environmental management standards is, amongst others, of interest to the protection of the marine environment. It gives rise to implementation in all areas of activities, including in the maritime transport. There are many other areas impacted by ISO standards such as freight containers, paints and varnish for ships, water quality testing for pollution. In the light of recent developments on the regulatory level, ISO 30000 series of standard on ship recycling management systems is also to be noted.

SECTION 3: WHERE ARE ENVIRONMENTAL REGULATIONS IMPACTING ON SHIPPING HEADING FOR?

0.10 Where do we stand at present?

Shipping is generally considered to be the most environmentally friendly means of transportation. During the last decades shipping has been subjected to dense regulation either in the form of new conventions or in the form of amendments to existing instruments, especially through MEPC resolutions. Global, i.e. international, action has been complemented by noteworthy regional action (e.g. on the level of the EU) or by individual policies on the part of a number of States. As it is mentioned below, it would be sensible to expect additional regulatory challenges for the sector as, in light of the risks affecting the environment, societal expectations become more and more demanding.

INTRODUCTORY CHAPTER

Against this background, despite dense regulation, enhanced levels of awareness and best practice guidance, the marine pollution agenda is far from being
settled. This is moreover the result of marine pollution incidents that occur from
time to time, and attract the attention of the public opinion in the light of catastrophic casualties. Marine pollution may be the result of accidents with more
than one contributing factor or the result of deliberate actions or omissions
involving the company, the master and/or the crew. Illegal discharges at sea may
be due to lack of awareness or inadequate training or negligence (e.g. marine
equipment poorly maintained). Deliberate actions may be prompted by economic incentives (e.g. deliberate actions based on savings of costs such as fees
for ship-generated waste disposal in relation to the use of port reception facilities
or savings of time due to the constraints related to the use of such facilities).[65]
Deliberate actions may be facilitated by loose enforcement mechanisms – related
mechanisms failing to function properly.[66] All these aspects are relevant to the
shaping and enforcement of regulations.

Increasing societal awareness of environmental issues has prompted further
action. An illustration can be found in the area of climate change. During its
Marine Environment Protection Committee (MEPC) meeting for its 70th session, the IMO decided to implement a global sulphur cap of 0.50% m/m (mass/
mass) in 2020. This would represent a significant reduction from the 3.5% m/m
global limit that applies at present. In addition to this, control of greenhouse gas
emissions from shipping is further enhanced through a roadmap (2017 through to
2023) for developing a comprehensive IMO strategy on reduction of GHG emissions from ships, which foresees an initial GHG strategy to be adopted in 2018.

On another level of action, ship recycling awareness has been progressing,
with the Hong Kong Convention for the Safe and Environmentally Sound Recycling of Ships, adopted on 15 May 2009, representing about 20% of world tonnage through the ratification of five contracting States.

0.11 Identifying possible drivers for the future

Numerous factors are likely to come into play and potentially impact on future
shipping regulations governing marine environment.[67] As already mentioned,
societal expectations tend to be more and more demanding, and experience up to
now reasonably suggests that this is likely to continue.

A possible direction in the discussion is the future growth of the shipping sector, and the demand for seaborne transport.

The growing development of information and communication technology, in
combination with the explosion of digitalised data, is an additional driver to new

---

65 See EMSA, *supra* note 7, p. 44 *et seq.*

66 The illegal practice commonly referred to as magic pipes is an illustration of such blatant
behaviours.

67 An excellent discussion on the future of shipping can be found in DNV GL, *The Future of
Shipping* (Høvik, 2014).

challenges in the area of energy-efficiency performance, marine environment protection and marine pollution control. The wider context presents additional challenges and demands new regulations: one may think of developments in the area of unmanned merchant ships, advanced ship design, new alternative fuel sources, etc.

BIBLIOGRAPHY

Andersson, K., Brynolf, S., Lindgren, J.F. and Wilewska-Bien, M. (Editors), *Shipping and the Environment* (Springer, Heidelberg, 2016)

Attard, D. J. (General Ed), *The IMLI Manual on International Maritime Law, Vol. I, The Law of the Sea & Vol. III, Marine Environment Law and Maritime Security Law* (OUP, Oxford, 2016)

Christodoulou-Varotsi, Iliana, *Maritime Safety Law and Policies of the European Union and the United States of America: Antagonism or Synergy* (Springer, Heidelberg, 2009)

Christodoulou-Varotsi, Iliana, 'Recent Developments in the EC Legal Framework on Ship-Source Pollution: The Ambivalence of the EC's Penal Approach' [2006] 33 TRANSP. L. J. Vol. 3,371

Clark, R.B., *Marine Pollution* (5th edition, OUP, Oxford, 2001)

Commission Regulation (EU) 788/2014 laying down detailed rules for the imposition of fines and period penalty payments and the withdrawal of recognition of ship inspection and survey organizations pursuant to Article 6 and 7 of Regulation (EC) No. 391/2009 of the European Parliament and of the Council (Text with EEA relevance) [2014] OJ L 214/12

DNV GL, *The Future of Shipping* (Høvik, 2014)

European Commission (EU) Communication to the European Parliament, the Council, the European Economic and Social Committee and the Committee of the Regions, *Strategic Goals and Recommendations for the EU's Maritime Transport Policy Until 2018* (Brussels 21.1.2009, COM(2009)8final)

European Commission (EU) Joint Communication to the European Parliament, the Council, the European Economic and Social Committee and the Committee of the Regions, *International Ocean Governance: an Agenda for the Future of Our Oceans* (Brussels, 10.11.2016, JOIN (2016)49final)

European Maritime Safety Agency (EMSA) *Addressing Illegal Discharges in the Marine Environment* (document date unavailable)

European Parliament and Council (EC) Directive 2009/15 on common rules and standards for ship inspection and survey organizations and for the relevant activities of maritime administrations (Recast) (Text with EEA relevance) [2009] OJ L 131/47

European Parliament and Council Directive (EC) 2008/56 establishing a framework for common action in the field of marine environmental policy (Text with EEA relevance) [2008] OJ L164/19

European Parliament and Council Regulation (EC) 391/2009 on common rules and standards for ship inspection and survey organizations (Recast) (Text with EEA relevance) [2009] OJ L 131/11

Gard Handbook on Protection of the Marine Environment (3rd edition, Edgar Gold, 2006)

IACS, *Classification Societies – What, Why and How?* (2011)

OECD, *Cost Savings Stemming from Non-Compliance with International Environmental Regulations in the Maritime Sector* (Maritime Transport Committee, 2003)

OECD, *Economic Aspects of Environmental Compliance Assurance, Proceedings from the OECD Global Forum on Sustainable Development* (2–3 December 2004)

Pamborides, G.P., *International Shipping Law*, (Kluwer Law International/Ant. N. Sakkoulas Publishers, Athens, 1999)

Tan, Alan Khee-Jin, *Vessel-Source Marine Pollution-The Law and Politics of International Regulation* (Cambridge University Press, Cambridge, 2005)

United Nations Conference on Trade and Development (UNCTAD), *Revue of Maritime Transport* (2015)

United Nations Conference on Trade and Development (UNCTAD), *Review of Maritime Transport* (2017)

CHAPTER 1

Marine Pollution From Oil

TABLE OF CONTENTS

Section 1	Identifying the subject area	32
1.1	General discussion – challenges relating to marine pollution by oil	32
	1.1.1 Pollution by oil and Port State Control findings	38
1.2	Key terms/definitions	39
Section 2	Main discussion of the regulatory framework (MARPOL Annex I)	41
1.3	Overview of the legal basis	41
1.4	Structure of the Annex I	42
1.5	Key resolutions (non-exhaustive list)	42
1.6	Construction requirements	44
1.7	Protection of fuel oil tanks	44
1.8	Control of operational discharges of oil from machinery spaces	45
1.9	Discharges from the cargo area of oil tankers	46
Section 3	Key management issues, including documentation	46
1.10	Surveys and certification	46
	1.10.1 Shipboard Oil Pollution Emergency Plan	47
	1.10.2 Oil Record Book	47
	1.10.3 International Oil Pollution Prevention Certificate	48
1.11	Relevance of the International Safety Management Code	48
1.12	Industry best practices	49
Section 4	Areas of special interest	50
1.13	Ship-to-ship transfer of crude oil and petroleum products	50
1.14	Recent developments: oil tankers operations in ice-covered waters (the Polar Code)	51
Section 5	Selected aspects concerning implementation and enforcement	52
1.15	Selected highlights on national jurisdictions	52

SECTION 1: IDENTIFYING THE SUBJECT AREA

1.1 General discussion – challenges relating to marine pollution by oil

The marine transportation of oil has been addressed by the international regulator long before other substances – an illustration is the International Convention for the Prevention of Pollution of the Sea by Oil (OILPOL 1954), which will be addressed later on in this chapter. MARPOL 73/78, the international instrument of reference on marine pollution by oil, defines oil as "petroleum in any form including crude oil, fuel oil, sludge, oil refuse and refined products [...]".[1]However, the range of sources of oil entering into the marine environment is broad and is not confined to ships: they range, amongst others, from marine pipelines and dry-docked vessels to coastal facilities (e.g. refineries, storage facilities, etc.), recreational boating, offshore oil and gas exploration and production, and natural marine seeps. Both chronic oil spills from ships' ordinary operations (e.g. at ports or in busy traffic lanes) and accidental oil spills resulting in small or costly large-scale spills constitute real challenges for regulators, and the oil and shipping industries. It is generally considered that newer ships are cleaner but the way operations are conducted may have an impact on pollution. If the focus is placed on operational discharges of oil from ships into the sea, relevant factors would notably include ship type, age, level of maintenance, use of appropriate equipment aboard and reception facilities ashore, level of awareness and training of the crew, tanker cargoes (for example, in relation to tank washing), etc.

At this point, it would be useful to mention that accidental spillage tends to be coastal and/or unintentional; "accidental" may be understood on the basis of the criterion of time as it results from incidents involving oil release from point sources over a relatively limited amount of time (e.g. hours or days) and can be contrasted with slow leakages of relatively small amounts of oil over longer periods such as months or years.[2] As suggested by authoritative studies, estimates on oil inputs at sea are a highly complex task involving questions on methodology, availability, credibility and treatment of data. According to estimates, for the period under examination (by the study), operational discharges from ships represented 45% of the input of 457,000 tonnes/yr. of oil entering the marine environment (ships); according to the same source, shipping accidents had a share of 36% of the input.[3]

---

1 See regulation 1 of MARPOL Annex I on definitions. The definition excludes from its scope "those petrochemicals which are subject to the provisions of Annex II of the present Convention [...]".

2 See GESAMP (Joint Group of Experts on the Scientific Aspects of Marine Environment Pollution), *Estimates of Oil Entering the Marine Environment from Sea-Based Activities* (Report No. 75, IMO/FAO/UNESCO-IOC-WHO/IAEA/UN/UNEP, 2007, p. 9). It is noted that GESAMP is a high-level advisory body working on marine pollution issues in collaboration, amongst others, with the IMO.

3 *Ibid*, p. VIII. The topic of oil inputs into North American waters has also been studied by the National Research Council, USA (see, amongst others, NRC, *Oil in the Sea III: Inputs, Fates and Effects* (2003 report)).

Against this background, the effects of pollution by oil on humans and on the environment have been widely recognised.[4] Despite the ability of the marine environment for progressive re-establishment through natural processes, harm may be caused by the oil. Harm may stem from the oil itself and/or the ensuing operations, i.e. response and clean-up. Food chain, marine life and natural resources may be negatively impacted by pollution by oil, thus causing ecological damage and adversely impacting on humans and on their activities (economy, tourism, etc.). There are numerous factors involved with the consequences of marine pollution by oil, including the type of oil concerned (light, heavy and medium oils react differently), the features of the location involved (are sensitive coastal zones and delicate ecosystems involved?), the amount of spillage, sea and weather conditions, time of year of the occurrence, etc.[5]

Despite the increase of transportation of oil in recent years, a noteworthy reduction during the last decades of oil spilt at sea is generally acknowledged. This positive development may be attributed to a number of factors such as:

- the effectiveness of regulations, including the imposition of strict sanctions that deter non-compliance;
- the advent of modern technologies (e.g. in relation to ship construction or oil recovery from casualties);
- environmental awareness enhancement, including training of the crew and personnel ashore;
- enhancement of the commitment of companies and their personnel aboard and ashore;
- the contribution of numerous stakeholders from the oil and shipping industries through various tools, including best industry practices that support implementation;
- the contribution of non-governmental organisations (NGOs).

Lessons learnt from past accidents also contribute to a better understanding of related risks and their handling. A number of casualties have shed light on problematic aspects and have proved to be the triggers of additional and/or better regulations (see, among others, the *Torrey Canyon*, 1967, and the *Exxon Valdez*, 1989, respectively in the UK and in the USA).

In the graph below the operation at time of incident for large oil spills greater than 700 tonnes (period 1970–2016) is identified. The causes of large spills (>700 tonnes) for the same period are described in the second graph.

---

4 Notably, see the following publications by the International Tanker Owners Pollution Federation (ITOPF): *Fate of Marine Oil Spills* (TIP 02); *Effects of Oil Pollution on the Marine Environment* (TIP 13); *Effects of Oil Pollution on Social and Economic Activities* (TIP 12). Also see National Ocean and Atmospheric Administration (NOAA, USA), http://response.restoration.noaa.gov (last visit 12 January 2017).

5 On the recovery of the marine environment following oil spills, see *supra* note 4, ITOPF (TIP 13), p. 3 *et seq.*

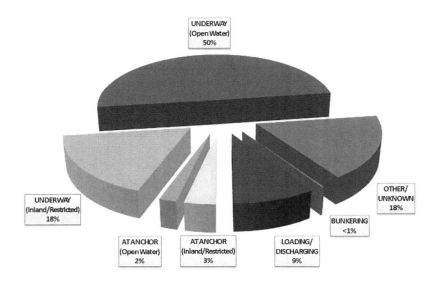

Graph 1.1 Operation at time of incident for large oil spills (>700 tonnes, 1970–2016)
Source: International Tanker Owners Pollution Federation, ITOPF (reproduced with permission)

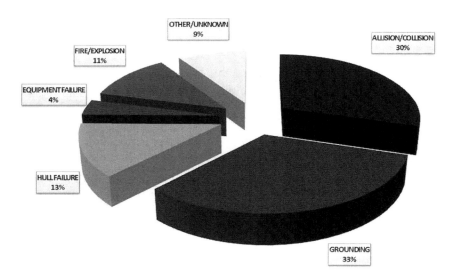

Graph 1.2 Causes of large oil spills (>700 tonnes), 1970–2016
Source: International Tanker Owners Pollution Federation, ITOPF (reproduced with permission)

MARINE POLLUTION FROM OIL

A number of large-scale oil accidents have drawn the attention of the public and have prompted regulatory changes internationally and/or regionally. Some of them, involving the shipping industry, are outlined below. Accidents having resulted in more limited spillages in recent years also contribute to the picture.[6] Selected accidents involving oil from the offshore sector are briefly touched upon in the chapter which deals with pollution from the oil and gas offshore sector.

- The *Torrey Canyon* accident (1967)

The *Torrey Canyon* accident involved an eight-year-old oil tanker flying the Liberian flag laden with crude oil, which ran aground on 18 March 1967 off Cornwall, UK. The vessel's hull had broken on a reef off the Isles of Scilly. The entire cargo, estimated at 119,000 tonnes of crude oil, was lost. A long section of the Cornish coast was heavily contaminated by the slick. Thousands of seabirds were killed and the accident had extensively impacted on the lives of local communities, tourism and other sectors; in the process, the oil polluted beaches and harbours in the Channel Islands and Brittany, France.

The accident had taken place in fine weather and was attributed to a navigational error.[7] The accident is generally presented as the first very serious tanker disaster that attracted the attention of the general public, including on the level of methods for mitigating the spill, and the risks related to the use of dispersants. As already mentioned, this catastrophic incident resulted in important regulatory developments on marine pollution prevention and compensation.

- The *Amoco Cadiz* accident (1978)

Built in 1974 and flying the Liberian flag, the *Amoco Cadiz* was laden with 223,000 tonnes of light crude oil and 4,000 tonnes of bunker fuel, when she encountered severe weather conditions and finally grounded off the coast of Brittany, France. The

---

6   Accidents involving tankers which took place in recent years and which resulted in more limited spillage, would be, amongst others, the following (in chronological order): *Athos I* accident occurred on 26 November 2004 in Delaware river, Philadelphia, USA. The 1983-built single hulled oil tanker *Athos I*, flying the Cypriot flag, had collided with a partly hidden anchor while preparing to dock at a refinery. The accident resulted in a spill of approximately 265,000 gallons of heavy crude oil into the Delaware river. Three States' shorelines were affected. The *Eagle Otome* accident took place on 23 January 2010. It involved a Singapore-flagged oil tanker which collided with two barges and their towing vessel in the Port Arthur, Texas, USA. The vessel was built in 1994. An estimated spillage of 1,440 MT of light crude oil is to be noted. The *Alfa I* was the first incident falling in the scope of the Supplementary Fund Protocol (third tier of compensation run by the IOPC Funds). The accident took place on 5 March 2012 in Elefsis Bay, Piraeus, Greece. It involved a Greek-flagged tanker (a converted double-hulled vessel) of 1,648 gross tonnes which was loaded with 1,800 tonnes of cargo. The quantity of oil released at sea was unknown. The *Nesa R3* accident involved a tanker under the flag of Saint Kitts and Nevis which took place on 19 June 2013 in Port Sultan Qaboos, Muscat, Sultanate of Oman. The quantity of spill in tonnes was estimated to be more than 250 tonnes. Some 40 kilometres of shoreline were affected by the spill. The accident involving the bulk carrier *M/V Summer Wind* and the oil tank-barge *Kirby* in the Galveston Bay near Texas City (USA) happened on 22 March 2014 and resulted in a spill of approximately 168,000 gallons. See www. iopcfunds.org and www.itopf.com (last visit 12 January 2017). Additional descriptions of spills may be found on the website of National Oceanic and Atmospheric Administration (NOAA) (see http:// response.restoration.noaa.gov/) (last visit 12 January 2017).

7   Philippe Boisson, *Safety at Sea – Policies, Regulations & International Law* (Edition Bureau Veritas, Paris, 1999, p. 250).

vessel was on her way from the Arabian Gulf to Europe. The accident happened on 16 March 1978, and was attributed to the failure of the vessel's steering mechanism. The entire cargo was spilled into the sea, causing a most extensive pollution problem to Brittany coastline. Once again, the attention of the media and the public opinion was geared towards this maritime disaster with huge ecological consequences. The casualty had resulted in the largest loss of marine life ever recorded after an oil spill at the time. The incident gave rise to useful lessons learnt insights on cleanup and impact analysis.[8]

- The *Exxon Valdez* accident (National Oceanic Atmospheric Administration and Environmental Protection Agency, 1989)

The US-flagged single hulled oil tanker *Exxon Valdez*, which was built in 1985, grounded on Bligh Reef, Alaska, on 24 March 1989, leaving its footprint on maritime history on account of its magnitude, exceptionally high costs for clean-up and litigation, and salient impact on the adoption of new regulations.[9]

The oil tanker was loaded with 180,000 tonnes of crude oil. She was travelling outside normal shipping lanes in order to avoid ice when she struck Bligh Reef in Prince William Sound. The accident caused major environmental problems and impacted on the health, well-being and economy of the local society (fishing, etc.). It resulted in approximately 38,500 tonnes of oil pouring into the Prince William Sound, Alaska (US), affecting 1,700 km of coastline.

Some of the probable causes of the grounding, pointed out during the investigation of the accident, were the following: human failure on numerous levels (proper manoeuvre of the vessel, proper navigation watch, etc.) possibly due to fatigue and excessive workload; failure of the shipping company to supervise the master and provide a rested and sufficient crew for the vessel; vessel traffic system-related failures; and lack of effective pilot and escort services.[10]

- The *Nakhodka* accident (1997)

The accident happened on the 2 January 1997 in the Sea of Japan. It involved the Russian 1970-built oil tanker *Nakhodka* (approximately 20,000 DWT). She was en route from China to the Russian Federation and she was laden with a cargo of 19,000 tonnes of medium fuel oil. The vessel broke into two sections in heavy weather and rough seas with 6,200 tonnes of oil at sea. In the process, the sections continued to leak oil. It is noteworthy that the vessel had broken up at a distance over 100 kilometres from the coast, which impacted on the extent of the pollution caused. Structural problems were notably associated with the casualty.[11]

---

8 Wilmot N. Hess (Editor), *The Amoco Cadiz Oil Spill: A Preliminary Scientific Report* (Washington, DC, 1 January 1978).

9 NOAA (Office of Response and Restoration), see Exxon Valdez page at: http://response.restoration.noaa.gov/oil-and-chemical-spills/significant-incidents/exxon-valdez-oil-spill (last visit 12 January 2017); John A. Wiens, *Oil in the Environment: Legacies and Lessons of the Exxon Valdez Oil Spill* (Cambridge University Press, Cambridge, 2013).

10 See *US National Transportation Safety Board Marine Accident Report on the Grounding of the US Tankship Exxon Valdez on Bligh Reef, Prince William Sound Near Valdez, Alaska* (24 March 1989, PB90–916405, NTSB/MAR-90/04).

11 Notably see H. Ohtsubo et al, Analysis on Accident of MV NAHKODKA, Conference Paper July 1999, 1999 ASME Offshore Mechanics and Arctic Engineering Conference, Newfoundland, Canada Volume Proceedings of OMAE'99, ASME, OMAE99/SR-6121, pp. 1–8.

MARINE POLLUTION FROM OIL

- The *Erika* accident (1999)

The oil tanker *Erika* sank off the coast of Brittany (France) on 12 December 1999. She was built in 1975 and was flying the Maltese flag. At the time of the accident she was laden with 30,884 tonnes of no. 2 heavy oil. The *Erika* encountered severe weather conditions and experienced a structure failure while she was crossing the Bay of Biscay. Following a list, she broke her back, and foundered off the coast of Brittany, France with both her sections eventually sinking.[12] Approximately 19,800 tonnes of heavy fuel oil had been discharged at sea, and 400 km of coastline had been polluted. Some of the factors that contributed to the accident related to the quality of management, as well as to flag State and class oversight on the level of implementation and enforcement. Criminal proceedings held in France resulted in uncommonly severe sanctions for French standards. The accident drew massive attention from the media and public opinion. It also triggered important developments on the international and regional regulatory level.

- The *Prestige* accident (2002)[13]

The single hulled oil tanker (42820 GT) *Prestige* was built in 1976 and was under the Bahamas flag. She was laden with a cargo of about 77,000 tonnes of heavy fuel oil, and on her way to Singapore via Gibraltar when she suffered hull damage, developed a severe list and began leaking oil. The accident happened on 13 November 2002 off the coast of Galicia, Spain. Towage and the granting of a place of refuge proved to be difficult tasks. During towage out into the Atlantic, the vessel broke in two and sank off the Spanish coast, contaminating the coasts of numerous countries (coast of Galicia in Spain, north coast of France, Channel Islands, etc.). Approximately 64,000 tonnes of cargo were released in the sea, while more than 13,000 tonnes of oil were in the wreck. Extensive clean-up operations had taken place both at sea and ashore, involving Spain, France and Portugal. The accident gave rise to massive legal proceedings. It drew special attention on the issue of preparedness, as well as on appropriateness of sanctions, including the challenges on crew criminalisation following an oil spill. The *Prestige* incident also prompted – alongside the *Erika* accident – regulatory developments on the level of the IMO and the European Union. The IMO, through its Marine Environment Protection Committee (MEPC), adopted amendments to MARPOL Annex I regulation 13G (subsequently renumbered 20) with a view to accelerating further the phasing-out of single hull oil tankers.

- The *Hebei Spirit* (2007)[14]

The collision of the Hong Kong-registered 1993-built single hull *Hebei Spirit* with the crane barge *Samsung No. 1* happened in poor weather conditions in the vicinity of Daesan, Korea. The accident occurred on 7 December 2007 while the *Hebei Spirit*

---

12 See Permanent Commission of Enquiry into Accidents at Sea (CPEM), *Report of the Enquiry into the Sinking of the Erika off the Coasts of Brittany on 12 December 1999* (document date unavailable).

13 On the *Prestige*, see, amongst others, Commission of the European Communities, *Communication from the Commission to the European Parliament and to the Council on Improving Safety at Sea in Response to the Prestige Accident* (Brussels, 3.12. 2002, COM(2002)681 final).

14 See the Hong Kong Marine Accident Investigation Section, *Report of Investigation Into the Collision Between the Hong Kong Registered Ship "Hebei Spirit" and Korean Crane Barge "Samsung No. 1" on 7 December 2007* (document date unavailable).

was waiting for discharge. This very large crude oil carrier (VLCC) was carrying a full cargo of 263,541 tonnes of crude oil. At the time of accident, the crane barge was towed by two tugs (an anchor boat was also escorting the barge). Prior to the incident, the tugs had lost control of the crane barge in adverse weather conditions. The crane barge was drifted toward the oil tanker and, when the towing wires parted, the crane barge made contact with the *Hebei Spirit*, causing three breaches in *Hebei Spirit's* hull. The crew had taken measures to limit the pollution. However, according to estimates, about 10,000 tonnes of cargo oil had spilled into the Yellow Sea, and over 300 kilometres of shoreline were affected. The investigation which followed pointed to a number of contributing factors, including the decision to commence towage despite poor weather conditions, the loss of control of the towing convoy, etc.

1.1.1 *Pollution by oil and Port State Control findings*

REGULATION 11, MARPOL ANNEX I

Port State control on operational requirements

1. A ship when in a port or an offshore terminal of another Party is subject to inspection by officers duly authorized by such Party concerning operational requirements under this Annex, where there are clear grounds for believing that the master or crew are not familiar with essential shipboard procedures relating to the prevention of pollution by oil.
2. In the circumstances given in para. 1 of this regulation, the Party shall take such steps as will ensure that the ship shall not sail until the situation has been brought to order in accordance with the requirements of this Annex.
3. Procedures relating to port State control prescribed in article 5 of the present Convention shall apply to this regulation.
4. Nothing in this regulation shall be construed to limit the rights and obligations of a Party carrying out control over operational requirements specifically provided for in the present Convention.

MARPOL Annex I-related deficiencies fall in the scope of regional programmes on port State control (PSC).

To name but a few findings based on regional instruments, under Paris Memorandum of Understanding (MOU), the percentage of deficiencies relating to oil (Annex I) was the highest for the years 2013 to 2015, included, in comparison with the deficiencies observed in relation to the other annexes of MARPOL for the same period.[15] Furthermore, oil record book-related deficiencies were among the top five deficiencies during 2015 under the same instrument.

---

15 See Paris Memorandum of Understanding (MOU) on Port State Control, *Port State Control – Safer Entry of Enclosed Spaces Annual Report 2015*, p. 44. The percentage for MARPOL Annex I deficiencies for the year 2015 was 1.9%, as opposed to lower percentages for the other annexes. For the year 2014, relevant percentage was the same. For the year 2013, relevant percentage was higher, i.e. 2.2%.

In addition to the above, oil filtering equipment-related deficiencies (MARPOL Annex I) were among the most frequent detainable deficiencies under the Memorandum of Understanding of Port State Control in the Asia-Pacific Region (commonly referred to as Tokyo MOU) for the year 2015.[16]

According to data concerning port State control in west and central African region in relation to the year 2015, the percentage of total deficiencies for MARPOL Annex I was significantly higher than for the other annexes of MARPOL.[17]

The above findings suggest that proper implementation of the requirements of MARPOL Annex I raises more challenges for operators and the stakeholders concerned than the other annexes, and that there is room for improvements.

1.2 Key terms/definitions

Operational discharges of oil	Commonly generated by the ship's engines (fuel oil sludge, bilge oils) and tanker's cargoes.
Oil	For MARPOL Annex I purposes, in broad terms oil means petroleum in any form including crude oil, fuel oil, sludge, oil refuse and refined products.
Special areas	Sea areas where for recognised technical reasons (oceanographical and ecological condition/particular character of traffic) special obligatory methods for the prevention of sea pollution by oil are required. Defined special areas under MARPOL Annex I are the Mediterranean Sea, the Baltic Sea, the Black Sea, the Red Sea, the Gulf of Aden, the Antarctic area, etc.
Reception facilities	They are found outside and within special areas.[1] These are facilities outside special areas found at oil loading terminals, repair ports, and in other ports, for the reception of oily residues and oily mixtures from ships. Reception facilities within special areas may be found at oil-loading terminals and repair ports for the reception and treatment of all the dirty ballast and tank washing water from oil tankers; in addition, within special areas, all ports are held to be provided with adequate reception facilities for other residues and oil mixtures from all ships.
Condition assessment scheme (CAS)	Developed by the IMO, CAS is a survey method aimed at assessing the structural condition of a single hull oil tanker. CAS complements the so-called Enhanced Survey Programme, and seeks to provide an international standard for meeting the requirements of MARPOL Annex I (regulations 20.6, 20.7 and 21.6.1). It is noted at this point that regulation 20 addresses double hull and double bottom requirements for oil tankers delivered before 6 July 1996. This scheme was adopted by resolution MEPC.94(46) of 27 April 2001, as amended. For the purposes of CAS, oil tankers are divided into three categories (category 1, 2 and 3). CAS requirements apply to Category 2 and Category 3 only.

(Continued)

16 Memorandum of Understanding on Port State Control in the Asia-Pacific Region, *Annual Report on Port State Control in the Asia-Pacific Region 2015*, p. 17.

17 See Memorandum of Understanding (MOU) on Port State Control for West and Central African Region (Abuja MOU), *2015 Abuja MOU Annual Report*, p. 12. The percentage of 3.03 is reported, as opposed to 0.19% for MARPOL Annex IV, 0.76% for MARPOL Annex V, and 0.38% for MARPOL Annex VI.

(Continued)

Crude oil washing (COW)	Introduced in the shipping industry in the late 1970s, COW refers to the cleaning of oil tanks on a tanker with crude oil (instead of water) as a washing agent, i.e. the oil acting as a solvent (high-pressure flushing with crude oil). COW seeks to reduce the chances for marine pollution that would be generated from water washing of ship's tanks after discharge of cargo. Every crude oil tanker delivered after 1 June 1982 of 20,000 tonnes deadweight and above is required under regulation 33 of MARPOL Annex I to be fitted with a cargo tank cleaning system using crude oil washing.[2]
Segregated ballast tanks (SBT)	Ballast water introduced into a tank completely separated from the oil cargo and fuel system and permanently allocated to the carriage of ballast water.[3] SBT requirement was introduced by MARPOL Protocol of 1978. Ballast water contained in segregated ballast tanks will not come in contact with either cargo oil or fuel oil.
Oil discharge monitoring and control system (ODMCS)	ODME is a system which monitors the discharge into the sea of oily ballast or other oil-contaminated water from the cargo tank areas and which comprises specific items.[4] The ODMCS relates to the requirement[5] that every oil tanker of 150 gross tonnes and above must be fitted with a relevant system approved by the flag State administration. The design and installation of the said system must be in line with the guidelines and specifications for oil discharge monitoring and control systems for oil tankers developed by the IMO. Relevant IMO resolutions (non-exhaustive list) are MEPC.108(49) adopted on 18 July 2003, and MEPC.240(65) on 2013 Amendments to the Revised Guidelines and Specifications for Oil Discharge Monitoring and Control Systems for Oil Tankers.
Single hull/ Double hull	The distinction between single and double hulls pertains to construction requirements of tankers, an area governed by SOLAS Convention. The distinction is of interest to the protection of the marine environment, as double hulls are generally considered to provide greater protection in the event of collision or stranding in case of leakage of cargo oil (cargo tanks are surrounded with a second internal plate at a sufficient distance from the external layer). Double hulls were first introduced in the USA under the Oil Pollution Act (OPA 1990), and internationally in 1992 by the Marine Environment Protection Committee of the IMO (entry into force 6 July 1993). Relevant amendments made it mandatory for new oil tankers to have double hulls or an equivalent design standard; the phasing-in of existing tankers was also set out; schedules were revised in 2001 and 2003 with a view to accelerating the phasing out of single hulled tankers.
Oil tanker	For the purposes of MARPOL, it means "a ship constructed or adapted primarily to carry oil in bulk in its cargo spaces and includes combination carriers, any 'NLS tanker' as defined in Annex II of the present Convention and any gas carrier as defined in regulation 3.20 of chapter II-1 of SOLAS 74 (as amended), when carrying a cargo or part cargo of oil in bulk."[6]
Load on top (LOT) system	This system was developed by the oil industry in the 1960s, and it was provided for in the 1969 amendment to OILPOL 54. LOT was also recognised by the 1973 MARPOL Convention. It is a procedure based on settling and separation of the departure ballast water and the oil (the water layer is allowed to settle, and oil should flow to the top in a slop tank). The effectiveness of this method in practice is conditioned by a number of factors.

Ship-to-ship (STS) transfer	The term indicates the operation undertaken for the transfer of crude oil, petroleum products and liquefied gas between ocean-going vessels. The operation may take place when both ships are underway or at anchor. Oil tankers of 150 gross tonnage and above have been subjected, since 1 January 2011, to MARPOL regulations on the matter.

1 See MARPOL Annex I, regulation 38.
2 See MARPOL Annex I, regulation 33.
3 HELMEPA, *Pollution Prevention from Ships: 30 Years of HELMEPA and MARPOL* (December 2012), p. 28.
4 See IMO Resolution MEPC.108(49). Adopted 18 July 2003. Revised Guidelines and Specifications for Oil Discharge Monitoring and Control Systems for Oil Tankers.
5 See regulation 31, Chapter 4 (Requirements for the cargo area of oil tankers), MARPOL Annex I.
6 MARPOL Annex I, regulation 1.5.

SECTION 2: MAIN DISCUSSION OF THE REGULATORY FRAMEWORK (MARPOL ANNEX I)

1.3 Overview of the legal basis

The International Convention for the Prevention of Pollution of the Sea by Oil (OILPOL 1954), which was the first international instrument on the regulation of marine pollution by oil, was superseded by MARPOL.[18] OILPOL 1954 reflected the first substantial effort of the international regulator through a relatively concise text consisting of 21 articles and two annexes to address pollution from operational discharges of oil from tankers. It adopted a prescriptive approach to the problem, which to some extent characterised the instrument that followed, i.e. MARPOL 73/78. As already mentioned, MARPOL 73/78 superseded OILPOL 1954.[19]

MARPOL Annex I entered into force on 2 October 1983. Annex I has been amended by a number of MEPC resolutions.[20] In October 2004 MARPOL Annex I was further revised (entry into force 1 January 2007).

---

18 See MARPOL Article 9.
19 OILPOL 1954 came into force on 26 July 1958. As a general rule, its scope of material application included all seagoing vessels (amongst others, ships of less than 500 tons gross tonnage were excepted). OILPOL 1954 defined oil as crude oil, fuel oil, heavy diesel oil and lubricating oil (refined petroleum products were implicitly exempted) (see Article I). Amongst others, the discharge from any tanker of oil and oily mixtures of more than 100 ppm (parts per million) was prohibited; the instrument also set out zones up to 50 miles from the shoreline in which intentional discharges were prohibited, and provided for the requirement on oil record books, oily water separators and shore reception facilities. OILPOL 1954 also set out duties for the flag and port States, and addressed the question of penalties of polluters. Eight years after its adoption, the Convention was subject to amendments, in light of concerns on implementation and enforcement and the increase of movements of oil. The 1962 amendments were followed by the 1969 amendments; the latter gave international recognition of the so-called load-on-top (LOT) system, i.e. the technique used as an alternative prevention technology based on the settling and separation of residual oil and water from deballasting and tank washing in a slop tank, a technique which raised some difficulty from the standpoint of its effectiveness. Additional amendments took place in 1971 which did not enter into force.
20 MEPC amendments to Annex I are summarised in IMO MARPOL Consolidated Edition 2011 (sales publication), p. 2.

The general rule enshrined in the Annex is that all discharges of oil are prohibited. From this standpoint, the Annex contributes to the overall rationale of the Convention, which is the elimination of marine pollution. However, in recognition of the inadequacy of port reception facilities at the worldwide level, some operational discharges at sea had to be permitted under strict conditions and were therefore regulated.[21]

1.4 Structure of the Annex I

Chapter 1 (regulations 1–5)	General
	Definitions, application, exemptions and waivers, exceptions, equivalents, etc.
Chapter 2 (regulations 6–11)	Surveys and certification
	Initial, renewal, intermediate survey, and other surveys; issue, endorsement, duration and validity of the International Oil Pollution Prevention Certificate; Port state control (PSC) on operational requirements
Chapter 3 (regulations 12–17)	Requirements for machinery spaces of all ships
	Construction, equipment, control of operational discharge of oil
Chapter 4 (regulations 18–36)	Requirements for the cargo area of oil tankers
	Construction, equipment, control of operational discharges of oil
Chapter 5 (regulation 37)	Prevention of pollution arising from oil pollution incident Shipboard Oil Pollution Emergency Plan (SOPEP)
Chapter 6 (regulation 38)	Reception facilities
	Reception facilities outside special areas, reception facilities within special areas, general requirements
Chapter 7 (regulation 39)	Special requirements for fixed or floating platforms
Chapter 8 (regulations 40–42)	Prevention of pollution during transfer of oil cargo between oil tankers at sea
	Scope of application, general rules on safety and environmental protection, notification
Chapter 9 (regulation 43)	Special requirements for the use or carriage of oils in the Antarctic area
Appendices to Annex I Other	Annexes I to III

1.5 Key resolutions (non-exhaustive list)

Some key resolutions which relate to Annex I (non-exhaustive list) are identified below. It is noted that the practice of the IMO is to adopt resolutions whose content may supersede or amend the content of previous texts (for example, the revised

---

21 See Colin de la Rue and Charles B. Anderson, *Shipping and the Environment* (2nd edition, Informa, 2009) p. 825.

guidelines contained in resolution MEPC.107(49) mentioned below superseded the recommendations included in resolution MEPC.60(33)). Furthermore, a period of time is usually required for the entry into force of a resolution (e.g. Resolution MEPC.107(49) adopted on 18 July 2003 implemented from 1 January 2005). The status of IMO resolutions in a national legal system is commonly investigated before national maritime administrations. Attention of readers is drawn to possible amendments.

- Resolution MEPC.107(49) (adopted on 18 July 2003) Revised Guidelines and Specifications for Pollution Prevention Equipment for Machinery Space of Bilges of Ships;
- Resolution MEPC.108(49) adopted on 18 July 2003 "Revised Guidelines and Specifications for Oil Discharge Monitoring and Control Systems for Oil Tankers";
- Resolution MEPC.240(65) adopted on 17 May 2013 "2013 Amendments to the Revised Guidelines and Specifications for Oil Discharge Monitoring and Control Systems for Oil Tankers (Resolution MEPC.108(49))";
- Resolution MEPC.83(44) (adopted on 13 March 2000) Guidelines for Ensuring the Adequacy of Port Waste Reception Facilities;
- Resolution MEPC.94(46) on Condition Assessment Scheme (CAS) (adopted on 27 April 2001); Amended by Resolution MEPC.99(48) (adopted on 11 October 2002), MEPC.112(50) (adopted on 4 December 2003) Amendments to the Condition Assessment Scheme; MEPC.131(53) (adopted on 22 July 2005) Amendments to the Condition Assessment Scheme (CAS); and MEPC.155(55) (adopted 13 October 2006) Amendments to the Condition Assessment Scheme (CAS);
- Resolution MEPC. 95(46) (adopted on 27 April 2001) Amendments to the Annex of the Protocol of 1978 Relating to the International Convention for the Prevention of Pollution from Ships, 1973 (Amendments to regulation 13G of Annex I to Marpol 73/78 and to the Supplement to the IOPP Certificate);
- MEPC.139(53) (adopted on 22 July 2005) Guidelines for the application of the revised MARPOL Annex I requirements to Floating Production, Storage and Offloading Facilities (FPSOs) and Floating Storage Units (FSUs), as amended;
- IMO Resolution A.982(24) (adopted on 1 December 2005) Revised Guidelines for the identification and designation of Particularly Sensitive Sea Areas (PSSAs);
- IMO Resolution A.393(X) (adopted on 14 November 1977) Recommendation on international performance and test specification for oily-water separating equipment and oil content meters, as amended;
- MEPC.107(49) (adopted on 18 July 2003) Revised guidelines and specification for pollution prevention equipment for machinery space bilges of ships;
- MEPC.54(32) (adopted on 6 March 1992) Guidelines for the development of shipboard oil pollution emergency plans, as amended;
- A.446(XI) (adopted on 15 November 1979) Revised Specifications for the Design, Operation and Control of Crude Oil Washing Systems, as amended;

- MEPC.235(65) (adopted on 17 May 2013) Amendments to the Annex of the Protocol of 1978 Relating to the International Convention for the Prevention of Pollution from Ships, 1973 (Amendments to Form A and Form B of Supplements to the IOPP Certificate under MARPOL Annex I);
- MEPC.238(65) (adopted on 17 May 2013) Amendments to the Annex of the Protocol of 1978 Relating to the International Convention for the Prevention of Pollution from Ships, 1973 (Amendments to MARPOL Annexes I and II to make the RO Code mandatory);
- MEPC.246(66) (adopted on 4 April 2014) Amendments to the Annex of the Protocol of 1978 Relating to the International Convention for the Prevention of Pollution from Ships, 1973 (Amendments to MARPOL Annexes I, II, III, IV and V to make the use of the III Code mandatory);
- MEPC.248(66) (adopted on 4 April 2014) Amendments to the Annex of the Protocol of 1978 Relating to the International Convention for the Prevention of Pollution from Ships, 1973 (Amendment to MARPOL I on mandatory carriage requirement for a stability instrument);
- MEPC.256(67) (adopted on 17 October 2014) Amendment to the Annex of the Protocol of 1978 Relating to the International Convention for the Prevention of Pollution from Ships, 1973 (Amendment to MARPOL I, regulation 43).

1.6 Construction requirements

Among the first requirements of Annex I was the construction of all crude oil tankers above 20,000 DWT and all oil product tankers above 30,000 DWT with segregated ballast tanks (SBT).

In 1992 amendments were introduced concerning the mandatory design and construction of tankers of 5,000 DWT and above built after 6 July 1996/ordered after 6 July 1993 with double hulls (or an alternative design approved by the IMO). According to a schedule, the said requirement was subsequently extended to existing tankers (2001 amendments, following the *Erika* accident, setting out a stricter phasing-out schedule, entry into force in 2003; further amendments were adopted in 2003, which entered into force on 5 April 2005). The carriage of heavy grade oil (HGO) by single hulls was also regulated in a restrictive manner.

The flag State administration of a single hull SBT/PL tanker may allow its operation to continue until 2015 or until the date of its completion of 25 years since delivery, on the condition that the outcome of the Condition Assessment Scheme is satisfactory.

1.7 Protection of fuel oil tanks

MARPOL regulation 12A on oil fuel tank protection sought to prevent pollution by spillage of bunker fuel oil. "Oil fuel" is defined as any oil used as fuel in connection with the propulsion and auxiliary machinery of the ship in which such oil is carried. Regulation 12A is a highly technical provision. It was introduced through an amendment of Annex I in October 2004, and it entered into force on 1 January 2007.

The regulation applies to "all ships with an aggregate oil fuel capacity of 600 m^3 and above which are delivered on or after 1 August 2010". Ships concerned must be fitted with fuel tanks which are situated in protected locations, have a maximum capacity per tank specified by the instrument, and satisfy performance standards for accidental outflow.[22]

1.8 Control of operational discharges of oil from machinery spaces

- Discharges outside special areas
  "Any discharge into the sea of oil or oily mixture from ships of 400 gross tonnage and above shall be prohibited except when all the following conditions are satisfied:

  1. the ship is proceeding en route;
  2. the oily mixture is processed through an oil filtering equipment meeting the requirements of regulation 14 of this Annex;
  3. the oil content of the effluent without dilution does not exceed 15 ppm;
  4. the oily mixture does not originate from cargo pump-room bilges on oil tankers; and
  5. the oily mixture, in case of oil tankers, is not mixed with oil cargo residues."[23]

- Discharges in special areas
  "Any discharge into the sea of oil or oily mixtures from ships of 400 gross tonnage and above shall be prohibited except when all of the following conditions are satisfied:

  1. the ship is proceeding en route;
  2. the oily mixture is processed through an oil filtering equipment meeting the requirements of regulation 14.7 of this Annex;
  3. the oil content of the effluent without dilution does not exceed 15 ppm;
  4. the oily mixture does not originate from cargo pump-room bilges on oil tankers; and
  5. the oily mixture, in case of oil tankers, is not mixed with oil cargo residues."[24]

It is also noted that "in respect of the Antarctic area, any discharge into the sea of oil or oily mixtures from any ship shall be prohibited".[25]

---

22 *Ibid*, p. 827.
23 Extract from MARPOL Annex I, regulation 15.
24 *Ibid*
25 *Ibid*

1.9 Discharges from the cargo area of oil tankers

- Discharge outside special areas

  "Subject to the provisions of regulation 4 of this Annex [this is about discharges resulting from damage] and paragraph 2 of this regulation, any discharge into the sea of oil or oily mixtures from the cargo area of an oil tanker shall be prohibited except when all the following conditions are satisfied:

  1. the tanker is not within a special area;
  2. the tanker is more than 50 nautical miles from the nearest land;
  3. the tanker is proceeding en route;
  4. the instantaneous rate of discharge of oil content does not exceed 30 litres per nautical mile;
  5. the total quantity of oil discharged into the sea does not exceed for tankers delivered on or before 31 December 1979, as defined in regulation 1.28.1, 1/15,000 of the total quantity of the particular cargo of which the residue formed a part, and for tankers delivered after 31 December 1979, as defined in regulation 1.28.2, 1/30,000 of the total quantity of the particular cargo of which the residue formed a part, and;
  6. the tanker has in operation an oil discharge monitoring and control system and a slop tank arrangement as required by regulations 29 and 31 of this Annex."[26]

- Discharges in special areas

  "3 Subject to the provisions of paragraph 4 of this regulation, any discharge into the sea of oil or oily mixture from the cargo area of an oil tanker shall be prohibited while in a special area.

  4 The provisions of paragraph 3 of this regulation shall not apply to the discharge of clean or segregated ballast.

  5 Nothing in this regulation shall prohibit a ship on a voyage only part of which is in a special area from discharging outside the special area in accordance with paragraph 1 of this regulation."[27]

SECTION 3: KEY MANAGEMENT ISSUES, INCLUDING DOCUMENTATION

1.10 Surveys and certification

A survey is an inspection set out by law which seeks to ascertain whether certain requirements are met for the purposes of issuing a certificate. There is a distinction between class and statutory surveys. Certificates are issued by flag States which usually empower surveyors nominated for the purpose or recognised organisations; in practice the latter are often ship classification societies. In this context, surveys are an important tool for ensuring quality, implementation and enforcement. The flag administration fully guarantees the completeness and efficiency of the survey.

---

26 Extract from MARPOL Annex I, regulation 34.
27 *Ibid*

Furthermore, the flag State undertakes according to regulation 6 paragraph 3.4 of Annex I to ensure the necessary arrangements to satisfy this obligation.

Surveys provided by MARPOL Annex I, Chapter 2 ("Surveys and certification") include:

- initial survey;
- renewal survey;
- intermediate survey;
- annual survey;
- additional survey.

1.10.1 Shipboard Oil Pollution Emergency Plan

The requirement to carry onboard a shipboard oil pollution emergency plan (SOPEP) approved by the flag administration applies according to regulation 37 to every oil tanker of 150 gross tonnage and above and every ship other than an oil tanker of 400 gross tonnage and above. The plan consists of a number of items, including, at a minimum, the procedures to be followed for the reporting of an oil pollution incident, the list of contact persons and authorities to be contacted in case of an oil pollution incident, a detailed description of the action to be undertaken with a view to controlling oil discharge following the incident, and the procedures and point of contact on the ship for coordinating shipboard action with the authorities in combating pollution. It is noted that the shipboard oil pollution emergency plan must be based on IMO guidelines.

1.10.2 Oil Record Book

Vessels accumulate volumes of oily waste water in their bilges, engine rooms, and mechanical spaces. As it was briefly described above, MARPOL Annex I prohibits ships from discharging these wastes at sea, unless certain criteria are met. For example, a ship may only discharge *en route* if, amongst others, the discharged material is processed through specified oil filtration equipment that traps most of the oil. Vessels are also required to record all oil transfer operations in an oil record book that is kept on board and is available for inspection. False entries to conceal illegal discharges and/or the manipulation of existing equipment (a practice commonly referred to as "magic pipes") are only some of the aspects involved by the use of the oil record book. As it will be seen below under Section 5, maintaining an accurate oil record book is an area which has clearly given rise to litigation in a number of jurisdictions.

More specifically, regulation 17 sets out[28] that every oil tanker of 150 gross tonnage and above and every ship of 400 gross tonnage and above other than an oil tanker must be provided with an oil record book part I (machinery space

---

28 This is within Chapter 3 of MARPOL Annex I; it relates to requirements for machinery spaces of all ships.

operations). It is further stipulated in the same provision that this document may be part of the ship's official log-book or in the form specified in the appropriate appendix. The details concerning the completing of the oil record book part I are also set out in regulation 17.

In the event of discharge of oil or oily mixtures as provided in regulation 4 of Annex I which deals with exceptions or in the event of accidental or other exceptional discharge of oil not excepted, a statement must be made in the oil record book part I of the circumstances of, and the reasons for, the discharge.[29] Furthermore, any failure of the oil-filtering equipment shall be recorded in the book.

The said document must be kept, according to regulation 17.6, in such a place as to be readily available for inspection at all reasonable times and, except in the case of unmanned ships under tow, it shall be kept on board the ship.

In addition to the above, there is a requirement[30] that every oil tanker of 150 gross tonnage and above must be provided with an oil record book part II (cargo/ballast operations). The details of completing the book part II are set out in the same provision. Amongst others, any failure of the oil discharge monitoring and control system must be noted in the said book part II.

1.10.3 International Oil Pollution Prevention Certificate

The International Oil Pollution Prevention Certificate (IOPPC) is issued or endorsed, as appropriate, either by the flag administration or by any persons or organisation duly authorised by it, following an initial or renewal survey.[31] Oil tankers of 150 gross tonnage and above and any other ships of 400 gross tonnage and above which are engaged in voyages to ports or offshore terminals under the jurisdiction of other Parties to MARPOL are concerned.[32] Regulation 10 sets out the details concerning the duration and validity of the certificate. The certificate is issued for a period specified by the flag administration and, according to MARPOL, it shall not exceed five years.[33] A model is provided by the IMO concerning the form of the certificate.[34]

1.11 Relevance of the International Safety Management Code

The International Safety Management (ISM) Code will be discussed in more detail in the chapter which addresses the human element. For the purposes of this chapter which deals with marine pollution by oil, it may be recalled that the ISM Code introduces a managerial approach to safety, marine environment protection and labour standards, by treating the vessel and the corporate environment in which it operates as a whole (rather than in a fragmented manner). The Code

---

29 MARPOL Annex I, regulation 17.3.
30 Regulation 36 (This is within Chapter 4 on Requirements for the cargo area of oil tankers).
31 MARPOL Annex I, regulation 7.
32 *Ibid*
33 MARPOL Annex I, regulation 10.
34 MARPOL Annex I, regulation 9 and Appendix II.

was adopted in 1993 through IMO Resolution A.741(18), and was subsequently integrated within SOLAS. The Code sought to remedy the problem of poor management of ships, including sub-standard ships, following a number of major casualties such as the *Amoco Cadiz* in 1978 and *the Herald of Free Enterprise* in 1987. Since its adoption, the Code has been amended a number of times. The Code became mandatory for ships progressively between 1998 and 2002.

The Code is highly relevant to marine pollution control. It seeks to remedy the problems resulting from poor management (procedures, communication, etc.), and the situation where senior management and/or owners would seek to distance themselves from the adverse occurrences affecting their ship. As already mentioned, the instrument adopts a managerial approach to safety and marine pollution prevention policies. This means that, in addition to the technical requirements which are proper to maritime safety and marine pollution from the regulatory compliance package (e.g. SOLAS, MARPOL, etc.), the ISM Code requires the establishment of a safety culture supporting safe and environmentally friendly shipping. This approach is based on the rationale of self-regulation where safety and marine environment protection (alongside, in recent years, seafarers' rights) should be integrated in the values of each person working ashore or aboard.

Briefly viewed from the standpoint of marine pollution prevention, on the one hand the Code sets out that every company should develop, implement and maintain a safety management system which includes, amongst others, a safety and environmental-protection policy;[35] on the other hand, the Code introduces a requirement that "the Company should establish procedures, plans and instructions, including checklists as appropriate, for key shipboard operations concerning the safety of the personnel, ship and protection of the environment. The various tasks should be defined and assigned to qualified personnel".[36]

1.12 Industry Best practices

A number of institutional stakeholders in the shipping industry provide useful resources to the industry which support the goal of proper implementation of international requirements and dissemination of good practice, including in the field of marine pollution prevention and management and/or pollution by oil.

The International Chamber of Shipping (ICS), the International Shipping Federation (ISF), Oil Companies International Marine Forum (OCIMF), the Baltic and International Maritime Council (BIMCO), the International Association of Independent Tanker Owners (Intertanko), and other stakeholders work on standards through guidance[37] or other resources. Some of them are mentioned below:

- ICS Shipping Industry Guidance on Environmental Compliance;
- ICS Shipping and the Environment – A Code of Practice;

---

35 Para. 1.4.1 of the ISM Code on Functional requirements for a safety management system.
36 Para. 7 of the Code.
37 Information about relevant publications may notably be found at www.marisec.org (last visit 12 January 2017).

- ISC/ISF Guidelines on the Application of the IMO International Safety Management (ISM) Code;
- ICS/OCIMF/IAPH[38] International Safety Guide for Oil Tankers and Terminals (ISGOTT);
- ICS/OCIMF Ship to Ship Transfer Guide (Petroleum);
- ICS/OCIMF Prevention of Oil Spillages through Cargo Pump Room Sea Valves;
- Shipping industry guidance on the use of Oily Water Separators (published by Maritime International Secretariat Services Limited);
- ICS Model Shipboard Oil Pollution Emergency Plan (SOPEP);
- ICS/OCIMF Ship-to-ship transfer guide – petroleum;
- Energy Institute (London) HM (Hydrocarbon Management) 40 for the Crude Oil Washing of Ships' Tanks and the Heating of Crude Oil Being Transported by Sea (2004, 2nd edition)

"Companies should take steps to prevent deliberate non-compliance. This may involve installing monitoring equipment, using seals on overboard discharge lines, fitting unique tags on flanges, or fitting interlocks to prevent falsification of monitoring records."

Source: Shipping Industry Guidance on Environmental Compliance (ICS Shipping and the Environment – A Code of Practice, 2008)

"Ship operators have ultimate responsibility for establishing a compliance culture within their companies, and it is important that every effort is made to ensure that seafarers do not engage in any illegal conduct in the mistaken belief that it will benefit their employer. Every seafarer should be made fully aware of the severe legal consequences, both for the company and the seafarers themselves, of even minor non-compliance with environmental rules."

Source: Shipping Industry Guidance on the Use of Oily Water Separators

---

SECTION 4: AREAS OF SPECIAL INTEREST

In this section we have identified a topic of technical interest, and a topic which represents a recent development.

1.13 Ship-to-ship transfer of crude oil and petroleum products

MARPOL had to be amended in order to address the prevention of marine pollution during ship-to-ship (STS) oil transfer operations. The said amendments entered into force on 1 January 2011. It is not our intention to analyse such a

---

38 International Association of Ports and Harbours.

technical area as the ship-to-ship transfer of crude oil and petroleum products.[39] For the purposes of this chapter which describes basic directions about prevention of marine pollution by oil, let us stress from the outset that oil tankers of a specified tonnage involved with cargo transfer operation are required to have aboard an approved STS operations plan[40] describing, amongst others, step-by-step the said operations, emergency shutdown procedures, reporting oil spillages procedures, etc. The said plan may be part of the safety management system (SMS) required under the ISM Code (SOLAS Chapter IX). A risk assessment of STS operations should confirm, amongst others, the suitability of the oil tanker's personnel (e.g. training, qualification, etc.), and the adequacy of the personnel in terms of numbers to control and perform oil transfer operations. The operations should be performed according to certain standards which take into account best practice guidelines, and the Parties involved should be prepared to immediately discontinue the operation if necessary (e.g. under adverse weather and/or sea conditions, etc.). A qualified person in overall advisory control should be designated aimed at ensuring that the operations are conducted according to the plan, advising the master(s), ensuring the provisions of the contingency plan, etc. The selection of the STS transfer area should be made in recognition of safety considerations, including, wherever applicable, national requirements, and coordination with the authorities.

1.14 Recent developments: oil tankers operations in ice-covered waters (the Polar Code)

The Polar Code will be touched upon in different chapters as the book progresses. The International Code for Ships Operating in Polar Waters (Polar Code), was adopted by the IMO in November 2014 through the amendment of the SOLAS and MARPOL Conventions (in the latter case, the amendments were adopted in May 2015). The Code entered into force on 1 January 2017, and it represents a major development of the international regulatory agenda for the protection of the marine environment in polar waters.

The Code applies to ships which operate in Arctic and Antarctic waters as an additional instrument to MARPOL. It seeks to ensure the safe ship operation and the protection of the polar environment by addressing risks present in polar waters and not adequately mitigated by other instruments of the IMO. The first part of the Code deals with safety and the second part with marine pollution prevention. Each part contains respectively a mandatory and a recommendatory division. For the purposes of the Code, ships are divided into a number of categories.

---

39 For a detailed presentation of ship-to-ship transfer of crude oil and petroleum products while underway or at anchor, notably see IMO, *Manual on Oil Pollution, Section I – Prevention* (2011 edition, Chapter 6, pp. 61–80), and ICS/OCIMF, *Ship-to-Ship Transfer Guide – Petroleum* (4th edition, 2005).

40 According to regulation 41(3) of Chapter 8, MARPOL Annex I, "Any oil tanker subject to this chapter and engaged in STS operations shall comply with its STS operations Plan".

The Code addresses prevention of pollution by oil, by setting out structural and operational requirements.[41] A prohibition of the discharge into the Arctic waters of oil or oily mixture from any ship is notably spelled out, with an additional mention that this prohibition shall not extend to the discharge of clear or segregated ballast. Furthermore, operation in polar waters (which includes Arctic and Antarctic waters) shall be taken into account, according to the Code, "as appropriate, in the Oil Record Books, manuals and the Shipboard Oil Pollution Emergency Plan or the Shipboard Marine Pollution Emergency Plan as required by MARPOL Annex I". In the part which addresses structural requirements, a number of requirements are set out in relation to the category of ship concerned.

SECTION 5: SELECTED ASPECTS CONCERNING IMPLEMENTATION AND ENFORCEMENT

1.15 Selected highlights on national jurisdictions

Cases on marine pollution are commonly approached from the standpoint of legal liabilities, including limitation of liability, and the cost of clean-up operations. The highlights below constitute only a limited number of illustrations – some of them are notorious, others are of local interest. They come from varied national legal systems, and they are briefly presented with the focus on the implementation and enforcement of MARPOL I provisions on illegal discharges of oil. They should be assessed in light of the position of each court in the national court hierarchy, and the legal principles applicable in each system.[42] Readers are reminded at this point that Chapter 11 will deal with the legal repercussions of marine pollution, including limitation of liability. As already mentioned, the highlights below are presented because of their relevance with MARPOL Annex I.

United States v Abrogar[1]	The case pertained to the accuracy of the oil record book of a ship while in the US waters or in a US port. The question was discussed on the grounds of domestic legislation (Act to Prevent Pollution from Ships (APPS), 33 U.S.C. § 1901 *et seq.*) implementing MARPOL Annex I in the USA.
United States v Ionia Management[2]	The case explored the charges brought under APPS 33 U.S.C. §1908 based on the defendant's actions during a US Coast Guard inspection. The case involved, amongst others, the question of maintaining an accurate oil record book.

---

41 See Part II – A 'Pollution Prevention Measures' – Chapter 1 'Prevention of Pollution by Oil'.

42 For example, the Greek legal system is considered to be a civil/continental law system where the principle of binding precedent, as known, in the English legal system and in systems under the influence of common law, does not apply.

United States v Jho[3]	The case involved a foreign-flagged vessel and the question of maintaining an oil record book under 33 C.F.R § 151.23. The alleged offences pertained to the ship's pollution-detection equipment, and its capacity, following alleged actions on the part of the chief engineer, to recognise discharges with higher oil content than allowed under U.S. law. It is noted that in this case the coastguard was tipped off by a crew member. One of the arguments explored was whether international law prohibited the authorities from prosecuting relevant offences which, according to the defendants, had occurred on the high seas. The Fifth Circuit reversed the district court. Its reasoning was interesting: if the requirement to 'maintain' an ORB included only an obligation to record entries when discharges were made and not to keep the book accurate (a requirement at U.S. ports), then the regulation would be at odds with MARPOL and Congress' clear intent under domestic legislation to prevent pollution at sea according to the international instrument. Furthermore, the argument that international law limited the competency of the port State to prosecute violations of domestic law committed in port, was rejected. The court held that the obligation to "maintain" an ORB imposes a duty upon to foreign vessels to ensure that their oil record book is accurate (or at least not knowingly inaccurate) when they enter ports of navigable waters of the U.S.
Piraeus (Greece) Administrative Court of Appeal[4] judgment No. 390/2015	Case pertaining to marine pollution following an oil spill detected through air surveillance by military air forces around the stern of a cargo ship; the decision also explores the concept of pollution by oil and the use of means of evidence of the spill. According to Greek judges, the provisional alteration of natural characteristics of the sea through the discharge of liquids constitutes pollution, and it is not required that such substances must be harmful (State Council Decision No. 2083/07 is referred to on this point). A penalty had been imposed by the lower court under section 12 of the Presidential Decree 55/1998[5]on the Protection of the marine environment, which was not changed by the Administrative Court of Appeal.
Piraeus (Greece) Administrative Court of Appeal judgment No. 2149/2011	The case is of interest to marine pollution (MARPOL I, regulations 4 and 20). The case involved amongst others a contention on the omission to fully update the oil record book prescribed under MARPOL Annex I and the corresponding enacting provisions in Greece,[6] and an additional contention according to which the authorities would not be entitled to conduct controls of the ship any time, including while the ship was under repair.

(Continued)

(Continued)

Piraeus (Greece) three-member Administrative Court of First Instance[7] Decision No. 4711/2011	The case is part of wider legal proceedings involving the casualty of the cruise ship *Sea Diamond* in 2007 off the coast of Santorini island, in the Aegean Sea, Greece. In this case, the claimants/applicants (the master, the ship owner and the operator) challenged the fine imposed on them by the Greek Minister of Mercantile Marine. Amongst others, the case discusses the argument of the applicants that according to MARPOL 73/78 there is no pollution offence when the discharge of oil is due to the damage to the ship or its equipment (see regulation 4 on exceptions). According to Greek judges in the said case, this contention is not legally founded as "the provisions of the International Convention MARPOL 73/78 which was ratified by Greece with Law 1269/1982 apply only in the case of pollution of international sea waters, whereas in the present case the pollution was caused in a port and shores of a country as well as in Greek territorial waters and the (above-mentioned)[8] provisions of codified law 743/1977[9] shall apply".[10]
Hellenic State Council[11] judgments Nos 2706/2006, 1834/1988, 35/1989, 2952/1990, 865/1993 (Greece)	The cases in question explore, amongst others, the question of monetary fines imposed by the Greek administration in case of marine pollution. They point to the position that a fine is imposed when marine pollution is ascertained and that the ascertainment of leakage of specific quantity or the description of the kind or composition of the oily and other polluting substances which escaped at sea and caused the pollution in question are not a condition for the imposition of the fine.
Paris (France) Court of First Instance judgment of 16 January 2008[12] Paris (France) Court of Appeal judgment of 30 March 2010[13]; and French Supreme Court (Cour de Cassation) decision of 25 September 2012[14]	In the notorious case involving the *Erika*, the sinking of the Maltese oil tanker off the coast of Brittany (exclusive economic zone of France) in 1999 and the ensuing large-scale pollution (19,800 tonnes of heavy fuel oil discharged at sea, having impacted 400 km of coastline)[15], raised a number of questions revolving around limitation of liability under international conventions, and the interpretation of certain MARPOL provisions, including Article 4 on violations and regulation 4 of MARPOL Annex I on exceptions. According to MARPOL Convention, Article 4(4), the penalties specified under the law of a (State) party under this provision shall be "adequate in severity to discourage violations of the present Convention and shall be equally severe irrespective of where the violation occur". At the first and second level of legal proceedings in France, four defendants were held criminally liable, and were imposed monetary sanctions, namely: the representative of the owners, the technical managers, the classification society, and the cargo owner. This was additional to civil liability (with the cargo owner being considered at the second level of legal proceedings protected by the channeling provisions of international conventions on civil liability). On the

second level of proceedings, the Court of Appeal rejected the defendants' arguments that MARPOL seeks only the punishment of the shipowner and the captain, and the Court considered that MARPOL did not entail any restriction concerning the Parties likely to be sanctioned under French law. In a decision adopted on 25 September 2012, France's highest court (Cour de Cassation), upheld all convictions and ruled civil liability of cargo interests.

1   459 F.3d 430 (3d Cir.2006).
2   498 Supp. 2d 477 (D. Conn. 2007). It is noted that in subsequent litigation, the judgment of the District Court and the jury verdict were affirmed.
3   534 F.3d 398 (5th Cir. 2008).
4   Διοικητικό Εφετείο Πειραιά.
5   Α' 58.
6   Law 1269 of 21/21/7.1982 (Α'89).
7   Διοικητικό Πρωτοδικείο Πειραιά, 8ο Τριμελές.
8   Brackets put by us.
9   Law 743/1977 on the Protection of the Marine Environment (Α' 319).
10   Free translation by us.
11   Supreme Administrative Court of Greece.
12   Tribunal de Grand Instance de Paris, 11ème Chambre, 4ème section.
13   Cour d'Appel de Paris, Pole 4, Chambre 11E.
14   Cour de Cassation, 25 September 2012, arrêt no 3439 (10–82.938) de la Chambre Criminelle.
15   A lessons learnt approach of the casualty can be found in French Permanent Commission of Enquiry into Accidents at Sea (CPEM), *Report of the Enquiry Into the Sinking of the Erika Off the Coasts of Brittany on 12 December 1999* (available in French and English on the internet).

BIBLIOGRAPHY

Boisson, Ph., *Safety at Sea – Policies, Regulation & International Law* (Editions Bureau Veritas, Paris, 1999)

Camphuysen, C.J., *Chronic Oil Pollution in Europe, a Status Report* (Royal Netherlands Institute for Sea Research, commissioned by the International Fund for Animal Welfare (IFAW), 2007)

Courtney, Aaron, Fjelstad, Eric, and Wildman, Sloane Anders, 'Multijurisdictional Regulation of Cruise Ship Discharges' [2004] Natural Resources and the Environment 19(1), Summer

(de la) Rue, C., and Anderson, Ch. B., *Shipping and the Environment* (2nd edition, Informa, Lloyd's Shipping Law Library, London/New York 2009)

European Maritime Safety Agency (EMSA), *Addressing Illegal Discharges in the Marine Environment* (document data unavailable)

Gard, 'MARPOL Annex I, Regulations for the Prevention of Pollution by Oil – A Selection of Articles Published by Gard AS' (2011)

GESAMP (Joint Group of Experts on the Scientific Aspects of Marine Environment Pollution), *Estimates of Oil Entering the Marine Environment from Sea-Based Activities* (Report No. 75, IMO/FAO/UNESCO-IOC-WHO/IAEA/UN/UNEP, 2007)

Hellenic Marine Environment Protection Association (HELMEPA), *Pollution Prevention from Ships: 30 Years of HELMEPA and MARPOL* (December 2012)

Hydrocarbon Management HM 40 Guidelines for the Crude Oil Washing of Ships' Tanks and the Heating of Crude Oil Being Transported by Sea (2nd edition, Energy Institute, London, June 2004)

IMO, *MARPOL Consolidated Edition 2011* (and related supplements)

IMO, *Manual on Oil Pollution* (Section I-Prevention) (2011)

International Chamber of Shipping (ICS), *Shipping and the Environment: A Code of Practice* (4th edition, London, 2008)

International Tanker Owners Pollution Federation (ITOPF), Effects of Oil Pollution on Social and Economic Activities (*TIP 12*)

International Tanker Owners Pollution Federation (ITOPF), Effects of Oil Pollution on the Marine Environment (*TIP 13*)

International Tanker Owners Pollution Federation (ITOPF), Fate of Marine Oil Spills (*TIP 02*)

International Chamber of Shipping (ICS)/Oil Companies International Marine Forum (OCIMF)/The Society of International Gas Tanker and Terminal Operators (SIGTOO), *Ship to Ship Transfer Guide for Petroleum, Chemicals and Liquefied Gases* (London, 2013)

International Tankers Owner Pollution Federation (ITOPF), *Trends in Oil Spills from Tankers Over the Past Ten Years* (2015)

INTERTANKO, *A Guide for Correct Entries in the Oil Record Book (Part I, Machinery space ops)* (3rd edition, London, 2014)

International Chamber of Shipping (ICS), Oil Companies International Marine Forum (OCIMF), International Association of Ports and Harbours (IAPH), *International Safety Guide for Oil Tankers and Terminals* (ISGOTT) (5th edition, Witherby Seamanship International, Livingston, UK)

National Research Council, *The Double Hull Tanker Legislation: An Assessment of the Oil Pollution Act of 1990* (National Academies Press, Washington, DC, 1998)

OSPAR Commission, *North Sea Manual on Maritime Oil Pollution Offences* (London, 2010 (last update 26.3.2012))

Polish Register of Shipping, Informative Publication No. 23/1, Condition Assessment Scheme (CAS) for Single Hull Oil Tankers, Gdansk (2013)

Wilkins Tim, Intertanko, *MARPOL Annex I Regulations for the Prevention of Pollution by Oil – An Introduction to the International Regulations for the Prevention of Pollution by Oil* (PowerPoint presentation)

CHAPTER 2

The international regulation, prevention and management of marine environmental pollution created by the offshore oil and gas industry

WYLIE SPICER, Q.C. AND PETER L'ESPERANCE

TABLE OF CONTENTS

Section 1	The offshore oil and gas industry as a source of marine environmental pollution	58
2.1	The offshore oil and gas industry as a source of marine environmental pollution	59
2.2	Contextualising the problem: the offshore oil and gas industry's relative contribution to marine environmental pollution	60
2.3	Regulating marine environmental pollution from the offshore oil and gas industry	60
Section 2	Specific sources of marine pollution from offshore oil and gas operations	63
2.4	Pollution from seabed activities	64
2.4.1	Oil	64
2.4.2	Drilling fluid	64
2.4.3	Drill cuttings	65
2.4.4	Produced water	65
2.4.5	Chemicals	66
2.4.6	Sound production	66
2.4.7	Other sources	66
2.5	Pollution by dumping	67
2.6	Pollution from vessels	67
2.7	Atmospheric pollution	67
Section 3	International law and policy	68
2.8	International legal framework	68
2.8.1	Customary international law	69
2.8.2	1958 Geneva Conventions	69
2.8.3	*UNCLOS III*	70
2.8.3.1	State obligations to protect and preserve the marine environment	71
2.8.3.2	State obligations to regulate pollution from seabed activities	72

	2.8.3.3	State obligations to regulate dumping	72
	2.8.3.4	State obligations to regulate pollution from or through the atmosphere	74
	2.8.3.5	State obligations to regulate pollution from activities carried out in the area	75

2.9 International instruments addressing specific pollution sources   75
     2.9.1 *MARPOL 73/78*   75
         2.9.1.1 Annex I: regulations for the prevention of pollution by oil   76
         2.9.1.2 Annex V: regulations for the prevention of pollution by garbage from ships   79
         2.9.1.3 Annex VI: regulations for the prevention of air pollution by ships   80
     2.9.2 *London Convention, 1972*   81
     2.9.3 *1996 Protocol to the London Convention, 1972*   82
2.10 International instruments addressing liability, clean-up and compensation for environmental damage   83
     2.10.1 *UNCLOS III*   83
     2.10.2 *The 1974 Offshore Pollution Liability Agreement*   84
     2.10.3 *Convention on Civil Liability for Oil Pollution Damage resulting from Exploration for and Exploitation of Seabed Mineral Resources, 1977*   85
     2.10.4 *1990 International Convention on Oil Pollution Preparedness, Response and Cooperation*   85
2.11 International policy statements   86
     2.11.1 United Nations Conference on the Environment and Development Rio Declaration   86
     2.11.2 United Nations Environment Programme   87
     2.11.3 *Convention on Environmental Impact Assessment in a Transboundary Context*   88
     2.11.4 *2003 Protocol on Strategic Environmental Assessment*   89
2.12 Select regional agreements   89
     2.12.1 *OSPAR Convention*   89
Section 4   Conclusions   90
2.13 Limits of the international legal framework   90
2.14 Future directions   92

SECTION 1: THE OFFSHORE OIL AND GAS INDUSTRY AS A SOURCE OF MARINE ENVIRONMENTAL POLLUTION

This chapter addresses the international regulation, prevention and management of marine environmental pollution generated by the offshore oil and gas industry.

2.1 The offshore oil and gas industry as a source of marine environmental pollution

In October 1947, a floating rig drilled the first commercial offshore oil well in 14 feet of water off southeastern Louisiana in the Gulf of Mexico.[1] Since that time, the offshore oil and gas industry has proliferated and currently features an estimated 6,500 oil and gas installations operating in regions including the North Sea, the Canada's North Atlantic, the Gulf of Mexico, the Gulf Coast, South East Asia and off the coasts of Australia, New Zealand, China and Brazil.[2] Today, offshore production accounts for 37% of global oil production and 28% of global gas production, a share which may rise as geophysical exploration techniques and deep water drilling technology permit offshore oil and gas extraction from newly discovered prospects of high-yielding deep water fields.[3]

The unique processes required to locate, extract, process and export oil and gas in the offshore generate risks of marine environmental pollution. Such pollution can result from routine operations, for example, through the creation of drill cuttings as a by-product of the drilling process, produced water, gas venting, machinery exhaust and other operational discharges of hydrocarbons and other chemicals into the marine environment. Alternatively, pollution may result from accidental releases of oil, gas, chemicals, drilling fluid, among other harmful substances. In extreme cases, well failures or blow-outs can result in catastrophic oil spills causing extensive damage to marine and coastal ecosystems and the marine mammals, fish, birds and aquatic organisms which they are host to. Additionally, these incidents can cause loss of life, personal injury, and significant economic losses to affected commercial fisheries and tourism sectors. A recent example is provided by the explosion and sinking of the *Deepwater Horizon* rig in the Gulf of Mexico, and the subsequent failure of the Macondo well's blowout preventer, resulting in an estimated 4.9 million barrels of oil spilling into the marine environment over a 5-month period.[4] In a similar incident following an explosion on the Montara wellhead platform on 21 August 2009, an estimated 105,000 barrels of oil spilled into the Timor Sea over a 74-day period, until the damaged well was capped on 3 November 2009.[5]

---

1 Offshore Technology Magazine, 'History of the Offshore Industry' <www.offshore-mag.com/index/about-us/history-of-offshore.html> accessed 21 July 2016.

2 Zhiguo Gao, 'International Law on Offshore Abandonment: Recent Developments, Current Issues and Future Directions' in Zhiguo Gao (ed), *Environmental Regulation of Oil and Gas* (Kluwer Law International, 1998) 144 [*Gao, Environmental Regulation of Oil and Gas*]; Edgar Gold, *Gard Handbook on Protection of the Marine Environment* (3rd edition, Gard AS, 2006) 638 [Gold, *Gard Handbook*].

3 World Ocean Review, 'World Ocean Review 3: Oil and Gas from the Sea' *Maribus gBmbH*, 2014, p. 17.

4 Harry Weber, 'Blown Out BP Well Finally Killed at Bottom of Gulf', *Associated Press* (19 September 2010).

5 Meraiah Foley, 'As Oil Enriches Australia, Spill Is Seen as a Warning' *New York Times* (Asia-Pacific, 27 September 2009).

2.2 Contextualising the problem: the offshore oil and gas industry's relative contribution to marine environmental pollution

Massive oil spills occurring in the wake of well blowouts, often vividly portrayed by the media, illustrate the industry's potentially devastating and irreversible impacts on the marine environment. However, an accurate image of the industry's contribution to marine environmental pollution requires looking beyond isolated events and considering the industry's relative contribution to the broader problem of marine pollution.

The Joint Group of Experts on Scientific Aspects of Marine Environmental Protection (GESAMP) – established in 1969 to advise the United Nations (UN) on scientific aspects of marine environmental protection, completed the most authoritative assessment on the sources and types of marine pollution in 1990. The assessment estimates the offshore oil and gas industry's contribution to marine pollution to be 1% – the smallest source of marine pollution relative to land-based discharges (44%), atmospheric sources (33%), vessel pollution (12%), and dumping (10%).[6] There are sound reasons to believe GESAMP's estimates of different activities' contributions to marine environmental pollution have changed since 1990, specifically, the development of stricter regulations regarding ocean pollution and dumping.

A 2007 GESAMP study evaluates the relative contributions of *sea-based* activities to marine environmental pollution.[7] The study estimates that offshore oil and gas exploration and production released an average of 20,000 metric tonnes of oil into the marine environment annually based on data acquired between 1988 and 1997. In contrast, the study estimates that shipping released an average of 457,000 metric tonnes of oil into the marine environment annually over the same period.[8]

Empirical research suggests that although the offshore oil and gas industry's relative contributions to marine environmental pollution are small as a proportion of all pollution entering the marine environment, the industry's absolute contributions remain significant and deserving of regulatory attention.

2.3 Regulating marine environmental pollution from the offshore oil and gas industry

Currently, no single international agreement comprehensively regulates marine environmental pollution from offshore oil and gas activities.[9] In 1977, the Comité Maritime International (CMI) adopted a Draft Convention on Offshore Mobile Craft (the *Rio Draft*) designed to clarify the application of contemporary international treaties to offshore activities, including those addressing marine

---

6 IMO/FAO/UNESCO/WMO/WHO/IAEA/UN/UNEP Joint Group of Experts on the Scientific Aspects of Marine Pollution (GESAMP), *The State of the Marine Environment*, Report No. 39 (1990), cited in Donald R. Rothwell and Tim Stephens, *The International Law of the Sea* (Hart Publishing, 2010) 339.

7 GESAMP, *Estimates of Oil Entering the Marine Environment from Sea-Based Activities* (IMO, 2007) [GESAMP, 2007].

8 *Ib.*, at viii.

9 Hossein Esmaeili, *The Legal Regime of Offshore Oil Rigs in International Law* (Dartmouth Publishing Company, 2001) 150 [Esmaeili].

environmental pollution.[10] The CMI submitted the *Rio Draft* to the Legal Committee of the IMCO (the precursor to the International Maritime Organisation (IMO)). However, IMCO Parties declined adopting the draft.[11] Subsequent efforts to develop an international instrument regulating the offshore oil and gas industry's contributions to marine environmental pollution were equally unsuccessful. Accordingly, the task of regulating the sector's contributions to marine environmental pollution fell to a constellation of international legal sources, supplemented by regional and domestic legislation, regulations and policies.

This chapter considers the constellation of international legal sources relevant to the regulation, prevention and management of marine environmental pollution generated by the offshore oil and gas industry. To facilitate this inquiry, the following topics are explored:

Section 2: Specific sources of marine pollution generated by offshore oil and gas operations

Section 2 describes the specific processes involved at all stages of offshore oil and gas exploration and production that creates risks of marine environmental pollution. The section seeks to identify specific environmental issues accompanying offshore oil and gas activities to assess the international legal framework's effectiveness in addressing those issues.

Section 3: The international legal framework governing the regulation, prevention and management of marine pollution generated by offshore oil and gas operations

Section 3 explores the relevant international rules regulating marine pollution generated by the offshore oil and gas industry.

First, it considers the international legal framework establishing State obligations to protect and preserve the marine environment, specifically: customary international law, the *1958 Geneva Convention on the Continental Shelf*,[12] the *1958 Geneva Convention on the High Seas*,[13] and, the *1982 United Nations Convention on the Law of the Sea (UNCLOS III)*.[14]

Second, the section considers international instruments addressing specific pollution sources, including: The *International Convention for the Prevention of Pollution From Ships, 1973* as amended by the *1978 Protocol (MARPOL 73/78)*;[15] the *1972 Convention on the Prevention of Pollution by Dumping of Wastes and other Matter (London*

---

10 *CMI Documentation 1977* Vol I, 28; Vol III, p. 124, cited in Nicholas Gaskell, 'Compensation for Offshore Pollution: Ships and Platforms' in Malcolm Clarke (ed), *Maritime Law Evolving* (Hart Publishing, 2013) 79 [Gaskell, *Compensation for Offshore Pollution*].

11 *Ibid*, at 80.

12 *Geneva Convention on the Continental Shelf*, 29 April 1958, 499 UNTS 311 (entered into force 10 June 1964) [*Geneva Convention on the Continental Shelf*].

13 *Geneva Convention on the High Seas*, 29 April 1958, 450 UNTS 11 (entered into force 30 April 1962) [*Geneva Convention on the High Seas*].

14 *United Nations Convention on the Law of the Sea*, 10 December 1982, 1833 UNTS 3 (entered into force 16 November 1994) [*UNCLOS III*].

15 IMO, *International Convention for the Prevention of Pollution from Ships*, 2 November 1973, 1340 UNTS 184 (entered into force 2 October 1983), as amended by IMO, *Protocol of 1978 Relating to the International Convention for the Prevention of Pollution from Ships*, 17 February 1978 (entered into force 2 October 1983), as amended [*MARPOL 73/78*].

Convention, 1972),[16] and the *1996 Protocol* to the *London Convention, 1972 (1996 Protocol)*.[17]

Third, it considers instruments addressing liability, compensation and clean up for marine environmental damage created by the offshore oil and gas industry, specifically: the *1974 Offshore Pollution Liability Agreement (OPOL, 1974)*;[18] the not yet in force *Convention on Civil Liability for Oil Pollution Damage Resulting From Exploration for and Exploitation of Seabed Mineral Resources, 1977 (CLEE, 1977)*;[19] and, the *1990 International Convention on Oil Pollution Preparedness, Response and Cooperation (OPRC, 1990)*.[20]

Fourth, the section describes two international policy statements articulating the international community's commitment to enhancing regulation of marine environmental pollution generated by the offshore oil and gas industry, specifically: the *United Nations Convention on the Environment and Development Rio Declaration (Rio Declaration)*; and, the United Nations Environment Programme Regional Seas Programme.[21] Further, the section describes two multilateral conventions governing environmental impact assessment and strategic environmental assessment requirements for offshore hydrocarbon projects, specifically: the *Convention on Environmental Impact Assessment in a Transboundary Context*; and, the *2003 Protocol on Strategic Environmental Assessment*.[22]

Fifth, in an effort to depict the international legal regime's silence regarding regulating select operational discharges, this section concludes by briefly examining several OSPAR Commission Decisions addressing specific pollution sources more directly.[23]

Section 4: Conclusion

The conclusion examines the international legal regime's effectiveness in regulating, managing and preventing the unique sources of pollution generated by the offshore oil and gas sector. It evaluates the arguments for and against comprehensive, international regulation of the offshore oil and gas industry's contribution to marine environmental pollution.

---

16 *Convention on the Prevention of Marine Pollution by Dumping of Wastes and Other Matter*, 29 December 1972, 1046 UNTS 120 (entered into force 30 August 1975) [London Convention, 1972].

17 *1996 Protocol to the Convention on the Prevention of Marine Pollution by Dumping of Wastes and other Matter*, 7 November 1997, 36 ILM 1 (entered into force 3 March 2006) [*1996 Protocol*].

18 See the Offshore Pollution Liability Association Limited Website, 'About Us' <www.opol.org.uk/about.htm> accessed 21 July 2016.

19 *Convention on Civil Liability for Oil Pollution damage resulting from Exploration For and Exploitation of Seabed Mineral Resources, 1977*, 1 May 1977 (London, United Kingdom)[*CLEE, 1977*]. The Convention is not yet in force.

20 *1990 International Convention on Oil Pollution Preparedness, Response and Cooperation*, 30 November 1990, 1891 UNTS 51 (entered into force 13 May 1995) [OPRC, 1990]

21 United Nations, 'Report of the United Nations Conference on the Environment and Development' *Chapter 17: Protection of the Oceans, All Kinds of Seas, Including Enclosed and Semi-Enclosed Seas, and Coastal Areas and the Protection, Rational Use and Development of Their Living Resources* (Rio de Janeiro, 3–14 June 1992) [*Rio Declaration*].

22 *Convention on Environmental Impact Assessment in a Transboundary Context*, 25 February 1991 (entered into force 10 September 1997) [*Espoo Convention*]; and *2003 Protocol on Strategic Environmental Assessment*, 21 May 2003 (entered into force 11 July 2010).

23 The OSPAR Commission is the body responsible for administering the OSPAR Convention, the mechanism by which 15 Governments & the EU cooperate to protect the marine environment of the northeast Atlantic. See OSPAR Commission website, <www.ospar.org/about>, accessed 21 July 2016.

SECTION 2: SPECIFIC SOURCES OF MARINE POLLUTION FROM OFFSHORE OIL AND GAS OPERATIONS

The *UNCLOS III* defines "pollution of the marine environment" as: "The introduction by man, directly, or indirectly, of substances or energy into the marine environment, including estuaries, which results or is likely to result in such deleterious effects as harm to living resources and marine life, hazards of human health, hindrance to marine activities, including fishing and other legitimate uses of the sea, impairment of quality for use of sea water and reduction of amenities."[24]

Inevitably, the unique processes facilitating offshore oil and gas exploration and production can introduce substances or energy into the marine environment which result in or are likely to result in deleterious effects to living resources, marine life and human health. Deleterious ecological effects caused by operational or accidental discharges of hydrocarbons and other chemicals into the marine environment include physical damage to marine mammals, birds, fish and invertebrate species such as molluscs and corals caused by direct contact with sufficiently large quantities of oil, oily substances or other chemicals.[25] Additionally, deleterious ecological effects can include acute toxic effects to marine mammals, birds, fish, invertebrates and other marine organisms caused by contact with or exposure to oil, oily substances or other chemicals.[26] Further, environmental impacts caused by offshore construction and decommissioning operations include habitat disruption caused by the placement of structures on the seabed or smothering of marine benthic communities by the placement of offshore installations, pipelines and cutting pilings.[27]

The severity of deleterious ecological effects will vary according to whether the released substance is biodegradable or non-biodegradable. Those which are non-biodegradable, such as heavy metals, other chemicals and certain high molecular weight hydrocarbons, do not break down once released in the marine environment and may persist for several generations in marine animal or plant life.[28] Deleterious ecological effects will also vary according to the location of the discharge and the sensitivity of the receiving environment. Such effects will be more severe in higher latitude or polar regions than in temperate or tropical regions where a host of factors, including climate, water temperature, salinity and the microbial content of the receiving environment accelerate biodegradation rates.[29]

This section identifies the specific processes at each stage of an offshore oil and gas exploration and production facility's lifecycle and explains how those

---

24 *UNCLOS III*, *supra* note 14, art 1(1)(4).

25 OSPAR Commission, 'Assessment of Impacts of Offshore oil and gas activities in the North-East Atlantic' (OSPAR, 2009) 13 [*OSPAR Commission Offshore Oil and Gas Assessment*].

26 *Ibid.*

27 *Ibid.*

28 Maria Gavouneli, *Pollution from Offshore Oil Installations* (Graham & Trotman/Martinus Nijhoff, 1995) 35; See also IMO/FAO/UNESCO/WMO/WHO/IAEA/UN/UNEP Joint Group of Experts on the Scientific Aspects of Marine Pollution (GESAMP), *Impact of Oil on the Marine Environment* (FAO, 1997) 3.

29 Sergei V. Vinogradov and Jay Paul Wagner, 'International Legal Regime for the Protection of the Marine Environment Against Operational Pollution from Offshore Petroleum Activities' in *Gao, Environmental Regulation of Oil and Gas, supra* note 2 at 97 [Vinogradov and Wagner].

processes either create or risk creating marine pollution. The section considers the relevant categories of marine pollution articulated by the *UNCLOS III*: pollution from land-based sources,[30] pollution from seabed activities,[31] pollution by dumping,[32] pollution from vessels,[33] and pollution from or through the atmosphere.[34]

2.4 Pollution from seabed activities

2.4.1 Oil

Offshore oil and gas activities can release oil into the marine environment at multiple stages of the exploration and production process through operational and accidental discharges. The bulk of oil entering the marine environment is present in operational discharges of produced water (see below).[35] Other sources of operational oil discharges include deck drainage, oil dropout during well testing and flaring operations, and the escape of oil-based drilling fluids during drilling operations. Sources of accidental discharges include small and large-scale well blowouts, pipeline ruptures, and tanker spillage during loading, offloading and transhipment operations.[36]

2.4.2 Drilling fluid

Drilling operations require "drilling fluid" – or, drilling mud – to be injected into the bore hole to improve lubrication and stabilization of drilling operations. Drilling fluid is comprised of a liquid base, a weighted material and other chemical additives, which vary according to the drilling operations contemplated and the environmental or geological conditions in which those operations are carried out. Drilling fluids are essential for rotary drilling operations and perform multiple functions, including controlling formation pressures, removing drill cuttings, well sealing, maintaining well bore stability, cooling and lubricating the drill bit.[37] The specific drilling operations will dictate the drilling fluid used, of which there are three main types:

- water-based: typically containing seawater as the base liquid;
- oil-based: typically containing a base liquid of diesel or a low aromatic mineral oil; and
- synthetic-based: typically containing an organic oil base liquid.[38]

---

30 UNCLOS III, *supra* note 14, art 207.

31 *Ibid*, art 208.

32 *Ibid*, art 209.

33 *Ibid*, art 210.

34 *Ibid*, art 211.

35 *OSPAR Commission Offshore Oil and Gas Assessment*, *supra* note 25 at 13.

36 Vinogradov and Wagner, *supra* note 29 at 93.

37 Canadian Association of Petroleum Producers, *Offshore Drilling Waste Management Review* (February 2001), p. 4.

38 Torgeir Bakke, Jarle Klunsoyr, and Steinar Sanni, 'Environmental Impacts of Produced Water and Drilling Waste Discharges from the Norwegian Offshore Petroleum Industry' (2013) *Marine Environmental Research* 92, 154, 161 [Bakke, Klunsoyr, and Sanni].

Depending on their specific contents, drilling fluids can contaminate the cuttings piles generated by drilling operations and leach into the water column once those cuttings piles are deposited on the seabed. Historically, oil-based drilling fluids have been the main source of oil pollution entering the marine environment from offshore oil and gas activities.[39]

2.4.3 Drill cuttings

Drilling operations produce "drill cuttings" – rock fragments generated and carried to the surface by drilling operations. A sample of 98 wells drilled in United Kingdom suggested an average cuttings volume of 1,481 tonnes.[40] Although not inherently harmful in themselves, drill cuttings can suffocate the marine benthic communities if discharged of the seafloor as "cuttings piles". Moreover, if discharged untreated, drill cuttings can contain residual traces of hydrocarbons and other chemicals which leach into the marine environment over time.[41]

2.4.4 Produced water

Offshore oil and gas extraction generates "produced water", which comprises formation water naturally occurring in the rock structures of the subsoil, water injected into the formation to aid in the extraction of the hydrocarbons, crude oil constitutes, natural and added salts, organic chemicals, solids, heavy metals, and trace amounts of naturally occurring radioactive substances.[42] Produced water represents a significant proportion of the total fluid recovered from an offshore well and represents the largest volume waste by-product of the oil and gas exploration and production.[43] Produced water is separated from the recovered oil and gas in processing facilities either on land or on the offshore installation. It is then treated and discharged into the marine environment or injected into subsurface rock formations.[44]

Analysts predict that as an increasing number of fields reach maturity globally, the volume of produced water will increase commensurately.[45] This increase results from requirements to inject increasing volumes of seawater into reservoirs to maintain reservoir pressure and ensure breakthrough into production wells.[46] Projected increases in the volume of produced water necessary to recover offshore

---

39 *Ibid.*

40 OSPAR Commission Offshore Oil and Gas Assessment, *supra* note 25 at 15.

41 Bakke, Klunsoyr, and Sanni, *supra* note 38 at 161.

42 H. Whitehead, *An A–Z of Offshore Oil and Gas* (Gulf Publishing Company, 1983) 219, cited in Esmaeili, *supra* note 9 at 148.

43 Esmaeili, *supra* note 9 at 149; Argonne National Laboratory, 'Produced Water Volumes and Management Practices in the United States' prepared for the U.S. Department of Energy (September 2009) 15.

44 For an analysis of the environmental impacts of produced water on the marine environment, see: Bakke, Klunsoyr, and Sanni, *supra* note 38.

45 Vinogradov and Wagner, *supra* note 29 at 97.

46 *Ibid.*

oil and gas resources suggest a growing hazard to the marine environment flowing from operational discharges of produced water.

2.4.5 Chemicals

Chemicals are essential to offshore oil and gas extraction. They are primarily used for drilling and production functions, including:

- rig and turbine washes;
- lubricants;
- solvents;
- hydraulic fluids used to control wellheads, subsea valves, and blowout preventers;
- chemicals used in hydrocarbon extraction and processing;
- drilling fluids; and
- cementing chemicals.

Chemicals may enter the marine environment in trace amounts through routine discharges of drilling mud, produced water or deck wash.[47] They may also enter the marine environment through accidental spills.

2.4.6 Sound production

Activities associated with offshore oil and gas operations generate noise energy which can adversely impact marine mammals, fish and other organisms which rely on acoustics for orientation, reproduction and other biological functions. Seismic surveying techniques used by offshore operators to search for evidence of oil and gas resources involve directing intense impulses of compressed air into the ocean at regular intervals. This technique generates intense sound, which may disrupt the habitat and sensory capacities of marine mammals, fish and other aquatic species.[48] Offshore construction and decommissioning operations involving pile driving and, in some applications, the use of explosives, can generate intense sound which propagates through the water column, seabed and subsoil. The machinery used in the regular operation of the installation, support vessels, storage tankers and shuttle tankers can also generate moderate yet persistent sound.[49]

2.4.7 Other sources

Other sources of marine pollution flowing from offshore oil and gas operations include deck drainage, domestic waste, and in some circumstances, the dumping

---

47 OSPAR Commission Offshore Oil and Gas Assessment, *supra* note 25 at 13.

48 Natural Resources Defence Counsel, 'Boom, Baby, Boom: The Environmental Impacts of Seismic Surveys' (May 2010).

49 Oil and Gas UK, 'About the Industry', Environment, Underwater Sound <http://oilandgasuk. co.uk/knowledgecentre/underwatersound.cfm> accessed 21 July 2016.

of garbage. Deck drainage consists of lubricating oils, spilled mud, deck wash, residual quantities of chemicals and solvents which drain from the offshore installation into the marine environment with the wind and weather.[50]

2.5 Pollution by dumping

Dumping waste from an offshore platform into the sea and disposing of or abandoning the platform itself during the decommissioning process are potential sources of marine pollution. Waste streams which are the by-product of offshore oil and gas exploration and production may contain concentrations of hydrocarbons and other chemicals which can damage the marine environment if that waste is dumped in an untreated form. Similarly, during the decommissioning process, the deliberate disposal of a platform or its auxiliary subsea systems such as pipelines and flow lines can damage the marine environment either directly, or through leaching residual hydrocarbons or chemicals into the water column or seabed.[51]

2.6 Pollution from vessels

Offshore oil and gas exploration and production activities require a fleet of diverse vessels whose operations can be a source of marine pollution. The range of vessels includes offshore construction vessels, heavy lift vessels, offshore support vessels, storage tankers, shuttle tankers, and others. The operational and accidental discharges associated with the use of these vessels are the subject of regulations governing vessel source marine pollution, rather than the offshore oil and gas sector specifically.

2.7 Atmospheric pollution

Offshore oil and gas exploration and production involves processes which generate marine pollution in the form of atmospheric emissions. These processes include: combustion required to generate electricity, operate pumps and compressors; diesel exhaust; flaring operations; venting during tank unloading; and incidental releases.[52] These processes result in the release of gases, including carbon dioxide, methane, nitrogen oxide, and sulphur.[53] When these gases enter the atmosphere, they contribute to anthropogenic climate change, stratospheric ozone depletion, and ocean acidification, among other environmental challenges.[54]

---

50 Esmaeili, *supra* note 9 at 149.
51 *Ibid* at 149.
52 Oil and Gas UK, 'Knowledge Centre: Atmospheric Emissions' <http://oilandgasuk.co.uk/atmospheric-emissions.cfm> accessed 21 July 2016.
53 *Ibid.*
54 *Ibid.*

SECTION 3: INTERNATIONAL LAW AND POLICY

2.8 International legal framework

Currently, no single international treaty comprehensively regulates marine environmental pollution from offshore oil and gas installations.[55] Rather, a patchwork of legal sources comprised of customary international law, international treaties, regional treaties, and domestic legal sources regulates marine environmental pollution generated by the sector.

Offshore oil and gas exploration and production activities primarily occur in maritime zones under coastal state jurisdiction, such as the territorial sea, which extends 12 nautical miles (NM) seaward from the baseline; the exclusive economic zone, which extends from the seaward limit of the territorial sea to the 200-NM limit measured from the baseline; the continental shelf or the extended continental shelf where applicable, which extends from the seaward limit of the territorial sea to the 200-NM limit or up to the 350-NM limit depending on the bathymetry of the coastal states' continental shelf.[56] Because the bulk of offshore activities occur in maritime zones where coastal States exercise primary legislative jurisdiction as an extension of their sovereignty or sovereign rights, the domestic legal sources of the relevant coastal state[s] will be the starting point for offshore operators seeking to ascertain the laws regulating marine environmental pollution from offshore activities.

Domestic legal sources will vary across States and across regions. For this reason, this chapter does not provide a comprehensive analysis of all legal rules regulating marine pollution and the offshore oil and gas industry. However, to the extent that international legal sources shape and inform domestic legislation, this article discusses those international legal sources under the following headings:

- international legal framework;
- international instruments addressing specific pollution sources;
- international instruments addressing liability, clean-up and compensation for environmental damage; and
- international policy statements.

This discussion attempts to show practitioners where international legal sources impose uniform requirements which the domestic laws of the relevant coastal State(s) must reflect. Further, it attempts to show where international legal sources inadequately regulate potential pollution sources generated by offshore oil and gas activities, flagging where practitioners should seek additional guidance from relevant regional or domestic legal sources.

---

55 Esmaeili, *supra* note 9 at 150.
56 UNCLOS III, *supra* note 14, arts 2, 56, 77.

2.8.1 Customary international law

The concept that states have a positive obligation to prevent marine environmental pollution is relatively recent. For this reason, it has been suggested that any obligation under customary international law is immature and vague.[57] Yet, broader principles exist under international law that may support state obligations to prevent marine environmental pollution. The most relevant of these principles provides that states cannot use their territories in such a manner as to cause damage to the territories of other states.[58] This principle is considered in a series of cases, such as the *Corfu Channel Case*,[59] the *Nuclear Test Case*,[60] and the *Trail Smelter Case*.[61] Moreover, the principle has been articulated in a number of international instruments, the most relevant being the *1972 Stockholm Declaration on the Human Environment*, which provides in Principle 21: "States have, in accordance with the Charter of the United Nations and Principles of international law ... **the responsibility to ensure that activities within their jurisdiction or control do not cause damage to the environment of other States or of areas beyond the limits of national jurisdiction**" (emphasis added)[62]

Principle 22 of the *1972 Stockholm Declaration* gives effect to the obligation to prevent environmental harm caused by activities under their jurisdiction through acknowledging the concepts of state responsibility, liability and compensation for extra-territorial damage: "States shall cooperate to develop further the international law regarding liability and compensation for the victims of pollution and other environmental damage caused by activities within the jurisdiction or control of such States to areas beyond their jurisdiction."[63]

The *1972 Stockholm Declaration* is not binding upon states. However, the Principles which it articulates, including Principle 21, are generally recognized as expressions of customary international law.[64]

2.8.2 1958 Geneva Conventions

The *1958 Geneva Convention on the Continental Shelf*[65] and the *1958 Geneva Convention on the High Seas*[66] are the first international instruments articulating the obligation to prevent marine environmental pollution flowing from offshore oil and gas activities. The general obligations expressed by the *1958 Geneva Convention on the Continental Shelf* and the *1958 Geneva Convention on the*

---

57 Esmaeili, *supra* note 10 at 150.

58 *Ibid.*

59 *Corfu Channel Case (United Kingdom v Albania)* [1949] ICJ Rep 4.

60 *Nuclear Test Case (New Zealand v France)* [1974] ICJ Rep 253.

61 *Trail Smelter Case (United States v Canada)* (1938–1941) RIAA vol III, pp. 1905–1982.

62 *Declaration of the United Nations Conference on the Human Environment*, 16 June 1972, 11 ILM 1416 (1972) [*1972 Stockholm Declaration*].

63 *Ibid*, principle 22.

64 Patricia Birnie, Alan Boyle, and Catherine Redgwell, *International Law and the Environment* (Oxford University Press, Oxford, 2009).

65 *Geneva Convention on the Continental Shelf, supra* note 12.

66 *Geneva Convention on the High Seas, supra* note 13.

High Seas were drafted prior to the offshore oil and gas industry's sustained development. Accordingly, although the relevant provisions anticipate general obligations to control pollution caused by offshore oil and gas exploration and production activities, the provisions remain general and do not fully address the environmental issues which evolved with the industry's growth.

Article 5(1) and (7) of the *1958 Geneva Convention on the Continental Shelf* provide:

> The exploration of the continental shelf and the exploitation of its natural resources must not result in any unjustifiable interference with navigation, fishing or the conservation of the living resources of the sea ...

[and]

> The coastal State is obliged to undertake, in the safety zones, all appropriate measures for the protection of the living resources of the sea from harmful agents.

Article 24 of the *1958 Geneva Convention on the High Seas* provides: "Every State shall draw up regulations to prevent pollution of the seas by the discharge of oil from ships or pipelines or resulting from the exploitation and exploration of the seabed and its subsoil, taking account of existing treaty provision on the subject."

2.8.3 UNCLOS III

The *UNCLOS III*, often referred to as the constitution for the world's oceans,[67] establishes an international framework governing the use of the world's oceans. The *UNCLOS III* replaced the Geneva Conventions for all signatory countries and has achieved nearly universal ratification.[68] Note, however, the *1958 Geneva Convention on the Continental Shelf* and the *1958 Geneva Convention on the High Seas* remain active for countries that have not ratified the *UNCLOS III* (see, for example, the USA). Moreover, even for non-party states, the provisions of the *UNLCOS III* remain relevant as they are generally accepted as reflecting customary international law.

The *UNCLOS III* contains a number of provisions which regulate either directly or indirectly marine environmental pollution from offshore oil and gas activities. This chapter considers those provisions under the following headings:

- State obligations to protect and preserve the marine environment (articles 192–196);
- State obligations to regulate pollution from seabed activities (articles 208 and 214);

---

67 The phrase "Constitution for the Oceans" is attributable to Tommy T. B. Koh of Singapore, President of the Third United Nations Conference on the Law of the Sea.

68 In 2014, 166 countries have ratified the *UNCLOS III* <www.un.org/depts/los/convention_agreements/convention_overview_convention.htm> accessed 21 July 2016; *UNCLOS III, supra* note 14, art 311.

INTERNATIONAL REGULATION OF MARINE POLLUTION

- State obligations to regulate dumping (articles 1, 210 and 214);
- State obligations to regulate pollution from or through the atmosphere (article 212); and
- obligations of States and the authority to regulate pollution from seabed activities in the area (articles 209(2) and 145(a)).

2.8.3.1 State obligations to protect and preserve the marine environment

Part XII of the *UNCLOS III* is dedicated to the "Protection and Preservation of the Marine Environment" (articles 192–196). Article 192 articulates the general obligation binding upon coastal and flag states "to protect and preserve the marine environment".

The language of article 192 suggests a dual obligation both to protect *and* preserve the marine environment. This dual obligation appears to be broader than any at customary international law regarding marine pollution because it imposes a positive obligation on States to protect the marine environment from prospective damage and a duty to preserve the marine environment generally.[69] Further, the obligation appears to be independent of environmental harm or damage to other states.

Significantly, the obligation articulated by article 192 co-exists with States' sovereign rights to exploit their natural resources under articles 56 and 80 of the *UNCLOS III* in their exclusive economic zones and continental shelf respectively. Article 193 of the *UNCLOS III* affirms this right in providing: "States have the sovereign right to exploit their natural resources pursuant to their environmental policies and in accordance with their duty to protect and preserve the marine environment."

Article 194 describes the measures all States are required to take to prevent, reduce and control pollution of the marine environment. The article applies to both flag and coastal States. The prescribed measures are non-exhaustive and apply to all sources of pollution. Article 194(3)(c) provides:

> The measures taken pursuant to this Part shall deal with all sources of pollution of the marine environment. These measures shall include, *inter alia*, those designed to minimize to the fullest possible extent … **pollution from installations and devices used in exploration or exploitation of the natural resources of the seabed and subsoil, in particular measures for preventing accidents and dealing with emergencies, ensuring the safety of operations at sea, and regulating the design, construction, equipment, operation and manning of such installations or devices.**

(emphasis added)

---

69 The obligation expressed by article 194, appears to be broader than that expressed in Principle 21 of the *1972 Stockholm Declaration on the Human Environment*, which gives States "the responsibility to ensure that activities within their jurisdiction or control do not cause damage to the environment". See *Stockholm Declaration, 1972, supra* note 62, Principle 21.

2.8.3.2 State obligations to regulate pollution from seabed activities

Article 208(1) requires coastal States to adopt laws regulating pollution arising from or in connection with seabed activities subject to their jurisdiction and from artificial islands, installations and structures under their jurisdiction, pursuant to articles 60 and 80 (internal waters, territorial sea, exclusive economic zone, continental shelf, archipelagic waters). Article 208(1) provides: "Coastal States shall adopt laws and regulations to prevent, reduce and control pollution of the marine environment arising from or in connection with seabed activities subject to their jurisdiction and from artificial islands, installations and structures under their jurisdiction, pursuant to articles 60 and 80."

Interpretation of Article 208(1) suggests that coastal States are required to regulate marine environmental pollution "arising from or in connection with seabed activities subject to their jurisdiction and from artificial islands, installations and structures" employed for the purposes in Article 60 and 80, i.e. the exploration and exploitation of the non-living resources of the seabed and subsoil. This suggests that regardless of the legal characterization of the vessel or installation engaged in offshore oil and gas activities, the coastal State will have primary legislative jurisdiction over marine pollution generated by those activities. This interpretation accords with Articles 56(1)(b)(iii) and 90, which gives the coastal State jurisdiction with regard to the protection and preservation of the marine environment in the exclusive economic zone and on the continental shelf respectively.

Article 214 requires coastal States to adopt and enforce rules and standards established through competent international organizations, such as the IMO, or diplomatic conference, to prevent, reduce and control marine environmental pollution arising from or in connection with seabed activities subject to their national jurisdiction. Article 214 provides:

> States shall enforce their laws and regulations adopted in accordance with article 208 and shall adopt laws and regulations and take other measures necessary to implement applicable international rules and standards established through competent international organizations or diplomatic conference to prevent, reduce and control pollution of the marine environment arising from or in connection with seabed activities subject to their jurisdiction and from artificial islands, installations and structures under their jurisdiction, pursuant to articles 60 and 80.

2.8.3.3 State obligations to regulate dumping

The *UNCLOS III* requires all states, including coastal and flag States, to adopt laws to prevent, reduce and control marine pollution caused by "dumping".[70] Article 1(1)(5)(a) of the *UNCLOS III* defines dumping to include: "(i) the deliberate disposal of wastes or other materials from vessels, platforms or other man-made structures at sea; and (ii) any deliberate disposal of vessels, platforms or other man-made structures at sea."

This definition covers the disposal of wastes from offshore oil and gas installations, as well as the deliberate disposal of disused installations or their

---

70 UNCLOS III, *supra* note 14, art 210.

components during the decommissioning process. Interpretation of the *UNCLOS III* definition of dumping suggests that it does not cover the *in situ* abandonment of offshore installations and their associated systems. Article 1(1)(5)(b) excludes from the definition of dumping:

> (i) **the disposal of wastes or other matter incidental to, or derived from the normal operations of vessels, aircraft, platforms or other man-made structures at sea and their equipment**, other than wastes or other matter transported by or to vessels, aircraft, platforms or other man-made structures at sea, operating for the purpose of disposal of such matter or derived from the treatment of such wastes or other matter on such vessels, aircraft, platforms or structures;
>
> (ii) placement of matter for a purpose other than the mere disposal thereof, provided that such placement is not contrary to the aims of this Convention [emphasis added].

Paragraph (i) states that dumping excludes the disposal of waste that is incidental to or derived from the normal operations of platforms or other man-made structures at sea, except where such waste is carried by vessels, aircraft or platforms operating for that express purpose, or where such waste is the product of a treatment process. This exception suggests that the discharge of "produced water" from offshore oil and gas activities falls within the definition of "dumping" provided by the *UNCLOS III*, specifically, as a discharge which is "derived from the treatment of such wastes or other matter on such vessels, aircraft, platforms or structures". However, there may be some ambiguity in this interpretation as the definition of dumping given by the *UNCLOS III* was premised on the definition of dumping of the 1972 *Convention on the Prevention of Marine Pollution by Dumping of Wastes and other Matter* which specifically exempts operational discharges from offshore oil and gas activities. Paragraph (ii) suggests the deliberate placement of matter will not amount to "dumping", for example, employing a disused installation to construct a breakwater or develop an artificial reef.

Article 210 requires all states, including coastal and flag States, to adopt laws to prevent, reduce and control marine pollution by dumping. The article does not prohibit dumping outright, but requires coastal state authorization for proposed dumping activities to be lawful. The article requires coastal State regulations concerning dumping to be no less effective than international standards. Finally, the article requires the coastal State to consult with other States potentially adversely affected by their decision to permit dumping. Article 210 provides:

> 1. **States shall adopt laws and regulations to prevent, reduce and control pollution of the marine environment by dumping.**
>
> 2. States shall take other measures as may be necessary to prevent, reduce and control such pollution.
>
> 3. Such laws, regulations and measures shall ensure that dumping is not carried out without the permission of the competent authorities of States.
>
> 4. States, acting especially through competent international organizations or diplomatic conference, shall endeavour to establish global and regional rules, standards and recommended practices and procedures to prevent, reduce and control such pollution. Such rules, standards and recommended practices and procedures shall be re-examined from time to time as necessary.
>
> 5. **Dumping within the territorial sea and the exclusive economic zone or onto the continental shelf shall not be carried out without the express prior**

approval of the coastal State, which has the right to permit, regulate and control such dumping after due consideration of the matter with other States which by reason of their geographical situation may be adversely affected thereby.

6. **National laws, regulations and measures shall be no less effective in preventing, reducing and controlling such pollution than the global rules and standards** [emphasis added].

Article 216 of the *UNCLOS III* requires flag States, coastal States, and other States to enforce applicable international rules and standards regulating dumping, developed under the auspices of the *UNCLOS III*. Those rules are explored in greater depth in sections 3.3 and 3.4, which respectively consider the *London Convention, 1972* and the *1996 Protocol*.

2.8.3.4 State obligations to regulate pollution from or through the atmosphere

Article 212 requires States to adopt laws and regulations to prevent reduce and control the prevention of the marine environment from or through the atmosphere, through providing:

> **States shall adopt laws and regulations to prevent, reduce and control pollution of the marine environment from or through the atmosphere, applicable to the air space under their sovereignty** and to vessels flying their flag or vessels or aircraft of their registry, taking into account internationally agreed rules, standards and recommended practices and procedures and the safety of air navigation.
>
> [emphasis added]

Several reasons exist to suggest the provision does not cover atmospheric emissions generated by offshore oil and gas exploration and production activities. First, the provision does not refer explicitly to offshore installations or structures. Second, certain interpretations suggest that the provision does regulate atmospheric emission generally but only those emissions resulting in pollution to the marine environment *from or through* the atmosphere.[71] Third, the provision only covers pollution from or through the atmosphere in "air space under [State] sovereignty". This suggests limited application to atmospheric emissions which enter the air space above the territorial sea, where coastal states enjoy full sovereignty. It is less certain whether the article applies to the atmospheric emissions generated by oil and gas operations located in the exclusive economic zone and on the continental shelf where coastal states enjoy sovereign rights but not full sovereignty.

Despite ambiguity in Article 212's application to atmospheric pollution generated by offshore oil and gas operations, commentators have suggested that interpreting the provision as applying to the industry is consistent with the *UNCLOS III*'s underlying objectives to address *all* sources of pollution affecting the marine environment.[72]

---

71 Vinogradov and Wagner, *supra* note 29 at 102.
72 *Ibid*.

2.8.3.5 State obligations to regulate pollution from activities carried out in the area

Article 209(2) imposes obligations on flag States to adopt laws regulating marine pollution from seabed activities carried out in the area, by providing:

> Subject to the relevant provisions of this section, States shall adopt laws and regulations to prevent, reduce and control pollution of the marine environment from activities in the Area undertaken by vessels, installations, structures and other devices flying their flag or of their registry or operating under their authority, as the case may be. The requirements of such laws and regulations shall be no less effective than the international rules, regulations and procedures referred to in paragraph 1.

Article 145(a) addresses the obligation of the authority to adopt measures to prevent, reduce and control marine environmental pollution caused by activities in the area, activities including offshore petroleum exploration and production. Article 145(a) provides:

> Necessary measures shall be taken in accordance with this Convention with respect to activities in the Area to ensure effective protection for the marine environment from harmful effects which may arise from such activities. To this end the Authority shall adopt appropriate rules, regulations and procedures for *inter alia*:
>
> (a) the prevention, reduction and control of pollution and other hazards to the marine environment, including the coastline, and of interference with the ecological balance of the marine environment, particular attention being paid to the need for protection from harmful effects of such activities as drilling, dredging, excavation, disposal of waste, construction and operation or maintenance of installations, pipelines and other devices related to such activities;
>
> (b) the protection and conservation of the natural resources of the Area and the prevention of damage to the flora and fauna of the marine environment.

2.9 International instruments addressing specific pollution sources

2.9.1 MARPOL 73/78

MARPOL 73/78 as amended is the primary international convention regulating the prevention and control of vessel-source marine environmental pollution.[73] To accomplish this task, *MARPOL 73/78*'s 6 annexes regulate specific discharges of harmful substances or effluents containing such substances.[74]

MARPOL 73/78 defines ships to include "fixed or floating platforms" signalling the presumptive application of the Convention's 6 annexes to offshore oil and gas operations, unless such operations are specifically exempted.[75] Despite

---

73 *MARPOL 73/78*, *supra* note 15.
74 *Ibid*, art 1(1).
75 *Ibid*, art 2(4).

this broad definition of "ship", the instrument limits its application to the offshore oil and gas industry by defining "discharge" to exclude:

> Release of harmful substances directly arising from the exploration, exploitation and associated offshore processing of sea-bed mineral resources.[76]

This exempts discharges of produced water, drilling fluids, and drill cuttings from regulation under *MARPOL 73/78* – discharges which historically have been the largest sources of pollution flowing from offshore oil and gas activities.[77] A 1993 United Nations report confirms "*MARPOL 73/78* has been interpreted as not applying to discharges arising from offshore sea bed activities, but only garbage under its Annex V."[78] Yet, amendments to *MARPOL 73/78* have extended the application of its annexes to the offshore oil and gas industry beyond annex V as will be explored below.

This section explores the applicability of the three *MARPOL 73/78* annexes which target the most significant sources of pollution generated by the offshore oil and gas industry: annex I, regulating oil pollution; annex V, regulating the discharge of garbage from ships; and, annex VI, regulating air pollution. For current and regularly updated commentary which clarify ambiguities in *MARPOL 73/78*'s application to the offshore oil and gas industry, consult regularly updated, unified interpretations prepared by the IMO and the International Association of Classification Societies.[79]

2.9.1.1 Annex I: regulations for the prevention of pollution by oil

As noted above, *MARPOL 73/78* does not cover what have historically been the most significant sources of marine environmental pollution generated by offshore oil and gas operations – operational discharges of oil present in produced water. Yet, *MARPOL 73/78*, annex I, regulation 39 regulates certain sources of oil pollution generated by offshore oil and gas installations in providing:

> 1   This regulation applies to fixed or floating platforms including drilling rigs, floating production, storage and offloading facilities (FPSOs) used for the offshore production and storage of oil, and floating storage units (FSUs) used for the offshore storage of produced oil.
>
> 2   Fixed or floating platforms when engaged in the exploration, exploitation and associated offshore processing of sea-bed mineral resources and other

---

76   *Ibid*, art 2(3)(b)(ii).

77   Bakke, Klunsoyr, and Sanni, *supra* note 38 at 161.

78   Law of the Sea. Report of the Secretary General (of the United Nations), 10 November 1993 with addendum of 30 November 1993 (UN Doc. a/48/527 and A/48527/Add.1). Note that this report pre-dates amendments to *MARPOL 73/78* providing for the instrument's broader application to offshore oil and gas activities.

79   See for example International Association of Classification Societies, *Interpretations of the International Convention for the Prevention of Pollution from Ships, 1973 as modified by the Protocol of 1978 relating thereto and its Annexes* (2015) <www.iacs.org.uk/document/public/Publications/Unified_interpretations/PDF/UI_MPC_pdf2774.pdf> accessed 21 July 2016; See also IMO, *Guidelines for the Application of the Revised MARPOL Annex I requirement to Floating Production, Storage and Offloading Facilities (FPSOs) and Floating Storage Units*, 22 July 2005, MEPC 53/24/Add.2 [*IMO, FPSO & FSU Guidelines*].

platforms shall comply with the requirements of this Annex applicable to ships of 400 gross tonnage and above other than oil tankers, except that:

1. they shall be equipped as far as practicable with the installations required in regulations 12 and 14 of this Annex;
2. they shall keep a record of all operations involving oil or oily mixture discharges, in a form approved by the Administration; and
3. subject to the provisions of regulation 4 of this Annex, the discharge into the sea of oil or oily mixture shall be prohibited except when the oil content of the discharge without dilution does not exceed 15 parts per million.

3. In verifying compliance with this Annex in relation to platforms configured as FPSOs or FSUs, in addition to the requirements of paragraph 2, Administrations should take account of the Guidelines developed by the Organization.[80]

MARPOL 73/78, annex I, regulation 39 provides that offshore oil and gas installations engaged in the exploration, exploitation and associated offshore processing of sea-bed mineral resources "**shall comply with the requirements of this Annex** applicable to ships of 400 gross tonnage and above other than oil tankers" (emphasis added).[81] The term "shall comply" suggests the mandatory application of the regulations of annex I, applicable to ships of 400 gross tonnage and above other than oil tankers, to offshore oil and gas installations engaged in exploration and production activities.

However, the regulation alters the mandatory application of prescribed regulations in providing that fixed and floating platforms "shall be equipped **as far as practicable** with the installations required in regulations 12 and 14 of this Annex" (emphasis added).[82] The term "as far as practicable" alters the mandatory application of regulations 12 and 14 of annex I to fixed and floating platforms, and suggests that the regulations are mandatory to the extent that they are practically or reasonably feasible. Regulation 12, annex I requires select ships to possess oil residue tanks and specifies technical design criteria for those tanks in providing: "Every ship of 400 gross tonnage and above shall be provided with a tank or tanks of adequate capacity, having regard to the type of machinery and length of voyage, to receive the oil residues (sludge) which cannot be deal with otherwise in accordance with the requirements of this Annex."[83]

Regulation 14, annex I requires select ships to possess oil filtering equipment and specifies technical design criteria for that equipment in providing: "Except as specified in paragraph 3 of this regulation, any ship of 400 gross tonnage and above by less than 10,000 gross tonnage shall be fitted with oil filtering equipment complying with paragraph 6 of this regulation. Any such ship which may

---

80 *MARPOL 73/78 supra* note 15, annex I, reg 39; For an elaboration on the limited application of *MARPOL 73/78* as amended to Floating Production, Storage and Offloading Facilities (FPSOs) and Floating Storage, see *IMO, FPSO & FSU Guidelines, supra* note 79.

81 *MARPOL 73/78 supra* note 15, annex I, reg 39, para. 2.

82 *Ibid*, annex I, reg 39, para. 2.1.

83 *Ibid*, annex I, reg 39, para. 1.

discharge into the sea ballast water retained in oil fuel tanks in accordance with regulation 16.2 shall comply with paragraph 2 of this regulation."[84]

MARPOL 73/78, annex I, regulation 15 controls operational oil discharges and prohibits the discharge into the sea of oil or oil mixtures subject to the exceptions listed in regulation 15,[85] and regulation 4.[86]

MARPOL 73/78, annex I, regulation 39, paragraph 2.3 prohibits fixed or floating platforms from discharging oil or oily mixtures into the sea "except where the oil content of the discharge without dilution does not exceed 15 ppm".[87]

Yet, recall that *MARPOL 73/78* excludes from the definition of "discharge" the "release of harmful substances directly arising from the exploration, exploitation and associated offshore processing of sea-bed mineral resources".[88] Depending on the interpretation given to "harmful substances **directly arising from** the exploration, exploitation and associated offshore processing of sea-bed mineral resources" (emphasis added),[89] substances such as offshore processing drainage, produced water discharge, and displacement discharge may not be subject to the 15 ppm prescribed maximum. Rather, *MARPOL 73/78*'s regulations on the maximum content of operational discharges only apply to deck drainage, comprising effluents from generators, fuel tanks and pumps. Note that, for certain installations which lack the capacity to separate effluent streams, meeting the 15 ppm maximum prescribed by *MARPOL 73/78* may not be practically feasible.[90]

---

84 *Ibid*, annex I, reg 14, para. 1.
85 *Ibid*, annex I, reg 15, para. 2 provides:

> Any discharge into the sea of oil or oil mixtures from ships of 400 gross tonnage and above shall be prohibited except when all of the following conditions are satisfied:

> .1 the ship is proceeding *en route*;
> .2 the oily mixture is processed through an oil filtering equipment meeting the requirements of reg 14 of this Annex;
> .3 the oil content of the effluent without dilution does not exceed 15 ppm;
> .4 the oily mixture odes not originate from cargo pump-room bilges on oil tankers; and; and
> .5 the oil mixture, in case of oil tankers, is not mixed with oil cargo residues.

86 *Ibid*, annex I, reg 4, provides:

> Regs 15 and 34 of this Annex shall not apply to:

> .1 the discharge into the sea of oil or oily mixture necessary for the purpose of securing the safety of a ship or saving life at sea; or
> .2 the discharge into the sea of oil or oily mixture resulting from damage to a ship or its equipment ...
> .3 the discharge into the sea of substances containing oil, approved by the administration, when being used for the purpose of combating specific pollution incidents in order to minimize the damage from pollution. Any such discharge shall be subject to the approval of any Government in whose jurisdiction is contemplated the discharge will occur.

87 *Ibid*, annex I, reg 39, para. 2.3.
88 *Ibid*, art 2(3)(b)(ii).
89 *Ibid*, art 2(3)(b)(ii).
90 Vinogradov and Wagner, *supra* note 29 at 106.

The IMO's Marine Environmental Protection Committee has developed voluntary *Guidelines for the Application of the Revised MARPOL Annex I Requirements to FPSOs and FSUs* (*FPSO & FSU Guidelines*).[91] The *FPSO & FSU Guidelines* clarify the application of Annex I regulations to FPSOs and FSUs, recognizing that: "the environmental hazards associated with the quantities of produced oil stored on board operational FPSOs and FSUs are similar to some of the hazards related to oil tankers and that relevant requirements of the revised MARPOL Annex I in relation to oil tankers could be adapted to address those hazards in an appropriate manner".[92]

The *FPSO & FSU Guidelines* acknowledge that functional similarities between oil tankers, FPSOs and FSUs give rise to corresponding similarities in the environmental risks associated with their operations. For this reason, the *FPSO & FSU Guidelines* subject FPSOs and FSUs to the more stringent set of regulations articulated by *MARPOL 73/78* applicable to oil tankers under prescribed circumstances: e.g. when FPSOs or FSUs are undertaking any voyage away from their operating station.[93] The *FPSO & FSU Guidelines* provide a detailed assessment of each annex I regulations' application to FPSOs and FSUs and should be consulted by practitioners where appropriate.[94]

2.9.1.2 Annex V: regulations for the prevention of pollution by garbage from ships

MARPOL 73/78's revised annex V regulates garbage management and disposal from ships, including fixed and floating platforms. Regulation 1(9) defines garbage as:

> all kinds of food wastes, domestic wastes and operational wastes, all plastics, cargo residues, incinerator ashes, cooking oil, fishing gear, and animal carcasses generated during the normal operation of the ship and liable to be disposed of continuously or periodically except those substances which are defined or listed in other Annexes to the present Convention.[95]

Regulation 1(12) defines "operational waste" in a manner which suggests that it does not include by-products of the offshore oil and gas production process, such as produced water or drilling fluid. This qualified definition of operational waste is consistent with the other exemptions present in *MARPOL 73/78*, and reads as follows:

> Operational wastes means all solid wastes (including slurries) not covered by other Annexes that are collected on board during normal maintenance or operations of a ship, or used for cargo stowage and handling. Operational wastes also includes

---

91 IMO, FPSO & FSU Guidelines, *supra* note 79. Note that "FPSO" is an abbreviation for floating production, storage and offloading facilities and "FSU" is an abbreviation for floating storage units.

92 *Ibid*, para. 6.

93 *Ibid*, para. 8.

94 *Ibid*, para. 6.

95 *MARPOL 73/78*, *supra* note 15, annex V, reg 1.9.

cleaning agents and additives contained in cargo hold and external wash water. Operational wastes does not include grey water, bilge water, or other similar discharges essential to the operation of a ship, taking into account the guidelines developed by the Organization.[96]

2012 Guidelines for the Implementation of MARPOL Annex V prepared by the IMO prohibit discharging other by-products of offshore oil and gas operations, including cleaning agents, turbine washes and machinery wastewater, unless such forms of operational waste satisfy the criteria of being "not harmful to the marine environment".[97]

Regulation 5 articulates special requirements for the discharge of garbage from fixed and floating platforms in providing:

> 1   Subject to the provisions of paragraph 2 of this regulation, **the discharge into the sea of any garbage is prohibited from fixed or floating platforms and from all other ships when alongside or within 500 m of such platforms**.
>
> 2   Food wastes may be discharged into the sea from fixed or floating platforms located more than 12 nautical miles from the nearest land and from all other ships when alongside or within 500 m of such platforms, but only when the wastes have been passed through a comminuter or grinder. Such comminuted or ground food wastes shall be capable of passing through a screen with openings no greater than 25 mm [emphasis added].[98]

Significantly, regulation 5 prohibits outright garbage disposal from fixed or floating platforms, with food wastes being the sole exemption from this prohibition under limited circumstances.

2.9.1.3 Annex VI: regulations for the prevention of air pollution by ships

MARPOL 73/78's annex VI regulates air pollutants in ship exhausts, such as sulphur oxides and nitrogen oxides, and prohibits deliberate emissions of ozone depleting substances.[99] Presumptively, the annex applies to offshore oil and gas installations, encompassing fixed and floating drilling rigs and other platforms.[100] Yet, regulation 3, annex VI exempts emissions generated by offshore exploration and production activities from *MARPOL 73/78*'s application in providing:

> 3.1   **Emissions directly arising from the exploration, exploitation and associated offshore processing of sea-bed mineral resources are,** consistent

---

96 *Ibid*, annex V, reg 1.12.

97 IMO, *2012 Guidelines for the Implementation of MARPOL Annex V*, 2 March 2012, MEPC 63/23/Add.1, annex 24. Para 1.7.5 of the *2012 Guidelines for the Implementation of MARPOL Annex V* provides that cleaning agents or additives will not be harmful to the marine environment where the following criteria are met:

> .1 is not a "harmful substance" in accordance with the criteria in MARPOL Annex III; and
>
> .2 does not contain any components which are known to be carcinogenic, mutagenic or reprotoxic (CMR).

98 *MARPOL 73/78, supra* note 15, annex V, reg 5.

99 IMO website, 'Marine Environment: Prevention of Air Pollution From Ships', <www.imo.org/en/OurWork/Environment/PollutionPrevention/AirPollution/Pages/Air-Pollution.aspx>, accessed 21 July 2016.

100 *MARPOL 73/78, supra* note 15, annex VI, reg 5.1.

INTERNATIONAL REGULATION OF MARINE POLLUTION

with article 2(3)(b)(ii) of the present Convention, **exempt from the provisions of this Annex**. Such emissions include the following:

(.1) emissions resulting from the incineration of substances that are solely and directly the result of exploration, exploitation and associated offshore processing of sea-bed mineral resources, including but not limited to the flaring of hydrocarbons and the burning of cuttings, muds, and/or stimulation fluids during well completion and testing operations, and flaring arising from upset conditions;

(.2) the release of gases and volatile compounds entrained in drilling fluids and cuttings;

(.3) emissions associated solely and directly with the treatment, handling, or storage of sea-bed minerals; and

(.4) emissions from diesel engines that are solely dedicated to the exploration, exploitation and associated offshore processing of sea-bed mineral resources [emphasis added].[101]

[...]

This exemption significantly limits *MARPOL 73/78* regulations' applicability to perhaps the most significant sources of atmospheric pollution generated by the offshore oil and gas industry. However, for emissions generated by the offshore sector not covered by these exemptions, annex VI regulations are presumptively applicable, including regulation 12 governing emissions of ozone-depleting substances, regulation 13 governing nitrogen oxide emissions,[102] and regulation 14 prescribing maximum sulphur oxide and particulate matter content for fuel oil.

This chapter focused on *MARPOL 73/78* annexes I, V and VI given their focus on what have historically been the largest pollution sources generated by the offshore oil and gas industry. Practitioners should note that *MARPOL 73/78*'s remaining annexes are presumptively applicable to offshore oil and gas activities, including annex II: regulations for the control of pollution by noxious liquid substances carried in bulk; annex III: regulations for the prevention of pollution by harmful substances carried by sea in packaged form; and, annex IV: regulations for the prevention of pollution by sewage from ships. Practitioners should consult these annexes in detail for the specific requirements applicable to offshore oil and gas activities.

2.9.2 London Convention, 1972

The *London Convention, 1972* seeks to promote the effective control of all sources of marine pollution and to implement all practicable steps to prevent marine pollution caused by the dumping of wastes and other matter.[103] The *London Convention, 1972* does not regulate discharges of by-products of the offshore oil and gas production process, such as produced water or drill cuttings.

---

101 *Ibid*, reg 3.1.

102 Note, however, that *MARPOL 73/78*, annex VI, reg 3.1.4 exempts from the application or regulation 13 nitrogen oxides emissions from "diesel engines that are solely dedicated to the exploration, exploitation and associated offshore processing of sea-bed mineral resources".

103 *London Convention, 1972*, *supra* note 16.

However, it does cover the deliberate disposal of disused installations or platforms into the sea.

The *London Convention, 1972* defines "dumping" to include "any deliberate disposal at sea of wastes or other matter from vessels, aircraft, platforms, or other man-made structures at sea", and "any deliberate disposal at sea of vessels, aircraft, platforms, or other man-made structures at sea".[104] However, the *London Convention, 1972* exempts: "The disposal of wastes or other matter directly arising from, or related to the exploration, exploitation and associated off-shore processing of sea-bed mineral resources will not be covered by the provisions of this Convention."[105]

Like *MARPOL 73/78*, this exemption is a significant limitation in so far as discharges of produced water and drill cuttings have historically been the largest sources of pollution flowing from offshore oil and gas activities.[106]

The *London Convention, 1972* prohibits the dumping of wastes prescribed in Annex I, including crude oil, radioactive wastes, persistent plastics and others.[107] However, the Convention allows the coastal State to authorize the dumping of wastes prescribed in annexes II and III by issuing a special or general permit. Materials listed in annex II include scrap metal and other bulky wastes liable to sink to the sea bottom, wastes containing significant quantities of arsenic copper, lead, and other metals. These materials ostensibly include disused offshore installations and their components.

The *London Convention, 1972* provides criteria guiding coastal states in their decision to permit ocean dumping, including:

- the characteristics and composition of the matter in question;
- the characteristics of the dumping site;
- the method of deposit;
- potential effects on marine life, other users of the sea; and
- the practical availability of alternative land-based methods of disposal.[108]

2.9.3 1996 Protocol to the London Convention, 1972

The *1996 Protocol* to the *London Convention, 1972* elaborates on the definition of "dumping" to include:

1. any deliberate disposal into the sea of wastes or other matter from vessels, aircraft, platforms or other man-made structures at sea;
2. any deliberate disposal into the sea of vessels, aircraft, platforms or other man-made structures at sea;
3. any storage of wastes or other matter in the seabed and the subsoil thereof from vessels, aircraft, platforms or other man made structures at sea; and

---

104 *Ibid*, art III.
105 *Ibid*, art III(1)(c).
106 Bakke, Klunsoyr, and Sanni, *supra* note 38 at 161.
107 *London Convention, 1972, supra* note 16, art 1(a).
108 *Ibid*, annex III(C).

INTERNATIONAL REGULATION OF MARINE POLLUTION

4 **any abandonment or toppling at site of platforms or other man-made structures at sea, for the sole purpose of deliberate disposal** [emphasis added].[109]

Like the *London Convention, 1972*, the *1996 Protocol* exempts: "The disposal or storage of wastes or other matter directly arising from, or related to the exploration, exploitation and associated off-shore processing of seabed mineral resources ...."[110]

Again, like the *London Convention, 1972*, the *1996 Protocol* prohibits dumping at sea but creates exceptions for prescribed materials, such as platforms or structures, where the coastal state approves the proposed dumping by issuing a special permit.[111] The second contribution of the *1996 Protocol* is its elaboration on the criteria guiding the issuance of dumping permits. Annex II to the *Protocol* sets out criteria and conditions which must be met before the decision to issue a dumping permit can be made, including a comprehensive impact evaluation and the establishment of a satisfactory ongoing compliance monitoring program.[112] Of special note is the content of the impact evaluation, which requires a waste prevention audit, consideration of waste management options, which includes a comparative assessment of the relative risks of alternative strategies with reference to impacts on human health and the environment.[113]

2.10 International instruments addressing liability, clean-up and compensation for environmental damage

2.10.1 UNCLOS III

Article 235 of the *UNCLOS III* requires States to fulfil international obligations to protect and preserve the marine environment and provides that States failing to fulfil their obligations will be liable in accordance with international law.[114] Article 235 requires States to adopt measures to ensure adequate compensation is available in respect of the damage caused by pollution of the marine environment.

> 2. States shall ensure that recourse is available in accordance with their legal systems for prompt and adequate compensation or other relief in respect of damage caused by pollution of the marine environment by natural or juridical persons under their jurisdiction.
>
> 3. With the objective of assuring prompt and adequate compensation in respect of all damage caused by pollution of the marine environment, States shall cooperate in the implementation of existing international law and the further development of international law relating to responsibility and liability for the assessment of and compensation for damage and the settlement of related disputes, as well as, where

---

109 *1996 Protocol, supra* note 17.
110 *Ibid*, art 1(4.3).
111 *Ibid*, art 4, annex I.
112 *Ibid*, annex II, para. 17.
113 *Ibid*, annex II, paras 2, 5, 11, 12.
114 UNCLOS III, *supra* note 14, art 235(1).

appropriate, development of criteria and procedures for payment of adequate compensation, such as compulsory insurance or compensation funds.[115]

Commentators have suggested that article 235 of the *UNCLOS III* provides for State liability for pollution damages to the marine environment caused by offshore oil and gas installations operating under State jurisdiction and control.[116] In all likelihood, States typically shift or modify that liability through legislation, regulations or other agreements with the operator. Regardless of where liability falls, however, Article 235 of the *UNCLOS III* generally confirms the principle of responsibility and liability for environmental damage to the marine environment, including environmental damage caused by offshore oil and gas exploration and production activities.

2.10.2 The 1974 Offshore Pollution Liability Agreement

The *1974 Offshore Pollution Liability Agreement* (*OPOL, 1974*) is a private agreement designed to provide compensation for oil pollution damage originating from installations operated by Parties to the agreement.[117] *OPOL, 1974* applies in EU coastal State waters, primarily those of the North Sea, northern Europe, Norway, the Isle of Man, and the Faroe Islands.[118] The *Agreement* may be amended from time to time. Moreover, it may accept new members operating in new jurisdictions, in accordance with *OPOL, 1974*'s internal procedures.

Under *OPOL, 1974*, companies party to the agreement accept strict liability for pollution damage and the cost of remedial measures, subject to limited exceptions, up to a maximum amount of US$250 million per incident.[119] The *Agreement* requires Parties to provide evidence of insurance from insurers with the financial strength rating prescribed in the *OPOL, 1974* rules, evidence of financial responsibility, a guarantee from a company with the financial strength rating prescribed in the *OPOL, 1974* rules, or evidence showing that the company is capable of qualifying as a self-insurer.[120] Parties agree to indemnify other Parties in the event of a default by other Parties to the agreement.

OPOL, 1974's primary intent is:

1. to provide an orderly means for the expeditious settlement of claims arising out of an escape or discharge of oil from offshore exploration and production operations;
2. to encourage immediate remedial action by the Parties;
3. to ensure the financial responsibility of the Parties to meet their obligations;

---

115 UNCLOS III, *supra* note 14, art 235(2), (3).

116 Esmaeili, *supra* note 10 at 171.

117 See The Offshore Pollution Liability Association Limited Website, 'About Us', online: www. opol.org.uk/about.htm.

118 Gold, *Gard Handbook*, *supra* note 2 at 664.

119 *Ibid.*

120 *Ibid.*

INTERNATIONAL REGULATION OF MARINE POLLUTION

4. to provide a mechanism for ensuring that claims are met up to the maximum liability under OPOL;

5. to avoid complicated jurisdictional problems.[121]

The London-based Offshore Pollution Liability Association Limited administers *OPOL, 1974.*

2.10.3 Convention on Civil Liability for Oil Pollution Damage resulting from Exploration for and Exploitation of Seabed Mineral Resources, 1977

In 1977, several European States attempted to create a comprehensive regime governing offshore oil and gas operators' liability for environmental damages and compensation obligations. Their attempt produced the *CLEE, 1977* – an instrument not yet in force and unlikely to enter into force anytime soon given its age.[122] Yet, the instrument offers a useful precedent for future efforts to draft a liability and compensation regime.

CLEE, 1977 establishes detailed rules on liability standards and limitation amounts. It defines installations to include all fixed and mobile offshore drilling units, as well subsea infrastructure such as wellheads, pipelines and storage facilities.[123]

The instrument provides for the individual and joint liability of the operator or operators of an installation or installations at the time of an incident for any pollution damage resulting from the incident, subject to limited exceptions.[124] The instrument limits operators' liability to a specified amount, yet preserves States' right to impose variations in liability standards and amounts. Commentators have suggested that this flexibility was one of the primary reasons for *CLEE, 1977*'s failure to gain widespread support.[125]

2.10.4 1990 International Convention on Oil Pollution Preparedness, Response and Cooperation

The *OPRC, 1990* requires State Parties to take all appropriate measures to prepare for and respond to an oil pollution incident.[126] Accordingly, the Convention's relevance to offshore oil and gas pollution consists in responding to accidental oil pollution incidents rather than operational discharges. The *OPRC, 1990* makes explicit provision for offshore oil and gas installations in article 2(4), which defines "offshore units" as:

> "Offshore unit" means any fixed or floating offshore installation or structure engaged in gas or oil exploration, exploitation or production activities, or loading or unloading of oil.

---

121 *Ibid.*
122 CLEE, 1977, *supra* note 20 (not yet in force).
123 *Ibid*, art 1(2).
124 CLEE, 1977, *supra* note 20, art 2.
125 Gold, *Gard Handbook*, *supra* note 2 at 665.
126 OPRC, 1990, *supra* note 21.

The *OPRC, 1990* requires State Parties to ensure that operators of offshore units have oil pollution emergency plans in place.[127] The *OPRC, 1990* requires persons in charge of offshore units to report oil pollution incidents to the relevant coastal State authority.[128] The instrument provides for the creation of national coastal State preparedness and response systems and provides for international cooperation in pollution response.[129] *OPRC, 1990* differs from the *UNCLOS III* by requiring States to impose specific measures in response to pollution from offshore oil and gas activities, for example, through requiring oil pollution emergency plans, rather than the general obligation expressed in the *UNCLOS III* to adopt laws to prevent marine environmental pollution from offshore oil and gas activities. However, *OPRC, 1990* focuses on pollution response measures rather than pollution prevention measures. Moreover, *OPRC, 1990* does address marine pollution from operational discharges.

2.11 International policy statements

2.11.1 United Nations Conference on the Environment and Development Rio Declaration

The United Nations Conference on Environment and Development (UNCED), occurring at Rio de Janeiro, Brazil in 1992, articulated international policy statements acknowledging the offshore oil and gas industry's impacts on the marine environment and the importance of regulating those impacts to achieve sustainable development. Although the relevant provisions are non-binding, the provisions can influence the development and interpretation of regulations on international, regional, and national levels.[130]

Chapter 17 of the *Rio Declaration* predominantly dealt with the improvement, adoption and implementation of existing rules, it also identified areas where new rules were required.[131] With respect to existing rules, the *Rio Declaration* recommended: the enhancement of management and environmental planning for integrated management and sustainable development of coastal and marine areas and their resources, at both the local and national levels; the maintenance of biological diversity and productivity of marine species and habitats under national jurisdiction; and, the endorsement of precautionary approaches.[132]

With respect to areas requiring additional rules, the *Rio Declaration* specifically identifies the offshore oil and gas industry as warranting additional environmental regulation, in providing:

> States, acting individually, bilaterally, regionally or multilaterally and within the framework of IMO and other relevant international organizations, whether

---

127 *Ibid*, art 3(2).
128 *Ibid*, art 4(1)(a)(ii).
129 *Ibid*, arts 6–7.
130 Gold, *Gard Handbook, supra* note 2 at 660.
131 *Rio Declaration, supra* note 21; Vinogradov and Wagner, *supra* note 25 at 112.
132 *Ibid*, chapters 17.6, 17.7, 17.21.

subregional, regional or global, as appropriate, should assess the need for additional measures to address degradation of the marine environment by assessing existing regulatory measures to address discharges, emissions and safety and assessing the need for additional measures.[133]

Further, the *Rio Declaration* recommends broader adoption of the *OPRC, 1990* as well as international cooperation to strengthen or establish, where necessary, regional oil/chemical-spill response centres and/or, as appropriate, mechanisms in cooperation with relevant subregional, regional or global intergovernmental organizations.[134]

2.11.2 United Nations Environment Programme

The United Nations Environment Programme (UNEP) has engaged with the issue of marine environmental pollution generated by the offshore oil and gas industry at multiple stages. In fact, the UNEP was one of the first international institutions to assess the environmental implications of the offshore oil and gas industry. In 1977, the UNEP initiated an extensive consultation process which formed the basis for the creation of non-binding guidelines designed to assist States in preventing, reducing, and managing the environmental effects of offshore oil and gas exploration and production activities.[135]

More recently, through its Regional Seas Programme, the UNEP has created a series of protocols to supplement select regional marine pollution prevention agreements. Two of those protocols, applicable to the Mediterranean and Persian/Arabian Gulf Regions, address the offshore oil and gas industry's contribution to marine environmental pollution:

- *Protocol for the Protection of the Mediterranean Sea Against Pollution Resulting From Exploration and Exploitation of the Continental Shelf and the Seabed and its Subsoil;*[136] and
- *Protocol Concerning Marine Pollution Resulting From Exploration and Exploitation of the Continental Shelf.*[137]

These protocols contain general undertakings mandating Parties to take "all appropriate measures to prevent, abate, combat and control pollution in the Protocol Area resulting from activities, inter alia by ensuring that the best available

---

133 *Ibid*, chapters 17.30(c).

134 *Ibid*, chapters 17.33, 17.34.

135 Vinogradov and Wagner, *supra* note 25 at 113–15.

136 UNEP, *Protocol for the Protection of the Mediterranean Sea Against Pollution Resulting from Exploration and Exploitation of the Continental Shelf and the Seabed and Its Subsoil*, 14 October 1994 (entered into force 24 March 2011).

137 UNEP, *Protocol Concerning Marine Pollution Resulting from Exploration and Exploitation of the Continental Shelf*, 29 March 1989 (entered into force 17 February 1990).

techniques, environmentally effective and economically appropriate, are used for this purpose".[138]

Perhaps more importantly, however, these protocols contain detailed provisions prescribing requirements for:

- work authorizations;
- environmental assessments as preconditions for regulatory approval;
- regulations addressing the discharge and disposal of harmful or noxious substances;
- regulations addressing the discharge and disposal of oil and oily mixtures from installations in the Protocol area; specifically, a maximum oil content for machinery space drainage not exceeding 15 mg per litre and for produced water, not exceeding 100 mg per litre;
- regulations addressing the disposal of sewage and garbage;
- regulations requiring contingency planning measures;
- regulations addressing monitoring;
- regulations addressing the removal of disused installations;
- regulations restricting operations in specially protected areas; and
- regulations establishing liability and compensation regimes.[139]

2.11.3 Convention on Environmental Impact Assessment in a Transboundary Context

The *Convention on Environmental Impact Assessment in a Transboundary Context* ("*Espoo Convention*") requires Parties to perform an environmental impact assessment ("EIA") of listed activities at an early stage of the planning process. The objective of the instrument is to prevent, reduce and control significant adverse transboundary environmental impacts.[140] Among activities for which an EIA is required, the *Espoo Convention* lists offshore hydrocarbon production likely to cause a significant adverse transboundary impact.[141]

The *Espoo Convention* entered into force in 1997. Parties include members of the EU but also the United States.[142] The significant offshore oil and gas indus-

---

138 UNEP, *Protocol for the Protection of the Mediterranean Sea Against Pollution Resulting From Exploration and Exploitation of the Continental Shelf and the Seabed and Its Subsoil*, 10 June 1995 (entered into force 9 July 2004), article 3(1).

139 UNEP, *Protocol for the Protection of the Mediterranean Sea Against Pollution Resulting from Exploration and Exploitation of the Continental Shelf and the Seabed and Its Subsoil*, 14 January 1994 (not yet entered into force).

140 *Convention on Environmental Impact Assessment in a Transboundary Context*, 25 February 1991, art 2.1(entered into force 10 September 1997) [*Espoo Convention*].

141 *Ibid*, art 2.3, Appendix I.

142 More specifically, *Espoo Convention* Parties include: EuropeanUnion, Albania, Armenia, Austria, Azerbaijan, Belarus, Belgium, Bulgaria, Canada, Croatia, Cyprus, Czech Republic, Denmark, Estonia, Finland, Former Yugoslav Republic of Macedonia, France, Germany, Greece, Hungary, Ireland, Italy, Kazakhstan, Kyrgyzstan, Latvia, Liechtenstein, Lithuania, Luxembourg, Moldova, Netherlands, Norway, Poland, Portugal, Romania, Slovakia, Slovenia, Spain, Sweden, Switzerland, Ukraine, United Kingdom, USA.

tries which have evolved in the maritime zones of *Espoo Convention* Parties signals the instrument's relevance in managing marine environmental pollution on a bilateral and multilateral basis within and between those jurisdictions.

The *Espoo Convention* articulates the content of Parties' obligations to notify and consult each other on all major projects under consideration that are likely to have a significant adverse environmental impact across boundaries.[143] The instrument's appendices offer guidance on the content of environmental impact assessment documentation, the environmental assessment itself, criteria to assist in the determination of the environmental significance of unlisted activities, post-project analysis, bilateral and multilateral cooperation and arbitration.[144]

2.11.4 2003 Protocol on Strategic Environmental Assessment

In 2003, Parties to the *Espoo Convention* adopted the *2003 Protocol on Strategic Environmental Assessment* ("*Kiev Protocol*"), which requires Parties to perform a strategic environmental assessment ("SEA") for listed plans and programmes likely to have significant environmental and health effects.[145] Among activities for which a SEA is required, the *Kiev Protocol* lists offshore hydrocarbon production likely to cause a significant adverse transboundary impact.[146]

Unlike project-based environmental assessments, SEAs look beyond single projects to proactively assess the environmental and socio-economic impacts of an industry sector, industrial development in a geographical region, or a specific plan, programme or policy. The *Kiev Protocol* elaborates on the application and content of SEA to listed plans or programmes, touching on scoping determinations, the role of public participation, transboundary consultations, decision making and monitoring.

2.12 Select regional agreements

2.12.1 OSPAR Convention

To illustrate the dearth of international regulations on operational discharges of offshore oil and gas activities, the *Convention for the Protection of the Environment of the North-East Atlantic* ("*OSPAR Convention*") and related OSPAR Commission decisions offer valuable perspective.[147] The *OSPAR Convention* establishes the modern framework for environmental protection and conservation in the European northeast Atlantic. The Convention is binding upon countries such as the United Kingdom, Norway and Denmark, responsible for regulating

---

143 *Espoo Convention*, appendix II.

144 *Espoo Convention*, appendices I–IV.

145 *2003 Protocol on Strategic Environmental Assessment*, 21 May 2003 (entered into force 11 July 2010).

146 *Ibid*, art 4.2, Annex I.

147 *Convention for the Protection of the Environment of the North-East Atlantic*, 22 September 1992, 2354 UNTS 67 (entered into force 25 March 1998) [*OSPAR Convention*].

the North Sea's mature oil and gas industry. Several decisions and recommendations established under the Convention regulate operational discharges of the offshore oil and gas industry, including drilling fluids, drill cuttings, produced water and other chemicals. Unlike the extant international legal regime governing pollution from the offshore sector, decisions adopted under the auspices of the *OSPAR Convention* target the specific sources of pollution flowing from offshore oil and gas operations. Relevant instruments include:

- OSPAR Decision 2000/3 on the Use of Organic Phase Drilling Fluids (OPF) and the Discharge of OPF-Contaminated Cuttings;[148]
- OSPAR Decision 2000/2 on a Harmonised Mandatory Control System for the Use and Reduction of the Discharge of Offshore Chemicals (as amended by OSPAR Decision 2005/1);[149]
- OSPAR Recommendation 2001/1 for the Management of Produced Water from Offshore Installations;[150]
- OSPAR Recommendation 2006/5 on a Management Regime for Offshore Cuttings Piles.[151]

SECTION 4: CONCLUSIONS

2.13 Limits of the international legal framework

Few international regulations target what have historically been the most significant sources of pollution generated by the offshore oil and gas sector: operational discharges of drill cuttings, drilling fluids, and produced water. This suggests that a practitioner's first point of reference should be regional or domestic legal sources governing the regulation, prevention, and management of marine environmental pollution generated by the offshore oil and gas industry. However, international legal sources nevertheless play a role by establishing the framework in which regional and domestic regulations operate, and informing the objectives and purposes of those regulatory efforts.

The *UNCLOS III* requires States to protect and preserve the marine environment. To fulfil this obligation, coastal States are required to adopt and enforce "laws and regulations to prevent, reduce and control pollution of the marine environment arising from or in connection with seabed activities subject to their jurisdiction and from artificial islands, installations and structures under their jurisdiction".[152] The *UNCLOS III* does not elaborate on the content of this and other obligations, nor does it provide detailed enforcement procedures.

---

148 Meeting of the OSPAR Commission, Copenhagen: 26–30 June 2000.
149 *Ibid.*
150 OSPAR Recommendation 2001/1 adopted by OSPAR 2001 (OSPAR 01/18/1, Annex 5) as amended.
151 Meeting of the OSPAR Commission, Stockholm: 26–30 June 2006.
152 UNCLOS III, *supra* note 14, art 208(1).

MARPOL 73/78 as amended regulates different sources of pollution generated by a range of marine activities, including offshore oil and gas operations. However, *MARPOL 73/78* does not cover the "release of harmful substances directly arising from the exploration, exploitation and associated off-shore processing of sea-bed mineral resources", encompassing operational discharges of oil, drill cuttings, drilling fluids and produced water. Further, *MARPOL 73/78* does not regulate atmospheric emissions directly arising from the exploration, exploitation and associated offshore processing of sea-bed mineral resources.

The *London Convention, 1972* and the *1996 Protocol* regulate the dumping of wastes from offshore installations into the sea, and the dumping or abandonment of offshore installations and their associated systems during the decommissioning process. The *London Convention* and *1996 Protocol* create a robust regulatory regime regulating decommissioning to prevent environmental damage during the abandonment phase of an installation's lifecyle. However, the fact that the Convention and the Protocol do not cover "the disposal or storage of wastes or other matter directly arising from, or related to the exploration, exploitation and associated off-shore processing of seabed mineral resources" limits the instruments' usefulness in regulating what have historically been the industry's largest contributions to marine environmental pollution – operational discharges of by-products of the drilling process, such as drill cuttings, drilling fluids, and produced water.[153]

Regarding liability, compensation and clean-up for environmental damage caused by oil spills from offshore installations, the *OPOL, 1974* provides some access to compensation where the damage results the within the prescribed areas and does not exceed the US$250 million liability cap.[154] The private agreement is limited in its geographical scope: it only applies to activities carried out in the offshore areas of northern Europe, Norway, the Isle of Man, and the Faroe Islands. Moreover, the private agreement is limited in its maximum liability amount: US$250 million. Arguably, the maximum liability amount does not reflect the scale of the damages likely to be incurred in the event of a large-scale oil spill. Limits in geographical scope and maximum liability amounts confirm *OPOL, 1974*'s inability to serve as an adequate liability and compensation regime in today's global offshore oil and gas industry.

The *OPRC, 1990* requires State Parties to take all appropriate measures to prepare for and respond to an oil pollution incident.[155] The *OPRC, 1990* specifically applies to offshore oil and gas installations.[156] Significantly, the instrument articulates specific provisions regarding oil pollution response requiring State Parties to ensure that operators of offshore units have oil pollution emergency plans in place and requiring persons in charge of offshore units to report oil

---

153 *1996 Protocol, supra* note 17, art 1(4.3).

154 See The Offshore Pollution Liability Association Limited Website, 'About Us' <www.opol. org.uk/about.htm> accessed 25 July 2016.

155 OPRC, 1990, *supra* note 20.

156 *Ibid*, art 2(4).

pollution incidents to the relevant coastal State authority.[157] However, the *OPRC, 1990* focuses on pollution response measures rather than pollution prevention measures.

Finally, the international legal framework is silent regarding the specific regulations addressing sound production as a source of marine environmental pollution,

2.14 Future directions

This chapter considers international law's role in regulating marine environmental pollution in the offshore oil and gas industry. The authors suggest that although existing legal instruments successfully address some sources of marine pollution generated by the industry, they under address or fail to address others, often, sources which have historically represented the industry's largest contribution to marine environmental pollution. Underscoring the international legal framework's incomplete development are regional instruments, including those enacted under the UNEP and the OSPAR Convention, which target and regulate specific sources of pollution generated by offshore oil and gas operations, specifically, operational discharges of oil, drilling fluid, drill cuttings, produced water, chemicals, atmospheric emissions and sound production. Further evidence of the international regulatory framework's incomplete development is provided by contrasting the sophisticated legal framework governing civil liability and compensation for vessel source pollution which has evolved in the international shipping industry, with the failed and fragmentary efforts to do the same in the offshore oil and gas industry in the form of the *CLEE, 1977* and *OPOL, 1974*.

When one considers the international regulatory framework's failure to directly regulate the sources of pollution generated by the offshore oil and gas industry discussed in section 2 of this chapter, it raises the question: is the international legal framework's incomplete and fragmented application a function of the inherent superiority of regional instruments or domestic legal sources in addressing marine environmental pollution generated by offshore oil and gas operations? Or, is the greater comprehensiveness of regulations at national and regional levels simply a response to the inadequacies of the international regulatory framework?

In an effort to engage with this question, the incomplete character of the current international regulatory framework can be partially explained by the practical reality that most offshore operations occur within the coastal jurisdiction of specific states. Accordingly, regulations of offshore oil and gas operations have occurred on either a bilateral level between the coastal State and the operator(s), or, on a regional level between neighbouring coastal States and the operator(s).[158] This makes sense as the operating conditions and environmental conditions faced by offshore oil and gas operators may vary widely regionally. Second, the incomplete character of the current international regulatory framework is in part the

---

157 *Ibid*, arts 3(2), 4(1)(a)(ii).
158 Gold, *Gard Handbook, supra* note 2 at 645.

result of industry opposition to comprehensive, international regulations.[159] In some cases, coastal states with established safety and environmental protection regimes have joined industry in opposing the development of an international regime, due to concerns that standards developed at an international level may fall below those developed nationally.[160] Third, query the comparative responsiveness of international regulations versus those enacted nationally or regionally to the rapidly evolving technology employed by the offshore oil and gas industry.

Despite the reasons favouring domestic or regional regulation, sound reasons favour international regulation. First, the global character and size of the offshore oil and gas industry confirms its potential for non-negligible environmental impacts both in terms of operational and accidental discharges of oil and other chemicals, as well as habitat disruption caused by offshore construction activities. Second, the transboundary character of environmental pollution generated by offshore oil and gas operations favours uniform rules regulating pollution generated by the industry. Third, as near-shore petroleum reservoirs are depleted and the industry seeks to expand exploration and production activities to deep water and ultra-deep-water locations, environmental risks may increase commensurately.

A 2007 GESAMP study estimates that the industry releases approximately 17,000 tonnes of oil into the marine environment annually through operational discharges and small-scale accidents.[161] As articulated above, the adverse ecological impacts to marine life caused by *any* exposure to oil, chemicals and other substances favours implementing regulations. The question for law makers, industry and relevant organizations remains: whether environmental regulation is most efficiently and effectively accomplished at the national, regional or international levels?

BIBLIOGRAPHY

Bakke, Torgeir, Klunsoyr, Jarle, and Sanni, Steinar, 'Environmental Impacts of Produced Water and Drilling Waste Discharges from the Norwegian Offshore Petroleum Industry' [2013] *Marine Environmental Research* 92, 154

Birnie, Patricia, Boyle, Alan, and Redgwell, Catherine, *International Law and the Environment* (Oxford University Press, Oxford, 2009)

Esmaeili, Hossein, *The Legal Regime of Offshore Oil Rigs in International Law* (Dartmouth Publishing Company, England, 2001)

Foley, Meraiah, 'As Oil Enriches Australia, Spill Is Seen as a Warning' *New York Times* (Asia-Pacific, 27 September 2009)

Gao, Zhiguo, 'International Law on Offshore Abandonment: Recent Developments, Current Issues and Future Directions' in Zhiguo Gao (ed), *Environmental Regulation of Oil and Gas* (Kluwer Law International, London/The Hague/Boston, 1998)

---

159 *Ibid.*
160 *Ibid.*
161 GESAMP, 2007, *supra* note 7 at viii.

Gaskell, Nicholas, 'Compensation for Offshore Pollution: Ships and Platforms' in Malcolm Clarke (ed), *Maritime Law Evolving* (Hart Publishing, Oxford, 2013)

Gavouneli, Maria, *Pollution from Offshore Oil Installations* (Graham & Trotman/Martinus Nijhoff, 1995)

GESAMP, *Estimates of Oil Entering the Marine Environment from Sea-Based Activities* (IMO, London, 2007)

Gold, Edgar, *Gard Handbook on Protection of the Marine Environment* (3rd edition, Gard AS, Norway, 2006)

IMO/FAO/UNESCO/WMO/WHO/IAEA/UN/UNEP Joint Group of Experts on the Scientific Aspects of Marine Pollution (GESAMP), *The State of the Marine Environment*, Report No. 39 (1990)

Law of the Sea, *Report of the Secretary General (of the United Nations)*, 10 November 1993 with addendum of 30 November 1993 (UN Doc. a/48/527 and A/48527/Add.1)

Natural Resources Defence Counsel, 'Boom, Baby, Boom: The Environmental Impacts of Seismic Surveys' (May 2010)

Offshore Technology Magazine, 'History of the Offshore Industry' <www.offshore-mag.com/index/about-us/history-of-offshore.html> accessed 21 July 2016

Oil and Gas UK, 'About the Industry', Environment, Underwater Sound <http://oilandgasuk.co.uk/knowledgecentre/underwatersound.cfm> accessed 21 July 2016

Oil and Gas UK, 'Knowledge Centre: Atmospheric Emissions' <http://oilandgasuk.co.uk/atmospheric-emissions.cfm> accessed 21 July 2016

OSPAR Commission, *Assessment of Impacts of Offshore Oil and Gas Activities in the North-East Atlantic* (OSPAR, London, 2009)

Rothwell, Donald R., and Stephens, Tim, *The International Law of the Sea* (Hart Publishing, Oxford, 2010)

Weber, Harry, 'Blown Out BP Well Finally Killed at Bottom of Gulf' *Associated Press* (19 September 2010)

Whitehead, H., *An A–Z of Offshore Oil and Gas* (Gulf Publishing Company, Houston, 1983)

World Ocean Review, 'World Ocean Review 3: Oil and Gas from the Sea' *Maribus gBmbH* (2014)

CHAPTER 3

Marine oil pollution in the United States of America

A framework for prevention and response to marine oil pollution incidents

ANTONIO RODRIGUEZ AND JAKE RODRIGUEZ

TABLE OF CONTENTS

Section 1	The Oil Pollution Act of 1990 and the Clean Water Act	95
3.1	Introduction	95
3.2	Civil liability	96
3.3	Financial responsibility	98
Section 2	Prevention of pollution	99
3.4	Vessel response plans	99
3.5	Port State Control	101
3.6	Penalties for failure to comply	102
Section 3	Response	102
3.7	The National Contingency Plan	102
3.8	Spill notification requirements	103
3.9	Civil and criminal penalties	104
Section 4	Conclusions	105

SECTION 1: THE OIL POLLUTION ACT OF 1990 AND THE CLEAN WATER ACT

3.1 Introduction

While not a signatory to many of the international marine pollution conventions,[1] the United States has extensively legislated in this area, and most of the requirements of the various international conventions are directly or indirectly covered

---

1 In 1973, the International Maritime Organisation ("IMO") adopted the International Convention for the Prevention of Pollution by Ships, as subsequently modified by Protocol in 1978. Widely referred to as MARPOL 73/78, the Convention's objective is to minimize ship-borne pollution by restricting operational pollution and reducing the possibility of accidental pollution. Currently, the U.S. is signatory to Annexes I, II, III, V and VI of MARPOL 73/78.

by U.S. law. The U.S. legal landscape for marine pollution encompasses both federal and state law and regulations intended to safeguard the navigable waters of the U.S. and to respond to and address any pollution events that occur. It is critically important for maritime industry operators to be well versed in U.S. marine pollution laws, regulations and requirements.

3.2 Civil liability

The Oil Pollution Act of 1990 ("OPA"), enacted in the wake of the 1989 *Exxon Valdez* grounding off the coast of Alaska and the resulting oil spill, established a comprehensive liability and compensation regime for oil discharges upon the navigable waters of the U.S., the adjoining shorelines, and the exclusive economic zone.[2] OPA applies broadly to discharges of "oil of any kind or in any form, including petroleum, fuel oil, sludge, oil refuse, and oil mixed with wastes other than dredged spoil".[3] The Federal Water Pollution Control Act ("FWPCA" or "Clean Water Act") was amended by OPA, but continues to cover discharges of hazardous materials other than oil.[4]

OPA provides that "each responsible party for a vessel or a facility from which oil is discharged, or which poses the substantial threat of a discharge of oil, into or upon the navigable waters or adjoining shorelines or the exclusive economic zone is liable for the removal costs and damages ... from such incident".[5] U.S. navigable waters include the territorial seas, which extend three miles from the coast.[6] The exclusive economic zone extends up to 200 nautical miles offshore.[7]

The "responsible party" with respect to vessels is "any person owning, operating, or demise chartering [a] vessel".[8] A lender that finances a vessel and holds title to a vessel simply to protect its security interest, but does not participate in the management of the vessel, is not a responsible party under the statute.[9] The Code of Federal Regulations provides guidance on who may be deemed an "operator," defining it as:

> [A] person who is an owner, a demise charterer, or other contractor, who conducts the operation of, or who is responsible for the operation of, a vessel. A builder, repairer, scrapper, lessor, or seller who is responsible, or who agrees by contract to become responsible, for a vessel is an operator. A time or voyage charterer that does not assume responsibility for the operation of a vessel is not an operator.[10]

---

2 33 U.S.C. § 2702(a).
3 33 U.S.C. § 2701(23).
4 33 U.S.C. §§ 1251 *et seq.*
5 33 U.S.C. § 2702(a).
6 33 U.S.C. § 2701(21), (35).
7 33 U.S.C. § 2701(8); Presidential Proclamation 5030, Exclusive Economic Zone of the United States of America, 48 Fed. Reg. 10605 (10 Mar. 1983).
8 33 U.S.C. § 2701(32)(A).
9 33 U.S.C. § 2701(26)(B)(ii).
10 33 C.F.R. § 138.20.

OPA contains a strict liability standard, which means that the responsible party is liable without regard to fault or negligence.[11] However, OPA also statutorily caps the monetary amount that a responsible party must pay. The cap amount for vessels varies depending on the type of vessel and, in the case of tankers, whether it is equipped with a single or double hull. The highest cap is for single-hull tank vessels, which have a higher risk of spills.[12] Because of the pollution risk, single-hull tankers have been phased out in recent years. Tankers in U.S. waters are now required to have a double hull.[13] The Limitation of Liability Act, which allows vessel owners to limit their liability to the value of the vessel and pending freight in certain circumstances, does not apply to oil pollution removal costs or damages.[14]

There are several exceptions to the liability limits under OPA, and these exceptions are sufficiently broad as to make it easy for responsible Parties to lose their right to limit their liability. First, the limits do not apply if the incident was caused by the responsible party's gross negligence, willful misconduct, or violation of an applicable federal safety, construction, or operating regulation. For the purposes of this exception, the responsible party includes such party's agents or employees, or persons acting pursuant to a contract with the responsible party.[15] This means that the negligent or grossly negligent acts of a single crew member could result in unlimited liability, even if the owner or operator acted properly. Second, the limits do not apply if the responsible party: (1) knows of the incident but fails to report it, (2) fails to provide reasonable removal assistance requested by an authority, or (3) without sufficient cause, fails to comply with an order issued by an authority.[16] Third, the limits do not apply to the removal costs incurred by a federal, state or local government in connection with a discharge of oil from an outer Continental Shelf facility or a vessel carrying oil as cargo from such a facility. Such removal costs must be paid by the owner or operator of such facility or vessel without regard to the statutory limit of liability.[17]

OPA establishes responsible party liability for "removal costs and damages".[18] Removal costs – including the costs to prevent, minimize, or mitigate oil pollution – are those that are incurred by the U.S., a state, or an Indian tribe under the Clean Water Act or under state law, or those incurred by any person for acts that are consistent with the National Contingency Plan.[19] The federal, state, and/ or local governments may recover damages for (1) injury to natural resources,

---

11 *Water Quality Insurance Syndicate v United States*, 522 F. Supp. 2d 220, 226 (D.D.C. 2007) ("The OPA imposes strict liability on Parties that discharge oil into the navigable waters of the United States").

12 33 U.S.C. § 2704(a); 33 C.F.R. § 138.230.

13 46 U.S.C. § 3703(a).

14 *Metlife Capital Corp. v M/V EMILY* S, 132 F.3d 818, 819 (1st Cir. 1997) (citing 33 U.S.C. § 2702(a)). See also 3 Benedict on Admiralty, at 9–112[a][4].

15 33 U.S.C. § 2704(c)(1).

16 33 U.S.C. § 2704(c)(2).

17 33 U.S.C. § 2704(c)(3).

18 33 U.S.C. § 2702(a).

19 33 U.S.C. § 2702(b)(1); 33 U.S.C. § 2701(31); discussed *infra* at Section 3.

(2) loss of taxes and other revenue due to the injury or destruction of property or natural resources, and (3) costs of providing additional public services during or after removal.[20] Property owners or lessors may recover damages for injury to real or personal property, including economic losses resulting from destruction of such property.[21] Any claimant may recover damages for loss of subsistence use of natural resources and/or for lost profits or earning capacity due to the injury or loss of property or natural resources.[22]

There are only three narrow defenses under OPA. A responsible party is not liable for removal costs or damages if the discharge was caused solely by: (1) an act of God, (2) an act of war, or (3) an act or omission of a third party if the responsible party exercised due care and took precautions against foreseeable acts or omissions of third Parties.[23] Because a responsible party must demonstrate preparedness in order to avail itself of the defense that a third party was solely at fault, it is important that vessel owners have adequate plans in place at all times. Also, it is imperative that responsible Parties comply with the reporting requirements and cooperate with authorities following a spill, because the three limited defenses are not available if the responsible party fails to report the incident, fails to provide reasonable assistance with removal, or fails to comply with an order issued by authorities.[24] In cases where a discharge was caused solely by a third party, the responsible party can either: (1) establish that a third party was the sole cause and liable for any removal costs and damages, in which case the third party will be treated as the responsible party; or (2) allege that a third party was the sole cause, pay the claims, and then file suit to recover the money that was paid.[25]

3.3 Financial responsibility

OPA mandates that the responsible party for certain types of vessels maintain evidence of financial responsibility in an amount equal to the maximum amount of limited liability to which the responsible party could be exposed.[26] This requirement applies to (1) all vessels over 300 gross tons, and tank vessels over 100 gross tons, using any place subject to U.S. jurisdiction, except non-self-propelled

---

20 33 U.S.C. § 2702(b)(2).

21 *Ibid.*

22 *Ibid.*

23 33 U.S.C. § 2703(a). "Act of God" is narrowly defined as an "unanticipated grave natural disaster or other natural phenomenon of an exceptional, inevitable, and irresistible character the effects of which could not have been prevented or avoided by the exercise of due care or foresight". *Ibid* at § 2701(1).

24 33 U.S.C. § 2703(c).

25 33 U.S.C. § 2702(d)(1); *Marathon Pipe Line Co. v LaRoche Indus.*, 944 F. Supp. 476, 479 (E.D. La. 1996); *Dune Energy, Inc. v FROGCO Amphibious Equip., LLC*, 2013 U.S. Dist. LEXIS 61515, *8 (E.D. La. Apr. 29, 2013) ("OPA allows for third party liability in one of two ways. First, the third party may be treated as the responsible party. Second, the responsible party may be entitled by subrogation to pursue all rights the claimant and the United States government had against the third party") (Citations omitted).

26 33 U.S.C. § 2716(a).

vessels that do not carry oil as cargo or fuel, and (2) any vessels using the exclusive economic zone to transship or lighter oil destined for a place subject to U.S. jurisdiction.[27] If a responsible party owns multiple vessels, it need only have evidence of financial responsibility in an amount that would meet the maximum liability applicable to the vessel that would have the highest liability limit.[28] Evidence of financial responsibility may be in the form of insurance, surety bond, guarantee, letter of credit, qualification as a self-insurer, or other suitable security.[29]

Failure to comply with the financial responsibility requirements can result in sanctions. If the responsible party does not provide evidence of financial responsibility, the vessel can be detained or denied entry into U.S. waters. Any vessel that is found in U.S. navigable waters without evidence of financial responsibility is subject to seizure and forfeiture.[30] And, any person that is found to have violated the financial responsibility requirements is subject to a civil penalty in the maximum amount of $25,000 per day of violation.[31] In addition, the Attorney General may secure relief necessary to compel compliance with the financial responsibility requirements, including a court order terminating operations.[32]

SECTION 2: PREVENTION OF POLLUTION

3.4 Vessel response plans

Owners or operators of tank vessels and non-tank vessels, as defined by statute, are required to prepare and submit to the United States Coast Guard ("USCG") detailed response plans for responding to a "worst case discharge" of oil or hazardous materials, and to a substantial threat of such a discharge.[33] The failure to comply with the regulations regarding such vessel response plans ("VRPs") can result in civil penalties and/or vessel detention.

Tank vessels that are storing or transporting oil on U.S. waters, or that are transferring oil in any place subject to U.S. jurisdiction, must operate in compliance with an approved VRP.[34] A "tank vessel" is defined as a vessel that carries "oil or hazardous material in bulk as cargo or cargo residue" and that (1) is a vessel of the U.S.; (2) operates on U.S. navigable waters; or (3) transfers oil or hazardous material in a place that is subject to U.S. jurisdiction.[35] More recently, the USCG implemented requirements related to non-tank vessels.[36] Non-tank vessels may not operate on U.S. navigable waters unless they are in compliance

---

27 33 U.S.C. § 2716(a).
28 *Ibid.*
29 33 U.S.C. § 2716(e).
30 33 U.S.C. § 2716(b); 33 C.F.R. § 138.40.
31 33 U.S.C. § 2716a(a); 33 C.F.R. § 138.40.
32 33 U.S.C. § 2716a(b); 33 C.F.R. § 138.40.
33 33 U.S.C. § 1321(j)(5)(A).
34 33 C.F.R. § 155.1025(a).
35 46 U.S.C. § 2101(39).
36 78 FR 60100 (2013).

with an approved VRP.[37] A "non-tank vessel" is defined as a self-propelled vessel that is at least 400 gross tons, carries oil as fuel for propulsion, and operates on the navigable waters of the U.S.[38]

VRPs must identify a qualified individual that has full authority to implement removal actions and must require such individual to immediately communicate with federal officials and persons providing equipment and personnel to respond to a discharge or threat of discharge.[39] The vessel owner or operator must provide each qualified person a document specifying that such person has authority to contract with oil spill response organizations, act as a liaison with the federal on-scene coordinator, and expend funds on response activities.[40] The VRP must identify the personnel and/or equipment which have been secured by contract, necessary to remove a worst case discharge.[41] The VRP must also describe the training, equipment testing and drills that will be conducted in order to ensure the safety of the vessel and to mitigate or prevent a discharge.[42]

A VRP must be written and divided into the specific sections that are listed in the Code of Federal Regulations. Such sections include notification procedures, a list of contacts, training procedures, emergency procedures, and geographic-specific appendices for the captain of the port ("COTP") zones in which the vessel operates.[43] The specific information to be provided in the VRP sections is determined by whether the vessel is a tank vessel or a non-tank vessel, manned or unmanned, and whether it is carrying oil as a primary or secondary cargo.[44] The vessel owner or operator must submit the VRP to the USCG for approval at least 60 days before a tank vessel intends to store, transport or lighter oil in areas subject to U.S. jurisdiction or 60 days before a non-tank vessel intends to operate upon U.S. navigable waters.[45] Once the VRP is approved, the vessel owner or operator must maintain a copy of the plan and the approval letter on the vessel, and must also provide them to the persons identified as qualified individuals.[46]

Tank and non-tank vessels carrying group I-IV oils must also include salvage and marine firefighting requirements in their VRPs.[47] Such vessels must identify specific salvage and marine firefighting resources, as listed in the regulations, and list the resource providers that they have contracted with to provide those services.[48] The vessel owner/operator must ensure that the listed resource providers are capable of providing the services within the timeframes listed in the

---

37 33 C.F.R. § 155.5021(a).

38 33 U.S.C. § 1321(a)(26).

39 33 U.S.C. § 1321(j)(5)(D).

40 33 C.F.R. §155.1026.

41 33 U.S.C. §1321(j)(5)(D)(iii).

42 33 U.S.C. § 1321(j)(5)(D)(iv).

43 33 C.F.R. §§ 155.1030, 155.1055, 155.5030, 155.5035.

44 *See* 33 C.F.R. §§ 155.1035, 155.1040, 155.1045, 155.1050, 155.1052, 155.5035.

45 33 C.F.R. §§ 155.1065, 155.5065.

46 33 C.F.R. §§ 155.1030, 155.5030. The USCG's Homeport website contains useful reference material on VRPs: http://homeport.uscg.mil/mycg/portal/ep/home.do (choose "Environmental," then "Vessel Response Plan Program").

47 33 C.F.R. § 155.4015.

48 33 C.F.R. § 155.4030.

regulations.[49] The vessel owner must obtain written consent from all of the listed resource providers, stating that the provider agrees to provide the listed services and is capable of arriving within the required response times.[50] Vessel owners and operators are also required to conduct both announced and unannounced exercises and drills to ensure that the plan will stand up to an emergency. The regulations detail the types and frequency of such drills and exercises.[51]

As the U.S. legislation implementing MARPOL 73/78, the Act to Prevent Pollution from Ships[52] empowers the USCG to administer and enforce the MARPOL annexes to which the U.S. is a party.[53] MARPOL requires certain vessels to maintain an international shipboard oil pollution emergency plan ("SOPEP"). The SOPEP requirements, as implemented in the U.S., apply to U.S. oceangoing ships that are oil tankers of 150 gross tons or more, other ships that are 400 gross tons or more, or drilling rigs and platforms when not engaged in exploration or processing, and that (1) engage in international voyages, (2) are certificated for ocean service, (3) are certificated for coastwise service beyond three nautical miles, or (4) operate at any time seaward of the outer boundary of the territorial sea.[54] A SOPEP must contain six mandatory sections, each containing specified information and instructions for the master and officers in dealing with a pollution incident or threat of such incident.[55] The SOPEPs must be submitted to the USCG for approval.[56] An owner or operator with multiple ships that are subject to the SOPEP requirements may submit a single plan for each type of ship, but must include a ship-specific appendix for each vessel covered by the SOPEP.[57] The SOPEP requirements are considered to be met if a U.S. flag vessel holds a USCG-approved VRP and provides evidence of compliance with the VRP requirements.[58]

3.5 Port State Control

Under MARPOL 73/78, a state party must issue certificates to vessels operating under their authority certifying compliance with the Convention. For U.S. flag vessels, the authority to issue such international oil pollution prevention ("IOPP")

---

49 33 C.F.R. § 155.4040.
50 33 C.F.R. § 155.4045.
51 33 C.F.R. § 155.4052.
52 33 U.S.C. §§ 1901 *et seq.*
53 Currently, the U.S. is a signatory to: Annex I – Regulation for the Prevention of Pollution by Oil (entered into force October 2, 1983); Annex II – Regulations for the Control of Pollution by Noxious Liquid Substances in Bulk (entered into force October 2, 1983); Annex III – Prevention of Pollution by Harmful Substances Carried by Sea in Packaged Form (entered into force July 1, 1992); Annex V – Prevention of Pollution by Garbage from Ships (entered into force December 31, 1998); and Annex VI – Prevention of Air Pollution from Ships (entered into force May 19, 2005).
54 33 C.F.R. § 151.09(a)(1)–(4), (c).
55 33 C.F.R. § 151.26(b)(8).
56 33 C.F.R. § 151.27.
57 33 C.F.R. § 151.27(c).
58 33 C.F.R. §§ 151.09(d)(2), 155.1030(k), 155.5030(k).

certificates is delegated to the USCG.[59] A party to MARPOL may inspect any vessel entering ports within its jurisdiction, but such inspections must be "limited to verifying that there is on board a valid certificate," unless there are "clear grounds for believing that the condition of the ship or its equipment does not correspond substantially with the particulars of that certificate,"[60] If the USCG finds that a vessel is not in compliance with pollution prevention requirements (including SOPEP and/or VRP requirements) or if the ship or its equipment is not in agreement with the IOPP certificate or other documentation, the vessel may be detained until it is capable of returning to sea without presenting a threat to the marine environment. The USCG's inspection may include an examination of the oil record books, which are required under MARPOL, and must contain details of all oil discharge or transfer operations.[61]

3.6 Penalties for failure to comply

The consequences for failure to comply with response plan requirements can be severe. If a vessel does not have an approved response plan, the vessel can be denied entry to a U.S. port or can be detained and prevented from leaving.[62] In addition, substantial penalties of up to $190,000 may be assessed.[63] Penalties may also be imposed for violations of crew licensing requirements or navigation regulations.[64]

There is a right of appeal for any person against whom penalties have been assessed. Such person can appeal the assessment by filing a notice of appeal in the appropriate U.S. District Court or U.S. Court of Appeals (depending upon whether it was a Class I or Class II penalty) within 30 days from the date the civil penalty order was issued.[65]

SECTION 3: RESPONSE

3.7 The National Contingency Plan

The Clean Water Act, as amended by OPA, requires the preparation of a "National Contingency Plan for removal of oil and hazardous substances,"[66]

---

59 33 C.F.R. § 151.07. U.S.-flagged oil tankers of 150 gross tons or more and other U.S. ships of 400 gross tons or more that engage in voyages into the jurisdictions of other MARPOL Parties must have on board a valid IOPP certificate. 33 C.F.R. § 151.19(a). Oil tankers of 150 gross tons or more and other vessels of 400 tons or more that are operated under the authority of other Parties to MARPOL must also have a valid IOPP certificate. 33 C.F.R. § 151.19(b).

60 International Convention for the Prevention of Pollution From Ships, art. 5(2).

61 33 C.F.R. §§ 151.23–25. Each year, the USCG publishes an Annual Report on Port State Control in the United States, which contains the statistics related to enforcement of international conventions. The 2016 Annual Report is available at http://www.dco.uscg.mil/Portals/9/DCO%20 Documents/5p/CG-5PC/CG-CVC/CVC2/psc/AnnualReports/annualrpt16.pdf.

62 33 U.S.C. § 1321(b)(12); 46 U.S.C. § 60105.

63 33 U.S.C. § 1321(b)(6)(A), (B); 33 C.F.R. § 27.3.

64 33 U.S.C. § 1236; 46 U.S.C. § 8702; 33 C.F.R. § 27.3.

65 33 U.S.C. § 1321(b)(6)(G).

66 33 U.S.C. § 1321(d)(1).

providing for the "efficient, coordinated, and effective action" to minimize the damages from such discharges.[67] OPA expanded the role and breadth of the National Contingency Plan ("NCP") by establishing a multi-layered planning and response system to improve preparedness and response to spills in marine environments.

The purpose of the NCP is to "provide the organizational structure and procedures for preparing for and responding to discharges of oil and releases of hazardous substances, pollutants, and contaminants".[68] The NCP establishes the National Response Team and delineates its roles and responsibilities, including planning and coordinating responses. The National Response Team is headed by the Environmental Protection Agency ("EPA") and consists of representatives of other agencies, including the USCG and Federal Emergency Management Agency ("FEMA").[69] For marine environments, the USCG designates a federal on-scene coordinator ("FOSC") that is responsible for coordinating and directing response and removal.[70] Once an FOSC receives a report of a discharge, he must investigate the threat, classify the size and type of spill, and determine the course of action to ensure effective and immediate removal, mitigation, or prevention of the discharge.[71] The FOSC must also investigate and determine whether a discharge presents a substantial threat to the public health or welfare of the U.S., including fish, wildlife, other natural resources, and beaches and shorelines. If such a threat is perceived, the FOSC is given broad authority to act in response to such a discharge.[72]

3.8 Spill notification requirements

The Clean Water Act, as amended by OPA, requires any person in charge of a vessel to immediately notify the National Response Center upon knowledge of a reportable quantity discharge of oil or hazardous substance from the vessel.[73] The National Response Center then relays the information to the appropriate FOSC.[74] In addition to the severe civil and criminal penalties for failure to report a spill, a responsible party will not be able to avail itself of any defenses or liability limits if the responsible party knows or has reason to know of the incident but fails to report as required by law.[75]

---

67 33 U.S.C. § 1321(d)(2).
68 40 C.F.R. § 300.1.
69 40 C.F.R. §§ 300.110, 300.175(b).
70 40 C.F.R. § 300.5.
71 40 C.F.R. § 300.320.
72 40 C.F.R. § 300.322.
73 33 U.S.C. § 1321(b)(5); 40 C.F.R. § 300.125.
74 40 C.F.R. § 300.125. If reporting to the National Response Center is not practicable, reports may be made to the USCG or FOSC for the geographic area where the discharge occurs. The FOSC may also be contacted through the regional 24-hour emergency response telephone number 1–800–424–8802. The person in charge of the vessel must still notify the National Response Center as soon as possible. 40 C.F.R. § 300.300.
75 33 U.S.C. §§ 2703(c), 2704(c)(2).

3.9 Civil and criminal penalties

An oil spill can give rise to both criminal and civil penalties, under both state and federal law.[76] Under the Clean Water Act, administrative penalties ranging from $15,000 to $190,000 may be imposed.[77] An owner or operator of a vessel from which there is a prohibited discharge is subject to a civil penalty of $1,100 per barrel of oil discharged or up to $40,000 per day.[78] An owner or operator that fails to properly remove the discharge or fails to comply with an order issued by an authority is subject to a civil penalty of up to $40,000 per day or up to three times the costs incurred by the Oil Spill Liability Trust Fund.[79] If a spill is the result of a vessel owner or operator's gross negligence or willful misconduct, such person is subject to a penalty of at least $130,000 and not more than $4,000 per barrel of oil discharged.[80] However, if penalties have already been assessed pursuant to 33 U.S.C. §§ 1319 or 1321(b)(6), duplicative penalties under § 1321(7) may not be assessed.[81] Penalties pursuant to the FWPCA and OPA are paid into the Oil Spill Liability Trust Fund.[82]

Violators of oil pollution statutes may also be subject to criminal sanctions. A "negligent violation" may be punished by a fine of up to $25,000 per day of violation, or by imprisonment for up to one year, or both. A "knowing violation" is punishable by a fine of $5,000 to $50,000 per day, or by imprisonment of up to three years, or both. "Knowing endangerment", when a person knowingly violates the statute and knows that such violation places a person in imminent danger of death or serious bodily injury, is punishable by a fine of up to $250,000 (or $1,000,000 if the violator is a corporation), and up to 15 years in prison. Any person who knowingly makes false material statements in a report or document filed or required to be maintained under the Clean Water Act is subject to a maximum $10,000 fine and up to two years' imprisonment. The above criminal penalties, both fines and imprisonment terms, are doubled after a first conviction.[83] The failure of a person in charge of a vessel to report a discharge as required by law is punishable by a fine and up to five years in prison.[84] Violators may also be subject to the general fine provisions of 18 U.S.C. § 3571, which provides for varying fines depending on whether the violation is a misdemeanor or a felony. Criminal charges may also be brought under other statutes, such as the Refuse Act,[85] the

---

76 OPA specifically states that it does not preempt any state laws with respect to oil pollution. 33 U.S.C. § 2718(a). For a discussion of state oil pollution laws, see 3 Benedict on Admiralty, at 9–113.

77 33 U.S.C. § 1321(b)(6)(A), (B); 33 C.F.R. § 27.3.

78 33 U.S.C. § 1321(b)(7); 33 C.F.R. § 27.3.

79 33 U.S.C. § 1321(b)(7)(C); 33 C.F.R. § 27.3. The Oil Spill Liability Trust Fund ("OSLTF") is a billion-dollar trust fund established to pay removal costs and damages resulting from oil spills or substantial threats of oil spills to navigable waters of the U.S. The OSLTF is used for costs not directly paid by the statutory responsible party. The fund is also used to pay costs to respond to mystery spills for which the source has not been identified.

80 33 U.S.C. § 1321(b)(7)(D); 33 C.F.R. § 27.3.

81 33 U.S.C. §§ 1321(b)(7)(F), 1321(b)(11).

82 26 U.S.C. § 9509.

83 33 U.S.C. § 1319(c)(1)–(4).

84 33 U.S.C. § 1321(b)(5).

85 The Refuse Act prohibits the discharge of "refuse ... of any kind or description whatever", which has been held to include oil, into U.S. navigable waters. 33 U.S.C. § 407; *United States v*

Migratory Bird Treaty Act,[86] and the Act to Prevent Pollution from Ships.[87] In addition, polluters may be prosecuted under Title 18 of the U.S. Code for crimes in connection with falsifying oil record books and otherwise concealing unlawful discharges, as in the so-called "magic pipe" cases.[88]

SECTION 4: CONCLUSIONS

Over the past several decades, the U.S. has developed a comprehensive statutory regime to address virtually all aspects of marine pollution, from prevention and preparedness, to response and civil and criminal liability. The consequences for non-compliance with U.S. law in these areas can be severe. The United States has a substantial record of aggressively enforcing compliance with marine environmental laws, with both entities and individuals – from owners to operators, managers and shore-side personnel, and even corporate officers – being subject to the full spectrum of civil and criminal liability.

A detailed working knowledge of the U.S. marine pollution regime, while critically important, is merely a first step in ensuring compliance. Vessel owners and managers operating in U.S. waters would be well served to consider adopting a proactive posture in the establishment of enhanced measures to strengthen compliance regimes, thereby minimizing legal exposure to the greatest extent practicable. In this regard, increasing dedicated resources, training and shore-side management oversight can serve to foster and enhance environmental compliance.

BIBLIOGRAPHY

Force, Robert, Davies, Martin, and Force, Joshua S., 'Deepwater Horizon: Removal Costs, Civil Damages, Crimes, Civil Penalties, and State Remedies in Oil Spill Cases' [2011] Tulane Law Review 85, 889.

Rodriguez, Antonio J., and Rodriguez, H. Jake, 'Marine Oil Pollution' [2015] Benedict on Admiralty, Ch. IX, 3

Schoenbaum, Thomas J., *Admiralty & Maritime Law*, Ch. 18 (5th edition, Thomson West, Eagan, 2011).

Sump, David, 'The Oil Pollution Act of 1990: A Glance in the Rearview Mirror' [2011] Tulane Law Review 85(4), 1101–1119.

Standard Oil Co., 384 U.S. 224, 226 (1966).

86 16 U.S.C. § 703.

87 33 U.S.C. § 1908(a): "A person who knowingly violates the MARPOL [provisions] or the regulations issued thereunder commits a class D felony".

88 Such crimes include making false statements (18 U.S.C. § 1001), obstruction of proceedings (18 U.S.C. § 1505), and falsification of records in federal investigations (18 U.S.C. § 1519), The "magic pipe" cases involve a pipe that is temporarily installed to bypass the vessel's oily water separator, allowing oily waste to be discharged unlawfully into the ocean. The oil record books are then falsified to conceal the illegal discharges. *Chalos & Co., P.C. v Marine Managers, Ltd.*, 2015 U.S. Dist. LEXIS 144199, *4–5 (E.D. La. 23 Oct. 2015); *see also* U.S. Department of Justice, *Chief Engineer of U.S. Ship Pleads Guilty to Concealing Deliberate Pollution in "Magic Pipe" Case* (28 Feb. 2008), www.justice.gov/archive/opa/pr/2008/February/08_enrd_151.html.

CHAPTER 4

Marine pollution from sewage

TABLE OF CONTENTS

Section 1	Identifying the subject area	107
4.1	The meaning of "sewage" and the challenges for the marine environment	107
4.2	Key terms and definitions	109
Section 2	Overview of the legal basis	110
4.3	Main discussion	110
	4.3.1 Control of discharges of sewage into the sea	113
	4.3.2 Reception facilities	115
	4.3.3 Selected insights on items of regional interest	116
Section 3	Key management issues, including documentation	120
4.4	Surveys and certification	120
	4.4.1 International Sewage Pollution Prevention Certificate	120
4.5	Best practice	121
Section 4	Areas of special interest in relation to the legal framework	121
4.6	The IMO Member State Audit Scheme	121

SECTION 1: IDENTIFYING THE SUBJECT AREA

4.1 The meaning of "sewage" and the challenges for the marine environment

Sewage wastes (also called black water) are produced for most part from land-based resources such as municipal sewers or treatment facilities, and to a lesser extent by ships. Sewage and grey water[1] are generated by all vessels and may end up at sea either in treated or untreated form; sewage may also be retained

---

1 Grey water means drainage from dishwater, showers, laundries, etc. Grey water is not considered sewage or garbage under, respectively, MARPOL Annex IV and V. Regulating grey water has been a rather controversial issue (in the context of Antarctic waters, see, for example, XXXVI Antarctic Treaty, *Discharge of Sewage and Grey Water from Vessels in Antarctic Treaty Waters* (Consultative Meeting, Brussels, 2013).

aboard until it is discharged ashore to reception facilities. Due to their composition, uncontrolled sewage discharges at sea, especially near the coasts, may impair public health and ecosystems. According to scientists, pollutants such as metals, endocrine disrupters or pathogens may be present in sewage discharges.[2] In this context, a number of adverse phenomena have been associated with sewage, including, for example, oxygen depletion. The adverse aesthetic impact of sewage waste at sea can also be considered an issue.

Inevitably, the largest volumes of sewage are related to vessels carrying the greatest number of persons and consumables aboard. As a result, the challenges raised by the control of sewage waste are especially relevant to cruise ships, because of the amount of sewage waste produced by them. In the framework of a survey, an average cruise ship was reported to produce approximately 50 tonnes of sewage per day – between 20 and 40 litres per person per day.[3] In the framework of another survey conducted by the US Environmental Protection Agency (EPA), an average sewage generation rate of 79,000 litres per day per cruise vessel was reported.[4] If one narrows down the focus, for example, on a sea region such as the Baltic Sea, an illustration of the volumes of sewage waste potentially generated and the ensuing challenges, would be the following: the vast majority (80%) of the cruisers in the Baltic Sea have a maximum capacity of 3,000 persons or less; 7.5% are very large ships which can carry more than 4,000 persons (passengers and crew).[5]

According to regional Port State Control findings, as stated in the annual reports of relevant regional memoranda of understanding (MOUs), deficiencies relating to MARPOL Annex IV on sewage control from shipping, were reported to be 0.7% during the years 2013 and 2014, and 0.8% during the year 2015 (Paris MOU).[6] In the last case, this was, for example, in contrast to 1.9% during the same year (2015) for Marpol Annex I (oil) deficiencies, or 1.5% for Marpol Annex V (garbage) deficiencies.[7] Furthermore, in the context of the Memorandum of Understanding on Port State Control in the Asia-Pacific Region, commonly referred to as the Tokyo MOU, 1,301 deficiencies were reported in 2015 in relation to sewage (Annex IV), as opposed, for example, to 1,607 deficiencies in relation to MARPOL Annex I (oil) and 1252 deficiencies in relation to MARPOL Annex V (garbage) for the same year.[8]

---

2 See www.epa.gov/vessels-marinas-and-ports/vessel-sewage-discharges-homepage (last visit 3 April 2017).

3 Nickie Butt, 'The Impact of Cruise Ship Generated Waste on Home Ports and Ports of Call: A Study of Southampton' [2007] Marine Policy 31, cited in European Maritime Safety Agency (EMSA), *Addressing Illegal Discharges in the Marine Environment* (2013, p. 38).

4 United States Environmental Protection Agency (EPA), *Cruise Ship Discharge Assessment Report* (December 2008).

5 Helcom (Baltic Marine Environment Protection Commission), *Baltic Sea Sewage Port Reception Facilities, Helcom Overview 2014* (2015), p. 3.

6 2015 Annual Report Paris MOU on PSC, p. 44.

7 *Ibid.*

8 2015 Annual Report Tokyo MOU on PSC, p. 48.

The IMO has regulated sewage discharges and related issues through MAR-POL Annex IV, and via a number of Marine Environment Protection Committee (MEPC) resolutions which introduced changes to the said Annex. Special regimes exist in relation to specific sea areas (MARPOL Annex IV designated special areas and Polar waters). In some cases, there may be regional or domestic regulatory approaches to the problem of sewage discharges and management.[9] Last, but not least, it is noted that according to Article 14 of MARPOL Convention, MARPOL Annex IV is optional. Relevant provision sets out that "A State may at the time of signing, ratifying, accepting, approving or acceding to the present Convention declare that it does not accept any one or all of Annexes III, IV and V ("hereinafter referred to as "Optional Annexes") of the present Convention. Subject to the above, Parties to the Convention shall be bound by any Annex in its entirety."

4.2 Key terms and definitions

Sewage	It means drainage and other wastes from any form of toilets and urinals; drainage from medical premises (dispensary, sick bay, etc.) via wash basins, wash tubs and scuppers located in such premises; drainage from spaces containing living animals, or other waste waters when mixed with the drainages defined above.[1]
Grey water	It generally means wastewater from ship's sinks, showers, baths, laundries and galleys.
Special area	It means a sea area where for "recognized technical reasons in relation to its oceanographical and ecological condition and to the particular character of its traffic the adoption of special mandatory methods for the prevention of sea pollution by sewage is required";[2] the Baltic Sea area has been recognised as a special area for the purposes of MARPOL IV.
Sewage treatment plant	Sewage treatment plants are a component of sewage systems set out by MARPOL Annex IV for regulatory compliance purposes. A sewage treatment plant must be of a type approved by the flag State Administration, taking into account the standards and test methods developed by the IMO.[3] A related instrument (non-exhaustive list) is Resolution MEPC.227(64) adopted on 5 October 2012[4] whose Guidelines superseded those set out in MEPC.159(55).
Passenger ship	Ship which carries more than 12 passengers.[5]
Reception facilities in special areas	Facilities in ports and terminals within a special area to be used by passenger ships for the reception of sewage. In practice, port reception facilities may be fixed, floating or mobile. They should be capable of receiving ship-generated sewage. Furthermore, they should be adequate to meet the needs of those passenger ships, and operated so as not to cause undue delay.
Effluent	Treated wastewater produced by a treatment sewage plant[6].

(Continued)

---

9   On the status of MARPOL Annex IV in IMO Member States, see the website of the IMO.

(Continued)

Fast ice	Sea ice which forms and remains fast along the coast, where it is attached to the shore, to an ice wall, to an ice front, between shoals or grounded icebergs (see Polar Code, paragraph 4.3 below)
Polar Code	As already mentioned in the introductory chapter, the International Code for Ships Operating in Polar Waters (Polar Code), was adopted by the IMO in November 2014 and in May 2015 through the amendment of the SOLAS and MARPOL Conventions; the Code entered into force on 1 January 2017. It applies to ships which operate in Arctic and Antarctic waters as an additional instrument to MARPOL. It is aimed at ensuring safe ship operation and the protection of the polar environment by addressing risks present in polar waters and not adequately mitigated by other instruments of the IMO. The first part of the Code deals with safety and the second part with marine pollution prevention. Each part contains respectively a mandatory and a recommendatory division. Amongst others, the Code is of interest to the prevention of pollution by sewage from ships.
Ice-shelf	Floating ice sheet of considerable thickness showing 2 to 50 m or above sea-level, attached to the coast (see Polar Code, paragraph 4.3 below)

1 See MARPOL Annex IV, regulation 1.3.
2 MEPC.200(62) adopted on 15 July 2011 "Amendments to the Annex of the Protocol of 1978 relating to the international convention for the prevention of pollution from ships, 1973".
3 See regulation 9.1.1 of MARPOL Annex IV.
4 MEPC.227(64) adopted on 5 October 2012 "2012 Guidelines on Implementation of Effluent Standards and Performance Tests for Sewage Treatment Plants". The said Guidelines address the design, installation, performance and testing of sewage treatment plants required by regulations 9.1.1 and 9.2.1 of MARPOL Annex IV.
5 See the above-mentioned MEPC.200(62).
6 See 2012 Guidelines on Implementation of Effluent Standards and Performance Tests for Sewage Treatment Plants.

SECTION 2: OVERVIEW OF THE LEGAL BASIS

4.3 Main discussion

MARPOL Annex IV entitled "Regulations for the prevention of pollution by sewage from ships" entered into force on 27 September 2003. It is noteworthy that, since then, the Annex has been subject to revisions, notably including amendments adopted by resolution MEPC.200(62) (entry into force 1 January 2013). A requirement that ships be equipped with either an approved sewage treatment plant or an approved sewage comminuting and disinfecting system or a sewage holding tank has been set out.[10]

The Annex also tackles the following matters:

- control of discharges of sewage into the sea;
- port reception facilities;

10 See regulation 9.

- surveys and certification;
- Port State Control.

MARPOL Annex IV applies to the following ships engaged in international voyages,[11] namely:

- new ships of 400 gross tonnage and above; and
- new ships of less than 400 gross tonnage which are certified to carry more than 15 persons; and
- existing ships of 400 gross tonnage and above, five years after the date of entry into force of the Annex; and
- existing ships of less than 400 gross tonnage which are certified to carry more than 15 persons, five years after the date of entry into force of this Annex.

Furthermore, the above-mentioned resolution MEPC.200(62) added some new provisions to Annex IV and replaced a number of regulations with new ones. The Resolution also amended the form of the International Sewage Pollution Prevention Certificate. The added value of the Resolution is the designation of the Baltic Sea as a special area and the reshaping of a number of requirements. Some selected highlights from MEPC.200(62) are given below:

NEW REGULATION 11: DISCHARGE OF SEWAGE

   A   *Discharge of sewage from ships other than passenger ships in all areas and discharge of sewage from passenger ships outside special areas*

     1   Subject to the provisions of regulation 3 of this Annex,[12] the discharge of sewage into the sea is prohibited, except when:

       .1 the ship is discharging comminuted and disinfected sewage using a system approved by the Administration in accordance with regulation 9.1.2 of this Annex at a distance of more than 3 nautical miles from the nearest land, or sewage which is not comminuted or disinfected at a distance of more than 12 nautical miles from the nearest land, provided that, in any case, the sewage that has been stored in holding tanks, or sewage originating from spaces containing living animals, shall not be discharged instantaneously but at a moderate rate when the ship is *en route* and proceeding at not less than 4 knots; the rate of discharge shall be approved by the Administration based upon standards developed by the Organisation; or

       .2 the ship has in operation an approved sewage treatment plant which has been certified by the Administration to meet the operational requirements referred to in regulation 9.1.1 of this Annex, and the effluent shall not produce visible floating solids nor cause discoloration of the surrounding water.

---

11 Regulation 2.
12 It is noted that regulation 3 of MARPOL Annex IV deals with exceptions.

> 2 The provisions of paragraph 1 shall not apply to ships operating in the waters under the jurisdiction of a State and visiting ships from other States while they are in these waters and are discharging sewage in accordance with such less stringent requirements as may be imposed by such State.
>
> B *Discharge of sewage from passenger ships within a special area*
>
> 3 Subject to the provisions of regulation 3 of this Annex, the discharge of sewage from a passenger ship within a special area shall be prohibited:
>
>   .1 for new passenger ships on [...]; and
>
>   .2 for existing passenger ships on [...],
>
> except when the following conditions are satisfied:
>
> the ship has in operation an approved sewage treatment plant which has been certified by the Administration to meet the operational requirements referred to in regulation 9.2.1 of this Annex, and the effluent shall not produce visible floating solids nor cause discoloration of the surrounding water.
>
> C *General requirements*
>
> 4 When the sewage is mixed with wastes or waste water covered by other Annexes of MARPOL, the requirements of those Annexes shall be complied with in addition to the requirements of this Annex."
>
> 4 New regulation 12bis is added as follows:
>
> "12bis Reception facilities for passenger ships in Special Areas
>
> .1 Each Party, the coastline of which borders a special area, undertakes to ensure that:
>
>   .1 facilities for the reception of sewage are provided in ports and terminals which are in a special area and which are used by passenger ships;
>
>   .2 the facilities are adequate to meet the needs of those passenger ships; and
>
>   .3 the facilities are operated so as not to cause undue delay to those passenger ships.
>
> .2 The Governments of each Party concerned shall notify the Organisation of the measures taken pursuant to paragraph .1 of this regulation. Upon receipt of sufficient notifications in accordance with paragraph .1, the Organization shall establish a date from which the requirements of regulation 11.3 in respect of the area in question shall take effect. The Organization shall notify all Parties of the date so established no less than twelve months in advance of that date. Until the date so established, ships while navigating in the special area shall comply with the requirements of regulation 11.1 of this Annex.

In relation to special areas, it is noteworthy that under the tacit acceptance procedure, discussed in the introductory chapter, IMO Resolution MEPC.274(69) (adopted on 22 April 2016[13]) with anticipated entry into force on 1 September 2017

---

13 The said MEPC Resolution is entitled "Amendments to the Annex of the International Convention for the Prevention of Pollution from Ships, 1973, as Modified by the Protocol of 1978

introduces amendments concerning the Baltic Sea Special Area and the appendix to MARPOL Annex IV concerning the Form of the International Sewage Pollution Prevention Certificate. Furthermore, under MEPC.275(69), adopted on the same date,[14] the introduction of the Baltic Sea Special Area requirements is set in 2019 for new passenger ships and 2021 for existing passenger ships.[15]

Resolution MEPC.227(64) also deserves a special mention.[16] It was adopted on 5 October 2012 and introduced the "2012 Guidelines on Implementation of Effluent Standards and Performance Tests for Sewage Treatment Plants". The said Resolution superseded the Revised Guidelines on implementation of effluent standards and performance tests for sewage treatment plants (adopted by resolution MEPC.159(55)). The purpose of the 2012 Guidelines and specifications is to address the design, installation, performance and testing of sewage treatment plants required by specific regulations of MARPOL Annex IV. The 2012 Guidelines aim at a uniform interpretation of the requirements of regulations 9.1.1 and 9.2.1 of MARPOL Annex IV, at assisting maritime administrations in determining appropriate design, construction and operational testing and performance parameters for sewage treatment plants when such equipment is fitted in ships flying their flag, and at providing guidance for installation requirements. An approved sewage treatment plant should meet, according to the instrument, the technical specifications set out by it[17] and the tests outlined in relevant Guidelines. Furthermore, testing of the operational performance of a sewage treatment plant should be conducted in line with the Guidelines. Governments are invited by the Resolution to implement the Guidelines and apply them on or after 1 January 2016; furthermore, they are invited to provide the IMO with feedback on their application.

4.3.1 Control of discharges of sewage into the sea

As mentioned above, there is a prohibition of discharge of sewage into the sea.[18] This can be viewed as the hard core of the Annex; it aligns with the approach on regulation of discharges from other substances under the rest of the annexes of MARPOL.

Against this background, regulation 3 of MARPOL Annex IV, states that this prohibition shall not apply to:

Relating Thereto" (Amendments to MARPOL Annex IV – Baltic Sea Special Area and Form of ISPP Certificate).

14 The said MEPC Resolution is entitled "Establishment of the Date on Which Regulation 11.3 of MARPOL Annex IV in Respect of the Baltic Sea Special Area Shall Take Effect".

15 More specifically, the following dates are set out in MEPC.275(69): "1 June 2019 for new passenger ships; 1 June 2021 for existing passenger ships other than those specified in paragraph 1.3 below, and 1 June 2023 for existing passenger ships en route directly to or from a port located outside the special area and to or from a port located east of longitude 12°10' E within the special area that do not make any other port calls within the special area."

16 It is noted that MEPC.227(64) superseded MEPC.159(55).

17 Section 4 of the Guidelines.

18 Regulation 11 of MARPOL Annex IV.

- the discharge of sewage from a ship which is necessary for securing the safety of a ship and those on board or saving life at sea; or
- the discharge of sewage resulting from damage to a ship or its equipment if all reasonable precautions have been taken before and after the occurrence of the damage, for the purpose of preventing or minimising the discharge.

The rationale of regulations on this point is that discharge of sewage at sea must be exceptional. Discharge may be legal only under stringent conditions set out by the instrument, i.e. when the ship uses an approved sewage treatment plant or when the ship is discharging comminuted and disinfected sewage using an approved system at a distance of more than three nautical miles from the nearest land. Concerning sewage that is not comminuted or disinfected, it may be discharged at a distance of more than 12 miles under conditions.[19] Relevant provisions shall not apply, according to the Annex, as amended, to "ships operating in the waters under the jurisdiction of a State and visiting ships from other States while they are in these waters and are discharging sewage in accordance with such less stringent requirements as may be imposed by such States".

In the graph below, a summarised framework of the prohibitions of discharge can be identified.[20]

Moreover, the discharge of sewage from passenger ships within a special area is, in principle, prohibited.[21] This is according to the timetable set out by the amended Annex. The distinction between new and existing passenger ships is to be noted in

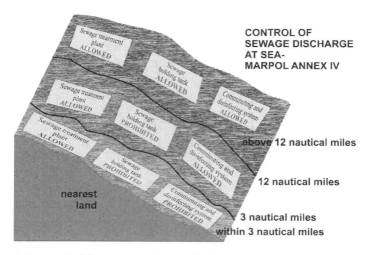

Graph 4.1 Summarised framework of the prohibitions of discharge of sewage from ships other than passenger ships in all areas and discharge of sewage from passenger ships outside special areas (Note: the provisions of MARPOL prevail)

---

19 See regulation 11.1 MARPOL Annex IV.
20 Readers are encouraged to access the instrument for the full picture and related details.
21 See regulation 11.3 of MARPOL Annex IV.

that regard. The exception set out by relevant regulations stems from the use of an approved sewage treatment plant and related conditions on effluents.[22]

4.3.2 Reception facilities

Reception facilities are central to the level of protection sought by the Annex. Governments of contracting States which require compliance with the regulations on the discharge of sewage, "undertake to ensure" the provision of facilities at ports and terminals for the reception of sewage. They should do so, according to regulation 12 of MARPOL Annex IV, without causing delay to ships. Furthermore, such infrastructure should be adequate to meet the needs of ships using them.

A new requirement was added via Resolution MEPC.200(62)[23] on reception facilities for passenger ships in special areas.

IMO Guide to Good Practice for Port Reception Facility Providers and Users deserves a special mention at this point.[24] The Guide uses the generic term "MARPOL residues/wastes" to refer collectively to all waste streams produced aboard a ship during normal operations and during cargo operations, governed by MARPOL, notably including MARPOL Annex IV sewage.

EXTRACT FROM THE IMO GUIDE TO GOOD PRACTICE FOR PORT RECEPTION FACILITY (PRF) PROVIDERS AND USERS[25]

It is noted that the Guide is aimed at providing guidance for ships' crews who seek to deliver MARPOL residues/wastes ashore. The Guide is also intended for port reception facility providers who seek to provide timely and efficient port reception services to ships. As already mentioned, the Guide uses the term residues/wastes to cover collectively all waste streams generated aboard ships during normal operations and during cargo operations governed by MARPOL Annex I, II, IV (sewage), V, and VI. The short extract below addresses the obligations of ships and port operators.

16. Keeping the seas and oceans clean should be seen as the overriding obligation for the use and provision of PRFs. MARPOL includes regulations aimed at preventing and minimizing pollution from ships – both accidental pollution and that from routine operations. The basis for providing and using PRFs is incorporated in the Annexes of MARPOL and implementing laws and regulations of States Parties. The following summarizes the basic obligations under MARPOL and includes other considerations that ship and port operators should take into account. For specific legal requirements, users of this Guide should refer directly to the MARPOL Protocols and Annexes or implementing regulations of individual States Party to the Convention.

---

22 *Ibid.*

23 New regulation 12bis entitled Reception facilities for passenger ships in Special Areas.

24 The Guide is incorporated MEPC.1/Circ.671/Rev.1 of 1 July 2013. The said Circular supersedes MEPC.1/Circ.671.

25 MEPC.1/Circ.671/Rev.1, 1 July 2013. Readers should bear in mind that MEPC.1/Circ.671/Rev.1 was superseded by IMO Circular MEPC.1/Circ.834, 15 April 2014, on Consolidated Guidance for Port Reception Facility Providers and Users.

17   To complement residue/waste minimization and management practices on board the ship (see section 6), the shipping industry needs access to adequate PRFs to enable compliance with the provisions of the Convention. Therefore, MARPOL places an obligation on States Parties to provide adequate reception facilities in their ports. The following regulations stipulate this requirement for each type of MARPOL residue/waste identified:

    .1   regulation 38 of Annex I;

    .2   regulation 18 of Annex II;

    .3   regulations 12 and 12*bis* of Annex IV;

    .4   regulation 8 of Annex V; and

    .5   regulation 17 of Annex VI.

18   In addition to the basic rules in the MARPOL Annexes, ships' operators should be aware that individual port States have implemented national and regional requirements which may mandate that ships discharge certain types of MARPOL residues/wastes to port reception facilities. Individual port States may also specify the means of disposal to meet quarantine and other regulatory requirements. Operators should therefore ensure they have a complete and up-to-date overview of national and regional requirements relating to PRFs. Such information may be gained directly from the port State authorities, or via agents in the port, or trade associations representing the shipping and/or port industries.

19   General obligations under each of the regulations listed above also state that Parties should communicate information on their PRFs to the Organization. To this end, the Organization has established the Port Reception Facilities Database (PRFD) within its Global Integrated Ship Information System (GISIS). The PRFD relies on up-to-date information being provided by port States. Port State authorities are encouraged to regularly seek accurate and up-to-date information from reception facility operators and port authorities and to maintain entries on the PRFD. Reception facility operators and port authorities should also be proactive in communicating updated information to port State authorities. This two-way communication will facilitate the dissemination of PRF information to the shipping industry.

20   Ship masters/owners/operators can use the PRFD on the GISIS website to obtain information on specific port reception facilities. PRF operators are encouraged to maintain and update on regular basis current and accurate information regarding their facilities and to provide such information to authorities so as to ensure the accuracy of information on the PRFD and that current information is available to ship masters and shipowners/operators. Ships' agents, acting on behalf of owners/operators may also access the public GISIS website PRF information.

4.3.3 Selected insights on items of regional interest

- The Baltic Sea

On the regional level, information on the status and use of sewage port reception facilities in the Baltic Sea area in 2014, with the focus placed on international cruise traffic, is provided by HELCOM (Baltic Marine Environment Protection Commission – Helsinki Commission)[26] on the basis of sources including regional AIS data, the shipping industry, port authorities and national administrations. A joint survey was launched in the Baltic Sea region for summer 2014 by HELCOM and the Cruise Lines International Association (CLIA), aimed at the collection of detailed data on sewage delivery needs and the facilities available in Baltic Sea ports. According to relevant findings, there were 79 international cruise ships operating in the Baltic Sea in 2014. It is noted that 80% of the cruise ships operating in the said region have a maximum capacity of 3,000 persons or less. Interestingly, the HELCOM CLIA survey 2014 suggests that 30% of the cruise ships in the Baltic Sea used sewage port reception facilities when available.

- The European Union (EU) approach

The adequacy or smooth operation of port reception facilities has attracted interest on the regional level. In the EU context, Directive 2000/59/EC of the European Parliament and of the Council of 27 November 2000 on port reception facilities for ship generated waste and cargo residues[27] gives the definition of "ship-generated waste". The last means all waste, including sewage, and residues other than cargo residues, which are generated during the service of a ship and fall in the scope of Annexes I, IV and V to MARPOL 73/78 and cargo associated waste as defined in the Guidelines for the Implementation of Annex V to MARPOL 73/78. The Directive, as amended, requires vessels to land the waste they produce during voyages to and between EU ports to Port Reception Facilities (PRF).

Let us mention at this point that EU Directives set out goals that Member States are held to implement within specified deadlines and according to means they consider fit for the purpose. With the aim of giving a clear picture of the functioning of port reception facilities in the EU in the framework of the transposition of the above-mentioned Directive, the European Maritime Safety Agency (EMSA), which is the technical arm of the European Commission for matters relating to shipping, had launched a study. This is the Study on the Availability and Use of Port Reception Facilities for Ship-Generated Waste, which was conducted on the basis of visits to and inputs from 50 major European ports, including on the level of port waste management plants, national harmonisation measures and legislation.[28]

The study pointed out, amongst others, that the level of implementation from one Member State to another differed, including on the level of cost recovery systems for the operation of port reception facilities and on the level of the incentives given for the use of relevant facilities. Relevant findings suggested that 50 ports had defined and implemented almost 50 different systems based on various approaches. These findings shed light on the quality of implementation of existing measures, and point to possible areas for improvements.

---

26 Helcom (Baltic Sea Marine Environment Protection Commission), *Baltic Sea Sewage Port Reception Facilities – Helcom Overview 2014* (revised second edition, 2015).

27 European Parliament and Council (EC) Directive 2000/59 on port reception facilities for ship generated waste and cargo residues [2000] OJ L 332/81.

28 Report issued by Carl Bro following interviews with port authorities in different Member States (December 2005).

In addition to the above, the Guidance for Ship Inspection under the Port Reception Facilities Directive (Directive 2000/59/EC) published by EMSA on 25 November 2016, is aimed at facilitating ship inspections undertaken by EU Member States for the purpose of the enforcement of the Directive.

- In the USA
- In polar waters (Arctic and Antarctic waters)

In the USA, interesting data on cruise ship discharges, including sewage, is provided by the United States Environmental Protection Agency (EPA). Special mention is made of the EPA Cruise Ship Discharge Assessment Report (2008). Amongst others, the report discusses possible options and alternatives to address sewage from cruise ships:

- prevention and reduction (e.g. decrease of the volume of untreated sewage or treated sewage effluent);
- control through discharge standards, including the review of discharge standards of treated sewage effluent (e.g. by requiring periodic sampling and testing);
- control via geographic restrictions on discharge (e.g. by prohibiting discharges on the basis of a certain distance from shore);
- enforcement and compliance assurance through a multifaceted process which includes monitoring, reporting, inspection and enforcement.

As observed by a number of stakeholders, on the one hand, as ship traffic (e.g. cruise ships) has developed in polar waters, the challenges raised by the discharge of sewage from ships have increased;[29] on the other hand, discharge restrictions based purely on shoreline proximity could be inadequate in the case of waters surrounding the two poles, as important ecological features and wildlife populations can also be found far offshore.[30]

Some of these concerns have been addressed by the International Code for Ships Operating in Polar Waters (Polar Code). The Code acknowledges the similarities and differences of Arctic and Antarctic waters. As already mentioned, it entered into force on 1 January 2017 following amendments of MARPOL and SOLAS. The instrument is highly relevant to the discussion on the legal regime and management governing discharges of sewage at sea notably through its Chapter 4 entitled "Prevention of Pollution by Sewage from Ships".

The Code applies to ships (divided for this purpose in three categories) which operate in Arctic and Antarctic waters as an additional instrument to MARPOL. It is aimed at safe ship operation and protection of the polar environment by addressing risks present in polar waters and not adequately mitigated by other international instruments. Amongst others, the Code sets out certification requirements (e.g. a valid Polar Ship Certificate). Viewed from a technical point of view, the instrument

---

29 FOEI, IUCN, Greenpeace, IFAW and WWF, *DE 53/18/3 Shipping Management Issues to be Addressed* (20 November 2009). Cited in Antarctic and Southern Ocean Coalition (ASOC) (Lead author, Dr. Sian Prior), *Discharge of Sewage and Grey Water from Vessels in Antarctic Treaty Waters* (XXXVI Antarctic Treaty Consultative Meeting, Brussels, paper a submitted on 23 April 2013).

30 ASOC paper, *ibid.*, p. 5.

contains an introduction with obligatory provisions and a main body which is divided into two parts. The first part deals with safety measures and the second part with marine pollution prevention measures. Each part contains respectively a mandatory and a recommendatory division.

The main principle is enshrined in paragraph 4.2 (Chapter 4) of the Code which deals with operational requirements. Sewage discharges within polar waters are prohibited except when performed in accordance with MARPOL Annex IV and the requirements set out by the Code.

The basic directions of the said regime can be summarised in the extract which follows:[31]

Extract from Chapter 4 of the Polar Code on Prevention of Pollution by Sewage from Ships

Operational requirements

Discharges of sewage within polar waters are prohibited except when performed in accordance with MARPOL Annex IV and the following requirements:

.1 **the ship is discharging comminuted and disinfected sewage in accordance with regulation 11.1.1 of MARPOL Annex IV at a distance of more than 3 nautical miles from any ice-shelf or fast ice and shall be as far as practicable from areas of ice concentration exceeding 1/10; or**

.2 **the ships is discharging sewage that is not comminuted or disinfected in accordance with regulation 11.1.1 of MARPOL Annex IV and at a distance of more than 12 nautical miles from any ice-shelf or fast ice and shall be as far as practicable from areas of ice concentration exceeding 1/10; or**

.3 **the ship has in operation an approved sewage treatment plant certified by the Administration to meet the operational requirements in either regulation 9.1.1 or 9.2.1 of MARPOL Annex IV, and discharges sewage in accordance with regulation 11.1.2 of Annex IV and shall be as far as practicable from the nearest land, any ice-shelf, fast ice or areas of ice concentration exceeding 1/10".**

In the context of the Polar Code, Resolution MEPC.265(68) was adopted on 15 May 2015 (entry into force 1 January 2017)[32] with a view to introducing amendments to MARPOL Annexes I (oil), II (noxious liquid substances in bulk), IV (sewage) and V (garbage).

---

31 See Chapter 4, para. 4.2.1 of the Polar Code for the details.

32 Resolution MEPC.265(68) adopted on 15 May 2015 "Amendments to the Annex of the Protocol of 1978 Relating to the International Convention for the Prevention of Pollution from Ships, 1973" – Amendments to MARPOL Annexes I, II, IV and V (To make use of environment-related provision of the Polar Code mandatory).

SECTION 3: KEY MANAGEMENT ISSUES, INCLUDING DOCUMENTATION

4.4 Surveys and certification

Chapter 2 of MARPOL Annex IV deals with surveys and certification.

Ships required to comply with the Annex shall be subject to specific surveys,[33] i.e. initial survey, renewal survey and additional survey.

In broad terms, the initial survey is conducted before the ship is put in service or before the International Sewage Pollution Prevention Certificate is issued for the first time. The initial survey ensures that the structure, equipment, systems, fittings, arrangements and materials are fully in line with the requirements of the Annex. A renewal survey is conducted at intervals set out by the flag State administration but not exceeding, in principle, five years. The renewal survey ensures that the structure, equipment, systems, fittings, arrangements and materials fully comply with the requirements of Annex IV. Additional surveys are also provided for, which may be general or partial, according to the circumstances.

Surveys are conducted by the officers of national administrations or are entrusted to nominated surveyors or to recognised organisations (in practice, classification societies). The powers of the nominated surveyor or recognised organisation are set out by the instrument. Amongst others, when they determine that the condition of the ship or its equipment does not correspond substantially with the particulars of the International Sewage Pollution Prevention Certificate or is such that the ship is not fit to proceed to sea without presenting threat of harm to the marine environment, they must ensure that corrective action is taken and shall notify in due course the flag State.[34]

It is noteworthy that, like in other areas, in the context of marine pollution control from sewage discharges, national administration fully guarantees "the completeness and efficiency of the survey".[35] The condition of the vessel, including its equipment, shall be maintained to comply with MARPOL. The ship must remain fit to proceed to sea "without presenting an unreasonable threat of harm to the marine environment".[36]

Reporting duties to the flag State are also set out.[37]

4.4.1 *International Sewage Pollution Prevention Certificate*

An International Sewage Pollution Prevention Certificate is provided in regulation 5 of the Annex. The Certificate, whose period of validity is specified by the flag State, and which shall not exceed five years,[38] shall be issued after an initial

---

33 See regulation 4.
34 See regulation 4.5.
35 See regulation 4.6.
36 See regulation 4.7.
37 See regulation 4.9.
38 See regulation 8.1.

or renewal survey to any vessel engaged in voyages to ports or offshore terminals under the jurisdiction of other Parties to MARPOL. The Certificate shall be issued or endorsed either by the flag State administration or by any person or organisation empowered in that regard (in practice, as already mentioned, this commonly means a classification society). In the latter case, however, the flag State Administration continues to assume full responsibility for the Certificate.

Amongst others, the Certificate certifies that the ship has been surveyed, as appropriate, and that it is equipped with a sewage treatment plant/comminuter/holding tank and a discharge pipeline in compliance with specific provisions of Annex IV.

IMO Resolution MEPC.200(62), which was adopted, as already mentioned, on 15 July 2011, amended the form of the International Sewage Pollution Prevention Certificate. Furthermore, IMO Resolution MEPC.274(69), adopted on 22 April 2016, and its corrigendum introduced changes to the regime on discharge of sewage from passenger ships within a special area as well as to the ISPP format.[39]

4.5 Best practice

Recommended management standards in relation to sewage stem, amongst others, from the International Chamber of Shipping. Such recommendations are intended to be incorporated into company safety management systems. They notably include a recommendation to ensure as a minimum compliance with Annex IV of MARPOL 73/78, and a recommendation to ensure that on board sewage treatment facilities are well maintained and operated in accordance with approved standards.[40]

Furthermore, good practices for port reception facility operators are set out in the above-mentioned IMO Guide to Good Practice for Port Reception Facility Providers and Users.[41] The Guide uses the generic term "MARPOL residues/wastes" to refer collectively to all waste streams produced aboard a ship during normal operations and during cargo operations, governed by MARPOL, notably including MARPOL Annex IV sewage.

SECTION 4: AREAS OF SPECIAL INTEREST IN RELATION TO THE LEGAL FRAMEWORK

4.6 The IMO Member State Audit Scheme

It should be noted from the outset that the IMO Member State Audit Scheme (IMSAS) does not specifically address sewage at sea but it is relevant to the

---

39 MEPC.274(69) adopted on 22 April 2016 "Amendments to the Annex of the International Convention for the Prevention of Pollution from Ships, 1973, as modified by the Protocol of 1978 relating thereto" (Amendments to MARPOL Annex IV) (Baltic Sea Special Area and Form of ISPP Certificate).

40 See International Chamber of Shipping (ICS), 'Shipping and the Environment: A Code of Practice' (4th edition, 2008 p. 20).

41 See *supra* 24 and 25.

question. The Scheme was set out in the so-called III Code (IMO Instruments Implementation Code), and was intended by its drafters to improve the implementation and enforcement of shipping regulations covered by the Scheme. The last has passed from a voluntary phase to a mandatory one (the mandatory audit scheme of all Member States commenced from 1 January 2016). Audited IMO Member States are thus given a tool for assessing their performance, including identifying how well they implement and administer relevant IMO regulations, or how effective their control and monitoring mechanisms are.

Amongst numerous amendments relating to IMO instruments (e.g. to SOLAS, via the addition of a new Chapter, i.e. Chapter XIII), amendments by the Marine Environment Protection Committee adopted in April 2014 to MARPOL Annexes, including MARPOL Annex IV on sewage, are to be noted. The amendments aimed at making the auditing of Member States mandatory.

BIBLIOGRAPHY

Alaska Department of Environmental Conservation (ADEC), *Assessment of Cruise Ship and Ferry Wastewater Impacts in Alaska* (Juneau, AK, 2004)

Antarctic and Southern Ocean Coalition (ASOC) (Lead author, Dr. Sian Prior), *Discharge of Sewage and Grey Water from Vessels in Antarctic Treaty Waters* (XXXVI Antarctic Treaty Consultative Meeting, Brussels, paper submitted 23.4.2013).

Butt, Nickie, 'The Impact of Cruise Ship Generated Waste on Home Ports and Ports of Call: A Study of Southampton' [2007] Marine Policy 31

Cruise Lines International Association (CLIA), *Cruise Industry Waste Practices and Procedures* (CLIA, Fort Lauderdale, 2006)

European Maritime Safety Agency (EMSA), 'Guidance for Ship Inspection Under the Port Reception Facilities Directive' (Directive 2000/59/EC) published on 25.11.2016

European Maritime Safety Agency (EMSA), 'Addressing Illegal Discharges in the Marine Environment' (2012)

European Maritime Safety Agency (EMSA)/RAMBOLL, 'Final Report EMSA Study on the Delivery of Ship-Generated Waste and Cargo Residues to Port Reception Facilities in EU Ports' (2012)

European Maritime Safety Agency (EMSA), 'A Study on the Availability and Use of Port Reception Facilities for Ship-Generated Waste' (December 2005)

Helcom (Baltic Marine Environment Protection Commission), 'Baltic Sea Sewage Port Reception Facilities, Helcom Overview 2014' (2015)

IMO, 'MARPOL Consolidated Edition' (2017)

Maritime and Coastguard Agency (MCA), UK, *Marine Guidance Note MGN 385 (M+F)*, *'Guidance on the Shipping (Prevention of Pollution by Sewage and Garbage from Ships) Regulations 2008* (available on the internet)

MEPC.1/Circ.671/Rev.1 of 1st July 2013 'IMO Guide to Good Practice for Port Reception Facility Providers and Users'; superseded by IMO Circular MEPC.1/Circ.834, 15 April 2014, on Consolidated Guidance for Port Reception Facility Providers and Users

MEPC.200(62) adopted on 15 July 2011 'Amendments to the Annex of the Protocol of 1978 Relating to the International Convention for the Prevention of Pollution from Ships, 1973'

MEPC.227(64) adopted on 5 October 2012 '2012 Guidelines on Implementation of Effluent Standards and Performance Tests for Sewage Treatment Plants'

MEPC.274(69) adopted 22 April 2016 'Amendments to the Annex of the International Convention for the Prevention of Pollution from Ships, 1973, as Modified by the Protocol of 1978 Relating Thereto' (Amendments to MARPOL Annex IV-Baltic Sea Special Area and Form of ISPP Certificate)

Paris MOU, 'Annual Report' (2015)

Paris MOU, 'Annual Report' (2016)

Rees, G., 'Health, Implications of Sewage in Coastal Waters – the British Case' [1993] Marine Pollution Bulletin 26(1), 14–19

Sweeting, J.E.N., and Wayne, S.L., 'A Shifting Tide: Environmental Challenges and Cruise Industry Responses' in R.K. Dowling (ed), *Cruise Ship Tourism* (Wallingford, CABI, 2006)

United States Environmental Protection Agency (US EPA), 'Cruise Ship Discharge Assessment Report' (December 2008)

West, Anna, 'Marine Pollution from Vessel Sewage in Queensland' [2004] MLAANZ Journal 18

CHAPTER 5

Marine pollution from wastes

TABLE OF CONTENTS

Section 1	Overview of the challenges raised by marine pollution from wastes		125
5.1	Identifying the problem of marine pollution from wastes: setting the scene		125
5.2	Key terms and definitions		128
Section 2	General (non-shipping specific) regulatory framework		131
5.3	Legislative background and discussion		131
	5.3.1	In relation to marine pollution from dumping of wastes	133
	5.3.2	In relation to transboundary movements of hazardous wastes and their disposal	138
Section 3	MARPOL Annex V regulations for the prevention of pollution by garbage from ships		140
5.4	General discussion and overview		140
5.5	Key management issues, including documentation		144
	5.5.1	Garbage Management Plan	144
	5.5.2	Placards	145
	5.5.3	Garbage Record Book	146
	5.5.4	Good practices for shipmasters, shipowners and operators	147
5.6	Areas of special interest		151
	5.6.1	Adequacy of port reception facilities	151
	5.6.2	Port State Control findings	152
	5.6.3	The impact of the Polar Code	152

SECTION 1: OVERVIEW OF THE CHALLENGES RAISED BY MARINE POLLUTION FROM WASTES

5.1 Identifying the problem of marine pollution from wastes: setting the scene

For most maritime practitioners, the main discussion on wastes centers upon garbage regulations under MARPOL Annex V. The latter is undoubtedly the reference in the shipping world as it regulates garbage generated during shipping operations. In the interest of a global understanding of marine pollution from wastes, it is meaningful to point out land-based sources of wastes, sea-based sources other than shipping operations (e.g. dumping) or even transboundary movements of hazardous wastes which may end at sea. There is a general belief that about 80% of marine litter stems from land-based sources. Even though this finding does not appear to have been confirmed by scientists,[1] it nevertheless suggests that shipping is not the principal contributor to the problem of wastes at sea. In the graph below (graph 5.1), key land and ocean-based sources of marine debris can be identified.

Despite waste reduction, recycling and other processes (see graph 5.2 below), waste disposal at sea raises a number of challenges nowadays for regulators, civil society and the shipping industry.[2]

Waste disposal is far from being confined to industrialised societies. Marine debris or marine litter can be found nowadays in all waters, including in those surrounding remote islands. Carried through currents and winds, marine debris is considered to be an international problem. Even though statistics on the international level are not crystallised and data collection, including on the level of distribution of debris on the seabed, are challenges, according to the United Nations Environment Programme (UNEP), estimates suggest that 13,000 pieces of plastic litter float on average on every square kilometer of the ocean. As it will be seen below, the term "garbage" is given a specific meaning by the international regulator. Marine litter can be understood as "any persistent, manufactured or processed solid material discarded or disposed of or abandoned in the marine and coastal environment".[3]

Marine debris stemming from land-based or ocean-based sources end up in the oceans, they float on the water or accumulate on the coasts or seabed, and may cause the death or injury of marine mammals, seabirds and other species. Marine species are entangled in the marine debris or ingest marine debris by mistake. Furthermore, these solid wastes may become potential dangers for maritime safety and the aesthetic view of the water and coastlines. According to scientists,

---

1 See Joint Group of Experts on the Scientific Aspects of Marine Environmental Protection (GESAMP), 'Pollution in the Open Oceans 2009–2013: A Report by a GESAMP Task Team' (GESAMP Reports and Studies No. 9, 2015), p. 39.

2 On the level of the European Union, for example, the European Commission recognises that marine litter is a major threat to the oceans and proposes an action in view of fighting marine litter and the "sea of plastic" (see European Commission Joint Communication to the European Parliament, the Council, the European Economic and Social Committee, and the Committee of the Regions on International Ocean Governance: an Agenda for the Future of our Oceans, Brussels (JOIN(2016)49 final, 10.11.2016); also, see Greenpeace/M. Allsopp, A. Walters, D. Santillo, and P. Johnston, *Plastic Debris in the World's Oceans* (document date unavailable).

3 United Nations Environment Programme (UNEP), *Marine Litter: An Analytical Overview* (2005, p. 3).

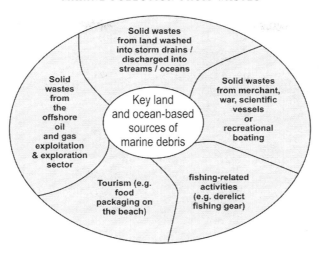

Graph 5.1 Key land and ocean-based sources of marine debris

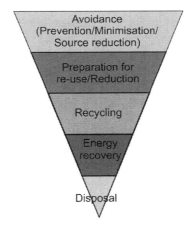

Graph 5.2 Waste management hierarchy showing priority and less preferred options

plastics make up 60–80% of all marine debris.[4] In addition to this, there are estimates suggesting that the vast majority of marine debris in the oceans originates from land-based sources.

From a legal standpoint, even though there is more than one legal definition of "waste", "wastes" are commonly understood to signify substances or objects

---

4 See J.G.B. Derraik, 'The Pollution of the Marine Environment by Plastic Debris: A Review' [2002] Marine Pollution Bulletin 44, 842–852, cited in Greenpeace, *supra* note 2, p. 9.

disposed of, intended to be disposed of or required to be disposed of under applicable provisions. In the 1996 Protocol to the Convention on the Prevention of Marine Pollution by Dumping of Wastes and Other Matter (commonly referred to as the London Protocol), there is a generic definition of wastes. "Wastes or other matter", according to this instrument, means "material and substance of any kind, form or description".[5] IMO MARPOL Annex V uses the term "garbage". It defines it as "all kinds of food wastes, domestic wastes and operational wastes, all plastics, cargo residues, cooking oil, fishing gear, and animal carcasses generated during the normal operation of the ship and liable to be disposed of continuously or periodically except those substances which are defined or listed in other Annexes to the present Convention". The term "wastes" is used in the same Annex in relation to domestic and operational wastes, which are also defined by the text. Under the 1989 Basel Convention, which is the international instrument of reference governing the control of transboundary movements of hazardous wastes, "wastes are substances or objects which are disposed of or are intended to be disposed of or are required to be disposed of by the provisions of national law".[6] The Convention was adopted in 1989 and entered into force in 1992 under the umbrella of the United Nations. The Convention sought to tackle the problem of "toxic trade" (including from developed countries to certain African countries), and therefore to protect human health and the environment. Wastes here are based on their origin and/or composition, their characteristics, as well as on a classification referred to as "other wastes", i.e. household waste and incinerator ash.[7] Furthermore, European Union (EU) legislation defines waste as "any substance or object which the holder discards or intends or is required to discard".[8]

The question raises numerous questions for regulators and the industry, including the following: awareness of the public, adequacy of land-based facilities to receive litter, effectiveness of waste management processes, littering practices in shipping, etc. The MARPOL Convention is the legal instrument of reference on the problem from the standpoint of shipping. Before addressing MARPOL, it is essential to explore basic definitions and the overall legal framework at the international level.

5.2 Key terms and definitions

The key concepts which follow borrow elements both from the area of discharge of garbage through ship's operation (MARPOL Annex V) and dumping of wastes

---

5 See Article 1, para. 8 of the London Protocol. As it will be seen later on, this instrument addressed the question of dumping of wastes on the basis of a general prohibition of dumping of wastes, which is complemented by a list of wastes that may be considered for dumping.

6 See Article 2 of the Basel Convention.

7 Article 1 and Annexes I, III, VIII and IX of the Basel Convention. See K. Kummer Peiry, 'Basel Convention on the Control of Transboundary Movements of Hazardous Wastes and their Disposal' [2010] United Nations Audiovisual Library of International Law. In relation to household waste and incinerator ash, see Article 1 and Annex II.

8 European Parliament and Council Directive (EC) 2008/98 of the 19 November 2008 on waste and repealing certain Directives (The 2008 Waste Framework Directive) (Text with EEA relevance) [2008] (OJ L312).

at sea from sources other than ship's operation (1972 London Convention and 1996 London Protocol).

Garbage	Garbage is given a specific meaning by the IMO.[9] It means all kinds of food wastes (i.e. spoiled or unspoiled food substances), domestic wastes (i.e. wastes not covered by other MARPOL Annexes generated in the accommodation spaces aboard) and operational wastes (i.e. all solid wastes not covered by other MARPOL Annexes collected aboard during normal maintenance or operations of a ship or used for cargo stowage and handling), plastics in any form (including incinerator ashes from plastic products), cargo residues (i.e. remnants of cargo which remain on the deck or in the holds following loading or unloading and that they are not covered by other MARPOL Annexes), cooking oil, fishing gear, and animal carcasses generated during the normal operation of the ship and liable to be disposed of continuously or periodically. The substances that are defined or listed in other Annexes to MARPOL do not fall in the above-mentioned definition according to the Resolution (IMO Resolution MEPC.201(62)).
Garbage management	In our context, "management" broadly means the collection, transport and disposal of wastes. Garbage management includes numerous aspects: they range from waste minimisation to shipboard handling, garbage collection and processing to storage and discharge. In the shipping context, IMO 2012 Guidelines for the Implementation of MARPOL Annex V provide[10] elements of garbage management.
Grey water	Grey water, according to 2012 Guidelines for the Implementation of MARPOL Annex V, is not included in the definition of garbage. Grey water is described by the instrument as drainage from dishwater, shower, laundry, bath and washbasin drains.
Sewage	Sewage from ships' operation is a distinct subject matter and is regulated by MARPOL Annex IV. Consequently, drainage from toilets, urinals, hospitals, and animal spaces does not fall in the scope of definition of garbage as set out in MARPOL Annex V. The 1972 London Convention[11] and the 1996 London Protocol, as amended, which pertain to dumping (see the definition of dumping below – dumping not including the disposal at sea of wastes or other matter incidental to or derived from the normal operations of vessels) address sewage sludge which does not derive from ship's operations. For example, sewage sludge may be considered for dumping under Annex I of the Protocol.

---

9 See IMO Resolution MEPC.201(62) adopted on 15 July 2011 entitled 'Amendments to the Annex of the Protocol of 1978 Relating to the International Convention for the Prevention of Pollution from Ships, 1973' (Revised MARPOL Annex V).

10 Resolution MEPC.219(63) adopted 2 March 2012.

11 Convention on the Prevention of Marine Pollution by Dumping of Wastes and Other Matter 1972.

Wastes	From a legal standpoint, the definition of the term "waste" is very broad. In the context of the 1972 London Convention, and the 1996 London Protocol, as amended, "wastes and other matter" means "material and substance of any kind, form or description".
	In the Annex I of the 1972 London Convention a list of prohibited wastes is set out which notably includes persistent plastics, crude oil and its wastes, radioactive wastes, materials in whatever form (e.g. solids, liquids, etc.) produced for biological and chemical warfare, industrial waste, i.e. waste material generated by manufacturing or processing operations, etc.
	According to the 1996 London Protocol, examples of wastes (or other matter) that may be considered for dumping are the following, namely: dredged material, sewage sludge, fish waste or material resulting from fish processing operations, vessels and platforms or other man-made structures at sea, etc.
	In the context of the so-called Basel Convention on the control of transboundary movements of hazardous wastes and their disposal, wastes are defined as substances or objects which are disposed of or are intended to be disposed of or are required to be disposed of by the provisions of national law.
	In the context of shipping and IMO instruments: the term "waste" is not defined in the IMO Resolution MEPC.201(62) of 15 July 2011 revising MARPOL Annex V. Nor does the IMO Resolution MEPC. 219(63) adopted on 2 March 2012 containing the 2012 Guidelines for the Implementation of MARPOL Annex V provide such a definition. Resolution MEPC.201(62) defines "operational wastes' (see below).
Operational wastes	According to the IMO instrument revising MARPOL Annex V on garbage (MEPC.201(62)), the term signifies all solid wastes, including slurries, not covered by other MARPOL Annexes collected onboard during normal maintenance or operations of a vessel or used for cargo stowage and handling.
	It should be noted that according to the same source, the term is extended so as to include cleaning agents and additives contained in cargo hold and external wash water.
	"Operational wastes" do not include according to relevant Resolution grey water or bilge water.
ISO 21070	Standard for the management and handling of shipboard garbage; it outlines best management practices for shipboard garbage management.
Dumping	The 1972 London Convention and the 1996 London Protocol, as amended, point to similar features in the definition of dumping. However, the Protocol goes further by including additional items in the definition.
	More specifically, under both instruments dumping is defined as any deliberate disposal into the sea of wastes or other matter from vessels, aircraft, platforms or other man-made structures at sea. Dumping also includes, according to both instruments, any deliberate disposal at sea of vessels, aircraft, platforms or other man-made structures at sea.

	Under the 1996 Protocol, dumping also includes the following: – any storage of wastes or other matter in the seabed and the subsoil thereof from vessels, platforms, etc.; and – any abandonment or toppling at site of platforms or other man-made structures at sea, for the sole purpose of deliberate disposal. Under both instruments dumping does not include (amongst others) the disposal at sea of wastes or other matter "incidental to, or derived from the normal operations of vessels, aircraft, platforms or other man-made structures at sea and their equipment […]".
Port reception facility	It generally means any facility capable of receiving ship-generated wastes or cargo residues. It can be fixed (e.g. ashore), floating or mobile. The problem of the adequacy of port reception facilities is deeply connected with the effective application of existing requirements on garbage.
Special area	These are sea areas where due to varied reasons (e.g. ecological, etc.) "special mandatory methods" apply. There are "designated" special areas under MARPOL V (e.g. Baltic Sea, North Sea, etc.). Most of them are also effective.
Cargo residues	Remnants of cargo which remain on the deck or in the holds following loading/unloading or entrained in wash water, not falling into the scope of other MARPOL Annexes. According to Resolution MEPC.201(62), cargo dust remaining on the deck after sweeping or dust on the external surfaces of the ship is not included in the definition of cargo residues.
Transboundary movement	In the context of the so-called Basel Convention which is discussed below it means any movement of hazardous wastes or other wastes from an area under the national jurisdiction of one State to or through an area under the national jurisdiction of another State or to or through an area not under the national jurisdiction of any State, provided at least two States are involved in the movement.

SECTION 2: GENERAL (NON-SHIPPING SPECIFIC) REGULATORY FRAMEWORK

5.3 Legislative background and discussion

There are numerous international instruments of a legal nature governing solid wastes. The instrument of reference for shipping is MARPOL Convention, Annex V. However, the interest of the other texts is noteworthy for at least two reasons: Firstly, they complement environmental protection through additional subjects, including land-based pollution or non-shipping sources and aspects of marine pollution other than those regulated by MARPOL Annex V; secondly, in some cases there is clearly a synergy between a regional or subject-specific instrument and generally recognised rules such as MARPOL Annex V. For example, in the case of the Jeddah Convention (1982) (see table above), it is set out that the Contracting Parties shall take all appropriate measures in line with the Convention

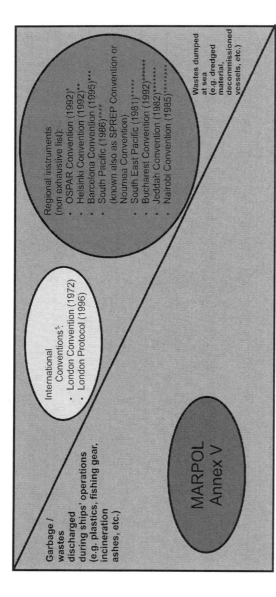

Figure 5.1 Regulation of discharges and dumping at sea (non-exhaustive list of related instruments)

and "with generally recognized international rules" to prevent, abate and combat pollution in the sea area caused by intentional or accidental discharges from ships and shall ensure effective compliance in the sea area with generally recognised rules relating to the control of this type of pollution including load-on-top, segregated ballast and crude oil wasting procedures from tankers.[12] Additional articles in the case of the Jeddah Convention pertain to pollution caused by dumping from ships and aircraft, pollution from land-based sources, pollution resulting from exploration and exploitation of the bed of the territorial sea, the continental shelf and the sub-soil, pollution from other human activities, etc.[13]

In the limited confines of this chapter, we have chosen to place the focus on the legal regime governing dumping of waste and the transboundary movements of hazardous wastes and their disposal as well as on MARPOL Annex V on regulation of discharges of garbage at sea.

5.3.1 In relation to marine pollution from dumping of wastes

Unregulated dumping of waste at sea in the 1960s and 1970s was one of the problems that the 1972 Convention on the Prevention of Marine Pollution by Dumping of Wastes and Other Matter, commonly referred to as the London Convention, sought to remedy.

Before discussing further the Convention, mention of Article 210 of UNCLOS III would be useful. As already mentioned in other chapters, UNCLOS III is the instrument of reference in international law of the sea, and was adopted ten years after the 1972 Convention. UNCLOS III implicitly reflects the 1972 instrument on waste by requiring that national regulation must not be less effective than the rules and standards set globally.[14] Against this background, Article 210 deals with pollution by dumping. States are held to adopt provisions for preventing, reducing and controlling pollution of the marine environment by dumping; they must also take other measures, as necessary. Furthermore, States, according to the same provision "shall endeavour to establish global and regional rules, standards and recommended practices and procedures to prevent, reduce and control such pollution"; the same provision also sets out synergies between coastal States sharing interests because of their geographical situation, and provides that domestic regulations must not be "less effective in preventing, reducing and controlling such pollution than the global rules and standards".

In this context, the London Convention 1972 (entry into force on 30 August 1975) constitutes an important tool for the protection of the marine environment from dumping of waste and other matter "that is liable to create hazards to human health, to harm living resources and marine life, to damage amenities

---

12 See Article IV on Pollution from Ships.

13 See Article V *seq.*

14 Birnie and Boyle, *International Law* (1992, p. 320), cited in Olav Schram Stokke, 'Beyond Dumping? The Effectiveness of the London Convention' [1998/99] Yearbook of International Co-operation on Environment and Development, p 40.

or to interfere with other legitimate uses of the sea".[15] It is noteworthy that the instrument acknowledges the duty of the States "to promote the effective control of all sources of pollution of the marine environment".[16] The term "dumping" is defined by the Convention as the deliberate disposal at sea of wastes and other matter from vessels, aircraft, platforms or other man-made structures. The term also includes the deliberate disposal at sea, amongst others, of vessels or platforms.

According to the IMO, dredged material constitutes about 80–90% of all reported dumped material, and 250 to 500 million tonnes of dredged material are dumped annually on a worldwide basis in waters which fall in the scope of the London Convention; 10% of this dredged material is reported to be contaminated from shipping, industrial and municipal discharges, and land run-off.[17] Sewage sludge, decommissioned vessels, organic materials (e.g. food and beverage processing wastes), fish wastes and mining wastes are additional materials dumped in the oceans.[18]

THE LONDON 1972 CONVENTION

The rationale of the London Convention reflects a blend of prohibited and allowed actions, which take into account the classifications and prescriptions set out by its Annexes.[19]
More specifically, there is:

- Prohibition of dumping of specified wastes or other matter in the so-called "black list" the Convention sets out in Annex I the dumping of wastes for which no permit may be granted (e.g. organohalogen compounds; mercury and mercury compounds; crude oil and its wastes, refined petroleum products, petroleum, distillate residues, and any mixtures containing any of these, taken on board for the purpose of dumping; persistent plastics, radioactive wastes, materials produced for chemical warfare, etc.).
- Permission of dumping of specified wastes (or other matter) upon prior special permit – relevant items here "require special care" and constitute what is referred to as the "grey list". The Convention sets out in Annex II the dumping of wastes or other matter requiring prior special permit; "special permit" according to the Convention means the permission granted specifically on application in advance in line with related Annexes; and
- Prior general permit-related dumping of other wastes (or other matter). General permit means permission granted in advance in line with Annex III.

The characteristics and composition of the matter (e.g. total amount and average composition of matter dumped over a specific period, the form, etc.), the features of

---

15 See Article I of the Convention.
16 *Ibid.*
17 IMO/HELCOM Regional Workshop for Promotion of the London Protocol and Helsinki Convention, Coenen R./IMO, 'London Convention and Protocol: Introduction, Achievements and Points for Comparison' [2011], Tallinn/Estonia, 6–8 April 2011.
18 *Ibid.*
19 See Article IV.

> dumping site and deposit method (e.g. location, rate of disposal per specific period, etc,), and general considerations and conditions (e.g. possible effects on amenities, possible effects on marine life, etc.) are set out in Annex III of the Convention.
>
> The Convention is not so detailed as the 1996 Protocol about dispute resolution. It provides in Articles X and XI that the Contracting Parties undertake to develop procedures for the assessment of State liability for damage to the environment of other States or to any other area of the environment, and the settlement of disputes concerning dumping. Procedures for the settlement of disputes in relation to the interpretation and application of the Convention were to be considered by the Contracting Parties in the process.
>
> In addition to the above, a number of resolutions were adopted by State Parties to the Convention banning incineration at sea of industrial wastes and dumping into sea of low-level radioactive wastes and setting out the phasing out of dumping of industrial wastes at sea.
>
> Commentators point to a number of challenges in relation to the Convention. Some of the challenges include the degree and quality of implementation.

A protocol introducing amendments, known as the London Protocol, which was adopted in 1996 with a view to eventually replacing the Convention, entered into force on 24 March 2006. The Protocol, which has been subject to a few amendments, is more restrictive than the Convention. The rationale of the Protocol is that all dumping is prohibited unless expressly permitted. Possibly acceptable wastes are included in the so-called "reverse list", and require permit. States that have ratified the Convention include the USA, the Russian Federation, Brazil, and other countries. The Protocol has been ratified, amongst others, by Australia, China, Japan, Canada, the UK, etc.

> ## THE 1996 LONDON PROTOCOL, AS AMENDED[20]
>
> Adopting a precautionary approach to the problem of marine pollution, which was complemented by the polluter-pays principle, the 1996 London Protocol had as a departing point a prohibition. According to Article 4, the Parties to the Convention have the obligation to prohibit dumping of any wastes or other matter with the exception of those listed in Annex 1 (this is the so-called "reverse list" containing possibly acceptable waste). "Sea", which was defined in the London Convention as all marine waters other than internal waters of States is given a broader meaning here, and also includes the seabed and the subsoil.
>
> However, dumping of wastes or other matter included in Annex 1 requires a permit, which will have to be granted in advance and in accordance with specified measures.
>
> Transfer of damage (or likelihood of damage) from one part of the environment to another (or transformation of one type of pollution into another) is put under control, as

---

20 As of 9 February 2016, the London Protocol was amended in 2006, 2009 and 2013.

Contracting Parties are held to act so as not to effect such transfers.[21] Furthermore, Contracting States are held to prohibit incineration at sea.[22] Export of wastes to other countries for dumping or incineration at sea purposes is also prohibited.[23] Reporting,[24] compliance[25] and technical cooperation[26] are additional aspects addressed by the Protocol.

Concerning application, it is noteworthy that the Protocol operates on more than one level and it involves the flag, port and coastal State. More specifically, a Contracting Party (State) is held to apply the measures required under the instrument to:[27]

- all vessels and aircraft registered in its territory or flying its flag;
- all vessels and aircraft loading in its territory the wastes or other matter to be dumped or incinerated at sea;
- all vessels, aircraft and platforms/structures believed to be engaged in dumping or incineration at sea in areas within which it has jurisdiction under international law.

Annex 2 addresses the assessment of wastes or other matter that may be considered for dumping. It is noted that "the acceptance of dumping under certain circumstances shall not remove the obligations under this Annex to make further attempts to reduce the necessity for dumping".[28] In this context, the main axes of the Annex are the following:

- waste prevention audit;
- consideration of waste management options;
- chemical, physical and biological properties;
- action list;
- dump-site selection;
- assessment of potential effects;
- monitoring;
- permit and permit conditions.

Having seen the main framework, the next thing to mention is settlement of disputes.[29] The Protocol states that disputes concerning the interpretation or application of the instrument shall be resolved in the first instance through negotiation, mediation or conciliation, "or other peaceful means chosen by Parties to the dispute". The Protocol does not define the meaning of the terms "mediation" or "conciliation" (it is noted that conciliation is addressed in Annex V of UNCLOS 1982). In the context where no resolution is possible within, in principle, 12 months after one Contracting Party has notified another that a dispute exists between them, the difference will be subjected to the arbitral procedure set out in Annex 3 of the Protocol. Article 16 also sets out the alternative of using the procedures provided by the United Nations Convention on the Law of the Sea.[30] The Arbitral Tribunal "decides its own rules of

---

21 Article 3.3.
22 Article 5.
23 Article 6.
24 Article 9.
25 Article 11.
26 Article 13.
27 Article 10(1).
28 Para. 1, Annex 2.
29 Article 16.
30 See Article 16(2) of the Protocol which mentions Article 287(1) of UNCLOS III.

procedure".[31] It is held, in principle, to render a reasoned award within five months from the time of its establishment. This is a final award without appeal. The Annex says in Article 9 (of Annex 3) that the arbitral award shall be communicated to the Secretary-General who shall inform the Contracting Parties, and "the Parties to the dispute shall immediately comply with the award".

The 1996 London Protocol has been subject to amendments, which triggered the adoption of a number of guidelines.

In addition to the above, in 2006, an amendment was adopted in relation to the sequestration of CO_2 streams and their storage in sub-seabed geological formations (entry into force on 10 February 2007).[32] At its simplest, the question of carbon dioxide capture and storage is commonly associated with the effort on the mitigation of the climate impact from burning of fossil fuels and industrial processes through permanent storage in underground geological formations and aquifers.[33]

Carbon dioxide streams from carbon dioxide capture processes for sequestration is included in the reverse list contained in Annex 1 alongside the other items that may be considered for dumping.

A further amendment on CO_2 export was adopted in 2009. It may be recalled on this point that, according to Article 6, export of wastes or other matter to other countries for dumping or incineration at sea is prohibited. The amendment, which has not entered into force yet, adds a second paragraph to Article 6. It sets out that the "export of CO2 for disposal in accordance with Annex 1 may occur, provided an agreement or arrangement has been entered into by countries concerned".

Having touched upon the basic points of a huge subject, the next thing to note as a general remark is that the Convention and the Protocol function as global instruments for the control of more than one source of marine pollution, which can be viewed as a positive thing for marine environment protection; while the regime set out is complex, it can clearly be viewed as contributing to stopping unregulated dumping by subjecting dumping to a licensing regime. Some of the challenges ahead are the need for wider participation on the part of States and the need for further compliance; both challenges would require more technical, legal and administrative support.[34]

---

31 Article 7, Annex 3.

32 See the additions resulting in para. 1.8 and para. 4 in Annex 1. On carbon dioxide capture and storage, a user-friendly resource for the understanding of the subject is Intergovernmental Panel on Climate Change (IPCC) Special Report 'Summary for Policymakers -A Special Report of Working Group III of the Intergovernmental Panel on Climate Change' [2005].

33 www.greenpeace.org/international/en/campaigns/climate-change/coal/carbon-capture-and-storage/ (last visit 18 March 2016).

34 Relevant to this point is the report 'Barriers to Compliance', Final Report, LC 29/INF.2 cited in David L. Vander Zwaag and Anne Daniel, 'International Law and Ocean Dumping: Steering a Precautionary Course Aboard the 1996 London Protocol, but Still an Unfinished Voyage; in The Future of Ocean Regime' Aldo Chircop, Ted L. MacDorman, Susan J. Rolston (eds), *Building Essays in Tribute to Douglas M. Johnston* (Martinus Nijhoff Publishers, Leiden/Boston 2009) p. 546.

Before the discussion on MARPOL Annex V, let us touch upon an additional instrument which is not proper to shipping. This is the so-called Basel Convention.

5.3.2 In relation to transboundary movements of hazardous wastes and their disposal

Hazardous wastes have the potential to impair human health, the environment or both. The management of hazardous wastes, i.e. the collection, transport and disposal of hazardous wastes, including after-care of disposal sites, presents an interest to marine pollution control. In the absence of appropriate measures, substances subject to transboundary movement may end up at sea. A number of cases on the deposit of toxic wastes in developing countries imported from abroad had prompted in the 1980s the awakening of the environmental dimension of the problem and contributed to the involvement of the international regulator.[35] Broad categories of wastes are concerned by the Basel Convention. They range from wastes originated from production processes to wastes stemming from medical care in hospitals or domestic garbage. Among hazardous wastes, there are by-products that are explosive, flammable, radioactive or liable to spontaneous combustion, or wastes containing harmful compounds such as mercury, lead, etc.[36]

The Convention regulates specified categories of hazardous wastes. It can be viewed as the leading international instrument in this area.[37] The Basel Convention was adopted in 1989 and entered into force on 5 May 1992. It sets out general obligations for its Contracting Parties, including prior written consent of the State of import.[38] It is noted that the Convention also regulates wastes collected from households and residues stemming from incineration of household wastes, if they are subject to transboundary movement. Radioactive wastes do not fall in the scope of the Convention. So are excluded wastes stemming from the normal operation of ships covered by international conventions.

It is essential to stress that the Convention concerns transboundary movements of hazardous wastes, i.e. movements of wastes across international frontiers (see the definition of "transboundary movement" under para 5.2 above). The right of every party to prohibit the import of hazardous wastes or other wastes for disposal is also set out.

---

35 Also see the Rotterdam Convention on the Prior Informed Consent Procedure for Certain Hazardous Chemicals and Pesticides in International Trade (adopted in 1998; entry into force 24 February 2004), and the Stockholm Convention on Persistent Organic Pollutants (adopted in 2001; entry into force on 17 May 2004).

36 See UNEP Training Manual on Environmental Law, Chapter 11 on Hazardous Wastes, p 125 *et seq.*

37 See Katharina Kummer Peiry, 'Basel Convention on the Control of Transboundary Movements of Hazardous Wastes and Their Disposal' United Nations Audiovisual Library of International Law [2010] (www.un.org/law/avl); Katharina Kummer Peiry, *International Management of Hazardous Wastes: The Basel Convention and Related Legal Rules* (Oxford University Press, Oxford, 1995/99). Also note additional documents relating to the Basel Convention available at: www.basel. int.

38 See Article 4 of the Convention.

ARTICLE 1

SCOPE OF THE CONVENTION

1. The following wastes that are subject to transboundary movement shall be "hazardous wastes" for the purposes of this Convention:

   (a) Wastes that belong to any category contained in Annex I, unless they do not possess any of the characteristics contained in Annex III; and

   (b) Wastes that are not covered under paragraph (a) but are defined as, or are considered to be, hazardous wastes by the domestic legislation of the Party of export, import or transit.

2. Wastes that belong to any category contained in Annex II that are subject to transboundary movement shall be "other wastes" for the purposes of this Convention.

3. Wastes which, as a result of being radioactive, are subject to other international control systems, including international instruments, applying specifically to radioactive materials, are excluded from the scope of this Convention.

4. Wastes which derive from the normal operations of a ship, the discharge of which is covered by another international instrument, are excluded from the scope of this Convention.

The main axes of the instrument are spread over the following:

- reduction of hazardous wastes generation;
- promotion of environmentally sound management of hazardous wastes;
- subjecting transboundary movements of hazardous wastes to restrictions;
- regulating permissible transboundary movements of hazardous wastes.

Adopted in 1995, the "Ban Amendment",[39] which has not entered into force, prohibits the export of all hazardous wastes which fall in the scope of the Convention intended for final disposal, reuse, recycling and recovery from countries listed in Annex VII to the Convention (broadly speaking, developed countries) to all other countries.

Furthermore, the Basel Protocol on Liability[40] which was adopted in 1999 and not in force yet, governs civil liability for damage resulting from the said transboundary movements, including their different stages.

It can be said that even though the international system has not opted for the absolute prohibition of transboundary movements of hazardous wastes, existing international regulations set out a regime which seeks to control such movements. The effectiveness of the controls depends, however, on numerous factors: some

---

39 Amendment to the Convention on the Control of Transboundary Movements of Hazardous Wastes and Their Disposal.

40 Basel Protocol on Liability and Compensation for Damage Resulting from Transboundary Movements of Hazardous Wastes and their Disposal.

of them pertain to the ratification of the instrument by States in order to make it applicable in national legal systems; other factors pertain to the quality of implementation and the necessary oversight.

Up to this point, we have touched upon the regimes on wastes which do not specifically pertain to shipping operations – even though some of them may not exclude shipping from their scope. Let us now examine in a little greater detail how the main instrument which governs marine pollution control from shipping addresses the challenges raised by the discharges of garbage from ship operation. This is where MARPOL Annex V comes into play.[41]

SECTION 3: MARPOL ANNEX V REGULATIONS FOR THE PREVENTION OF POLLUTION BY GARBAGE FROM SHIPS

5.4 General discussion and overview

MARPOL Annex V is the international instrument of reference on marine pollution by garbage from ships. It is noted that this Annex is optional for Member States, as according to Article 14 of MARPOL Convention, "A State may at the time of signing, ratifying, accepting, approving or acceding to the present Convention declare that it does not accept any one or all of Annexes III, IV and V (hereinafter referred to as 'Optional Annexes') of the present Convention. Subject to the above, Parties to the Convention shall be bound by any Annex in its entirety."

The Annex entered into force on 31 December 1988. It is noted from the outset that IMO Resolution MEPC.201(62), dated 15 July 2011, revised MARPOL Annex V (entry into force on 1 January 2013). Concerning the term garbage, in the meaning of the Annex, it does not comprise the substances defined or listed in other MARPOL Annexes. Furthermore, when garbage is mixed with or contaminated by other substances prohibited from discharge or which are subject to different discharge requirements, the more stringent requirements shall apply.

The amendments introduced by MEPC.201(62) entered into force through the tacit acceptance procedure. As you may recall, this is the procedure which facilitates a realistic speed in the entry into force of IMO amendments. It can be viewed in simple terms as operating "by default". In other terms, amendments to IMO instruments are considered to have been accepted by a specified date, unless not less than a specified number of the Parties (i.e. States) or Parties the combined merchant fleets of which constitute not less than a specified percentage of the gross tonnage of the international merchant fleet, have expressed their objection to the amendments.

The Annex to the Resolution is, technically speaking, the "tool" of said revision. It is made up of a number of regulations which deal with the matter, and an Appendix which includes the form of the garbage record book which will be touched upon below. Resolution MEPC.201(62) is complemented, amongst others, by:

---

41 See IMO MARPOL Annex V, Discharge Provisions (2017 Edition, London).

- MEPC.Resolution 219(63) of 2 March 2012 containing the 2012 Guidelines for the Implementation of MARPOL Annex V **(The 2017 Guidelines for the Implementation of MARPOL Annex V, adopted on 7 July 2017, and Resolution MEPC.277(70) on the Amendments to MARPOL Annex V (HME substances and form of Garbage Record Book) are to be noted but are not discussed in the chapter)**; and
- MEPC.Resolution 220(63) of the same date, containing the 2012 Guidelines for the Development of Garbage Management Plans.

Attention should be drawn to the continued review of IMO legislation through amendments stemming from the MEPC, and the alertness needed with regard to applicable international legislation.

Against this background, let us touch upon some key regulations. The definition of key terms is given in regulation 1. The following terms are defined by the instrument (you can consult directly MEPC.201(62); the glossary under para 5.2 above describes some selected concepts). The categories below stem from the form of garbage record book (Appendix to Resolution MEPC.201(62)).

- Plastics
- food wastes
- domestic wastes (e.g. aluminium soft drink cans)
- cooking oil
- incinerator ashes
- operational wastes (e.g. ash and clinkers from shipboard operations and coal-burning boilers; steel wire for timber packaging; oily rags, etc.)
- animal carcasses
- fishing gear
- cargo residues

The Annex has a broad material scope, as it applies to all ships.[42]

The departing point in the revised Annex is a general prohibition of discharge of garbage into the sea.[43] Once this general prohibition is set out, some exceptions are provided by the instrument, which operate under conditions. It is noteworthy, that fixed or floating platforms, i.e. structures located at sea which are engaged in the exploration, exploitation or associated offshore processing of sea-bed mineral resources – discussed in another chapter of the book – are also included in the scope of the instrument. The summary of applicable legal regime as it stems from MEPC.219(63) is set out in Table No. 1 of the 2012 Guidelines (see below), and it is helpful for the understanding of the matter in addition to the provisions themselves which should always be the reference.

Some of the challenges raised for shipowners/operators go into different directions: regulatory compliance, environmentally sound garbage management,

---

42 Revised MARPOL Annex V, regulation 2.
43 Revised MARPOL Annex V, regulation 3.

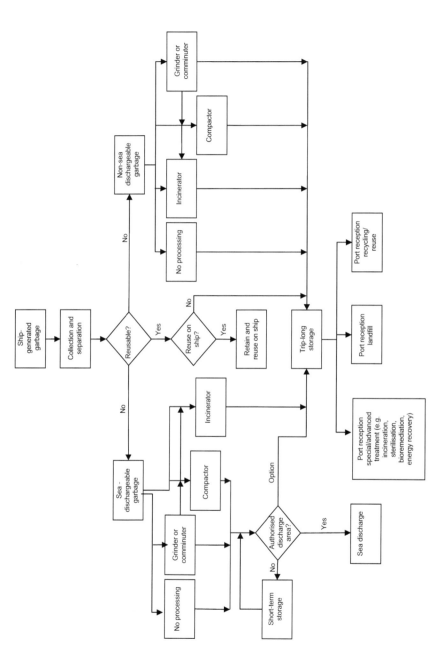

Graph 5.3 Options for shipboard handling and discharge of garbage
Source: MEPC.219(63)

Table 5.1 Summary of restrictions to the discharge of garbage into the sea under regulations 4, 5 and 6 of MARPOL Annex V

Garbage type[1]	All ships except platforms[4]		Offshore platforms located more than 12 nm from nearest land and ships when alongside or within 500 metres of such platforms[4] Regulation 5
	Outside special areas Regulation 4 (Distances are from the nearest land)	Within special areas Regulation 6 (Distances are from nearest land or nearest ice-shelf)	
Food waste comminuted or ground[2]	≥3 nm, en route and as far as practicable	≥12 nm, en route and as far as practicable[3]	Discharge permitted
Food waste not comminuted or ground	≥12 nm, en route and as far as practicable	Discharge prohibited	Discharge prohibited
Cargo residues[5,6] not contained in washwater	≥12 nm, en route and as far as practicable	Discharge prohibited	Discharge prohibited
Cargo residues[5,6] contained in washwater		≥12 nm, en route and as far as practicable (subject to conditions in regulation 6.1.2)	
Cleaning agents and additives[6] contained in cargo hold washwater	Discharge permitted	≥12 nm, en route and as far as practicable (subject to conditions in regulation 6.1.2)	Discharge prohibited
Cleaning agents and additives[6] in deck and external surfaces washwater	Discharge permitted		
Animal Carcasses (should be split or otherwise treated to ensure the carcasses will sink immediately)	Must be en route and as far from the nearest land as possible. Should be >100 nm and maximum water depth	Discharge prohibited	Discharge prohibited
All other garbage including plastics, synthetic ropes, fishing gear, plastic garbage bags, incinerator ashes, clinkers, cooking oil, floating dunnage, lining and packing materials, paper, rags, glass, metal, bottles, crockery and similar refuse	Discharge prohibited	Discharge prohibited	Discharge prohibited

1 When garbage is mixed with or contaminated by other harmful substances prohibited from discharge or having different discharge requirements, the more stringent requirements shall apply.

2 Comminuted or ground food wastes must be able to pass through a screen with mesh no larger than 25 mm.

3 The discharge of introduced avian products in the Antarctic area is not permitted unless incinerated, autoclaved or otherwise treated to be made sterile.

4 Offshore platforms located 12 nm from nearest land and associated ships include all fixed or floating platforms engaged in exploration or exploitation or associated processing of seabed mineral resources, and all ships alongside or within 500 m of such platforms.

5 Cargo residues means only those cargo residues that cannot be recovered using commonly available methods for unloading.

6 These substances must not be harmful to the marine environment.

Note: The table is intended as a summary reference. The provisions in MARPOL Annex V, as amended, Table 5.1, prevail. Our note to readers: The 2017 Guidelines for the Implementation of MARPOL Annex V should be noted.

Source: MEPC.219(63) (adopted 2 March 2012)

restraints relating to costs, etc. In this respect, a combination of approaches may be adopted, comprising, amongst others, reduction at source, reuse or recycling, onboard processing, limited discharge of garbage at sea, wherever this is legal, and appropriate use of port reception facilities. In the graph below the options for shipboard handling and discharge of garbage can be identified.

5.5 Key management issues, including documentation

There are three important documents (non-exhaustive list) which support the system established by the revised Annex, and which are described below. These are the following, namely:

- Garbage Management Plan;
- Garbage Record Book;
- placards.

5.5.1 Garbage Management Plan

Garbage Management Plans aboard constitute a mandatory requirement. They are set out in the amendments to the Annex (Resolution MEPC.201(62)) and they are specifically addressed in the 2012 Guidelines for the Development of Garbage Management Plans.[44]
Regulation 10.2 of revised MARPOL Annex V stipulates that:

- every ship of 100 gross tonnage and above; and
- every ship certified to carry 15 or more persons; and
- fixed or floating platforms

shall carry a garbage management plan "which the crew shall follow".
The Plan must set out written procedures for the following:

- minimising;
- collecting;
- storing;
- processing;
- disposing of garbage; and
- training.

The use of the equipment on board must also be provided for.
As already mentioned, according to the same provision, the crew shall follow relevant Plan, which must be based on relevant IMO guidelines and must be written in the working language of the crew. Furthermore, the Plan shall designate the person or persons in charge of carrying it out.

---

44 MEPC.220(63) of 2 March 2012.

An effective Garbage Management Plan requires that it is practical and easy for use. Those with related functions aboard must be acquainted with it; furthermore, alike all documents aboard which pertain to regulatory compliance, it must be constantly reviewed and updated, and put to the test at regular intervals.

5.5.2 Placards

The obligation to display placards which notify the crew and passengers of the key discharge requirements of Annex V is provided for ships of 12 m or more in length overall and fixed or floating platforms.[45] It is provided that the placards shall be written in the working language of the ship's crew. Furthermore, for ships on voyages to ports or offshore terminals under the jurisdiction of other Contracting Parties to the Convention, it is required by the same provision that the placard shall also be in English, French or Spanish.

Table 5.2 Sample placard targeting crew and shipboard operations

Discharge of all garbage into the sea is prohibited except provided otherwise
The MARPOL Convention and domestic law prohibit the discharge of most garbage from ships. Only the following garbage types are allowed to be discharged and under the specified conditions.
Outside Special Areas designated under MARPOL Annex V:

- Comminuted or ground food wastes (capable of passing through a screen with openings no larger than 25 millimetres) may be discharged not less than 3 nautical miles from the nearest land.
- Other food wastes may be discharged not less than 12 nautical miles from the nearest land.
- Cargo residues classified as not harmful to the marine environment may be discharged not less than 12 nautical miles from the nearest land.
- Cleaning agents or additives in cargo hold, deck and external surfaces washing water may be discharged only if they are not harmful to the marine environment.
- With the exception of discharging cleaning agents in washing water, the ship must be en route and as far as practicable from the nearest land.

Inside Special Areas designated under MARPOL Annex V

- More stringent discharge requirements apply for the discharges of food wastes and cargo residues; AND
- Consult Annex V and the shipboard garbage management plan for details.

For all areas of the sea, ships carrying specialized cargos such as live animals or solid bulk cargoes should consult Annex V and the associated Guidelines for the implementation of Annex V.
Discharge of any type of garbage must be entered in the Garbage Record Book
Violation of these requirements may result in penalties.

Source: MEPC.219(63)

---

45 See revised MARPOL Annex V, regulation 10.

Table 5.3 Sample placard targeting fixed or floating platforms and ships operating within 500 metres of such platforms

Discharge of all garbage into the sea is prohibited except provided otherwise
The MARPOL Convention and domestic law prohibit the discharge of all garbage into the sea from fixed or floating platforms and from all other ships when alongside or within 500 metres of such platforms.
Exception: Comminuted or ground food wastes may be discharge from fixed or floating platforms located more than 12 miles from the nearest land and from all other ships when alongside or within 500 metres of such platforms.
Comminuted or ground food wastes must be capable of passing through a screen no larger than 25 millimetres.
Discharge of any type of garbage must be entered in the Garbage Record Book
Violation of these requirements may result in penalties.

Source: MEPC.219(63)

5.5.3 Garbage Record Book

In addition to the above, regulation 10 paragraph 3 sets out garbage record-keeping. Every ship of 400 gross tonnage and above and every ship which is certified to carry 15 or more persons engaged in voyages to ports or offshore terminals under the jurisdiction of another Party to the Convention and every fixed or floating platform shall be provided with a Garbage Record Book. The form of the latter is specified in the appendix to Annex V. It can be a part of the ship's official log-book or otherwise.

EXTRACT FROM REGULATION 10 PARAGRAPH 3

3 [...]

.1 Each discharge into the sea or to a reception facility, or a completed incineration, shall be promptly recorded in the Garbage Record Book and signed for on the date of the discharge or incineration by the officer in charge. Each completed page of the Garbage Record Book shall be signed by the master of the ship. The entries in the Garbage Record Book shall be at least in English, French or Spanish. Where the entries are also made in an official language of the State whose flag the ship is entitled to fly, the entries in that language shall prevail in case of a dispute or discrepancy;

.2 The entry for each discharge or incineration shall include date and time, position of the ship, category of the garbage and the estimated amount discharged or incinerated;

.3 The Garbage Record Book shall be kept on board the ship or the fixed or floating platform, and in such a place as to be readily available for inspection at all reasonable times. This document shall be preserved for a period of at least two years from the date of the last entry made in it;

.4 In the event of any discharge or accidental loss referred to in regulation 7 of this Annex an entry shall be made in the Garbage Record Book, or in the case of any ship of less than 400 gross tonnage, an entry shall be made in the ship's official log-book, of the location, circumstances of, and the reasons for the discharge or loss, details of the items discharged or lost, and the reasonable precautions taken to prevent or minimize such discharge of accidental loss.

4   The Administration may waive the requirements for Garbage Record Book for:

.1 Any ship engaged on voyages of one (1) hour or less in duration which is certified to carry 15 or more persons; or

.2 Fixed or floating platforms.

5   The competent authority of the Government of a Party to the Convention may inspect the Garbage Record Book or ship's official log-book on board any ship to which this regulation applies while the ship is in its ports or offshore terminals and may make a copy of any entry in those books, and may require the master of the ship to certify that the copy is a true copy of such an entry. Any copy so made, which has been certified by the master of the ship as a true copy of an entry in the ship's Garbage Record Book or ship's official log-book, shall be admissible in any judicial proceedings as evidence of the facts stated in the entry. The inspection of a Garbage Record Book or ship's official log-book and the taking of a certified copy by the competent authority under this paragraph shall be performed as expeditiously as possible without causing the ship to be unduly delayed.

[...]

5.5.4 *Good practices for shipmasters, shipowners and operators*

GOOD PRACTICES FOR SHIPMASTERS, SHIPOWNERS AND OPERATORS

(Extract from Consolidated Guidance for Port Reception Facility Providers and Users, MEPC.1/Circ.834, 15 April 2014)

Considerations prior to delivery of MARPOL residues/wastes ashore

26   Efficient delivery of MARPOL residues/wastes ashore relies on advance planning. The following sections outline ways in which considerations for delivery of MARPOL residues/wastes ashore can be integrated into a ship's operating procedures in order to minimize delays and unexpected costs and improve environmental management practices. Good waste management strategies should be incorporated into voyage planning.

Logistical and commercial arrangements

27   Consideration should be given to the logistical and commercial arrangements which may be specified in shipping contracts (charter party agreements) between ship operators and cargo owners. Such arrangements should take into account the need to discharge MARPOL residues/wastes ashore

to reception facilities and should not compromise, but rather facilitate, the ship operator's ability to comply with obligations under MARPOL. Examples of logistical and commercial considerations might include allowing sufficient time in port to complete transfer of MARPOL residues/wastes and ensuring that disposal costs are accounted for in charter agreements when appropriate. Such considerations are especially important when cargo tank pre-washes are required for certain Annex II residues and when charter agreements specify tank or cargo hold cleaning after discharging cargoes.

Minimization and management of ship-generated residue/waste

28 Although not a direct requirement of MARPOL, minimizing the residue/waste generated on board ships represents an environmental best practice, and should be considered in a ship's overall waste management practices.

29 The most effective way of reducing ship-generated residue/waste is to reduce materials that become waste at the source. Efforts should be made to minimize packaging from ship stores, for example, by establishing an agreement with the supplier to accept the return of the packaging upon delivery, or to reduce the amount of packaging.

30 Developing an agreement with suppliers and manufacturers is not only important for more general waste categories such as plastics, but essential for other maritime specific wastes such as time expired pyrotechnics; used ropes, tails and wires; time expired medicine; and batteries. The supplier and/or manufacturer should be able to provide the specialist facilities for treatment or disposal of these products and materials.

31 Onboard waste management will also assist in minimizing ship-generated waste. Ship operators and shipbuilders should consider further the design of new ships to enhance waste treatment on board and consider introducing operational measures which can improve efficiency for existing ships. Further information on shipboard garbage handling and storage procedures and minimizing the amount of potential garbage is provided in the 2012 Guidelines for the Implementation of MARPOL Annex V (resolution MEPC.219(63)). In addition, an ISO standard for the management and handling of shipboard garbage (ISO 21070:2011) has been developed. For ships of 100 gross tonnage and above, and ships which are certified to carry 15 persons or more, information with regard to onboard management of garbage will also be included in the Garbage Management Plan (2012 Guidelines for the Development of Garbage Management Plans (resolution MEPC.220(63)).

32 In relation to the minimization of oily waste, an increased familiarity with the ship's engine-room treatment systems coupled with the crew's training in oily waste management and recording will assist in reducing the amount of waste produced and improve the overall on-board management of oily waste. The use of the Integrated Bilge Water Treatment System (IBTS) will facilitate segregation of oily waste, allowing for the storage of oil sludge, oil-water mixtures and clean water separately.

MARINE POLLUTION FROM WASTES

33 Ships' crew need to understand the correct use of, and entries to, the Oil Record Book, Cargo Record Book and the Garbage Record Book. This will help to ensure that any management system implemented can be easily monitored and audited. Industry associations such as INTERTANKO and ICS may provide useful guidance on the correct use of such record books.

34 If space permits, onboard waste management plans should take into account the possibility of being able to recycle certain garbage types. The segregation of garbage according to the requirements of MARPOL Annex V (e.g. plastics; food wastes; domestic wastes (e.g. paper products, rags, glass, metal, bottles, crockery, etc.); cooking oil; incinerator ashes; operational wastes; cargo residues; animal carcass(es); fishing gear) should also allow for the delivery of garbage in certain recyclable categories.

35 To facilitate the landing of recyclable residues/waste, ship operators should consider establishing contracts with facilities in ports that are visited on a regular basis. This will fulfil both the need to use a reputable supplier as per most environmental management systems and facilitate the discharge of segregated waste ashore on each port visit. Where appropriate reception facilities for segregated and/or recyclable wastes are not provided in a port, shipowners/operators are encouraged to request that such facilities are developed in conjunction with the recycling capability of the locality or region.

Communication and advance notification

36 Individual ports may need to comply with varying local requirements for specialized handling (such as quarantine) of certain types of MARPOL waste, such as animal, plant and food wastes generated on board the ship. Therefore, ship operators should check with local agents, port authorities, harbour masters or reception facility providers for port-specific requirements prior to arrival in order to plan for and accommodate any special handling requirements for that particular port, including any additional segregation that may need to take place on board well in advance of arrival. This information should be incorporated into the company's environmental management plan and should be taken into consideration in voyage planning.

37 As noted in paragraph 19, IMO's PRF Database, accessible online through the GISIS website, can be a good source of information about the reception facilities available at ports worldwide. Users must first register by creating a username and password.

38 In some ports, for logistical reasons, the providers of port reception facilities may require advance notification from the ship of its intention to use the facilities. Further information on this requirement is provided in section 4 of the Guidelines for ensuring the adequacy of port waste reception facilities (resolution MEPC.83(44)). Providing advance notification to the reception facility of the type and quantity of MARPOL residues/wastes on board and the type and quantity intended to be delivered will greatly assist the reception facility operator in receiving the materials while minimizing any delay to the vessel's normal port operation. General recommended practice is to provide at least 24 hours' notice, although specific require-

ments may vary by reception facility. If a ship visits a port on a regular basis, a standing arrangement with the PRF may prove to be most efficient. Shipmasters are recommended to use the standardized Advance Notification Form as developed by IMO (appendix 2). Port authorities, agents and facility operators are urged to accept the standardized format; however, some operators may require an alternate form.

Considerations during MARPOL residues/wastes delivery

39 During delivery of MARPOL residues/wastes, appropriate procedures as drawn up in the ship's Safety Management System (ISM Code) should be followed.

40 Following delivery, the master should request a Waste Delivery Receipt to document the type and quantity of MARPOL residues/wastes actually received by the facility. IMO has standardized the format of this document to facilitate its use and application and in order to provide uniformity of records throughout the world (appendix 3). Corresponding records, receipts or certificates of the delivery should be kept in the Garbage Record Book (for a minimum of two years) and the Oil Record Book (part I for all ship types and part II for oil tankers) and the Cargo Record Book for chemical tankers.

41 Ship operators play a critical role in assisting port States with their obligation to provide adequate PRFs for ships. Since the possibility for improving reception facilities is dependent, at least partly, on the receipt of adequate information about alleged inadequacies, shipping companies should be encouraged to include the provisions for reporting alleged inadequacies of port reception facilities in their procedures for shipboard operations required under section 7 of the ISM Code. As part of the ship's Safety Management System, the master should be required to complete a report on encountering an inadequate PRF. The format for such a report is provided in appendix 1, which is also available through the Port Reception Facility section of the GISIS website. Completed reports should be forwarded to the flag Administration and, if possible, to the Authorities of the port State.

42 Flag States are requested to distribute the format in appendix 1 to ships and urge masters to use it to report alleged inadequacies of port reception facilities to the Administration of the flag State and, if possible, to the Authorities of the port State. Flag States are also requested to notify IMO, for transmission to the Parties concerned, of any case where facilities are alleged to be inadequate, and to inform the port State of the alleged inadequacies.

43 Notification should be made as soon as possible following the completion of the alleged inadequacies reporting format and should include a copy of the master's report, together with any supporting documentation.

44 Port States should ensure the provision of proper arrangements to consider and respond appropriately and effectively to reports of inadequacies, informing IMO and the reporting flag State of the outcome of their investigation.

45 The alleged inadequacy report together with the follow-up action received from the port State is published on the IMO's PRF Database.

5.6 Areas of special interest

States are required to demonstrate their leadership at least in three directions: firstly, in order to conduct an effective port State control; secondly, on the level of the enforcement of MARPOL Annex V; and thirdly, for the ensuring adequate port reception facilities for proper implementation of relevant provisions.

5.6.1 Adequacy of port reception facilities

For the reception of garbage without undue delay to ships, the Annex says that Parties "undertake to ensure" the provision of "adequate" facilities at ports and terminals.[46] The adequacy of port reception facilities is essential for proper implementation of MARPOL Annex V, and central to the protection sought by special areas which are subject to a more stringent regime. Adequacy is not specifically defined in the Annex. Some features of adequacy are set out, however, in the Annex and in related instruments:[47] the facilities should meet the needs of ships using the port without causing them undue delay; their use should not constitute a disincentive to use; they should contribute to the improvement of the marine environment, and they must allow for the ultimate disposal of ships' waste to take place in an environmentally appropriate way.

Cases of inadequacy are to be notified by States to the IMO with a view of being transmitted to Contracting Parties concerned. Furthermore, the Annex tackles the issue of reception facilities within special areas, calling upon each party whose coastlines borders a special area, to undertake to ensure "that as soon as possible, in all ports and terminals within the special area, adequate facilities are provided, taking into account the needs of ships operating in these areas". In this respect, a duty of notification to the IMO of related measures is set out. This aspect is related to the activation of the requirements of regulation 6 on the discharge of garbage within special areas.[48]

As at December 2016, the following designated areas had become effective as special areas, namely:

- Mediterranean Sea;
- Baltic Sea;
- "Gulfs" area;
- North Sea;
- Antarctic area (south latitude 60 degrees south);
- Wider Caribbean region including the Gulf of Mexico and the Caribbean Sea.

It is noted that as at December 2016, the Black Sea and the Red Sea which are were also designated special areas, have not become effective yet.

---

46 MARPOL Annex V as revised, regulation 8.

47 Notably see Guidelines for ensuring the adequacy of port waste reception facilities (resolution MEPC.83(44)), and MEPC.1/Circ.834, dated 15 April 2014, Consolidated Guidance for Port Reception Facility Providers and Users.

48 See MARPOL Annex V as revised, regulation 8, para. 3(2).

As already mentioned, the issue of port reception facilities raises a number of challenges for contracting States and private operators. Some of the challenges include their adequacy, which is generally viewed as rather low, costs, etc.

5.6.2 Port State Control findings

Port State control findings generally point to a satisfactory level of implementation of MARPOL Annex V as compared with other areas subject to controls. That said, there is a general belief that there are discrepancies and room for improvements concerning implementation and enforcement, including on the level of the contribution of States.

Some illustrations of port State control findings are provided below.

Under Paris MOU, during the year 2015, deficiencies relating to MARPOL Annex V amounted to 1.5%, as opposed to 1.9% for MARPOL Annex I on oil. The percentage of 1.5% was slightly higher than for MARPOL Annex V in 2014 (1.3%), and lower than for MARPOL Annex V in 2013 (1.8%).[49]

Under PSC in the Asia-Pacific Region 2015 (Tokyo MOU) MARPOL Annex V gave rise to 1,252 deficiencies, in contrast to 1,607 deficiencies for MARPOL Annex I on oil, and 1,301 for MARPOL Annex IV on sewage.[50]

In the framework of Black Sea MOU, the findings relating to 2015 indicate that MARPOL V deficiencies represent 1.11% of total deficiencies. This is in contrast to 1.39% for MARPOL I on oil and 0.40% for MARPOL IV on sewage.[51]

5.6.3 The impact of the Polar Code

As already mentioned in previous chapters, the International Code for Ships Operating in Polar Waters (Polar Code, entry into force on 1 January 2017), was adopted by the IMO in November 2014 (safety provisions) and in May 2015 (environmental provisions) through the amendment of the SOLAS, MARPOL and STCW Conventions. The Code applies to ships which operate in Arctic and Antarctic waters. From our standpoint, which is marine pollution control, it operates as an additional instrument to MARPOL. The Code aims to ensure safe ship operation and the protection of the polar environment by addressing risks present in polar waters and not adequately mitigated by other instruments of the IMO. Safety is addressed in the first part of the Code; the second part of the instrument deals with marine pollution prevention. Each part contains respectively a mandatory and a recommendatory division.

Amongst others, the Code is of interest to the prevention of pollution by garbage from ships.[52] Additional requirements to regulation 4 of MARPOL Annex V are set out in relation to discharge of garbage into the sea in Arctic waters.[53]

---

49 2015 Annual Report Paris MOU on PSC, p. 44.
50 2015 Annual Report on PSC in the Asia-Pacific Region (Tokyo MOU), p. 32.
51 2015 Annual Report on PSC in the Black Sea Region, p. 18.
52 See Chapter 5 of the Polar Code.
53 See para. 5.2 of the Polar Code on Operational requirements (MEPC.264(68), adopted on 15 May 2015).

For example, food wastes shall not be discharged into the ice, and discharge of animal carcasses is prohibited.

Furthermore, additional requirements to those set out in regulation 6 of MARPOL Annex V are set out in relation to the discharge of garbage into the sea in the Antarctic area.[54]

In addition to the above, garbage-related documentation must take into account operation in polar waters, i.e. in the garbage record book, garbage management plan and relevant placards.[55]

It is also noted that in light of the Polar Code, Resolution MEPC.265(68), adopted on 15 May 2015,[56] introduced amendments to MARPOL Annexes I (oil), II (noxious liquid substances in bulk), IV (sewage) and V (garbage).

BIBLIOGRAPHY

Derraik, J.G.B., 'The Pollution of the Marine Environment by Plastic Debris: A Review' [2002] Marine Pollution Bulletin 44, 842–852

European Commission Joint Communication to the European Parliament, the Council, the European Economic and Social Committee, and the Committee of the Regions, *International Ocean Governance: An Agenda for the Future of Our Oceans Brussels* (JOIN(2016)49 final, 10.11.2016)

European Parliament and Council Directive (EC) 2008/98 of the of 19 November 2008 on Waste and Repealing Certain Directives (The 2008 Waste Framework Directive) (Text with EEA relevance) (22.11.2008) (OJ L312)

Greenpeace/Allsopp, M., Walters, A., Santillo, D., and Johnston, P., *Plastic Debris in the World's Oceans* (document date unavailable)

IMO/HELCOM Regional Workshop for Promotion of the London Protocol and Helsinki Convention, Coenen R./IMO, 'London Convention and Protocol: Introduction, Achievements and Points for Comparison' [2011], Tallinn/Estonia, 6–8 April 2011

IMO MARPOL Annex V Discharge Provisions (2017 Edition, London)

Intergovernmental Panel on Climate Change (IPCC) Special Report, 'Summary for Policymakers: A Special Report of Working Group III of the Intergovernmental Panel on Climate Change' [2005]

Joint Group of Experts on the Scientific Aspects of Marine Environmental Protection (GESAMP), *Pollution in the Open Oceans 2009–2013: A Report by a GESAMP Task Team* (GESAMP Reports and Studies No. 9, 2015)

Kummer Peiry, K., 'Basel Convention on the Control of Transboundary Movements of Hazardous Wastes and Their Disposal' [2010] United Nations Audiovisual Library of International Law

Lloyd's Register Marine, 'Lloyd's Register Guidance Notes, Garbage Management According to the Revised MARPOL Annex V' (January 2014)

---

54 See para. 5.2.2 of the Polar Code.

55 See para. 5.2.3 of the Polar Code.

56 Resolution MEPC.265(68) (adopted on 15 May 2015) 'Amendments to the Annex of the Protocol of 1978 Relating to the International Convention for the Prevention of Pollution from Ships, 1973' – Amendments to MARPOL Annexes I, II, IV and V (To make use of environment-related provision of the Polar Code mandatory).

MEPC.1/Circ.834, 15 April 2014 'Consolidated Guidance for Port Reception Facility Providers and Users'

MEPC.220(63), 2012 Guidelines for the Development of Garbage Management Plans. Adopted 2 March 2012

Peiry, Katharina Kummer, *International Management of Hazardous Wastes: The Basel Convention and Related Legal Rules* (Oxford University Press, Oxford, 1995/99).

Peiry, Katharina Kummer, 'Basel Convention on the Control of Transboundary Movements of Hazardous Wastes and Their Disposal' [2010] United Nations Audiovisual Library of International Law (www.un.org/law/avl)

Report 'Barriers to Compliance', Final Report, LC 29/INF.2 cited in Zwaag, David L. Vander, and Daniel, Anne, 'International Law and Ocean Dumping: Steering a Precautionary Course Aboard the 1996 London Protocol, but Still an Unfinished Voyage; in the Future of Ocean Regime' Aldo Chircop, Ted L. MacDorman, and Susan J. Rolston (eds), *Building Essays in Tribute to Douglas M. Johnston* (Martinus Nijhoff Publishers, Leiden/Boston, 2009)

Resolution MEPC.201(62) (adopted on 15 July 2011) 'Amendments to the Annex of the Protocol of 1978 Relating to the International Convention for the Prevention of Pollution from Ships, 1973' (Revised MARPOL Annex V)

Resolution MEPC.219(63) (adopted 2 March 2012) '2012 Guidelines for the implementation of MARPOL Annex V'

Resolution MEPC.264(68) (adopted on 15 May 2015) 'International Code for Ships Operating in Polar Waters (Polar Code)'

Resolution MEPC.265(68) (adopted on 15 May 2015) 'Amendments to the Annex of the Protocol of 1978 Relating to the International Convention for the Prevention of Pollution from Ships, 1973' – Amendments to MARPOL Annexes I, II, IV and V (To make use of environment-related provision of the Polar Code mandatory)

Resolution MEPC.83(44) (adopted 13 March 2000) 'Guidelines for Ensuring the Adequacy of Port Waste Reception Facilities'

United Nations Environment Programme (UNEP), *Marine Litter: An Analytical Overview* [2005]

CHAPTER 6

Frameworks governing marine pollution from the transportation of chemicals by sea

TABLE OF CONTENTS

Section 1	Carriage of chemicals by sea	156
6.1	Introductory remarks	156
6.2	Glossary	160
6.3	Selected systems of classification	161
	6.3.1 Globally Harmonized System of Classification and Labelling of Chemicals	161
	6.3.2 Standard European Behaviour Classification	163
	6.3.3 GESAMP hazard profiles	163
	6.3.4 European Union Regulation 1272/2008	164
6.4	United Nations Recommendations on the Transport of Dangerous Goods – Model Regulations	165
Section 2	Overview of MARPOL Annex II	166
6.5	Material scope of application	167
6.6	Categorisation of Noxious Liquid Substances	167
6.7	Design and construction	168
6.8	Discharge prohibitions	169
6.9	Verification of compliance – recently adopted Chapter IX of MARPOL Annex II	170
6.10	Polar Code – recently adopted Chapter X of MARPOL Annex II	170
Section 3	Overview of MARPOL Annex III	171
6.11	Material scope of application	171
6.12	Substantial requirements (packing, marking, labelling, stowage)	172
6.13	Quantity limitations	172
6.14	Exceptions	172
Section 4	Certification, Port State Control on operational requirements and other aspects stemming from MARPOL Annex II and Annex III	173
6.15	In relation to MARPOL Annex II	173
	6.15.1 Surveys and certificates	173

		6.15.1.1	The International Pollution Prevention Certificate for the Carriage of Noxious Liquid Substances in Bulk (NLS certificate)	173
		6.15.1.2	Procedures and Arrangements Manual	174
		6.15.1.3	Cargo Record Book	174
		6.15.1.4	Shipboard Marine Pollution Emergency Plan for Noxious Liquid Substances	174
	6.15.2	Port State Control on operational requirements		174
	6.15.3	Port reception facilities		175
6.16	In relation to MARPOL Annex III			176
	6.16.1	Documentation		176
	6.16.2	Port State Control on operational requirements		177

SECTION 1: CARRIAGE OF CHEMICALS BY SEA

6.1 Introductory remarks

Following the overview governing transportation of oil (Chapter 1), an overview of the framework governing chemical transportation is provided below. Ranging from chemicals with very severe environmental and safety hazards to edible vegetable oils and fats, chemicals covered by this chapter give rise to lengthy regulations at the international, regional and national level, complemented by industry best practice. Transported by sea in bulk (liquids and solids) or in packaged form (e.g. in drums stored in a container aboard a container ship), chemicals are necessary to modern life and represent an increasing volume of global trade. While not all chemicals are considered hazardous, according to estimates, more than 50% of packed goods and bulk cargoes moved by sea nowadays may be considered as dangerous, hazardous or harmful to the environment.[1] Interestingly, according to estimates, of about 37 million different chemicals used by man approximately 2,000 are carried regularly by sea.[2]

Chemicals are gases, liquids or solids carried by a variety of ships: bulk carriers, chemical, parcel or product tankers, gas carriers, container ships, general cargo vessels or roll-on roll-off vessels. The properties of hazardous chemicals (referred to by experts under the terms flammability, explosivity, toxicity, infection, reactivity, corrosivity and radioactivity) and their behaviours (classified as dissolvers, floaters, sinkers, gases or evaporators) are a challenge for safety and the marine environment. The impact of hazardous chemicals on the marine

---

1 Reported in Meltem Deniz Guner-Ozbek, *The Carriage of Dangerous Goods by Sea* (Springer, 2008, Berlin-Heidelberg, p. 1).

2 Reported in Dr. Karen Purnell, ITOPF, 'Are HNS Spills More Dangerous Than Oils Spills?' (White Paper, Interspill Conference, 4th IMO Research and Development Forum, Marseille, May 2009).

environment has been researched to a lesser extent than in the case of oil, thus many aspects remain unknown.[3] Substances which may appear inoffensive in the eyes of the public (e.g. palm oil) may have an impact on the marine environment and/or may be required to be carried by chemical tankers (e.g. vegetable oils). In this context, the description which follows is a brief introduction to the legal and, on some points, managerial framework governing transportation of chemicals by sea and related matters; the description does not engage in scientific research, and is not intended to be exhaustive.[4]

The legal regime governing transportation of hazardous chemicals by sea had to be addressed by the international regulator, and stems from the SOLAS Convention, the instrument *par excellence* on safety, MARPOL, which focuses on the marine environment, and from other texts or codes adopted by the IMO or other bodies. IMO Codes on the matter are safety-oriented but are relevant to the environment; they apply in conjunction with a number of factors, including the form of the chemical transported by sea, the type of ship involved, etc. (a number of IMO codes are identified in the Glossary below under paragraph 6.2).

It should be clear from the outset that hazardous and noxious substances (HNS) are subject to more than one definition depending on the legal instrument involved. At this point it may useful to shed light on some basic definitions which are additional to those presented in the main Glossary:

- The term "dangerous goods" is given a specific meaning by SOLAS Convention, i.e. dangerous goods mean "the substances, materials and articles covered by the IMDG Code", i.e. the International Maritime Dangerous Goods Code; Part A of SOLAS Chapter VII says that the carriage of dangerous goods in packaged form must comply with the provisions of the IMDG Code.[5] Furthermore, in order to ensure that all modes of transport classify dangerous goods in the same way, the Globally Harmonized System of Classification and Labelling of Chemicals (GHS) was developed by the United Nations (see paragraph 6.3.1 below); GHS divides dangerous goods into nine hazard classes in conjunction with the hazard presented by the goods in transport (e.g. Class 1: explosive substances and articles; Class 2: gases, etc.).

- The term "harmful substance" is defined by MARPOL as "any substance which, if introduced into the sea, is liable to create hazards to human health, to harm living resources and marine life, to damage amenities or to interfere with other legitimate uses of the sea, and includes any

---

3 *Ibid.*

4 Readers interested, amongst others, in the radioactive material transport, may read World Nuclear Transport Institute, Radioactive Materials Transport the International Safety Regime (An Overview of Safety Regulations and the Organizations Responsible for their Development) (Revised July 2006).

5 SOLAS Chapter VII on the Carriage of Dangerous Goods, Regulation 1.2. Part A is entitled Carriage of Goods in Packaged Form.

substance subject to control by the present Convention".[6] The same Convention defines "harmful substances" for the purposes of Annex III on the prevention of pollution by harmful substances carried by sea in packaged form as "those substances which are identified as marine pollutants in the International Maritime Dangerous Goods Code (IMDG Code) or which meet the criteria in the Appendix of this Annex".[7]

- Concerning the term "marine pollutant": dangerous goods identified as satisfying the test criteria for hazardous to the marine environment are labeled as "marine pollutant".[8]

Returning to the definition of HNS, according to the Protocol on Preparedness, Response and Coordination to Pollution Incidents by Hazardous and Noxious Substances, 2000 (the HNS-OPRC Protocol, entry into force 14 June 2007, is examined in Chapter 9), HNS are substances other than oil which, if introduced into the marine environment, are likely to create hazards to human health, to harm living resources and marine life, to damage amenities or to interfere with other legitimate uses of the sea. The HNS Convention 2010, which has not entered into force at this stage, and which is the international text governing liability and compensation in relation to HNS (see Chapter 11) defines HNS by reference to various conventions and codes: this definition includes the Appendix I of Annex I of MARPOL (oils carried in bulk), the IBC Code,[9] Appendix II of Annex II to MARPOL (bulk liquids), IGC Code[10] (gases), dangerous goods described in the IMDG Code,[11] and solid cargoes covered by the BC Code.[12]

According to the IMO, 2,000 types of HNS are regularly transported by sea – the list including, amongst others, sulphuric acid, hydrochloric acid, caustic soda, LPG/ LNG, ammonia, etc.

Accidents in recent years involving HNS notably include the following:[13]

- *CMA Djakarta* (1999) (calcium hypochlorite);
- *Ievoli Sun* (2000) (styrene, etc.);
- *Adamandas* (2003) (deoxidised iron balls);
- *Napoli* (2007) (explosives, flammables, pollutants, etc.);
- *Princess of the Stars* (2008) (pesticides);
- *Bareli* (2012) (heavy fuel oil and dangerous goods);

---

6   MARPOL Article 2.2.

7   MARPOL Annex III, regulation 1.1.1.

8   IMO Manual on Chemical Pollution, Section 2: Search and Recovery of Packaged Goods Lost at Sea (2007 edition) p. 7.

9   International Bulk Chemical Code.

10 International Code for the Construction and Equipment of Ships Carrying Liquefied Gases in Bulk.

11 IMO International Maritime Dangerous Goods Code.

12 Code of Safe Practice for Solid Bulk Cargoes.

13 Also see J.M. Häkkinen and A.I. Posti, 'Overview of Maritime Accidents Involving Chemicals Worldwide and in the Baltic Sea', in A. Weintrit and T. Neumann (eds), *Marine Navigation and Safety of Sea Transportation – Maritime Transport and Shipping* (CRC Press, London, 2013).

- *MOL Comfort* (2013) (containers and fuel);
- *Jabalenoor* (2015) (potash fertiliser)

HNS accidents have the potential to impair human life (e.g. death due to explosion, injury resulting from absorption via skin contact, etc.), the environment (e.g. impact on wildlife, marine species, etc.), safety (e.g. by requiring the evacuation of local communities), and/or the economy (e.g. adverse impact on marine resources, tourism, etc.). In this context, flag States have an important role to play by ensuring the implementation and enforcement of international regulations that they are Parties to, a task which is complemented by the contribution of port States in the framework of Port State Control. It may be appreciated that ships may be under the obligation to or should follow the practice of notifying port authorities in advance of the details of HNS aboard;[14] furthermore, shippers of packaged dangerous goods are held to declare specific information in relation to HNS to be transported by sea, and ensure the correct packaging and labelling – these formalities being relevant to stowage plans for the cargo, thus to the safety of the vessel. Additional obligations may stem from charterParties prohibiting the shipment of any goods of a dangerous, injurious, flammable or corrosive nature.[15] Against this background, it may be relevant to note that a number of maritime casualties involving hazardous chemicals have been associated with undeclared or inaccurate declarations of consignments.[16]

The risks associated with the transport, handling and use of chemicals have been acknowledged by the international community and have given rise to classification systems. The last ones identify hazardous chemicals and provide information about related hazards through standard symbols and phrases. Before addressing these aspects, a number of useful terms are defined below.

---

14 See IMO's *Revised Recommendation on the Safe Transport of Dangerous Cargoes and Related Activities in Port Areas* (2007 edition). On the European Union level, according to Directive 2010/65/EU (see Article 4) Member States are held to ensure that the master or any other person duly authorised by the operator of the ship provides notification (in principle) at least 24 hours in advance, prior to arriving in a port situated in an EU Member State, of specific information to the competent authority. Reporting formalities, i.e. information set out in the Annex of the Directive which must be provided for administrative and procedural purposes when a ship arrives in or departs from a port in that Member State, include, amongst others, notification of dangerous or polluting goods carried on board, etc. European Parliament and Council Directive (EU) 2010/65 on reporting formalities for ships arriving in and/or departing from ports of the Member States and repealing Directive 2002/6/EC (Text with EEA relevance) [2010] (OJ L 283/1).

15 The *CMA Djakarta* case is relevant in that regard (*CMA CGM S.A. v Classica Shipping Co. Ltd.* [2004] 1 Lloyd's Rep. 460). Following explosions and fire apparently caused by calcium hypochlorite (bleaching powder), the shipowner of the vessel took the charterer to court on the grounds of breach of contract (NYPE), as there was a clause in the charterparty prohibiting the shipment of any goods of a dangerous, injurious, flammable or corrosive nature.

16 According to experts, it is important to obtain, amongst others, the information on health hazards associated with the cargo; in the context of chemical spills experience suggests that cargo information is often not readily available aboard or from the ship management company. See T, Hoefer, P. Charlebois, S. Le Floch, M. Morrissette, 'Cargo Information Needed During the Initial Stages of a Chemical Spill' (Interspill 2015, White Paper).

6.2 Glossary

Ballasting and de-ballasting	Process by which when the vessel is at a port or at sea, sea water is taken in and discharged from the ship for the purposes of stability and trim.
BCH (Bulk Chemical) Code	IMO Code for the Construction and Equipment of Ships Carrying Dangerous Chemicals in Bulk; it applies to bulk solid cargoes. Applicable to chemical tankers built before 1 July 1986.
Chemical tanker	Defined by MARPOL Annex II as a ship constructed or adapted for the carriage in bulk of any liquid product listed in Chapter 17 of the International Bulk Chemical Code.
CSS Code	Code of Safe Practice for Cargo Stowage and Securing.[17]
GESAMP	UN Advisory Body. Joint Group of Experts on the Scientific Aspects of Marine Environmental Protection of IMO/FAO/ UNESCO/ WMO/ WHO/ IAEA/UN/UNEP.
GHS	Globally Harmonized System of Classification and Labelling of Chemicals; it was developed by the United Nations and is intended to be used internationally.
Hazard Class (GHS)	According to GHS, this is defined as the nature of the physical, health or environmental hazard (e.g. carcinogen, oral acute toxicity, etc.).
IBC (International Bulk Chemical) Code	International Code for the Construction and Equipment of Ships Carrying Dangerous Chemicals in Bulk; it sets out an international standard for the safe carriage by sea of dangerous chemicals and noxious liquids in bulk, thus reducing the risk to the ship, crew and the environment. It contains provisions governing the design, construction, etc. of new built or converted chemical tankers (It is noted that the IBC Code followed the BCH Code, i.e. Code for the Construction and Equipment of Ships Carrying Dangerous Chemicals in Bulk[18]).
IGC Code	International Code for the Construction and Equipment of Ships Carrying Liquefied Gases in Bulk.[19]
IMDG Code	International Maritime Dangerous Goods Code. Initially adopted in 1965 as a recommendatory text; it became mandatory under SOLAS (Chapter VII) from 1 January 2004. It operates as a uniform international tool for the transportation of dangerous goods by sea, and contains detailed technical specifications. It is updated every two years;[20] the Code aims to enhance safe transportation of dangerous goods, protect the marine environment and

---

17 IMO 2011 Edition.

18 The BCH Code applies to chemical tankers built or converted before 1 July 1986.

19 IMO IGC Code (2016 Edition).

20 The IMDG Code (2014 Edition) entered into force on 1 January 2016 for two years; the IMDG Code (2016 Edition) is to be noted (entry into force 1 January 2018; applied voluntarily from 1 January 2017).

	facilitate the movement of dangerous goods. Dangerous goods are classified into classes in conjunction with their properties. Dangerous goods are identified by a unique 4-digit UN Number and an internationally recognised name, referred to as the Proper Shipping Name (PSN). As noted, the IMDG Code is relevant to marine pollutants.
IMSBC Code	International Maritime Solid Bulk Cargoes Code.[21]
INF Code	International Code for the Safe Carriage of Packaged Irradiated Nuclear Fuel, Plutonium and High-Level Radioactive Wastes on Board Ships.
Noxious liquid substance (NLS)	Any substance indicated in the Pollution Category column of chapter 17 or 18 of the International Bulk Chemical Code or provisionally assessed under the provisions of regulation 6.3 as falling into category X,Y or Z.[22]
Pictogram	According to the GHS (see Glossary), it means a graphical composition including a symbol plus other graphic elements intended to provide specific information.[23]
Safety Data Sheets (SDS)	In the GHS (see the Glossary) they aim to provide to employers and employees comprehensive information at the workplace about hazards, including environmental hazards, of a substance or mixture; they also constitute a source of information for seeking advice on safety precautions.[24]

6.3 Selected systems of classification

The need to ensure consistent information on chemicals or dangerous goods for the purposes of protection of the public and the environment prompted international and regional approaches on the level of classification and labelling.

6.3.1 Globally Harmonized System of Classification and Labelling of Chemicals

The United Nations (UN) Globally Harmonized System of Classification and Labelling of Chemicals (GHS), mention of which was made above, constitutes an internationally-harmonised approach to classification and labelling designed for the global trade of chemicals. It classifies chemicals in conjunction with hazard types and uses labels and safety data sheets.[25]

In a nutshell, the GHS is aimed at facilitating trade and protecting human health and the environment by identifying the intrinsic hazards found in substances and mixtures and by providing hazard information about related hazards. In this respect, the GHS harmonises the criteria for hazard classification. The meaning of harmonisation in this context is the establishment of "a common

---

21 (Code and Supplement) 2016 Edition.

22 MARPOL Annex II, Chapter I, regulation 1.10.

23 Pictograms for the transport of dangerous goods can be found at www.unece.org (last visit 13 November 2017).

24 For more information on SDS under the GHS, see *infra* note 26, p. 35 *et seq.*

25 See www.unece.org/trans/danger.html (last visit 13 November 2017).

and coherent basis for chemical hazard classification and communication, from which the appropriate elements relevant to means of transport, consumer, worker and environment protection can be selected".[26]

> The GHS goes into two directions:
> - It provides harmonised criteria for the classification of substances and mixtures according to their health, environmental and physical hazards; and
> - It provides harmonised hazard communication elements, including labelling and safety data sheets requirements.[27]

The GHS uses hazard pictograms, i.e. graphical compositions including a symbol or other graphic elements in order to convey specific information; in transport regulations they are commonly referred to as labels.

Legally speaking, the GHS is a voluntary agreement and, as such, it requires to be introduced in national legal systems through an appropriate legal instrument. It may be appreciated that on the European Union level this aspect has been dealt with by Regulation 1272/2008 (see below under paragraph 6.3.4), referred to as the CLP Regulation.

The first edition of the GHS dates to 2002, and has been subject to revisions.[28]

In the table below the standard hazard symbols used in the GHS can be identified.

Flame	Flame over circle	Exploding bomb
Corrosion	Gas cylinder	Skull and crossbones
Exclamation mark	Environment	Health hazard

Figure 6.1 Standard hazard symbols (GHS)

Source: From Globally Harmonized System of Classification and Labelling of Chemicals (GHS) by the United Nations © (2017) United Nations. Reprinted with the permission of the United Nations.

---

26 See GHS Rev.7 (2017) (7th revised edition, United Nations, New-York/Geneva), para. 1.1.1.6(c).
27 GHS Rev.7 (2017).
28 Amongst others, see GHS Rev.7 (2017).

6.3.2 Standard European Behaviour Classification

The Standard European Behaviour Classification (SEBC) for chemicals spilt into the sea determines the theoretical behaviour of a substance through examination of physical and chemical properties, and categorises HNS in 12 groups by considering four basic behaviours, namely:

- floaters;
- sinkers;
- dissolvers;
- evaporators.

As noted by experts, the SEBC gives a set of criteria for the evaluation of short-term distribution between water and air.

6.3.3 GESAMP hazard profiles

GESAMP (Joint Group of Experts on the Scientific Aspects of Marine Environmental Protection) is a high profile advisory body to the United Nations established in 1969 and tasked to provide scientific advice on marine pollution. GESAMP evaluates the hazards of liquids transported in bulk by ships. The list of about 900 chemicals is updated every year by GESAMP through the IMO.[29] GESAMP has published The Revised GESAMP Hazard Evaluation Procedure for Chemical Substances Carried by Ships;[30] this document revises the first edition dating to 2002. The document is concerned with the evaluation criteria of hazards to health and the marine environment of chemical substances that may be released into the marine environment from ships (operational discharges, accidental spillage or loss overboard). It is noteworthy that the evaluation procedure was designed to assist with the implementation of MARPOL as well as with carriage requirements for the maritime transport of bulk liquid chemicals. Furthermore, the Revised GESAMP Hazard Evaluation Procedure for Chemical Substances Carried by Ships also takes into account the GHS.

The so-called GESAMP Hazard Profile identifies the hazard characteristics of a substance. It is on the basis of the Profile and other elements that carriage requirements for the substance carried onboard (chemical substances and mixtures in liquid form as governed by MARPOL Annex II and the IBC Code) are assigned by the IMO.[31] It is noted that GESAMP Hazard Profiles are determined by a specialised working group[32] of GESAMP.

---

29 See T. Hoefer, P. Charlebois, S. Le Floch, and M. Morrissette, 'Cargo Information Needed During the Initial Stages of a Chemical Spill' (Interspill 2015, White Paper).

30 GESAMP, Revised GESAMP Hazard Evaluation Procedure for Chemical Substances Carried by Ships (IMO/FAO/ UNESCO-IOC/WMO/IAEA/UN/UNEP/UNIDO/UNDP) Joint Group of Experts on the Scientific Aspects of Marine Environmental Protection, Rep. Stud. GESAMP No. 64 (2nd edition, 2014).

31 *Ibid.*, p. 6.

32 Working Group on the Evaluation of the Hazards of Harmful Substances Carried by Ships (GESAMP/EHS).

The following categories are used by GESAMP:

- bioaccumulation and biodegradation;
- aquatic toxicity;
- acute mammalian toxicity;
- irritation, corrosion and long-term health effects; and
- interference with other uses of the sea.[33]

6.3.4 *European Union Regulation 1272/2008*

In the European Union, the classification and labelling of hazardous chemicals is regulated by Regulation (EC) 1272/2008 on classification, labelling and packaging of substances and mixtures (referred to as the CLP Regulation).[34] The Regulation incorporates into the law of the European Union the GHS. More specifically, the Regulation, which is an act directly applicable into the legal systems of Member States of the EU, seeks to determine which properties of substances and mixtures should lead to a classification as hazardous, in order for the hazards of substances and mixtures to be properly identified and communicated. According to the drafters of the instruments, such properties should include physical hazards as well as hazards to human health and to the environment, including hazards to the ozone layer.[35]

As it can be seen below, the Regulation does not apply, in principle, to the transport of dangerous goods by air, sea, road, rail or inland waterways.

ARTICLE 1: PURPOSE AND SCOPE

1. The purpose of this Regulation is to ensure a high level of protection of human health and the environment as well as the free movement of substances, mixtures and articles as referred to in Article 4(8) by:
    (a) harmonising the criteria for classification of substances and mixtures, and the rules on labelling and packaging for hazardous substances and mixtures;
    (b) providing an obligation for:
        (i)   manufacturers, importers and downstream users to classify substances and mixtures placed on the market;
        (ii) suppliers to label and package substances and mixtures placed on the market;
        (iii) manufacturers, producers of articles and importers to classify those substances not placed on the market that are subject to registration or notification under Regulation (EC) No. 1907/2006;

---

33 See *supra* note 30.

34 Regulation (EC) 1272/2008 of the European Parliament and of the Council of 16 December 2008 on classification, labelling and packaging of substances and mixtures, amending and repealing Directives 67/548/EEC and 1999/45/EC, and amending Regulation (EC) 1907/2006 (Text with EEA relevance) [2008] OJ L 353/1.

35 See Recital 10 of Regulation 1272/2008.

> (c) providing an obligation for manufacturers and importers of substances to notify the [European Chemicals] Agency of such classifications and label elements if these have not been submitted to the Agency as part of a registration under Regulation (EC) No. 1907/2006;
>
> (d) establishing a list of substances with their harmonised classifications and labelling elements at Community level in Part 3 of Annex VI;
>
> (e) establishing a classification and labelling inventory of substances, which is made up of all notifications, submissions and harmonized classifications and labelling elements referred to in points (c) and (d).
>
> 2. This Regulation shall not apply to the following:
>
> [..]
>
> 6. Save where Article 33[36] applies this Regulation shall not apply to the transport of dangerous goods by air, sea, road, rail or inland waterways.

In addition to the international and/or regional efforts on harmonisation of classification, model regulations have been drafted by the United Nations in order to facilitate uniform approaches in national legal systems.

6.4 United Nations Recommendations on the Transport of Dangerous Goods – Model Regulations

Not only regulation of transport of dangerous goods is necessary for the prevention of accidents to persons or property and damage to the environment; it is also necessary for the protection of the means of transport used during transportation and other goods. An additional concern is the need to avoid hurdles to the movement of goods acceptable for transportation. In light of the challenges raised by the need to regulate the transport of dangerous goods, and in recognition of the need to harmonise regulations in this area, the United Nations have developed recommendations referred to as Model Regulations. The last ones are intended for Governments and other stakeholders such as intergovernmental or international organisations.[37] It should be noted from the outset that the model recommendations, presented in the form of Model Regulations on the Transport of Dangerous Goods, are addressed to all means of transport[38] but they do not apply to the bulk transport of dangerous goods in sea-going or inland navigation bulk carriers or tank-vessels, which is subject to special international or national regulations.[39]

---

36 Article 33 of Regulation 1272/2008 is entitled 'Specific rules for labelling of outer packaging, inner packaging and single packaging'.

37 UN Recommendations on the Transport of Dangerous Goods – Model Regulations (2015) (19th revised edition (Volume I) (ST/SG/AC.10/1/Rev.19)).

38 *Ibid.*, para. 5.

39 *Ibid.*, para. 1.

Model regulations exist in many subject areas; they should be understood as a recommendatory basic and uniform scheme of provisions with a given format and content which allows the adoption of national provisions, including special requirements. They are revised by the United Nations, and can also be revised by their users with the expectation that the core principles of the recommendations will be respected (so as to preserve uniformity).

In this context, the Model Regulations on the Transport of Dangerous Goods pertain to many areas, including classification of goods according to the hazard presented, definition of classes (explosives, gases, flammable liquids, flammable solids, oxidising substances and organic peroxides, toxic and infectious substances, radioactive material, corrosive substances, miscellaneous dangerous substances, including environmental hazardous substances), listing of principal dangerous goods, exceptions, etc.

With the above background information in mind, a brief overview of MARPOL Annex I and MARPOL Annex II, which are the texts of reference on the prevention of pollution by chemicals transported by sea, is provided below.

SECTION 2: OVERVIEW OF MARPOL ANNEX II

Prevention of pollution from noxious liquid substances (NLS) carried in bulk is regulated by MARPOL Annex II (entry into force on 6 April 1987). In addition to the risk of accidents involving ships carrying NLS,[40] NLS discharged into the sea from tank cleaning or deballasting operations represent an operational challenge. It can be said that the Annex is centered around categorisation of relevant substances (X, Y, etc.), typology of chemical tankers according to environmental and safety hazards (IMO ship type 1, etc.), and operational requirements.[41] Like the rest of IMO legislation, the Annex has been subject to numerous amendments stemming from the Marine Environment Protection Committee (MEPC). The revised Annex II, which became effective on 1 January 2007, introduced a new categorisation system for NLS (see paragraph 6.6 below); furthermore, in recognition of environmental challenges, the revision changed the way certain products are required to be transported, and set out lower permitted discharge levels of certain products. It may be appreciated that the carriage of chemicals by sea, including in bulk, is also regulated by SOLAS Chapter VII, which goes beyond the confines of the discussion – the focus of the discussion being placed on marine environment rather than safety.

Chemical tankers built after 1 July 1986 and carrying specific substances have to comply with the International Bulk Chemical (IBC) Code, which is a Code adopted under SOLAS. The bulk carriage of any liquid product other than those defined as oil (governed by MARPOL Annex I) is prohibited unless the product has been evaluated and categorised for inclusion in Chapter 17 or 18 of the

---

40 This risk appears to be under control (see EMSA, *Annual Overview of Marine Casualties and Incidents 2017*, p. 43, figure 48).

41 E.g. stripping performance requirements, which are not discussed in the present chapter.

IBC Code. Chemical tankers built on or after 1 July 1986 carrying substances listed in Chapter 17 of the IBC Code are required to follow the requirements governing design, construction, equipment and operation of ships set out by the Code. As to chemical tankers constructed before 1 July 1986, they need to be compliant with the predecessor of the IBC Code which is the BCH Code (Code for the Construction and Equipment of Ships Carrying Dangerous Chemicals in Bulk).

MARPOL Annex II comprises ten chapters, which deal respectively with the items which follow. That said, the chapter on verification of compliance with MARPOL and the one on the Polar Code resulted from relatively recent amendments. Appendices to MARPOL Annex II include the procedures, equipment, etc. which apply to the ships to which the Annex applies. The list with the chapters is given below:

- general;
- categorisation of noxious liquid substances;
- surveys and certification;
- design, construction, arrangement and equipment;
- operational discharges of residues of noxious liquid substances;
- measures of control by port States;
- prevention of pollution arising from an incident involving noxious liquid substances;
- reception facilities;
- verification of compliance with the provisions of MARPOL;
- International Code for Ships Operating in Polar Waters.

Annex II is of a technical nature. Selected key points relating to MARPOL Annex II are identified below.

6.5 Material scope of application

In principle, Annex II applies to all ships certified to carry NLS in bulk.[42] Furthermore, when cargo regulated by MARPOL Annex I (oil) is carried in a cargo space of an NLS tanker, the appropriate requirements of Annex I shall also apply.[43]

A number of exceptions, identified in paragraph 6.8 below, exemptions[44] and equivalents[45] are set out by the Annex.

6.6 Categorisation of Noxious Liquid Substances

Chapter 2 deals with the categorisation of NLS. When NLS are discharged into the sea from tank cleaning or deballasting operations, they are considered to present various degrees of hazard to marine resources or human health (e.g. major or minor hazard) which are correlated with discharge prohibitions.

---

42 Regulation 2.1.
43 Regulation 2.2.
44 Regulation 4.
45 Regulation 5.

In this respect, NLS are divided into the following four categories, namely:

- Category X: NLS, which, if discharged into the sea from tank cleaning or deballasting operations, are considered to present a major hazard to the marine environment or human health, justifying prohibition of discharge into the marine environment;
- Category Y: NLS, which, if discharged into the sea from tank cleaning or deballasting operations, are considered to present a hazard to marine resources or human health, or cause harm to amenities or other legitimate uses of the sea and therefore justify a limitation on the quality and quantity of their discharge at sea;
- Category Z: NLS, which, if discharged into the sea from tank cleaning or deballasting operations, are considered to present a minor hazard to marine resources or human health and therefore justify less stringent restrictions on the quality and quantity of their discharge into the marine environment;
- and "Other substances" (OS): substances evaluated to fall outside the above-mentioned categories because they are deemed to present no harm to marine resources, human health, amenities, or other legitimate uses of the sea when discharged into the sea from tank cleaning or deballasting operations.[46]

It is noted that for each cargo including a NLS, the above-mentioned IBC Code sets out provisions governing the design, construction and outfitting of new built or converted chemical tankers. As already mentioned, the Code is aimed at minimising the risks to the ship, its crew and the environment with due consideration of the nature of the products aboard. The Code also determines ship types for transportation purposes, the risks presented for ship's safety and its crew, tank aeration and gas detection requirements, methods for measuring cargo levels and firefighting procedures. A comprehensive review of the IBC Code was undertaken by the IMO in 2016 in order to bring the Code in line with the GHS and GESAMP hazard evaluation procedure for chemical substances carried by ships. Furthermore, carriage requirements for products listed in the IBC Code are being reassessed.

For ships constructed prior to 1 July 1986, the reference is the Code for the Construction and Equipment of Ships Carrying Dangerous Chemicals in Bulk (BCH Code), which is generally viewed as the predecessor of the IBC Code.

6.7 Design and construction

Provisions on design, construction and related matters can be found in Chapter 4 of MARPOL Annex II, which is of technical nature. In a nutshell, the chapter sets out that the design, construction, equipment and operation of ships certified

---

46 According to regulation 6.1.4, the requirements of Annex II do not apply to the discharge of bilge or ballast water or other residues or mixtures containing only "Other Substances".

to carry NLS in bulk are required, in conjunction with their age, to be in line with the International Bulk Chemical Code (IBC Code) or the Bulk Chemical Code (BCH Code).[47] There are additional provisions of a technical nature on pumping, piping, unloading arrangements and slop tanks[48] which go beyond our scope.

The relevance of the IBC Code should be stressed. The Code sets out standards for the construction and equipment of three types of chemical tankers (Type 1, 2 and 3). For example, Type 1 chemical tanker is intended to transport Chapter 17 of the IBC Code products with very severe environmental and safety hazards requiring maximum preventive measures. In other terms, this type is intended for the transportation of products deemed to present the greatest overall hazard. The quantity of cargo required to be transported in a Type 1 chemical should not exceed a specified volume in any one tank.

6.8 Discharge prohibitions

It should be noted from the outset that discharge prohibitions at sea of noxious liquid substances or mixtures containing such substances benefit from specific exceptions.

The first exception concerns the situation where the discharge is necessary for securing the safety of a ship or saving life at sea; furthermore, the exception covers under conditions discharges resulting from damage to a ship or its equipment. In this respect, all reasonable precautions must have been taken after the occurrence of the damage or the discovery of the discharge for the purpose of preventing or minimising the discharge. Furthermore, the exception does not work in the event where the owner or the master acted either with intent to cause damage, or recklessly and with knowledge that damage would probably result. A third case covered by the exception concerns discharges of NLS approved by the flag State and the Government in whose jurisdiction it is contemplated the discharge will occur – this would have to be for specific purposes (the provision identifies the case of combating specific pollution incidents with a view to minimising the damage from pollution).[49]

With the above in mind, discharge requirements are set out (Chapter V of Annex II entitled "Operational discharges of residues of noxious liquid substances"). The discussion of these criteria is highly technical goes beyond the scope of the chapter. It is noted, however, that discharges of residues of NLS are controlled through specific requirements. Amongst others, "the discharge into the sea of residues of substances assigned to category X, Y and Z or of those provisionally assessed as such or ballast water, tank washings or other mixtures containing such substances shall be prohibited unless such discharges are made in full compliance with the applicable operational requirements contained in this Annex".[50]

---

47 Regulation 11.
48 Regulation 12.
49 Regulation 3 on Exceptions.
50 Regulation 13.1.1 of MARPOL Annex II Chapter 5.

In addition to the above, there is a prohibition of discharge into the sea of NLS or mixtures containing such substances in the Antarctic Area, i.e. in the sea area south of latitude 60°S.[51]

6.9 Verification of compliance – recently adopted Chapter IX of MARPOL Annex II

Adopted on 4 April 2014, IMO Resolution MEPC.246(66)[52] amended MARPOL, including Annex II. The Resolution, which was activated through the tacit acceptance procedure, sought to introduce the requirements of the IMO Instruments Implementation Code (III Code).[53] The amendments introduced by MEPC.246(66) entered into force on 1 January 2016. As discussed in other chapters, the tacit acceptance procedure enables amendments to be considered to have been accepted by a certain date unless, prior to that date, not less than a specified number of Parties the combined merchant fleet of which constitutes not less than a specified percentage of the gross tonnage of the world's merchant fleet, have communicated to the IMO their objection to the amendments (in this case, one-third of the State Parties, the combined merchant fleets of which constitute not less than 50% of the gross tonnage of the international fleet). In practice, the use of objections by IMO Member States in the context of tacit acceptance procedure remains exceptional.

With the III Code, the nature of the audit that IMO Member States are subject to changes. Voluntary schemes under the previous regime are replaced with mandatory audit schemes. Audits for flag States are required every seven years.

In this context, a new Chapter 9 was added to Annex II. State Parties are required to use the provisions of the III Code in the execution of their obligations and responsibilities set out in Annex II.[54] Furthermore, periodic IMO audits in view of verifying compliance with and implementation of Annex II are provided for.[55]

Another recent change which impacted on MARPOL Annex II stems from the adoption of the Polar Code.

6.10 Polar Code – recently adopted Chapter X of MARPOL Annex II

The International Code for Ships Operating in Polar Waters[56] is addressed in more than one chapter of the book from the standpoint of the topics under discussion.

---

51 Regulation 13.8.

52 Resolution MEPC.246(66) (adopted on 4 April 2014) Amendments to the Annex of the Protocol of 1978 Relating to the International Convention for the Prevention of Pollution from Ships, 1973 (Amendments to MARPOL Annexes I, II, III, IV and V to make the use of the III Code mandatory).

53 IMO Resolution A.1070(28) (adopted 4 December 2013).

54 Regulation 19.

55 Regulation 20.

56 Resolution MEPC.265(68) adopted on 15 May 2015 'Amendments to the Annex of the Protocol of 1978 Relating to the International Convention for the Prevention of Pollution from Ships,

The so-called Polar Code was developed to supplement existing IMO instruments in recognition of the additional operational demands for ships operating in polar waters (Arctic and Antarctic waters) in relation to safety and marine environment protection. Not surprisingly, the goal of the Polar Code is to provide for safe ship operation and the protection of the polar environment by tackling risks that are present in polar waters, and are not adequately mitigated by other IMO instruments.

In this context, the Code sets out the prohibition of discharges into the sea in Arctic waters of NLS or mixtures containing such substances.[57] Furthermore, the Code also requires that operation in polar waters be taken into account in the Cargo Record Book, the Procedures and Arrangements Manual and the Shipboard Marine Pollution Emergency Plan for NLS (on these documents, see below under paragraph 6.15) or the shipboard marine pollution emergency plan as required by MARPOL Annex II.[58] Additional requirements are provided in relation to certain ships constructed on or after 1 January 2017.[59]

SECTION 3: OVERVIEW OF MARPOL ANNEX III

Annex III entered into force internationally on 1 July 1992. The Annex is aimed at preventing and minimising marine pollution by harmful substances in packaged form. In this context, the Annex spells out general requirements for the adoption of detailed standards on a number of issues such as packing, marking etc. (see paragraph 6.12 below).[60] The Annex sets forth a straightforward prohibition of the carriage of harmful substances (as defined by the said Annex), and regulates exceptions. It is noted that the revised regulations of MARPOL Annex III entered into force on 1 January 2014 through the tacit acceptance procedure. The changes of the Annex aimed at streamlining its provisions with the IMDG Code, which was also updated. Chemicals carried by sea in packaged form are also regulated by SOLAS Chapter VII.

6.11 Material scope of application

The regulations of the Annex apply to all ships carrying harmful substances in packaged form (on the meaning of "harmful substances" see paragraph 6.1 above). "Packaged form" signifies here the forms of containment specified for harmful substances in the IMDG Code.[61] Forms of containment covered include,

---

1973" – Amendments to MARPOL Annexes I, II, IV and V (To make use of environment-related provision of the Polar Code mandatory).

57 See Part II-A of the Polar Code on Pollution Prevention Measures, para. 2.1.1.

58 See Part II-A, para. 2.1.2.

59 See para. 2.1.3.

60 See Malgosia Fitzmaurice, 'The International Convention for the Prevention of Pollution from Ships (MARPOL)', in David J. Attard (General Ed), *The IMLI Manual on International Maritime Law* (Vol. III, Marine Environmental Law and Maritime Security Law, OUP 2016, p. 33 onwards).

61 Regulation 1.1.2.

for example, freight containers, portable tanks, etc. As it will be seen below, Annex III sets out substantial requirements in relation to packing, marking, labelling and stowage.

It may be appreciated that in contrast to Annex II, Annex III does not provide any pollution categories. A categorisation is effected by the IMDG Code, which, is intertwined with the Annex.

6.12 Substantial requirements (packing, marking, labelling, stowage)

There are a number of requirements relating to packing, marking and labelling, and stowage.[62] For example, packages containing harmful substances are required to be "durably marked or labelled to indicate that the substance is a harmful substance".[63] This must be made in accordance with the IMDG Code.[64] A reference is also made to the Code in relation to the method of affixing marks or labels on packages containing a harmful substance.[65] Furthermore, the Annex sets out requirements in relation to stowage and securing of harmful substances; the aim is to minimise the hazards to the marine environment with due consideration of safety.[66]

6.13 Quantity limitations

In addition to the above, it is also set out that certain harmful substances may need to be prohibited for carriage or be limited as to the quantity which may be carried aboard vessels. The limitation of the quantity should take into consideration the size, construction and equipment of the ship. Furthermore, the packaging and the inherent nature of the substances must also be taken into account.[67]

6.14 Exceptions

A prohibition to jettison harmful substances carried in packaged form is set out by the Annex.[68] However, there is an exception "where necessary for the purpose of securing the safety of the ship or saving life at sea".[69]

An appendix to the revised Annex III provides the criteria for the identification of harmful substances in packaged form.

In addition to the requirements which deal with prevention of pollution through prohibitions of discharge and other related aspects, Annex II and Annex III regulate certification and Port State Control.

---

62 See regulation 2 onwards.
63 Regulation 3.1.
64 *Ibid.*
65 Regulation 3.2.
66 Regulation 5.
67 Regulation 6.
68 Regulation 7.
69 Regulation 7.1.

FRAMEWORKS GOVERNING MARINE POLLUTION

SECTION 4: CERTIFICATION, PORT STATE CONTROL ON OPERATIONAL REQUIREMENTS AND OTHER ASPECTS STEMMING FROM MARPOL ANNEX II AND ANNEX III

6.15 In relation to MARPOL Annex II

6.15.1 Surveys and certificates

Chapter 3 of Annex II deals with surveys and certification. Ships carrying NLS in bulk are subjected to specified surveys for which specified requirements are formulated; the surveys are the following, namely: initial survey, renewal survey, intermediate survey, annual survey, and additional survey.[70] The usual provisions can be found concerning who is entitled to carry out ship surveys,[71] including a provision on national administrations being the guarantors of the completeness and efficiency of surveys.[72]

6.15.1.1 The International Pollution Prevention Certificate for the Carriage of Noxious Liquid Substances in Bulk (NLS certificate)

An International Pollution Prevention Certificate for the Carriage of Noxious Liquid Substances in Bulk (NLS certificate) is provided for in the same chapter.[73] The Certificate is issued to any ship intended to carry NLS in bulk engaged in voyages to ports or terminals under the jurisdiction of other States Parties to the Convention.[74] It certifies that the ship has been surveyed, as appropriate, that the survey showed that the structure, equipment, etc. of the ship and its condition are "in all respects satisfactory", and that the ship is compliant with the requirements of Annex II; furthermore, the Certificate certifies that the ship has been provided with a Procedures and Arrangements Manual (see paragraph 6.15.1.2 below) according to the Annex, and that it also complies with the requirements of Annex II for specified NLS "provided that all relevant provisions of Annex II are observed".[75]

The duration of the Certificate is specified by the national administration of the flag State and must not exceed five years.[76] Detailed provisions on duration and validity are also stated.[77]

In relation to chemical tankers, according to the IMO List of Certificates and Documents Required to be Carried on Board Ships dating to 19 July 2017,[78] the Certificate of Fitness for the Carriage of Dangerous Chemicals in Bulk (BCH Code), and

---

70 See regulation 8.1.
71 See regulation 8.2.1.
72 Regulation 8.2.6.
73 See regulation 9.1.
74 *Ibid.*
75 See Form of International Pollution Prevention Certificate for the Carriage of Noxious Liquid Substances in Bulk (Appendix III to MARPOL Annex II).
76 See regulation 10.1.
77 See regulation 10.
78 FAL.2/Circ.131, MEPC.1/Circ.873, MSC.1/Circ.1586, LEG.2/Circ.3.

173

the International Certificate of Fitness for the Carriage of Dangerous Chemicals in Bulk (IBC Code) shall have the same force and receive the same recognition as the NLS certificate.

6.15.1.2 Procedures and Arrangements Manual

Ships certified to carry substances categorised as X, Y or Z are required to have onboard an approved manual (Procedures and Arrangements Manual). The Manual is aimed to identify for the ship's officers the physical arrangements and all the operational procedures concerning cargo handling, tank cleaning, slops handling and cargo tank ballasting and deballasting which must be observed for compliance purposes with Annex II.[79] The Manual must be approved by the flag State administration and follow a specified form.[80]

In addition to the above, a Cargo Record Book is required.

6.15.1.3 Cargo Record Book

Ships carrying NLS in bulk must also have a Cargo Record Book. The latter can be part of the ship's official log-book or otherwise, in the form set out in an appendix to the Annex.[81] The list of items to be recorded is described in the form. Entries are required only for operations (e.g. loading of cargo, internal transfer of cargo, unloading of cargo, etc.) involving all categories of substances.

6.15.1.4 Shipboard Marine Pollution Emergency Plan for Noxious Liquid Substances

Ships certified to carry NLS in bulk of 150 gross tonnage and above are required to carry onboard an approved shipboard marine pollution emergency plan for NLS.[82] The minimum content of the plan is contained in Annex II. It notably includes:

- procedures to be followed notably by the master;
- the authorities or persons to be contacted in case of NLS pollution incident;
- action plan for the reduction or control of discharge of NLS following an incident;
- coordination with national and local authorities in combating the pollution.

6.15.2 Port State Control on operational requirements

MARPOL contains provisions on enforcement which are of interest to the control of marine pollution from NLS, and which relate to the enforcement powers of the

---

79 See regulation 14.
80 Appendix IV to Annex II.
81 See regulation 15.1.
82 Regulation 17.

flag State (e.g. Article 4 on violations). In addition to this, there are provisions on Port State Control which complement and support the goals and operation of Annex II.

Compliance of foreign vessels with operational requirements according to Annex II is verified by duly authorised officers in charge of inspections "where there are clear grounds for believing that the master or crew are not familiar with essential shipboard procedures relating to the prevention of pollution by noxious liquid substances".[83] This may potentially lead to detention. It should be noted at this point that Article 5 of MARPOL is also relevant.[84] This means that while in foreign ports or offshore terminals, a ship required to hold a certificate in accordance with MARPOL is subject to inspection by duly authorised officers which is limited, in principle, to verifying that there is on board a valid certificate.[85] Furthermore, inspections at foreign ports are provided for the purpose of verifying whether the ship has discharged any harmful substances in violation of relevant regulations.[86]

Recent findings under regional MOUs relating to MARPOL Annex II are expressed below as percent of total deficiencies (year under examination 2016). All things being equal, it may be appreciated that under other instruments (e.g. SOLAS) the percentage of deficiencies can be relatively high (e.g. in accordance with the findings of Riyadh MOU for the same year, deficiencies concerning lifesaving appliances for the same year amounted to 10.11%).

Paris MOU[1]	0.0%
Tokyo MOU[2]	25 deficiencies[3]
Black Sea MOU[4]	0.06%
Caribbean MOU[5]	0.00%
Riyadh MOU[6]	0.12%

1 Paris MOU Annual Report 2016.
2 Annual Report on Port State Control in the Asia-Pacific Region 2016.
3 As opposed to 1,609 deficiencies involving MARPOL Annex I.
4 Port State Control in the Black Sea Region, Annual Report 2016.
5 Caribbean MOU on Port State Control Annual Report 2016.
6 Riyadh MOU Annual Report 2016.

6.15.3 Port reception facilities

MARPOL Annex II also sets out the provision of port reception facilities.[87]

It may be recalled that the use of port reception facilities is central to the successful implementation of MARPOL, especially from the standpoint of reduction

---

83 Regulation 16.9.
84 This is stated in regulation 19.9.3 of MARPOL Annex II.
85 In case of clear grounds for believing that the condition of the ship or its equipment does not correspond substantially with the particulars of the certificate, or if the ship does not carry a valid certificate, the vessel may be prevented from sailing (see Article 5(2) of MARPOL Convention).
86 Article 6(2) of MARPOL.
87 Regulation 18.

and/or elimination of intentional marine pollution from ships. While improvements are noted on the level of the availability and use of port reception facilities, it is observed by the IMO that the efficient delivery of MARPOL residues/wastes ashore continues to be challenging. According to IMO Consolidated Guidance for Port Reception Facility Providers and Users (adopted on 15 April 2014) which aims to enable shipowners/operators and PRF operators to comply with MARPOL Convention, to complement residue/waste minimisation and management practices aboard the ship,[88] access by the industry to adequate PRF is needed.[89] According to the same document, "adequacy" as used in the Annexes of MARPOL signifies that the PRF satisfy the needs of ships using the ports without causing undue delay.[90]

States are called upon by MARPOL to provide adequate reception facilities in ports. In the context of Annex II this obligation can be found in regulation 18, as amended. More specifically, States "undertake to ensure" the provision of reception facilities according to the needs of ships using its ports, terminals or repair ports. According to the above-mentioned guideline, MARPOL residues and wastes in the context of Annex II include tanks washings and cargo residues containing NLS as defined in the Annex.

6.16 In relation to MARPOL Annex III

It is noted that there is no survey requirement under Annex III. However, a relevant requirement exists under SOLAS in relation to dangerous goods. Furthermore, there is no requirement on the provision of port reception facilities. MARPOL Annex III was amended by Resolution MEPC.193(61) dating to 1 October 2010.[91] The amendment entered into force through the tacit acceptance procedure on 1 January 2014.

6.16.1 Documentation

Transport information relating to carriage of harmful substances is subject to the IMDG Code. The said information is required to be made available to the person or organisation designated by the port State authority.[92] Ships carrying harmful substances are held to have a special list, manifest or stowage plan providing the harmful substances aboard and their location in accordance with the IMDG

---

88 The Guidelines note that waste minimisation is not a direct requirement under MARPOL but constitutes an environmental best practice.

89 MEPC.1/Circ.834, 15 April 2014. It is noted that guidance to Party State authorities and Governments for the implementation of port reception facilities under MARPOL is given in the IMO Comprehensive Manual on Port Reception Facilities (1999) and the Guidelines for Ensuring the Adequacy of Port Waste Reception Facilities (resolution MEPC.83(44)).

90 *Ibid.*, para. 6.

91 Resolution MEPC.193(61), adopted on 1 October 2010, Amendments to the Annex of the Protocol of 1978 relating to the International Convention for the Prevention of Pollution from Ships, 1973 (Revised MARPOL Annex III).

92 Regulation 4.1.

Code.[93] Furthermore, a copy of relevant documents is required to be made available before departure to the person or organisation designated by the port State authority.[94]

6.16.2 Port State Control on operational requirements

Regulation 8 of revised Annex III deals with Port State Control on operational requirements. The provision is additional to Port State Control procedures prescribed in Article 5 of the Convention.[95] Furthermore, it is stated that the rights and obligations of States on Port State Control over operational requirements under the Convention are not impaired by the provisions of regulation 8 on PSC.[96]

Furthermore, the right to inspect the ship concerning operational requirements at a foreign port (or offshore terminal) is spelt out. In case of clear grounds for believing that the master or crew are not familiar with shipboard procedures on pollution prevention by harmful substances, it is provided that the Party must take necessary steps. The steps in question include carrying out detailed inspection and, if required, ensuring detention until the situation is remedied in line with Annex III.[97]

Recent findings under regional MOUs relating to MARPOL Annex III expressed in percent of total deficiencies (year under examination 2016) point to the data below:

Paris MOU[1]	0.0%
Tokyo MOU[2]	12 deficiencies[3]
Black Sea MOU[4]	0.03%
Caribbean MOU[5]	0.00%
Riyadh MOU[6]	0.12%

1 Annual Report 2016.
2 Annual Report on Port State Control in the Asia-Pacific Region 2016.
3 As opposed to 1,609 deficiencies involving MARPOL Annex I.
4 Port State Control in the Black Sea Region Annual Report 2016.
5 Caribbean MOU on Port State Control Annual Report 2016.
6 Riyadh Memorandum of Understanding Annual Report.

BIBLIOGRAPHY

Annual Report Caribbean MOU on Port State Control (2016)
Annual Report Paris Memorandum of Understanding on Port State Control (2016)
Annual Report on Port State Control in the Asia-Pacific Region (2016)
Annual Report Port State Control in the Black Sea Region (2016)
Annual Report Riyadh Memorandum of Understanding on Port State Control (2016)

---

93 Regulation 4.2.
94 *Ibid.*
95 Regulation 8.3.
96 Regulation 8.4.
97 Regulation 8.2.

De la Rue, C., and Anderson, Ch. B., *Shipping and the Environment* (2nd edition, Informa, London/New York, Lloyd's Shipping Law Library, 2009)

Fitzmaurice, Malgosia, 'The International Convention for the Prevention of Pollution from Ships (MARPOL)' in David J. Attard (General Ed), *The IMLI Manual on International Maritime Law* (Vol. III, Marine Environmental Law and Maritime Security Law, OUP, Oxford, 2016)

GESAMP, Revised GESAMP Hazard Evaluation Procedure for Chemical Substances Carried by Ships (IMO/FAO/ UNESCO-IOC/WMO/IAEA/UN/UNEP/UNIDO/UNDP) Joint Group of Experts on the Scientific Aspects of Marine Environmental Protection, Rep. Stud. GESAMP No. 64 (2nd edition, 2014)

GHS Rev.7 (2017) (7th revised edition, United Nations, New York/Geneva)

Guner-Ozbek, Meltem Deniz, *The Carriage of Dangerous Goods by Sea* (Springer, Berlin-Heidelberg, 2008)

Häkkinen, J.M., and Posti, A.I., 'Overview of Maritime Accidents Involving Chemicals Worldwide and in the Baltic Sea' in A. Weintrit and T. Neumann (eds), *Marine Navigation and Safety of Sea Transportation – Maritime Transport and Shipping* (CRC Press, London, 2013)

Hoefer, Thomas, Charlebois, P., Le Floch, S., and Morrissette, M., 'Cargo Information Needed During the Initial Stages of a Chemical Spill' (Interspill 2015, White Paper)

Höfer, Thomas, 'Hazard Assessment for Chemicals Carried by Ships' (Interspill Conference 2009)

IMO Manual on Chemical Pollution, Section 2: Search and Recovery of Packaged Goods Lost at Sea (2007 edition)

IMO Manual on Chemical Pollution, Section 3: Legal and Administrative Aspects of HNS Incidents (2015 edition)

IMO MARPOL Consolidated Edition 2011 (and Supplements)

IMO's Revised Recommendation on the Safe Transport of Dangerous Cargoes and Related Activities in Port Areas (2007 edition)

International Chamber of Shipping (ICS), *Tanker Safety Guide (Chemicals)* (4th edition, London, 2014)

ITOPF (International Tanker Owners Pollution Federation) Response to Marine Chemical Incidents (Technical Information Paper 17) (document date unavailable)

Purnell, Karen, ITOPF, 'Are HNS Spills More Dangerous Than Oils Spills?' (White Paper, Interspill Conference, 4th Research and Development Forum, Marseille May 2009)

Transport Canada/Cedre, Understanding Chemical Pollution at Sea, www.chemical-pollution.com (last visit 6 November 2017)

Wilkins Tim (INTERTANKO), 'MARPOL Annex II-Regulations for the Control of Pollution by Liquid Noxious Substances in Bulk' (power point presentation)

World Nuclear Transport Institute, Radioactive Materials Transport the International Safety Regime (An Overview of Safety Regulations and the Organizations Responsible for their Development) (Revised July 2006)

CHAPTER 7

Air pollution from shipping

TABLE OF CONTENTS

Section 1	Identifying the subject area	180
7.1	What is the problem?	180
	7.1.1 The contribution of shipping to air pollution and climate change	181
7.2	Glossary	182
Section 2	Main discussion of the regulatory framework	183
7.3	The regulatory framework at the international level: MARPOL Annex VI	184
	7.3.1 Setting sulphur caps on the content of marine fuels with a view to reducing SOx and PM	185
	7.3.2 Emission Control Areas	185
	7.3.3 Control of emissions of NOx	186
	7.3.4 Regulation of ozone depleting substances	186
	7.3.5 Measures involving ship energy efficiency	186
	7.3.5.1 Energy Efficiency Design Index	187
	7.3.6 Identifying challenges	187
7.4	The regulatory framework at the EU level	188
	7.4.1 Overview	188
	7.4.2 Monitoring, Reporting and Verification Regulation (Regulation (EU) 2015/757)	190
	7.4.3 The future: is shipping heading towards an EU emission trading scheme?	191
Section 3	Key management issues, including surveys and certification	192
7.5	Surveys and inspections	192
7.6	Certificates and plans	193
	7.6.1 International Air Pollution Prevention Certificate	193
	7.6.2 International Energy Efficiency Certificate	193
	7.6.3 Ship Energy Efficiency Management Plan	194
7.7	Key management issues stemming from the EU regime	199
	7.7.1 MRV Regulation (EU) – related documentation	199
7.8	Port State Control	200

Section 4	Areas of special interest	201
7.9	Market-based approaches	201
Section 5	Developments underway	202
7.10	IMO's fuel consumption data	202
7.11	Recent development stemming from the European Union	202
7.12	Alternative solutions	202
7.12.1	Liquefied Natural Gas	202
7.12.2	Bioenergy/biofuels	203

SECTION 1: IDENTIFYING THE SUBJECT AREA

7.1 What is the problem?

In recognition of major concerns stemming from air emissions from shipping in relation to humans and the environment, marine pollution control was extended in recent years so as to cover air pollution from shipping. This is notably reflected in MARPOL Annex VI, entitled "Regulations for the prevention of air pollution from ships"; the Annex was adopted through a Protocol dating to 1997 (entry into force on 19 May 2005) and, since then, it has been subject to revisions. Annex VI deals with air emissions from vessels from the standpoint of specific air pollutants impairing air quality, and specific greenhouse gases (GHGs). With exhaust gases being the primary source of emissions from ships, as fuel combustion remains vital to ship movement and other operations, the use of marine bunker fuel oil is a key factor for air quality and becomes central to the discussion on air pollution from shipping – a ship using its main engine(s) on the open sea or while manoeuvring in ports, and running the main or auxiliary engines while at berth, loading or unloading cargo or passengers.[1] With this in mind, air emissions from shipping are recognised to contribute to air pollution and climate change, but in comparison with the non-transport sector and other modes of transportation, their contribution is generally acknowledged as significant but not major (this aspect will be dealt in more detail in the next paragraph).

Air emissions from shipping such as sulphur oxides (SOx), nitrogen oxides (NOx), volatile organic compounds (VOC), and particulate matter (PM) have been associated with negative effects on humans and the environment, and have been subjected to international and/or regional regulations.[2] Furthermore, GHG emissions such as carbon dioxide (CO_2), the most important GHG emitted by

---

1 See European Environment Agency (EEA), *The Impact of International Shipping on European Air Quality and Climate Forcing* (EEA Technical Report, No. 4/2013, ISSN 1725–2237, Copenhagen), p. 9.

2 See J. Harrison, 'Pollution of the Marine Environment from or through the Atmosphere', in David Joseph Attard (General Ed), *The IMLI Manual on International Maritime Law, Vol. III, Marine Environmental Law and Maritime Security Law* (pp. 169–192, OUP 2016).

ships, methane (CH_4), nitrous oxide (N_2O), ozone, and CFCs (chlorofluorocarbons) trap heat in the atmosphere and contribute to global warming and climate change. The various potential impacts of emissions from shipping on air quality, human health and ecosystems have been explored by scientists, even though many aspects remain unknown. It is noteworthy that nearly 70% of ship emissions occur within 400 km of coastlines with possible impacts further inland.[3]

It can be argued that, despite the existing regulations and policies on the matter, the question of air pollution from shipping continues to raise important questions for the future. This includes, amongst others, the dependency of regulators and policy makers on scientific findings which may not have fully crystallised, possible downsides of each new measure potentially compromising the overall goals sought by legal requirements (e.g. the risk of modal shift from sea transport to road transport, etc.), and possible changes on the picture of air pollution from shipping stemming from the potential use of unmanned or autonomous vessels in the near future.

7.1.1 The contribution of shipping to air pollution and climate change

While shipping contributes significantly less than the non-transport sector or other modes of transportation to the problem of air pollution and climate change, thus remaining an environmentally friendly mode of transportation, existing studies suggest that international and domestic shipping has some contribution to the problem.

The Second IMO Study on GHGs which dates to 2009 estimated the contribution of shipping to global emissions during 2007 to be 3.3%, with international shipping having contributed about 2.7% to the global emissions of CO_2 in the same year.[4] Additional insights were provided by the Third IMO GHG Study 2014: international shipping was considered to account (year 2012) for approximately 2.2% and 2.1% of global CO_2 and GHG emissions on a CO_2 equivalent (CO_2e) basis, respectively.[5]

On a regional level, emissions from shipping in European waters are considered to represent "a significant share" of worldwide ship emissions of air pollutants and GHGs[6] with the non-transport sector representing a clearly dominant contributor in relation to main air pollutants.[7]

It is noteworthy that a number of resources point out that unless measures were taken, shipping would risk to become a problematic contributor to air pollution

---

3 Endresen et al, 2003, cited in EEA, *supra* note 1, p. 38. For a detailed presentation, including an overview of scientific findings on air pollution from ships in the EU, see EEA, *ibid.*

4 Second IMO GHG Study 2009, p. 1.

5 Third IMO GHG Study 2014, p. 1.

6 See EEA, *supra* note 1, p. 5.

7 This is according to temporal coverage 2012 (National emissions reported to the Convention on Long-range Transboundary Air Pollution provided by the European Environment Agency; geographic coverage includes the EU Member States as well as Iceland, Liechtenstein, Norway, Switzerland and Turkey.

and global warming. In addition to this, the challenges encountered for the evaluation of the problem are to be noted; more than one methodology on the matter can be found, potentially leading to different findings on the actual contribution of shipping to air pollution and global warming, thus not providing a homogeneous basis for action to policy makers.[8]

On this point it is useful to briefly explain some key terms which are used in this subject area.

7.2 Glossary

Air pollutants	Some of them fall in the scope of MARPOL Annex VI which sets out limitations of emissions from sulphur oxides (SOx), nitrogen oxides (NOx), ozone-depleting substances (ODS), and volatile organic compounds (VOC) from tankers.
Climate change	"A change of climate which is attributed directly or indirectly to human activity that alters the composition of the global atmosphere and which is in addition to natural climate variability observed over comparable time periods" (UNFCCC[1]). The Earth's climate is changing not only due to natural but also due to anthropogenic factors (e.g. use of fossil fuels, deforestation, etc.). Scientific findings suggest that the Earth's average surface temperature has increased by more than $0.8°C$ ($1.4°F$) over the past 100 years.[2] Some of the wide-ranging effects of climate change are global warming, sea level rise, change of seasonal patterns, melting of snow and ice, etc. The above-mentioned United Nations Framework Convention on Climate Change (entry into force 1994), amended by the Kyoto Protocol (1997), sought to prevent dangerous human interference with the climate system.
Emission Control Areas (ECAs)	Sea areas designated under the IMO system where more stringent requirements apply in relation to the regulation of specified air emissions (emissions from SOx, NOx, and/or particulate matter (PM) are noted), thus the existence of Sulphur Emission Control Areas (SECAs) and Nitrogen Oxide Emission Control Areas (NECAs).
Emission trading scheme	In an emission trading scheme carbon is given a price as the system is based on the trading of pre-pollution permits in relation to specified pollutants. Examples of emission trading schemes are the Kyoto Protocol and the EU Emission Trading Scheme which works on the basis of the "cap and trade" principle and is the largest multi-country GHG emission trading scheme at present – companies receive or trade emission allowances within a specified cap, which they may trade.
Environmental sustainability/ sustainable development	Sustainability is commonly geared towards three directions, namely: the environment, society and economy. Environmental sustainability/ sustainable development advocates in favour of humans not impairing the needs of present and future generations.

---

8   Joint Research Centre (JRC) Reference Reports, European Commission and the Institute for Environment and Sustainability, Regulating Air Emissions from Ships – The State of the Art on Methodologies, Technologies and Policy Options, Miola et al, 2010, p. 15 *seq.*

Exhaust gas cleaning systems	Exhaust gas cleaning systems can be viewed as an expression of the possibility set out by regulation 4 of MARPOL Annex VI to use, subject to approval of the administration, alternative compliance methods which are at least as effective in terms of emission reductions as that required by the Annex (MEPC.259(68), adopted on 15 May 2015, introduced the 2015 Guidelines for Exhaust Gas Cleaning systems). It is noted that the term exhaust gas cleaning system is sometimes used to indicate scrubbers.
Fuel oil	In the context of MARPOL Annex VI, it means any fuel for combustion purposes, propulsion or operation of a ship, including distillate and residual fuels.[4]
Greenhouse gases (GHGs)	Gases of natural or anthropogenic origin that trap heat in the atmosphere and contribute to global warming (e.g. carbon dioxide, nitrous oxide, methane, etc.). According to the international text of reference, GHGs are "are those gaseous constituents of the atmosphere, both natural and anthropogenic, that absorb and re-emit infrared radiation".[3] Carbon dioxide is the most important GHG emitted by ships.
NOx Technical Code 2008	This is the Technical Code on Control of Emission of Nitrogen Oxides from Marine Diesel Engines. The Code aims to provide mandatory procedures for the testing, survey and certification of marine diesel engines so that manufacturers, shipowners and flag State administrations can make sure that all applicable marine diesel engines comply with relevant NOx, as emission limits. The NOx Technical Code was adopted in 1997 (entry into force 19 May 2005); revised in October 2008.
Ship energy efficiency	Ship energy efficiency at large is supported by technical and operational measures such as improved design, improved voyage planning, propeller cleaning, etc. The Energy Efficiency Design Index (EEDI), which is a technical measure on the use of less polluting equipment and engines, and the Ship Energy Efficiency Management Plan (SEEMP), which targets operations (both terms are further discussed below) are illustrations of ship energy efficiency measures which present an interest to air pollution from shipping.

1 UNFCCC (1992) stands for United Nations Framework Convention on Climate Change.
2 National Research Council of the National Academies (USA) – The National Academies Press, Washington D.C. (2012) "Climate Change: Evidence, Impact and Choices – answers to common questions about the science of climate change", p. 3.
3 United Nations Framework Convention on Climate Change (UNFCCC).
4 See MARPOL Annex VI, regulation 2.9.

SECTION 2: MAIN DISCUSSION OF THE REGULATORY FRAMEWORK

The regulatory framework governing air pollution from shipping is dominated by global regulations adopted at the IMO level. Nevertheless, it is clear that there is more than one institutional stakeholder involved working on the agenda of air emissions from vessels and climate change (see graph 7.1 below). While this factor enhances the discussion on air pollution and climate change, at the same time it may entail the risk of creating confusion, overlap or inconsistencies. Against this background, regulators and other bodies have included regulatory and non-regulatory approaches to the problem of air quality and climate change in relation to shipping, with the proposal of subjecting shipping to an emission trading scheme gaining momentum (see graph 7.2 below).

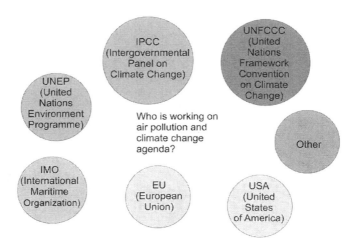

Graph 7.1 Who is working on air pollution and climate change agenda?

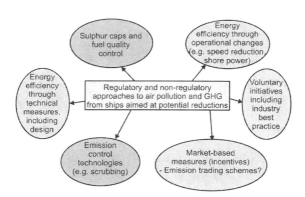

Graph 7.2 Regulatory and non-regulatory approaches to air pollution and GHG from ships aimed at potential reductions

7.3 The regulatory framework at the international level: MARPOL Annex VI

The breadth of MARPOL Annex VI from the standpoint of specified pollutants is briefly described below:

Regulation 12	Ozone depleting substances (ODS)
Regulation 13	Nitrogen oxides (NOx)
Regulation 14	Sulphur oxides (SOx) and particulate matter (PM)
Regulation 15	Volatile organic compounds (VOCs)
Regulation 16	Shipboard incineration
Regulation 21	CO_2 through the Energy Efficiency Design Index (EEDI)

It should be noted from the outset that Annex VI does not apply to emissions necessary for securing the safety of the vessel or saving life at sea or to emissions resulting from damage to a ship or its equipment. In the latter case, all reasonable precautions must have been taken after the damage or discovery of the emission for preventing or minimising the emission. Additionally, the owner or the master must not have acted "either with intent to cause damage, or recklessly and with knowledge that damage would probably result".[9]

7.3.1 Setting sulphur caps on the content of marine fuels with a view to reducing SOx and PM

Emissions from shipping as a result of the combustion of marine fuels with a high sulphur content have been considered as contributors to air pollution in the form of sulphur dioxide and particulate matter, with potentially negative effects on human health and the environment. The rationale adopted by MARPOL Annex VI in relation to sulphur oxides consists of mandatory requirements on the quality of marine fuels in recognition of the correlation between sulphur content of fuels and reduced sulphur emissions.

In this context, reduced SOx limits for marine bunker fuels have been set out by the Annex. With effect from 1 January 2012, the global cap was reduced from 4.5% to 3.5% m/m (mass/mass) outside Emission Control Areas. The IMO had undertaken a fuel availability study which would condition further reductions. In 2016, the IMO review of fuel availability was completed, concluding that sufficient compliant fuel oil would be available to satisfy the requirements on fuel oil. During its 70th session in London, the MEPC decided to implement a global sulphur cap of 0.50% m/m on or after 1 January 2020. This shift on the global level from 3.5% to 0.50% represents an important development which is likely to have a significant impact on health, the environment, and the business of private operators.

7.3.2 Emission Control Areas

Sulphur limits in the areas designated by the IMO as Emission Control Areas (ECAs) were set out at more stringent levels for SOx and PM, i.e. 1.00% from 1 July 2010 (from 1.50%), and they were further reduced to 0.10%, effective from 1 January 2015. At present, ECAs in relation to SOx concern the Baltic Sea, the North Sea, North American Area (SOx and PM), and United States Caribbean

---

9 See MARPOL Annex VI, regulation 3.1.

Sea area (SOx and PM). Emission Control Areas in the case of North America and United States Caribbean Sea also cover NOx. Mention is made of the control of emissions of nitrogen oxides below.

7.3.3 Control of emissions of NOx

Ships are required to gradually produce nitrogen oxides (NOx) emissions below certain levels.[10] This is sought through the mandatory use of a system structured over tiers which can be understood as levels of control, and which applies to marine diesel engines installed on ships according to the year of construction. In other terms, global NOx IMO regulations involve three tiers which progressively become increasingly stringent. Tier II level, for example, would require from ships built on or after 1 January 2011 a NOx emission reduction around 20%, whereas Tier III would lead to a reduction of 80%, and would involve NECAs and ships built after the implementation date of the relevant NECAs. It is noted that IMO NOx Tier III became effective from 1 January 2016 in the North America and US Caribbean Emission Control Area – the relevant requirement being applicable to all vessels with keel-laying on or after 1 January 2016 with a specified engine output.

7.3.4 Regulation of ozone depleting substances

Ozone depleting substances is a family of man-made compounds which are considered to deplete stratospheric ozone, thus contributing to ozone depletion. In the interest of clarity, it is noted that according to scientists a thinner ozone layer does not cause climate change. Yet, ozone depletion negatively impacts on humans and on the environment (in the case of human health, skin cancer has been associated with ODS). Principal ODS include, amongst others, chlorofluorocarbons (CFCs), hydrochlorofluorocarbons (HCFCs), methyl bromide, and bromofluorocarbons (halons).

Deliberate emissions of ozone-depleting substances are prohibited by the Annex.[11] Deliberate emissions comprise emissions which take place in the course of maintaining, servicing, repairing or disposing of systems or equipment; however, deliberate omissions do not include minimal releases associated with the recapture or recycling of an ozone-depleting substance. Furthermore, the question of emissions arising from leaks of an ozone-depleting substance, whether or not the leaks are deliberate, is left to the State Parties, as it is stated that they "may be regulated by Parties".

An ozone-depleting substances record book is set out.[12]

7.3.5 Measures involving ship energy efficiency

Ship energy efficiency aims at reduced greenhouse gas emissions. A new Chapter 4, entitled "Regulations on energy efficiency of ships" was added to MARPOL

---

10 MARPOL Annex VI, regulation 13.
11 MARPOL Annex VI, regulation 12.2.
12 MARPOL Annex VI, regulation 12.6.

Annex VI, via MEPC Resolution 203(62), adopted on 15 July 2011 (entry into force 1 January 2013). The Resolution amended the Annex through the inclusion of ship energy efficiency regulations. This legislative change represents a key development in the regulatory agenda of GHGs from shipping through mandatory technical and operational measures. The said measures have since then been under continued scrutiny, and they still attract a lot of attention.

7.3.5.1 Energy Efficiency Design Index

The Energy Efficiency Design Index (EEDI) is a performance-based approach to the problem of GHG emissions from shipping, through technical measures aimed at innovation.

The EEDI "estimates ship CO_2 emissions per ton-mile of goods transported relative to a reference average of similar ships".[13] The measure was adopted through the above-mentioned Chapter 4 of Annex VI, following long discussions. Since its adoption, it has been subject to amendments (e.g. so as to extend the requirement to more types of vessels). As already mentioned, the EEDI constitutes a technical approach to the problem of emissions of CO_2 by vessels, and is intended for new ships. Initially, the EEDI covered emissions from new tankers, bulk carriers, gas carriers, general cargo ships, container ships, refrigerated cargo carriers and combination carriers. LNG carriers, ro-ro cargo ships (vehicle carriers), ro-ro cargo ships, ro-ro passenger ships and cruise passenger ships having non-conventional propulsion were included at a subsequent stage.

Some of the salient features of the EEDI include the focus being placed on large ships and the EEDI score becoming increasingly stringent for the majority of new vessels. New ships were thus required to be more efficient beginning 2015, with their efficiency being increased by 2020 and from 2025. According to the International Council on Clean Transportation (ICCT), if implemented in line with the schedule, 263 million tonnes (Mt) of CO_2 are projected to be reduced annually by 2030.[14]

Ship energy efficiency will be further discussed below under the section on key management issues (para. 7.6.2) in relation to the Ship Energy Efficiency Management Plan (SEEMP).

7.3.6 Identifying challenges

Selected challenges stemming from the international regime governing emissions from shipping notably include the following:

- the ability of private operators to implement, including ensuring and evidencing compliance, thus avoid exposure to civil and criminal penalties; the ability also of private operators to ensure continued monitoring, and take corrective action, wherever needed;

---

13 The International Council on Clean Transportation (ICCT), Policy Update 15, 3 October 2011, p. 2.

14 *Ibid.*, p. 1.

- an aspect which amplifies the above is the smooth operation relating to the switch from high sulphur fuel to SECA-compliant marine fuel;
- the advisability, including credibility, costs, and long-term viability, of alternative solutions to low sulphur content fuels;
- the future of Emission Control Areas through the probable addition of new ECAs;
- the actual impact of international measures on protecting effectively air quality and slowing down climate change.

In addition to international regulations, air pollution from shipping has been subjected to European Union legislation; as it will be seen below, the latter impacts on EU-flagged ships as well as on ships calling at EU ports.

7.4 The regulatory framework at the EU level

7.4.1 Overview

On the one hand, the European Union supports global action on air pollution and climate change. In this context, the EU recognises that "emissions from shipping due to the combustion of marine fuels with high sulphur content contribute to air pollution in the form of sulphur dioxide and particulate matter, harming human health, damaging the environment, public and private property and cultural heritage and contributing to acidification".[15] Furthermore, the EU especially acknowledges the exposure of coastal populations to the problem, and considers that there are some advantages for ships through the reduction of the sulphur content of fuels such as operating efficiency and maintenance costs, as well as the facilitation of the effective use of certain emission abatement technologies.[16] As it will be seen below, the risk of modal shift from sea to land-based transport as a result of the costs of new requirements on sulphur content of fuels is also well noted by the EU.

On the other hand, the EU has clearly set its own regulatory agenda on the matter, and appears to be prepared for more regional action. It would be useful at this point to mention that EU Member States are bound by international regulations adopted by the IMO to the extent that they adhere to such regulations (e.g. through the ratification of a convention), whereas in the case of EU legislation, EU regulations are directly applicable in the EU Member States' legal system, and EU directives become operational through national transposition measures (i.e. an EU directive requires Member States to adopt appropriate national transposition measures making effective the EU directive in their system; a deadline is set out in that regard). The EU's regulatory agenda may seek to align EU requirements with the international regime or shape regional solutions to the problem of air pollution.

---

15 See Recital 4 Directive 2005/33/EC, *infra*, note 22.
16 *Ibid.*, Recital 7.

Applicable law stems from Directive (EU) 2016/802 ("the Sulphur Directive") of the European Parliament and of the Council of 11 May 2016 relating to a reduction in the sulphur content of certain liquid fuels.[17] Technically speaking, this text is a codification of Council Directive 1999/32/EC of 26 April 1999 on the reduction in the sulphur content of certain liquid fuels and on the amendment of Directive 93/12/EEC[18] (it is noted at this point that Directive 1999/32/EC had been amended a number of times, including, amongst others, by Directive 2005/33/EC[19] and Directive 2012/33/EU[20]). Like its predecessors, Directive 2016/802/EU seeks to reduce the emissions of sulphur dioxide from the combustion of certain types of liquid fuels, thus cutting the harmful effects of such emissions on humans and the environment.

In the above context, the purpose of Directive 1999/32/EC, which set out the maximum permitted sulphur content of heavy fuel oil, gas oil and marine gas oil used in the EU, was to reduce the emissions of sulphur dioxide resulting from the combustion of certain types of liquid fuels and, consequently, to reduce the harmful effects of such emissions on humans and the environment. The use of abatement technologies and economic incentives was also encouraged by Directive 1999/32/EC.[21]

Directive 2005/33/EC[22] amended the initial text as regards the sulphur content of marine fuels. Furthermore, SOx Emission Control Areas (Baltic Sea, North Sea and English Channel) were introduced by the same instrument. With effect from 1 January 2010, measures had to be taken under the Directive by Member States in order to ensure that inland waterways vessels and ships at berth in European Community ports do not use marine fuels with a sulphur content exceeding 0.1% by mass.[23]

Directive 2012/33/EU (whose implementation deadline expired on 18 June 2014) amended Directive 1999/32/EC as regards the sulphur content of marine fuels. In recognition of the risk that, without EU measures, "emissions from shipping would soon have been higher than emissions from all land-based sources",[24] Directive 2012/33/EU acknowledges air pollution caused by ships at berth as a major concern, and encourages the use of shore-side electricity.[25] Furthermore, the Directive points to the risk of modal shift from sea to land-based transport as a result of the costs of the new requirements to reduce SOx emissions.[26] Directive 2012/33/EU seeks to align the previous text, i.e. Direc-

---

17 [2016] OJ L132/58.

18 [1999] OJ L121/13.

19 European Parliament and Council (EC) Directive 2005/33 amending Directive 1999/32/EC [2005] OJ L191/59.

20 European Parliament and Council (EU) Directive 2012/33 amending Council Directive 1999/32/EC as regards the sulphur content of marine fuels [2012] OJ L327/1.

21 See Article 4c.

22 European Parliament and Council (EU) Directive 2005/33 amending Directive 1999/32/EC [2005] OJ L191/59.

23 Article 4b(1) of Directive 2005/33/EC.

24 See Recital 4 of the Directive.

25 See Recital 5 *et seq.* of the Directive.

26 See Recital 22 of the Directive.

tive 1999/32/EC, with the Annex VI to MARPOL, as revised in 2008; it may be recalled that the last one had introduced, inter alia, stricter sulphur limits for marine fuels in ECAs (1.00% as of 1 July 2010 and 0.10% as of 1 January 2015) and in the sea areas outside ECAs (3.50% as of 1 January 2012 and, in principle, 0.50% as of 1 January 2020).

As already mentioned, a codification directive is currently the reference, i.e. Directive 2016/802, which put together all relevant EU provisions.

7.4.2 Monitoring, Reporting and Verification Regulation (Regulation (EU) 2015/757)

The Monitoring, Reporting and Verification (MRV) Regulation, was adopted by the EU on 29 April 2015 (entry into force on 1 July 2015; it will become applicable from 1 January 2018[27]). As already mentioned, EU Regulations are directly applicable in the legal systems of EU Member States. The Regulation (Regulation 2015/757 of the European Parliament and of the Council of 29 April 2015 on the monitoring, reporting and verification of carbon dioxide emissions from maritime transport and amending Directive 2009/16/EC[28]) targets CO_2 emissions of large vessels regardless of flag using EU ports. According to European Commission's estimates, the regime set out by the Regulation is expected to cut CO_2 emissions by up to 2% compared to business-as-usual.[29]

Before having a closer look at the Regulation, let us bear in mind that the EU regime exists in parallel with the IMO roadmap (2017 through to 2023) on the reduction of GHGs from shipping and the fuel oil data collection system (Fuel Oil Data Collection System (FODCS)) decided by the IMO MEPC at its 70th meeting on 28 October 2016.

The EU Regulation is geared towards the reduction of CO_2 emissions from shipping at the EU level, through the setting up of a system requiring monitoring, reporting and verification of CO_2 emissions on the basis of fuel consumption of ships. This approach constitutes the first step of a staged approach on the part of the EU towards the inclusion in the future of maritime transport emissions in its regional GHG reduction commitment (alongside emissions from other sectors).[30] In emissions trading schemes (commonly referred to as cap-and-trade systems), carbon is given a price. The rationale of the EU is to view access to the emissions data as a first step for removing market barriers "that prevent the update of many cost-negative measures which would reduce greenhouse gas emissions from maritime transport".[31]

The Regulation applies to ships over 5,000 gross tonnes (GT) calling at EU ports from 1 January 2018. As noted in the Regulation, "All intra-Union voyages,

---

27 First reporting period starting on 1 January 2018.
28 [2015] OJ L123/55.
29 See Recital 13 of the Regulation.
30 See Recital 10 of the Regulation.
31 Ibid.

all incoming voyages from the last non-Union port to the first Union port of call and all outgoing voyages from a Union port to the next non-Union port of call, including ballast voyages, should be considered relevant for the purposes of monitoring."[32] Some exemptions are provided for: the Regulation does not apply to warships, naval auxiliaries, fish-catching or fish-processing ships, wooden ships of a primitive build, ships not propelled by mechanical means, or government ships used for non-commercial purposes.[33]

1 January 2018 is the date triggering the obligation of companies to monitor CO_2 emissions for each ship on a per-voyage and an annual basis.[34] A document of compliance is provided for, i.e. a ship-specific document issued to a company by a verifier, which confirms that the ship is MRV compliant for a specific reporting period.[35]

There are several important dates relevant to the application of the instrument notably including the following:

- By 31 August 2017: Drawing up of a monitoring plan to be reviewed by an accredited verifier for each ship grasped by the Regulation on the monitoring and reporting of their carbon emissions and transport work, i.e. commercial cargo transported multiplied by the distance sailed; it is noted at this point that the methods of calculation of the actual fuel consumption are set out by the instrument (e.g. bunker delivery note, bunker fuel tank monitoring, etc.). The content of the monitoring plan is also determined by the Regulation.[36]
- From 2019, by 30 April of each year: submission of a verified annual emissions report to the European Commission and to the authorities of the flag State;[37]
- From 2019, by 30 June of each year: collected data relating to emissions and efficiency parameters made publicly available by the European Commission.[38]

7.4.3 The future: is shipping heading towards an EU emission trading scheme?

The MRV Regulation clearly evidences the willingness of the EU to break market barriers to measures on GHGs reduction such as lack of reliable information on the fuel efficiency of ships. The Regulation is aimed at ensuring the conditions, through data collection, for placing CO_2 emissions from shipping in the scope of the EU's regional emissions trading scheme. Such development would risk to cause frictions with the international system, if the two systems (EU and IMO) are not aligned. A recent development dating to February 2017 is the adoption by

---

32 See Recital 14 of the Regulation.
33 Article 2(2).
34 Article 8.
35 See Chapter IV of the Regulation.
36 Article 6.
37 Article 11.
38 Article 21.

a majority of members of the European Parliament of a vote on the inclusion of shipping in the regional emissions trading scheme as of 2023 in the absence of comparable system on the IMO level by 2021.

SECTION 3: KEY MANAGEMENT ISSUES, INCLUDING SURVEYS AND CERTIFICATION

7.5 Surveys and inspections

Chapter 2 of MARPOL Annex VI deals with survey, certification and means of control. For compliance purposes, every ship of 400 gross tonnage and above[39] is subject to specified surveys, namely: initial, renewal, intermediate, annual, and additional.[40] For smaller vessels, i.e. vessels of less than 400 gross tonnage, the flag State may provide for appropriate measures in order to ensure that the applicable requirements for control of air emissions from ships are complied with.[41]

Concerning surveys, the Annex states, as usual, the conduct of surveys by officers of the flag State administration as well as the possibility of empowering third Parties (nominated surveyor or recognised organisation) for their conduct. This delegation does not invalidate the role of the administration as the full guarantor of the completeness and efficiency of the survey.[42] Mention is also made of the corrective action that must be ensured by these entities in case of substantial discrepancies between the condition of the equipment and the particulars of the certificate, as well as of the withdrawal of the certificate by the flag State administration in case no corrective action is taken.[43]

Furthermore, an obligation to maintain the equipment in conformity with the provisions of Annex VI is set out, as well as a prohibition to change the equipment or other items covered by the survey without the express approval of the flag State administration.[44] In case of accident or substantial defect affecting the efficiency of completeness of the equipment covered by Annex VI, there is an obligation on the master or shipowner to report "at the earliest opportunity" to the flag State, a nominated surveyor or recognised organisation responsible for issuing the relevant certificate.[45]

Following an amendment of Annex VI introduced by Resolution MEPC.203(62) (entry into force 1 January 2013),[46] additional surveys have been provided for in

---

39 Relevant provision also includes in its scope every fixed and floating drilling rig and other platforms (see MARPOL Annex VI, regulation 5).
40 See MARPOL Annex VI, regulation 5.1.
41 See MARPOL Annex VI, regulation 5.2.
42 See MARPOL Annex VI, regulation 5.3.4.
43 See MARPOL Annex VI, regulation 5.3.3.
44 See MARPOL Annex VI, regulation 5.5.
45 See MARPOL Annex VI, regulation 5.6.
46 Resolution MEPC.203(62) adopted on 15 July 2011. Amendments to the Annex of the Protocol of 1997 to amend the International Convention for the Prevention of Pollution from Ships, 1973, as modified by the Protocol of 1978 relating thereto (inclusion of regulations on energy efficiency for ships in MARPOL Annex VI).

relation to ships subject to ship energy efficiency requirements (the latter being introduced via the said Resolution, and having been included in Chapter 4 of the Annex).

7.6 Certificates and plans

7.6.1 International Air Pollution Prevention Certificate

The International Air Pollution Prevention Certificate (IAPPC) is dealt with in regulation 6 of the Annex. The Certificate is issued or endorsed by the flag State or any person or entity empowered by the flag State administration to do so.[47] Its period of validity is determined by the flag State but cannot exceed five years.[48]

The Certificate is issued following an initial or renewal survey to the following categories of ships, namely:

- any ship of 400 gross tonnage and above engaged in voyages to ports or offshore terminals under the jurisdiction of other Parties; and
- platforms and drilling rigs engaged in voyages to waters under the sovereignty or jurisdiction of other Parties.

The form of the certificate is given in an appendix to the Annex.

7.6.2 International Energy Efficiency Certificate

Valid, in principle, throughout the life of a ship,[49] the International Energy Efficiency Certificate (IEEC) was introduced by MEPC.203(62) (entry into force 1 January 2013),[50] and is issued by the flag State or a recognised organisation. The Certificate goes in two directions: it certifies that the ship has been surveyed for the purpose and that the ship complies with specified requirements.[51] As already mentioned, the IEEC is valid throughout the life of the ship.[52] It is issued or endorsed either by the flag State or by an entity empowered in that regard, following an appropriate survey.[53] The Certificate is relevant to ships of 400 gross tonnage and above before they engage in voyages to ports or offshore terminals under the jurisdiction of other Parties. The form of the certificate is set out in an appendix to the Annex in the form of a template.

---

47 See regulation 6.3. A provision addressing the issue of a certificate by another State Party at the request of the flag State is set out in regulation 7.

48 Regulation 9.1. Some clarifications are provided by the second paragraph of the provision concerning the duration of the IAPPC in relation to the date of conduct of the renewal survey and the expiry date.

49 See MARPOL Annex VI, regulation 9.10 and 9.11.

50 See MARPOL Annex VI, regulation 6.4.

51 Regulations 20, 21 and 22, addressing respectively the attained Energy Efficiency Design Index (Attained EEDI), the required EEDI, and the Ship Energy Efficiency Management Plan (SEEMP).

52 Subject to regulation 9.11.

53 See regulation 5.4 and 6.4.

The Certificate ceases to be valid if the ship is withdrawn from service or if a new certificate is issued following major conversion of the ship or upon transfer of the ship to the flag of another State.[54]

7.6.3 Ship Energy Efficiency Management Plan

The Ship Energy Efficiency Management plan (SEEMP) seeks to achieve less polluting ships from the standpoint of CO_2 emissions through strategies which optimise performance focused on operations. The SEEMP was provided for by MEPC.203(62) alongside the EEDI. Its scope includes new and existing ships. It is noted at this point that the importance of operational measures had been stressed prior to the adoption of the SEEMP by the Second IMO GHG Study (2009).

All ships or ship companies are required to develop and maintain a Plan to maximise the efficiency of ship operations. That said, while the SEEMP is mandatory, it does not set out specific requirements as to the result to be achieved.

The rationale of the SEEMP is based on planning, implementation, monitoring and self-evaluation/improvement. Each aspect is discussed in the 2012 Guidelines for the Development of a Ship Energy Efficiency Management Plan (SEEMP).[55] Part of the planning of the SEEMP is goal setting, which is voluntary; goal setting should be measurable and should seek to raise commitment and improvements. Any form can be given to the goal according to the above-mentioned guidelines, including the annual fuel consumption or a specific target of Energy Efficiency Operational Indicator (EEOI).

The EEOI is a voluntary monitoring tool for new and existing ships. It enables operators to measure the fuel efficiency of the ship in operation and the effect of any changes in operation.[56] In other words, it allows to obtain a quantitative indicator of a ship's and/or fleet's in operation energy efficiency.

Extracts from MEPC.213(63), adopted on 2 March 2012, Guidelines for the Development of a Ship Energy Efficiency Management Plan (SEEMP): **(Recently adopted 2016 Guidelines for the Development of a SEEMP are to be noted but are not discussed here)**.

---

5. GUIDANCE ON BEST PRACTICES FOR FUEL-EFFICIENT OPERATION OF SHIPS

5.1 The search for efficiency across the entire transport chain takes responsibility beyond what can be delivered by the owner/operator alone. A list of all the possible stakeholders in the efficiency of a single voyage is long; obvious Parties are designers, shipyards and engine manufacturers for the characteristics of the ship, and charterers, ports and vessel traffic management services, etc., for the specific voyage. All involved Parties should consider

---

54 Regulation 9.11.

55 MEPC.213(63), adopted on 2 March 2012.

56 MEPC.1/Cir.684, 17 August 2009, Guidelines for voluntary use of the ship Energy Efficiency Operational Indicator.

Fuel-efficient operations

Improved voyage planning

5.2 The optimum route and improved efficiency can be achieved through the careful planning and execution of voyages. Thorough voyage planning needs time, but a number of different software tools are available for planning purposes.

5.3 IMO resolution A.893(21) (25 November 1999) on "Guidelines for voyage planning" provides essential guidance for the ship's crew and voyage planners.

Weather routeing

5.4 Weather routeing has a high potential for efficiency savings on specific routes. It is commercially available for all types of ship and for many trade areas. Significant savings can be achieved, but conversely weather routeing may also increase fuel consumption for a given voyage.

Just in time

5.5 Good early communication with the next port should be an aim in order to give maximum notice of berth availability and facilitate the use of optimum speed where port operational procedures support this approach.

5.6 Optimized port operation could involve a change in procedures involving different handling arrangements in ports. Port authorities should be encouraged to maximize efficiency and minimize delay.

Speed optimization

5.7 Speed optimization can produce significant savings. However, optimum speed means the speed at which the fuel used per tonne mile is at a minimum level for that voyage. It does not mean minimum speed; in fact, sailing at less than optimum speed will consume more fuel rather than less. Reference should be made to the engine manufacturer's power/consumption curve and the ship's propeller curve. Possible adverse consequences of slow speed operation may include increased vibration and problems with soot deposits in combustion chambers and exhaust systems. These possible consequences should be taken into account.

5.8 As part of the speed optimization process, due account may need to be taken of the need to coordinate arrival times with the availability of loading/discharge berths, etc. The number of ships engaged in a particular trade route may need to be taken into account when considering speed optimization.

5.9 A gradual increase in speed when leaving a port or estuary whilst keeping the engine load within certain limits may help to reduce fuel consumption.

5.10 It is recognized that under many charter Parties the speed of the vessel is determined by the charterer and not the operator. Efforts should be made when agreeing charter party terms to encourage the ship to operate at optimum speed in order to maximize energy efficiency.

Optimized shaft power

5.11 Operation at constant shaft RPM can be more efficient than continuously adjusting speed through engine power (see paragraph 5.7). The use of automated engine management systems to control speed rather than relying on human intervention may be beneficial.

Optimized ship handling

Optimum trim

5.12 Most ships are designed to carry a designated amount of cargo at a certain speed for a certain fuel consumption. This implies the specification of set trim conditions. Loaded or unloaded, trim has a significant influence on the resistance of the ship through the water and optimizing trim can deliver significant fuel savings. For any given draft there is a trim condition that gives minimum resistance. In some ships, it is possible to assess optimum trim conditions for fuel efficiency continuously throughout the voyage. Design or safety factors may preclude full use of trim optimization.

Optimum ballast

5.13 Ballast should be adjusted taking into consideration the requirements to meet optimum trim and steering conditions and optimum ballast conditions achieved through good cargo planning.

5.14 When determining the optimum ballast conditions, the limits, conditions and ballast management arrangements set out in the ship's Ballast Water Management Plan are to be observed for that ship.

5.15 Ballast conditions have a significant impact on steering conditions and autopilot settings and it needs to be noted that less ballast water does not necessarily mean the highest efficiency.

Optimum propeller and propeller inflow considerations

5.16 Selection of the propeller is normally determined at the design and construction stage of a ship's life but new developments in propeller design have made it possible for retrofitting of later designs to deliver greater fuel economy. Whilst it is certainly for consideration, the propeller is but one part of the propulsion train and a change of propeller in isolation may have no effect on efficiency and may even increase fuel consumption.

5.17 Improvements to the water inflow to the propeller using arrangements such as fins and/or nozzles could increase propulsive efficiency power and hence reduce fuel consumption.

Optimum use of rudder and heading control systems (autopilots)

5.18 There have been large improvements in automated heading and steering control systems technology. Whilst originally developed to make the bridge team more effective, modern autopilots can achieve much more. An integrated Navigation and Command System can achieve significant fuel savings by simply reducing the distance sailed "off track". The principle is simple; better course control through less frequent and smaller corrections will minimize losses due to rudder resistance. Retrofitting of a more efficient autopilot to existing ships could be considered.

5.19 During approaches to ports and pilot stations the autopilot cannot always be used efficiently as the rudder has to respond quickly to given commands. Furthermore at certain stage of the voyage it may have to be deactivated or very carefully adjusted, i.e. heavy weather and approaches to ports.

5.20 Consideration may be given to the retrofitting of improved rudder blade design (e.g. "twist-flow" rudder).

Hull maintenance

5.21 Docking intervals should be integrated with ship operator's ongoing assessment of ship performance. Hull resistance can be optimized by new technology-coating systems, possibly in combination with cleaning intervals. Regular in-water inspection of the condition of the hull is recommended.

5.22 Propeller cleaning and polishing or even appropriate coating may significantly increase fuel efficiency. The need for ships to maintain efficiency through in-water hull cleaning should be recognized and facilitated by port States.

5.23 Consideration may be given to the possibility of timely full removal and replacement of underwater paint systems to avoid the increased hull roughness caused by repeated spot blasting and repairs over multiple dockings.

5.24 Generally, the smoother the hull, the better the fuel efficiency.

Propulsion system

5.25 Marine diesel engines have a very high thermal efficiency (~50%). This excellent performance is only exceeded by fuel cell technology with an average thermal efficiency of 60 per cent. This is due to the systematic minimization of heat and mechanical loss. In particular, the new breed of electronic controlled engines can provide efficiency gains. However, specific training for relevant staff may need to be considered to maximize the benefits.

Propulsion system maintenance

5.26 Maintenance in accordance with manufacturers' instructions in the company's planned maintenance schedule will also maintain efficiency. The use of engine condition monitoring can be a useful tool to maintain high efficiency.

5.27 Additional means to improve engine efficiency might include:
- Use of fuel additives;
- Adjustment of cylinder lubrication oil consumption;
- Valve improvements;
- Torque analysis; and
- Automated engine monitoring systems.

Waste heat recovery

5.28 Waste heat recovery is now a commercially available technology for some ships. Waste heat recovery systems use thermal heat losses from the exhaust gas for either electricity generation or additional propulsion with a shaft motor.

5.29 It may not be possible to retrofit such systems into existing ships. However, they may be a beneficial option for new ships. Shipbuilders should be encouraged to incorporate new technology into their designs.

Improved fleet management

5.30 Better utilization of fleet capacity can often be achieved by improvements in fleet planning. For example, it may be possible to avoid or reduce long ballast voyages through improved fleet planning. There is opportunity here for charterers to promote efficiency. This can be closely related to the concept of "just in time" arrivals.

5.31 Efficiency, reliability and maintenance-oriented data sharing within a company can be used to promote best practice among ships within a company and should be actively encouraged.

Improved cargo handling

5.32 Cargo handling is in most cases under the control of the port and optimum solutions matched to ship and port requirements should be explored.

Energy management

5.33 A review of electrical services on board can reveal the potential for unexpected efficiency gains. However care should be taken to avoid the creation of new safety hazards when turning off electrical services (e.g. lighting). Thermal insulation is an obvious means of saving energy. Also see comment below on shore power.

5.34 Optimization of reefer container stowage locations may be beneficial in reducing the effect of heat transfer from compressor units. This might be combined as appropriate with cargo tank heating, ventilation, etc. The use of water-cooled reefer plant with lower energy consumption might also be considered.

Fuel type

5.35 Use of emerging alternative fuels may be considered as a CO_2 reduction method but availability will often determine the applicability.

Other measures

5.36 Development of computer software for the calculation of fuel consumption, for the establishment of an emissions "footprint", to optimize operations, and the establishment of goals for improvement and tracking of progress may be considered.

5.37 Renewable energy sources, such as wind, solar (or photovoltaic) cell technology, have improved enormously in the recent years and should be considered for onboard application.

5.38 In some ports shore power may be available for some ships but this is generally aimed at improving air quality in the port area. If the shore-based power source is carbon efficient, there may be a net efficiency benefit. Ships may consider using onshore power if available.

5.39 Even wind assisted propulsion may be worthy of consideration.

5.40 Efforts could be made to source fuel of improved quality in order to minimize the amount of fuel required to provide a given power output.

Compatibility of measures

5.41 This document indicates a wide variety of possibilities for energy efficiency improvements for the existing fleet. While there are many options available, they are not necessarily cumulative, are often area and trade dependent and likely to require the agreement and support of a number of different stakeholders if they are to be utilized most effectively.

Age and operational service life of a ship

5.42 All measures identified in this document are potentially cost-effective as a result of high oil prices. Measures previously considered unaffordable or commercially unattractive may now be feasible and worthy of fresh consideration. Clearly, this equation is heavily influenced by the remaining service life of a ship and the cost of fuel.

Trade and sailing area

5.43 The feasibility of many of the measures described in this guidance will be dependent on the trade and sailing area of the vessel. Sometimes ships will change their trade areas as a result of a change in chartering requirements but this cannot be taken as a general assumption. For example, wind-enhanced power sources might not be feasible for short sea shipping as these ships generally sail in areas with high traffic densities or in restricted waterways. Another aspect is that the world's oceans and seas each have characteristic conditions and so ships designed for specific routes and trades may not obtain the same benefit by adopting the same measures or combination of measures as other ships. It is also likely that some measures will have a greater or lesser effect in different sailing areas.

5.44 The trade a ship is engaged in may determine the feasibility of the efficiency measures under consideration. For example, ships that perform services at sea (pipe laying, seismic survey, OSVs, dredgers, etc.) may choose different methods of improving energy efficiency when compared to conventional cargo carriers. The length of voyage may also be an important parameter as may trade specific safety considerations. The pathway to the most efficient combination of measures will be unique to each vessel within each shipping company.

7.7 Key management issues stemming from the EU regime

7.7.1 MRV Regulation (EU) – related documentation

A Monitoring Plan must be drawn up according to the above-mentioned MRV Regulation (EU). The Plan must indicate, amongst others, the method chosen to monitor and report CO_2 emissions for the ship concerned, which is dealt in detail in Annex I of Regulation (EU) 2015/757. The Monitoring Plan "shall consist of a complete and transparent documentation of the monitoring method".[57] The information which must be included at a minimum is also set out by the instrument, including, for example, a description of the CO_2 emission sources on board the ship (main engine, auxiliary engines, gas turbines, boilers and inert gas generators, and the fuel types used), a description of the procedures, systems and responsibilities used to update the list of CO_2 emissions sources over the reporting period, etc.

In addition to the above, a document of compliance must be issued to the company by a verifier, and must be kept aboard the vessel. The document confirms that the ship is compliant with the requirements of the Regulation for a specific reporting period. This is a ship-specific document which is issued to the company; the Directive defines the "company" as the shipowner or any other organisation or persons, such as the manager or the bareboat charterer, which has assumed the responsibility for the operation of the ship from the shipowner. The document of compliance is issued by a verifier on the basis of the verification report and must be kept on board ships in view of evidencing compliance with monitoring, reporting and verification obligations. The information to be included in the document of compliance is set out by Regulation (EU) 2015/757.[58] According to the Regulation, verifiers are held to inform then European Commission and the authority of the flag State of the issuance of such documents.[59]

Against this background, Port State Control, which is briefly presented below, constitutes a key tool for putting to the test the requirements governing the control and reduction of air emissions from shipping.

7.8 Port State Control

It may be relevant to note that provisions which present an interest for Port State Control provided for in the general part of MARPOL (e.g. Article 5 on certificates and special rules on inspection of ships) also apply to this context. Port State Control in the context under discussion is set out in regulation 10 of Annex VI, entitled "Port State control on operational requirements".

In summary, an inspection is set out when a ship is in a port or at an offshore terminal in a foreign country in case of clear grounds for believing that the master or crew are not familiar with essential shipboard procedures pertaining to the prevention of air pollution from ships.[60] Not surprisingly, the power of the port State to prevent the vessel from sailing until the situation has been brought to order in virtue of the Annex has also been provided for.[61]

A specific provision is dedicated to detection of violations and enforcement (regulation 11) which clearly states the duty of States Parties to MARPOL Annex

---

57 See article 6(3).
58 See article 17.
59 See article 17.
60 Regulation 10.1.
61 Regulation 10.2.

VI to cooperate in the detection of violations and the enforcement of the Annex is set out. This notably includes detection, monitoring and reporting. Furthermore, the right exercised at the discretion of the port State of a Party to inspect a ship to which Annex VI applies is also set out. The purpose here is to verify whether the ship has emitted any of the substances covered by the Annex in violation of the latter. To complete the picture, reporting to the flag State has also been provided for.[62]

A related provision is also concerned with the case where a ship (to which the Annex applies) enters the ports or offshore terminals under the jurisdiction of a State Party, for which an investigation request has been received by that Party.[63] The investigation request, however, must be accompanied with "sufficient evidence" that the ship has emitted any of the substances which fall within the scope of the Annex in any place in violation of the Annex.

SECTION 4: AREAS OF SPECIAL INTEREST

7.9 Market-based approaches

Market-based approaches to air pollution are often contrasted with prescriptive approaches, where regulators provide for specific duties ("command and control approach"). An illustration of a prescriptive approach would be the requirement of a specified sulphur content of fuels.

Market-based approaches are based on a different rationale, and they commonly go in two directions: Firstly, measures revolving around economic incentives (e.g. reduced fairway dues or other variable fees for rewarding environmentally friendly ships using, for example, air emission control technologies);[64] secondly, emission trading schemes, commonly referred to as cap-and-trade systems. Emissions trading, i.e. carbon trading, is aimed at combating climate change through limiting GHGs from human activities. It is based on the idea of accepted targets and allowed emissions; it is provided internationally by the Kyoto Protocol[65] and regionally on the EU level.[66] The latter is considered the largest world's cap-and-trade market, currently at its third stage. In these systems carbon is given a price, thus treated as a commodity. It is noted that at the present stage neither the international emission trading scheme nor the EU emission trading scheme include air emissions from shipping. Nevertheless, recent developments such as data collection systems at the regional and international level (see section 4 above) suggest that there is a strong possibility for shipping to be included in emission trading schemes in the near future.

---

62 Regulation 11.2.

63 Regulation 11.5.

64 See ICCT (The International Council on Clean Transportation) (2007) (authors: A. Friedrich & others) *Air Pollution and Greenhouse Gas Emissions from Ocean-Going Ships: Impacts, Mitigation Options and Opportunities for Managing Growth*, p. 56.

65 See http://unfccc.int/kyoto_protocol/mechanisms/emissions_trading/items/2731.php (last visit 12 May 2017).

66 See https://ec.europa.eu/clima/policies/ets_en (last visit 12 May 2017).

SECTION 5: DEVELOPMENTS UNDERWAY

7.10 IMO's fuel consumption data

As already mentioned, a mandatory Fuel Oil Data Collection System (FODCS) was decided by the IMO's Marine Environment Protection Committee (MEPC) on 28 October 2016. This development, which is currently going through the tacit acceptance procedure, is expected to take the form of an amendment to Chapter 4 of MARPOL Annex VI through the addition of a new regulation 22A (expected date of entry into force 1 March 2018). It may be recalled on this point that the tacit acceptance procedure allows amendments to enter into force "automatically" unless a specified number of IMO Member States object to them within a specified time period.

Under this amendment, ships of 5,000 GT and above will be required to submit annual reports on fuel consumption and transport work to their administration. It is noted that the methodology set out in the SEEMP will support the undertaking. The data collected will be reported to the administration of the flag State at the end of each calendar year. A statement of compliance will be issued following appropriate checks. It is noteworthy that the data collected that will be submitted to the IMO will give rise to anonymised publication.

7.11 Recent development stemming from the European Union

As discussed earlier, a majority of members of the European Parliament voted in February 2017 for the inclusion of shipping in the regional ETS as of 2023 in the absence of comparable system on the IMO level by 2021. This suggests that the agenda of the EU on CO_2 emissions from shipping is far from crystallising, and that it is reasonably expected to see more regional regulations ahead.

7.12 Alternative solutions

The use of liquefied natural gas and bioenergy are only some of the directions currently under discussion for less polluting ships and reduced GHGs. Viewed as alternative solutions, they raise different challenges and represent different stages in terms of acceptance and use by the industry.

7.12.1 Liquefied Natural Gas

Liquefied Natural Gas (LNG)has given rise to many discussions in recent years, and it is understood by some as the fuel of the future. LNG is a cleaner, sulphur-free fuel with almost no PM emissions. It produces highly reduced NOx emissions, and reduces GHG emissions by 20% from the vessel's stack. One of the problems relating to its use is the production of methane (CH_4), the on-board storage of the fuel in terms of space and availability in bunkering ports.

7.12.2 Bioenergy/biofuels

Biofuels are derived from organic matter that is available on a renewable or recurring basis (biomass).[67] The Second IMO Study GHG 2009 had already addressed the question of biofuels, including first generation biofuels produced from animal fats, vegetable oil, sugar or starch, second generation biofuels produced from residual non-food crops such as leaves, stems, or even industry waste, and third generation biofuels based on the use of algae.

Against this background, the use of biofuels raises a number of policy-making and technical issues. The study pointed out the limited potential of biofuels for reducing CO_2 emissions from shipping.[68]

In its Environmental Outlook to 2050, a paper dating to November 2011,[69] the Organisation for Economic Cooperation and Development (OECD) examines the climate change problem, makes projections and considers policy-making options. In broad terms, the important role of energy from food crops or inedible waste products (bioenergy) in mitigating climate change is recognised (use of bioenergy in the transport sector instead of fossil-energy based fuels expected to lead to lower CO_2 emissions). Nevertheless, in light of scientific findings, the potential to generate emissions comparable (or even higher) to those from fossil fuels in the processes associated with bioenergy, is also pointed out.

A conclusion of this section is that at the present stage, despite some progress concerning the use of LNG, there are high levels of uncertainty concerning alternative solutions to the use of liquid fuel, including on the use of bioenergy.

BIBLIOGRAPHY

Endresen, Q., Sørgård, E., Sundet, J.K., Dalsøren, S.B., Isaken, I.S.A., and Berglen, T.F., 'Emissions from International Sea Transportation and Environmental Impact' [2003] Journal of Geophysical Research 108, 4560. doi:10.1029/2002JD002898

European Commission, Joint Research Center (JRC) and Institute for Environmental Sustainability (IES), authored by Miola and others, *Regulating Air Emissions from Ships – the State of the Art on Methodologies, Technologies and Policy Options* (2010)

European Environment Agency (EEA), *The Impact of International Shipping on European Air Quality and Climate Forcing* (EEA Technical Report, No4/2013, ISSN 1725–2237, Copenhagen)

European Parliament and Council Directive (EC) 2005/33 amending Directive 1999/32/EC [2005] OJ L191/59

European Parliament and Council Directive (EU) 2012/33 amending Council Directive 1999/32/EC as regards the sulphur content of marine fuels [2012] OJ L 327/1

---

67 Renewable Fuel Standard – Potential Economic and Environmental Effects of US Biofuel Policy, National Research Council, National Academies Press, Washington, D.C., 2011.

68 Second IMO GHG Study 2009, p. 51.

69 OECD and DBL (Authors: Marchal et al), *OECD Environmental Outlook to 2050* [p. 67, pre-release version November 2011] Climate Change Chapter, www.oecd.org/environment/outlookto2050 (last visit 12 May 2017).

European Parliament and Council Regulation (EU) 2015/757 on the monitoring, reporting and verification of carbon dioxide emissions from maritime transport and amending Directive 2009/16/EC (Text with EEA relevance) [2015] OJ L123/55

ICCT, *Policy Update 15* (3 October 2011)

IMO, *MARPOL Annex VI and NTC (NOx Technical Code) 2008 with Guidelines for Implementation Edition 2013* (with September 2015 supplement)

IMO, *MARPOL Consolidated Edition 2017*

IMO, MEPC.1/Cir.684, 'Guidelines for Voluntary Use of the Ship Energy Efficiency Operational Indicator (EEOI)' (17 August 2009)

IMO, *Second IMO GHG Study 2009*

IMO, *Third IMO GHG Study 2014*

IMO Resolution MEPC.203(62), Amendments to the Annex of the Protocol of 1997 to amend the International Convention for the Prevention of Pollution from Ships, 1973, as modified by the Protocol of 1978 relating thereto (Inclusion of regulations on energy efficiency for ships in MARPOL Annex VI) (15 July 2011)

International Council on Clean Transportation (ICCT) Authors: Friedrich A. and others, *Air Pollution and Greenhouse Gas Emissions from Ocean-Going Ships: Impacts, Mitigation Options and Opportunities for Managing Growth* (2007)

National Research Council of the National Academies (USA), *Renewable Fuel Standard – Potential Economic and Environmental Effects of US Biofuel Policy* (The National Academies Press, Washington, DC, 2011)

National Research Council of the National Academies (USA), *Climate Change: Evidence, Impact and Choices – Answers to Common Questions About the Science of Climate Change* (The National Academies Press, Washington, DC, 2012)

OECD (Organisation for Economic Cooperation and Development) and DBL (Netherlands Environmental Assessment Agency) Authors: Marchal, V., Dellink, R., Van Vuuren (Detlef), Clapp, C., Chateau, J., Lanzi, E., Magné, B., Van Vliet, J., *OECD Environmental Outlook to 2050* (Climate Change Chapter) [pre-release version November 2011], www.oecd.org/environment/outlookto2050 OECD

CHAPTER 8

Other sources of marine pollution

Ballast water, harmful substances in anti-fouling systems, ship-breaking activities and other

TABLE OF CONTENTS

Section 1	Identifying the subject area	206
8.1	Potential sources of marine pollution outside the scope of MARPOL	206
8.2	Key terms/definitions	207
Section 2	Main discussion of the regulatory framework	207
8.3	Marine pollution from ballast water	207
8.3.1	International regulations	209
8.3.2	Key management issues, including documentation	213
8.3.2.1	Standards	213
8.3.2.2	Surveys and certification	214
8.3.2.3	Ballast Water Management Plan	214
8.3.2.4	Ballast Water Record Book	215
8.3.3	Port State Control	215
8.4	Harmful substances used in anti-fouling systems	216
8.4.1	What is the problem?	216
8.4.1.1	The International Convention on the Control of Harmful Anti-fouling Systems on Ships, 2001	217
8.4.1.2	Surveys and certification	218
8.4.1.3	Best management practices	218
8.4.1.4	The European Union approach: Regulation 782/2003 of 14 April 2003 and Regulation 536/2008 of 13 June 2008	219
8.5	Ship recycling	220
8.5.1	What is the problem?	220

8.5.2	The Hong Kong Convention 2009	220
	8.5.2.1 Documentation	224
8.5.3	European Union (EU) action	224
Section 3	Areas of special interest, including current developments	226
8.6	Ship strikes with marine mammals	226
8.7	Underwater noise emissions from vessels	227
8.7.1	On the IMO level	228
8.7.2	The action undertaken by the European Union	229
	8.7.2.1 Monitoring underwater energy of marine waters	229
	8.7.2.2 Monitoring impacts of individual projects	230

SECTION 1: IDENTIFYING THE SUBJECT AREA

8.1 Potential sources of marine pollution outside the scope of MARPOL

This chapter addresses policies and regulations governing marine pollution from various sources which are not within the confines of MARPOL. The transfer of living species from ships' ballast water, the use of harmful substances in paints used to prevent sea life from attaching to ships' hulls (anti-fouling paints), and ship-dismantling activities have been included in the discussion. The discussion is also extended to marine pollution from collisions between cetaceans and ships as well as to underwater noise from shipping. It is well established that sound propagates faster in water than in air. Noise sources of propeller-driven ships are numerous. One may think of propellers, main engines, auxiliary engines, etc. Underwater noise from shipping is of interest to the discussion on marine pollution as it represents a release of energy into the marine environment, which is grasped by the definition of pollution of the marine environment under the United Nations Convention on the Law of the Sea (UNCLOS) III.

As it will be seen below, this is a highly diverse subject area which gives rise to numerous challenges (e.g. the challenge of socially and environmentally sound management of ship recycling facilities), and distinct developments on IMO level. This is also an area clearly marked by a trend for regional (e.g. EU) or State regulatory developments.[1] A clear illustration is provided by EU provisions on ship recycling or by applicable provisions in the USA, including in the State of California, on ballast water standards. It can be said that the international community does not always achieve a uniform regulatory environment; this is suggested, for example, by the existence of international, regional and State regulations which sometimes overlap or create a lack of coherence in the field of ballast water management, an area touched upon below.

---

1   An overview of national requirements on ballast water management is provided in Lloyd's Register Marine, National Ballast Water Management Requirements, January 2014.

OTHER SOURCES OF MARINE POLLUTION

8.2 Key terms/definitions

Anti-fouling system	It means a coating, paint, surface treatment, surface or devise that is used on a ship to control or prevent attachment of unwanted organisms (IMO AFS Convention 2001).
Ballast water	According to the Ballast Water Management Convention, this means water with its suspended matter taken onboard a ship to control trim, list, draught, stability or stresses of the ship.
Ballast water management	According to the international instrument of reference which is discussed later on, the term means various processes (mechanical, physical, chemical and biological), either singularly or in combination, aimed to remove, render harmless or avoid the uptake or discharge of harmful aquatic organisms and pathogens within ballast water and sediments.
Biofouling	Accumulation of aquatic organisms such as micro-organisms, plants, and animals on surfaces and structures immersed in or exposed to the aquatic environment (source: IMO Resolution MEPC.207(62)[1]).
Fouling	Unwanted growth of biological material (e.g. algae) on ships' surface immersed in water.
Harmful aquatic organisms and pathogens	The Ballast Water Management Convention defines them as species that may create, once they are introduced into the water, hazards to the environment, human health, property or resources; they may impair biological diversity or interfere with other legitimate uses of the water.
Sediments	According to the international instrument of reference, this means matter settled out of ballast water within a ship.
Ship recycling	According to international regulations, it means activity of complete or partial dismantling of a ship in view of recovering components and materials for reprocessing and re-use, while taking care of hazardous and other materials, and associated operations (e.g. storage and treatment of components, etc.).
Ship recycling facility	The term is used in the Hong Kong Convention 2009; it means a defined area (site, yard or facility) that is used for ship recycling.

1 MEPC.207(62) adopted on 15 July 2011 "2011 Guidelines for the control and management of ships' biofouling to minimize the transfer of invasive aquatic species".

SECTION 2: MAIN DISCUSSION OF THE REGULATORY FRAMEWORK

8.3 Marine pollution from ballast water

It may be of assistance to indicate that ballast water is used by ships in order to ensure safe operating conditions and stability, including when cargo levels are low. At its simplest, with the use of ballast water ships attain the right depth of water. When new cargo is loaded, ballast water will have to be released. It is generally recognised that billion tonnes of ballast water is transferred around the world annually, which include non-native bacteria, microbes, aquatic plants or animal species. Unless certain precautions are taken, the use of ballast water has been considered by scientists as a potential means of distortion of biodiversity, human health and ultimately, the economy – the spread of invasive species being reported to represent a very high cost. It may be relevant to note at this point that the UNCLOS III sets out the duty of States to prevent the spread of alien species. These unwanted aquatic species travel with the ship's ballast water (see graph 8.1 below) and some of them, under conditions such as the level of environmental similarity between the ballast water source port and the ballast water receiving port, the water temperature, or salinity, will manage to survive and out-compete native species.[2] Some illustrations are zebra mussels, North American comb jellyfish (*Mnemiopsis leidyi*), water flea, the red mysid shrimp, the Chinese mitten crab, etc.; the European zebra mussel was introduced to the Great Lakes in the USA in ships' ballast water;[3] in the Black Sea, the Caspian Sea and the North Sea, the North American comb jellyfish should be mentioned.[4]

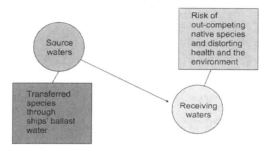

Graph 8.1 Simplified description of the interphase of transferred ballast water with the marine environment

It is not surprising that scientific findings are complex and sometimes unclear,[5] despite the question being known for more than 200 years.[6] In summary, despite some levels of uncertainty, the matter has been subjected to regulation, with technology developers being heavily involved. The relevant IMO instrument, which will be discussed below, takes note of the precautionary approach which flows from the Rio Declaration on Environment and Development.[7] Furthermore,

---

2 WWF International, Silent Invasion – The Spread of Marine Invasive Species Via Ships' Ballast Water (Gland, 2009), p. 3.
3 See GARD, *infra* note 5, p. 4.
4 WWF International, *supra* note 2, p. 5.
5 According to the National Oceanic and Atmospheric Administration (NOAA) in the USA, currents inevitably sweep over and carry off living organisms. In an insight by the P&I Club GARD dating to 1 August 1999 (insight 155), mention was made of a study by a biologist at the San Francisco Estuary Institute according to which there were at least 234 species in San Francisco Bay, and that not all of them had been introduced there through ballast water.
6 See Dandu Pughiuc, 'Ballast Water Management – an Overview of the Regulatory Process', p. 17, in N. Bellefontaine and Others (eds), GEF-UNDP-IMO GloBallast Partnerships Programme and the Global Industry Alliance 'Emerging Ballast Water Management Systems' Proceedings of the IMO-WMU Research and Development Forum, 26–29 January 2010, Malmö, Sweden.
7 Principle 15 of the Rio Declaration.

OTHER SOURCES OF MARINE POLLUTION

alternatives to the ballast water exchange and treatment are possible, to the extent that they ensure at least the same level of protection to humans, the environment, and resources, and are approved, in principle, by the IMO;[8] in practice, this means that research and development in this area should be encouraged.

8.3.1 International regulations

On the international level, the spread of unwanted aquatic species through ships' ballast water has given rise to a convention, the Ballast Water Management Convention 2004 (BWM Convention).[9] As the Convention makes mention on numerous points of "Guidelines developed by the Organisation", a number of guidelines had to be developed by the IMO, which complement the picture.

Non-exhaustive list of IMO guidelines:

MEPC.152(55) adopted on 13 October 2006 Guidelines for sediment reception facilities (G1)
MEPC. 173(58) adopted on 10 October 2008 Guidelines for ballast water sampling (G2)
MEPC. 123(53) adopted on 22 July 2005
Guidelines for ballast water management equivalent compliance (G3)
MEPC. 127(53) adopted on 22 July 2005
Guidelines for ballast water management and development of ballast water management plans (G4)
MEPC. 153 (55) adopted on 13 October 2006
Guidelines for ballast water reception facilities (G5)
MEPC. 124 (53) adopted on 22 July 2005
Guidelines for ballast water exchange (G6)
MEPC. 162(56) adopted on 13 July 2007
Guidelines for risk assessment under regulation A-4 of the BMW Convention (G7)
MEPC. 174(58) adopted on 10 October 2008
Guidelines for approval of ballast water management systems (G8)
MEPC. 169(57) adopted on 4 April 2008
Procedure for approval of ballast water management systems that make use of active substances (G9)
MEPC. 140(54) adopted on 24 March 2006
Guidelines for approval and oversight of prototype ballast water treatment technology programmes (G10)
MEPC. 149(55) adopted on 13 October 2006
Guidelines for ballast water exchange design and construction standards (G11)
MEPC. 209(63) adopted on 2 March 2012
Guidelines on design and construction to facilitate sediment control on ships (G12)
MEPC. 161(56) adopted on 13 July 2007
Guidelines for additional measures regarding ballast water management, including emergency situations (G13)
MEPC. 151(55) adopted on 13 October 2006
Guidelines on designation of areas of ballast water exchange (G14)

---

8   See regulation B-3, para. 7 of the Ballast Water Management Convention.
9   International Convention for the Control and Management of Ships' Ballast Water and Sediments (2004).

MEPC. 163(56) adopted on 13 July 2007
Guidelines for ballast water exchange in the Antarctic Treaty area

MEPC.252(67) adopted on 17 October 2014
Guidelines for Port State Control under the BWM Convention

MEPC.279(70) ADOPTED ON 28 OCTOBER 2016

2016 Guidelines for approval of Ballast Water Management Systems (G8)[10]
THE MARINE ENVIRONMENT PROTECTION COMMITTEE,

RECALLING Article 38(a) of the Convention on the International Maritime Organisation concerning the functions of the Marine Environment Protection Committee conferred upon it by the international conventions for the prevention and control of marine pollution from ships,

RECALLING ALSO that the International Conference on Ballast Water Management for Ships held in February 2004 adopted the International Convention for the Control and Management of Ships' Ballast Water and Sediments, 2004 (the Ballast Water Management Convention) together with four conference resolutions,

NOTING that regulation D-3 of the annex to the Ballast Water Management Convention provides that ballast water management systems used to comply with the Convention must be approved by the Administration, taking into account the guidelines developed by the Organization,

NOTING ALSO resolution MEPC.125(53) by which the Committee adopted the *Guidelines for approval of ballast water management systems* (the Guidelines (G8)), and resolution MEPC.174(58), by which the Committee adopted a revision to the Guidelines (G8),

NOTING FURTHER that, by resolution MEPC.174(58), the Committee resolved to keep Guidelines (G8) under review in the light of experience gained,

RECALLING the provisions for non-penalization of early movers contained in the *Roadmap for the implementation of the BWM Convention*, agreed at its sixty-eighth session (MEPC 68/WP.8, annex 2),

NOTING the Organization's established practice with regard to the validity of type approval certification for marine products (MSC.1/Circ.1221) that the Type Approval Certificate itself has no influence on the operational validity of existing ballast water management systems accepted and installed on board a ship and manufactured during the period of validity of the relevant Type Approval Certificate, meaning that the system need not be renewed or replaced due to expiration of such Certificate,

HAVING CONSIDERED, at its seventieth session, the outcome of the Intersessional Working Group on the Review of Guidelines (G8),

1   ADOPTS the *2016 Guidelines for approval of ballast water management systems* (G8), as set out in the annex to this resolution (the 2016 Guidelines (G8));

---

10 The table above does not make mention of the status of relevant resolutions. It is noted, however that MEPC.279(70) supersedes MEPC.174(58). Information on updates involving the status can be obtained from national maritime administrations and/or the website of the IMO.

2 AGREES to keep the 2016 Guidelines (G8) under review in the light of experience gained with their application;

3 RECOMMENDS that Administrations apply the 2016 Guidelines (G8) when approving ballast water management systems as soon as possible, but not later than 28 October 2018;

4 AGREES that ballast water management systems installed on ships on or after 28 October 2020 should be approved taking into account the 2016 Guidelines (G8);

5 AGREES that ballast water management systems installed on board ships prior to 28 October 2020 should be approved taking into account either the Guidelines (G8) as adopted by resolution MEPC.174(58), or preferably the 2016 Guidelines (G8) set out in the annex to this resolution;

6 AGREES that, for the purpose of operative paragraphs 4 and 5 of this resolution, the word "installed" means the contractual date of delivery of the ballast water management system to the ship. In the absence of such a date, the word "installed" means the actual date of delivery of the ballast water management system to the ship;

7 AGREES that the dates referenced in this resolution will be considered in the reviews carried out in accordance with regulation D-5 of the Ballast Water Management Convention, to determine whether a sufficient number of appropriate technologies are approved and available, taking into account the 2016 Guidelines (G8);

8 SUPERSEDES the *Guidelines for approval of ballast water management systems* (G8) adopted by resolution MEPC.174(58).

The BWM Convention was adopted on 16 February 2004 following many years of negotiations. The instrument aims at the minimisation and ultimate elimination of the transfer of harmful aquatic organisms and pathogens through the control and management of sea ballast water and sediments. The delayed entry into force of the instrument (8 September 2017) is noteworthy. This can be attributed to the controversy surrounding the actual benefits of its ratification, especially by maritime States which have a special weight in the ratification process from the standpoint of their participation in the required tonnage for entry into force purposes. Against this background, it should be noted that in the area of ballast water management, numerous States have set out their own requirements, and regulatory compliance does not therefore flow from a uniform framework. Furthermore, the above-mentioned date of entry into force of the Convention has been challenged in respect of some items. In this context, following the 71st session of the IMO Marine Environment Protection Committee in July 2017, draft amendments to regulation B-3 of the Convention were approved, setting out new deadlines for compliance with the D-2 discharge standard, i.e. the deadline on the installation of treatment systems.

The Convention defines ships as vessels of any type whatsoever operating in the aquatic environment. The definition specifically includes submersibles, floating craft, floating platforms, FSUs and FPSOs. The material scope of application of the Convention includes ships flying the flag of a State Party to the Convention and ships which operate under the authority of a Party. In this context, the instrument applies to the vast majority of vessels involved with international shipping. It should be noted from the outset that the Convention adheres to the principle of no more favourable treatment towards ships of non-Parties, which is also found in other international shipping regulations. This means that ships which fly the flag of States that have not ratified the Convention will be subjected to the requirements of the Convention when calling at ports of ratifying States.[11] The purpose of this principle is to avoid giving a competitive advantage to the vessels of countries that have not ratified the Convention.

Despite the broad material scope of the Convention, the latter states the following exclusions:[12]

- ships not designed or constructed to carry ballast water;
- ships, in principle, only operating in waters under the jurisdiction of a Party;
- ships of a Party which only operate in waters under the jurisdiction of another Party; this exclusion is subject to conditions, and requires the authorisation of the Party concerned;
- ships "which only operate in waters under the jurisdiction of one Party and on the high seas, except for ships not granted an authorisation pursuant to sub-paragraph (c), unless such Party determines that the discharge of Ballast Water from such ships would impair or damage their environment, human health, property or resources, or those of adjacent of other States";
- any warships, naval auxiliary or other ship owned or operated by a State, etc.;
- permanent ballast water in sealed tanks on ships, that is not subject to discharge.

As at March 2017, the Convention was ratified by 54 States representing 53.41% of the world fleet. Its entry into force required the ratification by at least 30 States with a fleet of 35% of the world tonnage. The absence of ratification of the Convention, up to this stage, by a number of maritime nations is noteworthy (as opposed, for example, to Liberia, Marshall Islands, Panama, and Norway, which have ratified the Convention).

Viewed from the standpoint of its structure, the Convention is articulated over 22 articles and an annex forming an integral part of the Convention, and containing technical standards in the form of regulations. The instrument contains numerous provisions in the form of soft law encouraging Parties towards a certain direction. Consequently, Parties "should ensure" that implementation practices undertaken by States do not cause greater harm than they prevent, or that Parties "should encourage" their ships which fall in the scope of the Convention "to avoid, as far as practicable", the uptake of ballast water with potentially harmful species.[13] On the same note, each Party "shall endeavour" to cooperate in view

---

11 See Article 3(3) of the BWM Convention.
12 See Article 3(2) of the BWM Convention.
13 See respectively Article 2(7) and (8).

of the effective implementation of the instrument;[14] furthermore, it "undertakes to ensure" that, in ports and terminals designated for the purpose, adequate sediment reception facilities are provided for the reception of sediments.[15] Scientific and technical research and monitoring are also encouraged by the Convention, which calls upon Parties to endeavour to take action in that regard.[16]

The salient features of the Convention from the standpoint of applicable requirements can be seen in the graph below.

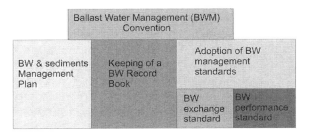

Graph 8.2 Applicable requirements under the Ballast Water Management (BWM) Convention

8.3.2 *Key management issues, including documentation*

8.3.2.1 Standards

Upon its entry into force, the Convention would require either D-1 (ballast water exchange) or D-2 (ballast water treatment) standard.[17] As already mentioned, the deadline governing the installation process of treatment systems has been extended by the 71st session of the MEPC.

That said, sanctions for the violations of the requirements of the Convention fall within the scope of the competency of the flag State, and this, "wherever the violation occurs".[18] It should be stressed, however, that violations within the jurisdiction of any Party lead to sanctions established under the law of that Party, which is entitled, under the Convention, to take legal proceedings in accordance with its law or provide necessary information and evidence to the flag State.[19] As far as the nature of sanctions is concerned, they are required to be adequate in severity to discourage violations of the Convention wherever they occur.[20]

Narrowing down the focus on standards for ballast water management, as already mentioned, they include ballast water exchange standard (Regulation

---

14 Article 2(4).
15 Article 5.
16 Article 6.
17 A technical overview of ballast water treatment technologies can be found in Bellefontane & Others (eds), *supra* note 4.
18 Article 8(1).
19 Article 8(2).
20 Article 8(3).

D-1), and ballast water performance standard (Regulation D-2). An efficiency of at least 95% volumetric exchange of ballast water is required from ships performing ballast water exchange in accordance with Regulation D-1. The provision also sets out details in relation to ships exchanging ballast water by the pumping-through method. Ships conducting ballast water management in accordance with ballast water performance standard (Regulation D-2) are required to discharge less than a specified quantity of viable organisms per cube metre.

8.3.2.2 Surveys and certification

Article 7 of the Convention and section E of the annex address surveys for the purposes of enforcement of the Convention and certification.

More specifically, ships of 400 gross tonnage and above to which the Convention applies are subject to initial, renewal, intermediate, annual and additional surveys. As regards floating platforms, floating storage units (FSUs) and floating production storage and offloading units (FPSOs), they are excluded.[21] The surveys are to be carried out by the officers of the flag State or duly empowered surveyors or recognised organisations. The flag State fully guarantees the completeness and efficiency of the surveys.[22]

Furthermore, the flag State assumes full responsibility for the International Ballast Water Management Certificate.[23] The latter is issued for a period specified by the administration not exceeding five years[24] after successful completion of a survey in accordance with regulation E-1; it is drawn up in the official language of the issuing Party[25] and in the form set out in an appendix to the Convention. The Certificate issued under the authority of a Party must be accepted, according to the Convention, by the other Parties. This means that it must be accepted by the other Parties and considered for all purposes covered by the Convention as having the same validity as a certificate issued by them.[26] The Convention contains detailed provisions under section E on the certificates, including the circumstances in which they cease to be valid.

8.3.2.3 Ballast Water Management Plan

A ship-specific Ballast Water Management Plan (BWM), approved by the flag State and taking into account relevant IMO Guidelines is required aboard each ship.[27] The content of the BWM plan is set out in the Convention. As a minimum, the following must be included, namely:

- safety procedures associated with BWM;
- detailed description of implementation actions of BWM requirements and supplemental practices;

---

21 Regulation E-1.
22 Regulation E-1, para. 8.
23 Regulation E-2, para. 2.
24 Regulation E-5, para. 1.
25 If the language used, according to the Convention, is neither English, French nor Spanish, the text shall include a translation into one of these languages (regulation E-4).
26 Regulation E-2, para. 1.
27 Regulation B-1 of the BWM Convention.

OTHER SOURCES OF MARINE POLLUTION

- procedures for the disposal of sediments at sea and to shore;
- procedures for coordinating shipboard BWM involving discharges to the sea with the authorities of the State concerned;
- designation of the officer on board in charge of the implementation of the Plan;
- reporting requirements;
- working language-related requirements.

8.3.2.4 Ballast Water Record Book

In addition to the above, each ship is required to have onboard and readily available for inspection a Ballast Water Record Book (electronic or integrated into another record book or system). Each operation concerning ballast water shall be "fully recorded without delay"[28] in the Book. In case of ballast water discharge according to regulations A-3,[29] A-4[30] or B-3.6[31] or in the event of other accidental or exceptional discharge of ballast water not covered by an exemption, an entry in the Ballast Water Record Book is required. The said entry must describe the circumstances of, and the reason for, the discharge.[32] The occasions which must be recorded in the Record Book are stated in an appendix to the Convention. According to the latter, entries shall be maintained on board the ship for a maximum period of two years after the last entry is made, and thereafter in the company's control for three years minimum.[33]

Clearly, BWM regulations have not been an easy task for regulators and practitioners, and the picture has not fully crystallised. This situation makes regulatory compliance more demanding and complex, especially on the level of Port State Control.

8.3.3 Port State Control

Port State Control is specifically addressed in this context in Article 9 of the Convention, which is reproduced below. Upon entry into force of the Convention, findings from regional memoranda of understanding will shed light on Port State Control in the context of the implementation of the Convention.

ARTICLE 9 OF THE CONVENTION ON BWM ON "INSPECTION OF SHIPS"

1. A ship to which this Convention applies may, in any port or offshore terminal of another Party, be subject to inspection by officers duly authorized by that Party for the purpose of determining whether the ship is in compliance

---

28 Regulation B-2, para. 5 of the BWM Convention.
29 Regulation A-3 pertains to exceptions.
30 Regulation A-4 pertains to exemptions.
31 Regulation B-3 pertains to ballast water management for ships; para. 6 is about ships discharging ballast water to a reception facility taking into account IMO Guidelines for such facilities.
32 Regulation B-2, para. 3.
33 Regulation B-2, para. 2.

with this Convention. Except as provided in paragraph 2 of this Article, any such inspection is limited to:

(a) verifying that there is onboard a valid Certificate, which, if valid shall be accepted; and

(b) inspection of the Ballast Water record book, and/or

(c) a sampling of the ship's Ballast Water, carried out in accordance with the guidelines to be developed by the Organization. However, the time required to analyse the samples shall not be used as a basis for unduly delaying the operation, movement or departure of the ship.

2. Where a ship does not carry a valid Certificate or there are clear grounds for believing that:

(a) the condition of the ship or its equipment does not correspond substantially with the particulars of the Certificate; or

(b) the master or the crew are not familiar with essential shipboard procedures relating to Ballast Water Management, or have not implemented such procedures;

a detailed inspection may be carried out.

3. In the circumstances given in para. 2 of this Article, the Party carrying out the inspection shall take such steps as will ensure that the ship shall not discharge Ballast Water until it can do so without presenting a threat of harm to the environment, human health, property or resources.

As already mentioned, this chapter is also concerned with harmful substances used in anti-fouling systems.

8.4 Harmful substances used in anti-fouling systems

8.4.1 What is the problem?

Unwanted growth of biological material on ships' surface immersed in water has given rise to the use of anti-fouling systems, including paints, aimed at preventing the problem of ship-fouling as well as the slowing down of ships. A risk of toxicity and other adverse impacts on health and the environment stemming from the use of certain anti-fouling systems, including the Tributyltin TBT-based anti-fouling paints, has been acknowledged by experts. TBT has been recognised by many as the most toxic chemical deliberately released into the marine environment.

Against this background, an international instrument was adopted by the IMO in order to ban marine paints used on ships' hulls containing compounds that are harmful to the marine environment. The international convention, which is briefly examined below, takes into account the precautionary principle expressed in the Rio Declaration on Environment and Development. It should be noted that the instrument operates in parallel with unilateral actions undertaken by individual States.

8.4.1.1 The International Convention on the Control of Harmful Anti-fouling Systems on Ships, 2001

The Anti-fouling Systems Convention (AFS Convention) was adopted by the IMO on 5 October 2001 in order to protect the marine environment and human health from the negative impacts of anti-fouling systems used on vessels. This was in recognition of scientific findings that certain anti-fouling systems used on ships may impair the aquatic environment. For the purposes of the Convention, a ship is considered to be a vessel of any type whatsoever operating in the marine environment; it includes hydrofoil boats, air-cushion vehicles, submersibles, floating craft, fixed or floating platforms, floating storage units (FSUs) and floating production storage and off-loading units (FPSOs).[34]

The Convention entered into force at the international level on 17 September 2008 and works in two directions: on the one hand, it phases out the use of harmful organotin compounds acting as biocides in anti-fouling paints; on the other hand, it sets out a mechanism for the prevention of potential future use of other harmful substances in anti-fouling systems.[35] A key element is that anti-fouling systems under control are described in Annex 1 of the Convention, which is subject to future reviews taking into account Article 6; the last provision sets out the process for proposing amendments to controls on anti-fouling systems. Furthermore, fixed dates have been adopted by the Convention for the prohibition of the application of organotin compounds on ships (last day for the application of organotin paints on ships set at 1 January 2003) and for the total phase out (1 January 2008). It is interesting to note that up to present, the only compound banned and phased out is TBT (organotin Tributyltin).[36]

In broad terms, the Convention applies to all ships.[37] Unless otherwise stated, it applies to ships entitled to fly the flag of a Party, ships not entitled to fly the flag of a Party, but which operate under the authority of a Party, and ships that enter a port, shipyard, or offshore terminal of a Party, but do not fall within the above categories. Warships, naval auxiliary, or other ships owned or operated by a Party and used only for governmental non-commercial purposes are excluded from the scope of the Convention. Like in other areas, the principle of no more favourable treatment is set out, which operates towards ships of non-Parties to the Convention. In this context, State Parties are held to apply the requirements of the Convention as may be necessary to ensure that no more favourable treatment is given to such ships.[38]

The instrument also pertains to wastes from the application or removal of TBT-based paints, which are required to be controlled in a safe and environmentally sound manner.

---

34 See Article 2 of the AFS Convention.

35 Article 6 addresses the process for proposing amendments to controls on anti-fouling systems.

36 It is noteworthy that according to a working document issued by the European Commission dating to 9 February 2017 a new substance (Cybutryne, also known as Irgarol) to be controlled by the AFS Convention was proposed to the Marine Environment Protection Committee of the IMO.

37 Article 3.

38 Article 3, para. 3.

A number of resolutions have been adopted through the IMO Diplomatic Conference in this area for future action to be adopted on the part of the Organisation as well as member States, including provisions on technical cooperation.

8.4.1.2 Surveys and certification

States are held to ensure that ships entitled to fly their flag or operating under their authority are surveyed and certified with the regulations set out in Annex 4.[39] The said annex, which is entitled "Surveys and certification requirements for anti-fouling systems", contains detailed provisions in the form of regulations on the matter, including on surveys, the issue or endorsement of an international anti-fouling system certificate, the issue or endorsement of an international anti-fouling system certificate by another Party, the validity of an International Anti-fouling System Certificate, and the Declaration on anti-fouling system. Model forms are also set out in the appendix to Annex 4.

The 2010 Guidelines for Surveys and Certification of Anti-fouling Systems on Ships,[40] which apply to ships of 400 gross tonnage and above engaged in international voyages, are concerned with the procedures for survey in order to ensure that a ship's anti-fouling system complies with the Convention. The Guidelines also provide the procedures necessary for issuance and endorsement of an International Anti-fouling System Certificate. Furthermore, guidance for compliant anti-fouling systems is also given.

It may also be relevant to note MEPC.104(49) setting out guidelines for brief sampling of anti-fouling systems on ships.[41]

8.4.1.3 Best management practices

Guidance on best management practices for removal of anti-fouling coatings from ships, including TBT hull paints, is given in an IMO Circular.[42]

Mention should also be made of the 2011 Biofouling Guidelines adopted on 15 July 2011 by the IMO through Resolution MEPC.207(62). It is noteworthy that while the focus of the AFS Convention is the addressing of adverse impacts from the use of anti-fouling systems on ships, the Guidelines have a different but related scope. They address the problem of accumulation of aquatic organisms on ships and the ensuing risk of transfer through a global managerial approach and practical guidance (biofouling management plan, biofouling record book, etc.). It should not be forgotten that factors which relate to biofouling are the design and history of the ship, operating speeds, places visited, training routes, etc.

That said, as it will be seen below, the AFS Convention has been transposed into EU legislation through regional mandatory instruments.

---

39 Article 10.
40 MEPC.195(61) adopted on 1 October 2010.
41 MEPC.104(49) adopted 18 July 2003.
42 AFS.3/Circ.3, 22 July 2009.

8.4.1.4 The European Union approach: Regulation 782/2003 of 14 April 2003[43] and Regulation 536/2008 of 13 June 2008[44]

In view of the above, let us briefly examine the problem on the regional level. If we place the focus on the EU Regulation 782/2003, the EU has acknowledged the harmful environmental effects of organotin compounds used as anti-fouling systems on ships, and in particular of TBT coatings. It can be recalled at this point that EU Regulations are directly applicable in the legal systems of EU Member States, and they do not require any national transposition measures.

The context in which the Regulation was adopted involves the period prior to the entry into force of the AFS Convention, and EU Member States' ratification. The Regulation sought to remedy anticipated uncertainty regarding the total prohibition of active TBT coatings, by considering that such uncertainty should not be accepted at Community level, and that "world-wide shipping industry [...] should be made aware clearly and in due time that as from 1 January 2008, ships bearing an active TBT coating on their hulls will no longer be allowed in Community ports".[45]

As an immediate follow-up to the AFS Conference, Commission Directive 2002/62/EC of 9 July 2002[46] was adopted in order to prohibit with effect from 1 January 2003 the marketing and use of organostannic compounds in anti-fouling systems for all ships, irrespective of their length. A key element is that the drafters of Regulation 782/2003 had taken notice that the EU instrument, which should seek solely to prohibit organotin compounds, should not duplicate the AFS Convention.[47] In the same vein, Regulation 782/2003 acknowledged the need for the definitions and requirements imposed by it to be as far as possible based upon those of the international instrument.

Adopted on 13 June 2008, i.e. prior to the entry into force of the AFS Convention, one of the purposes of European Commission Regulation 536/2008 was to set out measures allowing ships flying the flag of a third State at call at an EU port or offshore terminal to demonstrate their compliance with Article 5 of Regulation 782/2003.[48] It may be of assistance to indicate that the said article addresses the prohibition of the bearing of organotin compounds which act as biocides. In addition, Regulation 536/2008 also sought to establish procedures for control by the port State within the EU.

---

43 European Parliament and Council Regulation 782/2003 on the prohibition of organotin compounds on ships [2003] OJ L 115/1.

44 European Commission Regulation 536/2008 giving effect to Article 6(3) and Article 7 of Regulation (EC) 782/2003 on the prohibition of organotin compounds on ships and amending that Regulation [2008] OJ L 156/10.

45 Recital 14 of Regulation 782/2003.

46 European Commission Directive 2002/62/EC of 9 July 2002 adapting to technical progress for the ninth time Annex I to Council Directive 76/769/EEC on the approximation of the laws, regulations and administrative provisions of the Member States relating to restrictions on the marketing and use of certain dangerous substances and preparations (organostannic compounds) (Text with EEA relevance) [2002] OJ L 183/58. It is noted that Directive 2002/62/EC is no longer in force.

47 Recital 12 of Regulation 782/2003.

48 See Article 1 of Regulation 536/2008.

As discussed earlier, among the potential sources of marine pollution which are not addressed by MARPOL and give rise to a distinct legal regime, is ship dismantling. It will be seen below that environmentally sound management of ship-dismantling activities is an area with developments underway.

8.5 Ship recycling

8.5.1 What is the problem?

Despite the international ban on the use of certain hazardous materials on ships (e.g. asbestos, etc.), various hazardous materials continue to be found on vessels on the level of their construction or maintenance. In this context, uncontrolled ship-dismantling activities generate occupational health and safety risks; the risk of environmental pollution adversely affecting soil or air quality or generating marine pollution is an additional facet of the same problem. According to the EU, around 1,000 ships are dismantled worldwide every year, with most part taking place in South Asia.[49] Ships dismantled on beaches or river banks on the Indian sub-continent with little or no concern for health and/or the environment have been, at least up to the present stage, a common practice. An estimated 5.5 million tonnes of materials of potential environmental concern have ended up in dismantling yards from ships scrapped between 2006 and 2015 – materials including oil sludge, oils, paints, PVC and asbestos.[50] Adopted by the IMO on 15 May 2009, the Hong Kong International Convention for the Safe and Environmentally Sound Recycling of Ships constitutes the response of the international community to the environmental and other challenges raised by uncontrolled ship recycling.[51]

8.5.2 The Hong Kong Convention 2009

The Hong Kong Convention provides duties geared towards ships, ship-recycling facilities and flag States. A clear illustration is given, for example, by the requirement that ship recycling facilities have to be authorised; furthermore, they will have to be subjected to procedures aimed to prevent unsafe conditions, accidents, spills or emissions throughout the ship-recycling process likely to harm human health and/or the environment.[52]

The Convention has not entered into force. As at March 2017, the instrument was ratified by five States representing 19.99% of world tonnage. The

---

49 See www.emsa.europa.eu.

50 See Commission of the European Communities Green Paper on Better Ship Dismantling, Brussels 22.5.2007, COM(2007)269final, p. 2.

51 Before we touch upon the essentials of the Convention, it would be useful to mention that ships which constitute waste and which are subject to a transboundary movement for recycling fall within the scope of the Basel Convention of 22 March 1989, as amended, and on the EU level in the scope of Regulation (EC) 1013/2006 of 14 June 2006 on shipments of waste.

52 Regulation 19 on the Prevention of adverse effects to human health and the environment.

entry into force of the Convention requires ratification by 15 States representing 40% of world tonnage; an additional condition for its entry into force is the combined maximum annual ship recycling volume of the 15 ratifying States during the preceding ten years which must not be less than 3% of their combined tonnage.[53] Despite not being effective, in preparation of the potential entry into force of the Convention, a number of voluntary practices are observed on the part of the industry; this includes, for example, the issuance of Statements of Compliance (SOC) in relation to the Inventory of Hazardous Materials (IHM) required from ships or to the ship recycling facilities which already meet the requirements of the Convention. It may be relevant to note that upon its entry into force, the instrument will require, amongst others, the collection of voluminous data relating to the efficient maintenance of the IHM. Challenges that can be reasonably anticipated in relation to the potential entry into force of the Convention include the quality of implementation and the risk of red tape.

Like other instruments examined so far, the Convention takes into account the precautionary principle and clearly recognises that ship recycling contributes to sustainable development. The text aims at ensuring that ship recycling which brings to an end the operational life of a vessel does not put at risk human health, safety or the environment.

The Convention is intended to apply to ships entitled to fly the flag of a Party or operating under its authority, as well as to ship recycling facilities operating under the jurisdiction of a Party. Warships, naval auxiliary, or other ships owned or operated by a Party used only on government non-commercial service, are excluded from the material scope of the text.[54] Furthermore, ships of less than 500 GT or ships operating throughout their life "only in waters subject to the sovereignty or jurisdiction of the State whose flag the ship is entitled to fly"[55] are also excluded. Like in other regulated areas, ships flying the flag of non-Parties have been excluded from a more favourable treatment.[56]

It can be said that the instrument is centered on legal requirements which go in two directions: on the one hand, vessels are subject to appropriate surveys and certification; a key element in that regard is the International Certificate on Inventory of Hazardous Materials. On the other hand, ship recycling facilities are also regulated. The Convention is furthermore concerned with enforcement and violations. Controls relating to ship recycling are also provided for. The controls are on the shoulders of flag States as well as on the shoulders of State Parties with ship recycling facilities;[57] other provisions deal with ship inspection, detection of violations, violations and undue delay or detention of ships. An annex with technical regulations and seven appendices complement the

---

53 See Article 17 of the Hong Kong Convention 2009.
54 See Article 3, para. 2.
55 *Ibid*, para. 3.
56 *Ibid*, para. 4.
57 Article 4.

picture. Technical regulations included in the annex amplify numerous aspects, including the following:

- Design, construction, operation and maintenance of ships

"[…] each Party, shall prohibit and/or restrict the installation or use of Hazardous Materials listed in Appendix 1 on ships entitled to fly its flag or operating under its authority […]"[58]

"Each new ship shall have on board an Inventory of Hazardous Materials. The Inventory shall be verified by the Administration or by any person or organization authorized by it taking into account guidelines, including any threshold values and exemptions contained in those guidelines, developed by the Organization. The Inventory of Hazardous Materials shall be specific to each ship […] (paragraph 1)"[59]

"Existing ships shall comply as far as practicable with paragraph 1 not later than 5 years after the entry into force of this Convention, or before going for recycling if this is earlier, taking into account the guidelines developed by the Organization and the Organization's Harmonized System of Survey and Certification. The Hazardous Materials listed in Appendix 1, at least, shall be identified when the Inventory is developed. For existing ships a plan shall be prepared describing the visual/sampling check by which the Inventory of Hazardous Materials is developed, taking into account the guidelines developed by the Organization".[60]

- Preparation of ships in view of ship-recycling, including Ship Recycling Plan

"A ship-specific Ship Recycling Plan shall be developed by the Ship Recycling Facility(ies) prior to any recycling of a ship, taking into account the guidelines developed by the Organization[61] […]".

- Requirements

"Ships destined to be recycled shall:

- only be recycled at Ship Recycling Facilities that are authorized in accordance with this Convention, and fully authorized to undertake all the ship recycling which the Ship Recycling Plan specifies to be conducted by the identified Ship Recycling Facility(ies);
- conduct operations in the period prior to entering the Ship Recycling Facility in order to minimize the amount of cargo residues, remaining fuel oil, and wastes remaining on board […]
- be certified as ready for recycling by the Administration or organization recognised by it, prior to any recycling activity taking place".[62]

---

58 Regulation 4.
59 Regulation 5.
60 Regulation 5, para. 2.
61 Regulation 9.
62 Regulation 8.

OTHER SOURCES OF MARINE POLLUTION

- Authorisation of ship recycling facilities

> "1. Ship Recycling Facilities which recycle ships to which this Convention applies, or ships treated similarly pursuant to Article 3.4, shall be authorized by a Party taking into account the guidelines developed by the Organization.
> 2. The authorization shall be carried out by the Competent Authority(ies) and shall include verification of documentation required by this Convention and a site inspection. The Competent Authority(ies) may however entrust the authorization of Ship Recycling Facilities to organizations recognised by it
> [...]".[63]

- Ship recycling facility plan

> "Ship Recycling Facilities authorized by a Party shall prepare a Ship Recycling Facility Plan. The Plan shall be adopted by the board or the appropriate governing body of the Recycling Company, and shall include:
> .1 a policy ensuring workers' safety and the protection of human health and the environment [...];
> .2 a system for ensuring implementation of the requirements set out in this Convention, the achievement of the goals set out in the policy of the Recycling Company, and the continuous improvement of the procedures and standards used in the Ship Recycling operations;
> .3 identification of roles and responsibilities for employers and workers when conducting Ship Recycling operations;
> .4 a programme for providing appropriate information and training of workers for the safe and environmentally sound operation of the Ship Recycling Facility;
> .5 an emergency preparedness and response plan;
> .6 a system for monitoring the performance of Ship Recycling;
> .7 a record-keeping system showing how Ship Recycling is carried out;
> .8 a system for reporting discharges, emissions, incidents and accidents [...]
> .9 a system for reporting occupational diseases, accidents, injuries [...][64]".

- Reporting

> - "A shipowner shall notify the Administration in due time and in writing of the intention to recycle a ship in order to enable the Administration to prepare for a survey and certification required by this Convention[65] [...]".
> - "When the partial or complete recycling of a ship is completed in accordance with the requirements of this Convention, a Statement of Completion

---

63 Regulation 16.
64 Regulation 18.
65 Regulation 24, para. 1.

> shall be issued by the Ship Recycling Facility and reported to its Competent Authority(ies)[66] [...]".

8.5.2.1 Documentation

Not surprisingly, certificates issued under the authority of a State Party to the Convention must be accepted by the other Parties and treated as having the same validity.[67] The form of the certificates mentioned below is given in the appendices of the Convention.

The International Certificate on Inventory of Hazardous Materials is issued by the flag State administration or any other entity authorised by it following appropriate survey[68] for a period specified by the administration, which shall not exceed five years.[69] Regulation 11 addresses in detail the issuance and endorsement of certificates, including the International Ready for Recycling Certificate, with reference on numerous points to regulation 10 on surveys. The Convention also deals with the circumstances under which the International Certificate on Inventory of Hazardous Materials ceases to be valid.

Issued either by the flag State administration or any entity empowered in that regard, the International Ready for Recycling Certificate requires the successful completion of a final survey in line with the provisions of regulation 10. The Certificate will have to be issued to any ships to which the regulation 10 applies, taking into account, according to the Convention, the authorisation of the Ship Recycling Facility and the guidelines developed by the IMO. The Certificate is issued for a period specified by the administration, not longer than three months.[70]

As already mentioned, so far only a small number of countries have ratified the Convention. In that vein, the European Union adopted its own agenda on the matter, which in practice should facilitate ratification of the Hong Kong Convention by EU Member States.

8.5.3 European Union (EU) action

In recognition of the challenges raised by uncontrolled ship recycling activities of EU-flagged ships on humans and the environment, the EU regulator adopted Regulation (EU) 1257/2013 of 20 November 2013 on ship recycling.[71] The instru-

---

66 Regulation 25.
67 Regulation 11, para. 12.
68 Regulation 11.
69 Regulation 14, para. 2.
70 Regulation 14, para. 3.
71 European Parliament and Council Regulation (EU) No. 1257/2013 on ship recycling amending Regulation (EC) No. 1013/2006 and Directive 2009/16/EC [2013] OJ L 330/1. Regulation (EC) 1013/2006 implements the Basel Convention, as amended, while Directive 2009/16/EC deals with Port State Control. It is further noted that Regulation (EU) 1257/2013 on ship recycling is a text with EEA (European Economic Area) relevance, i.e. an instrument potentially affecting the legal systems of Norway, Iceland and Liechtenstein.

ment entered into force on 30 December 2013, and was subject to differentiated application dates depending on the subject matter extending up to 31 December 2020.[72] In this context, EU drafters acknowledged the lengthy time scale needed by the international community for the adoption of IMO instruments, as well as the inadequacy of current ship-recycling capacity in OECD countries for EU-flagged vessels, thus the need to take regional action. A key element is that, despite the prohibition on the transfer of end-of-life ships from industrial to developing countries under international law on the shipment of waste and the EC's Waste Shipment Regulation (i.e. Regulation 1013/2006[73] which implements on the EU level the Basel Convention on the control of the transboundary movements of hazardous wastes and their disposal), a number of notorious violations in recent years point to numerous challenges on the implementation level.

EU Regulation 1257/2013, which applies to EU-flagged ships but is also relevant to ships flying the flag of a third country (i.e. non-EU Member State) calling at a port or anchorage of a Member State of the EU,[74] is a multifaceted instrument with impacts on the international market of ship recycling; as such, it has met with criticism. In a nutshell, the instrument is intended to prevent and reduce accidents and other adverse effects on human health and the environment caused by ship recycling; in the same vein, it seeks to achieve this goal through the enhancement of safety, the protection of human health and the EU's marine environment during a ship's lifecycle. Secondly, the Regulation is concerned with the proper management of hazardous materials on ships. Thirdly, Regulation 1257/2013 is geared towards facilitation of the early ratification of the Hong Kong Convention "both within the Union and in third countries by applying proportionate controls to ships and ship recycling facilities on the basis of that Convention".[75] By building on the Hong Kong Convention, the EU instrument gives effect to the Convention despite the fact that the latter is not effective internationally. Last, but not least, the instrument has the ambition to reduce the disparities between operators in the EU, in OECD countries and in relevant third countries from the standpoint of health and safety at the workplace as well as from the standpoint of environmental standards. In this context, and in recognition of the need to increase the competitiveness of safe and environmentally sound recycling activities in Member States, a European list of ship recycling facilities satisfying the requirement of the Regulation was considered; the first European list of environmentally sound ship recycling facilities that are safe for workers was adopted by the European Commission in 2016. It included 18 shipyards located in the EU; applications from yards in third countries were reported to be in the process of being assessed.[76]

---

72 See Article 32 of the Regulation.

73 European Parliament and Council Regulation (EC) 1013/2006 on shipments of waste [2006] OJ L190/1.

74 See Article 12 of Regulation 1257/2013.

75 See recital 5 of the Regulation.

76 European Commission, News Release, Brussels, 20 December 2016. Relevant EU act is Commission Implementing Decision (EU) 2016/2323 of 19 December 2016 establishing the European list of ship recycling facilities pursuant to Regulation (EU) 1257/2013 of the European Parliament and of the Council on ship recycling (Text with EEA relevance) [2016] OJ L 345/119.

With the above in mind, according to the Regulation, "ship recycling" means "the activity of complete or partial dismantling of a ship at a ship recycling facility in order to recover components and materials for reprocessing, for preparation for re-sue or for re-use, whilst ensuring the management of hazardous and other materials, and includes associated operations such as storage, and treatment of components and materials on site, but not their further processing or disposal in separate facilities".[77] It is noteworthy that Regulation 1257/2013 gives a different definition of ship recycling than Directive 2008/98/EC on waste. On this point it would be useful to indicate that the EU instrument on ship recycling expressly takes note of the need to avoid duplication with Regulation 1013/2006 (Waste Shipment Regulation) and Directive 2008/98/EC on waste; as discussed, Regulation 1013/2006 implements at the EU level the Basel Convention on the control of the transboundary movements of hazardous wastes and their disposal. Regulation 1013/2006 applies to shipments of waste from the European Union, whereas Regulation 1257/2013 on ship recycling subjects ships which fall within its scope to controls throughout their lifecycle with a view to ensuring environmentally sound recycling of ships.[78] Furthermore, in order to ensure legal certainty, EU-flagged vessels covered by the Regulation on ship recycling would be excluded from the scope of the above-mentioned Waste Shipment Regulation.[79]

In view of the above, each new ship is required to have on board an inventory of hazardous materials; in broad terms, existing ships shall comply, "as far as practicable", with this requirement.[80] Furthermore, from a specified date onwards, "shipowners shall ensure that ships destined to be recycled, are only recycled at ship recycling facilities that are included in the European list".[81]

All in all, this is an area which has not settled at the EU level, and will have to be put to the test in practice in the very near future.

Another area of concern, which is of growing interest to the protection of the marine environment, is the collision of cetaceans with ships. This area is not specifically addressed by MARPOL.

SECTION 3: AREAS OF SPECIAL INTEREST, INCLUDING CURRENT DEVELOPMENTS

8.6 Ship strikes with marine mammals

The collision of cetaceans with ships is an issue of growing concern which impacts on the protection of the marine environment in varied ways. Strikes of

---

77 See Article 3, para. 1(6).

78 See recital 10 of Regulation (EU) 1257/2013.

79 See www.emsa.europa.eu.

80 See Article 5 of Regulation (EU) 1257/2013. It may be useful to note EMSA, *Best Practice Guidance Document on the Inventory of Hazardous Materials* (2017). The document provides best practice guidance on the development and maintenance of inventories of hazardous materials under Regulation (EU) 1257/2013.

81 See Article 6(2)(a) of Regulation (EU) 1257/2013.

ships with whales, dolphins and other cetaceans is likely to cause their injury or death, evidenced by carcasses at sea or blood in the water. Such strikes may also cause damage to vessels, including cracked hulls, damaged propellers, etc.

The challenge of protecting cetaceans from shipping has been addressed by the IMO through guidance (MEPC.1/Circ.674, 31 July 2009).[82] The circular provides guidance to Member Governments in reducing and minimising the risk of ship strikes of cetaceans through general principles that should be taken into account. The document also proposes possible actions at national and international level on the reduction of the risk of ship strikes of cetaceans.[83] It should not be forgotten that in this context maritime safety is also a concern, a concern which appears to be duly noted. A balance is sought between actions on minimising the risk of ship strikes with possible adverse impacts on the shipping industry.

Against this background, an IMO working document dating to 12 February 2016[84] provides information on recent outcomes regarding minimising ship strikes to cetaceans since the adoption of the IMO 2009 Guidance, where it is noted that the only proven, effective measures are avoidance of areas with known concentrations of whales and reduction of speed while transiting those areas. Furthermore, the prospect of designating some high risk areas as PSSAs (Particularly Sensitive Sea Areas) with associated routing measures on speed reduction, is touched upon. In addition to ship strikes with marine mammals, underwater noise emissions from vessels attract a great deal of attention at present.

8.7 Underwater noise emissions from vessels

There are numerous human sources of energy in the marine environment. These include shipping, the use of sonar systems by vessels, offshore oil and gas platform construction, dredging for shipping lanes, military activities, etc. Underwater noise produced by shipping and other activities in the oceans is considered to have adverse effects on natural processes. From this standpoint, addressing underwater noise emissions from vessels becomes an issue of environmental concern. It may be recalled on this point that under UNCLOS III, pollution of the marine environment means the introduction by man, directly or indirectly, of substances or energy into the marine environment, including estuaries, which results or is likely to result in such deleterious effects as harm to living resources and marine life, hazards to human health, hindrance to marine activities, including fishing and other legitimate uses of the sea, impairment of quality for use of sea water and reduction of amenities.[85] The question of noise produced from shipping has also been of interest to the IMO.

---

82 Guidance document for minimising the risk of shipstrikes with cetaceans.
83 See the introduction of the Circular.
84 MEPC 69/10/3 on the Identification and Protection of Special Areas and PSSAs – Information on recent outcomes regarding minimizing ship strikes to cetaceans – Submitted by the International Whaling Commission.
85 Article 1(1)(4).

8.7.1 On the IMO level

Noise produced from shipping has been dealt by the IMO from the standpoint of adverse impacts on the crew and the passengers (Code on Noise Levels on Board Ships, IMO Assembly Resolution A.468(XII) (November 1981)). SOLAS was amended on 1 July 2014 in order to make the Noise Code mandatory for new vessels. The Code aims at providing standards on preventing noise levels hazardous to human health and on reducing the exposure of seafarers to such noise levels.

The question of underwater noise emissions from vessels is a related question; it generates environmental concerns and has given rise to IMO guidance.

Incidental introduction of noise from commercial shipping operations in the marine environment nowadays attracts growing attention.[86] In addition to merchant ships, navy ships, seismic vessels, offshore survey vessels, and other types of ships produce noise and contribute to adverse effects on marine life. Interference with critical life functions of marine animals has been acknowledged by the IMO – sounds for critical life functions such as communicating, foraging, evading predators and navigating being produced and received by most marine animals. Furthermore, there are concerns that marine animals (e.g. large whales, many fish and some seals and sea lions) are especially vulnerable to adverse impacts from incidental shipping noise; this is because, according to scientists, they primarily use the same low frequency sounds as that generated by commercial ships for their communication and/or in order to perceive their environments (see graph 8.3 below). The expansion of shipping in recent decades and the long lifespan of a ship exacerbate this challenge which is currently a pending item on the international agenda.

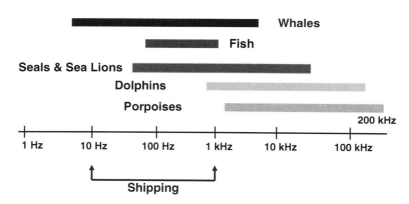

Graph 8.3 Frequency relationships between marine animal sounds and incidental noise from commercial shipping
Source: IMO MEPC. 58(19)

---

86 See the maritime press, including, amongst others, W. Laursen, Noise Control at Sea and in Port, Maritime Executive, 22 March 2017.

In view of the above, the IMO non-mandatory Guidelines for the reduction of underwater noise from commercial shipping were adopted on 7 April 2014; they aim to address adverse impacts on marine life, and can be applied to any commercial ship.[87] It may be relevant to note at this point that the introduction of noise from naval and war ships as well as the deliberate introduction of noise for other purposes such as sonar or seismic activities, is not covered by the Guidelines. The purpose of the document, which places the focus on primary sources of underwater noise associated with propellers, hull form, onboard machinery and operational aspects, is to provide general advice about reduction of underwater noise. Such advice is intended for designers, shipbuilders and ship operators. As a minimum, the optimal underwater noise mitigation strategy for ships should consider all relevant noise sources.

8.7.2 *The action undertaken by the European Union*

At the EU level, there are instruments on the monitoring of underwater energy in marine waters as well as on the monitoring of impacts of individual public and private projects. In prelude to their brief presentation, the EU project NoMEPorts is interesting to note. The project aims to develop a structured approach for mapping and managing noise in industrial seaport areas, and to contribute to action plans on the reduction of noise annoyance. The project is also concerned with the promotion of the use of a uniform guideline to be integrated in the EU Directive for the assessment and management of environmental noise (Directive 2002/49/EC).[88] At another level, the National Oceanic and Atmospheric Administration (NOAA) in the USA released in September 2016 the NOAA Noise Strategy Roadmap. The latter intends to give a roadmap over the next ten years by putting together essential steps that could be taken across this federal agency in order to achieve strategic goals on the management of noise impacts.

With the above in mind, let now have a closer look at the monitoring of underwater energy in marine waters at the EU level.

8.7.2.1 Monitoring underwater energy of marine waters

Adopted on 17 June 2008, the Marine Strategy Framework Directive (MSFD) (Directive 2008/56/EC)[89] views the marine environment as a "precious heritage", and seeks to integrate the environmental dimension in all relevant EU policies. The text is geared towards biodiversity. It is aimed at protecting more effectively the marine environment across Europe through the achievement by 2020 of good environmental status (GES) of the EU's marine waters. Thus, Member States are

---

87 MEPC.1/Circ.833, 7 April 2014.

88 European Parliament and Council (EC) Directive 2002/49 relating to the assessment and management of environmental noise-Declaration by the Commission in the Conciliation Committee on the Directive relating to the assessment and management of environmental noise [2002] OJ L189/12.

89 European Parliament and Council (EC) Directive 2008/56 establishing a framework for Community action in the field of marine environmental policy (Marine Strategy Framework Directive) (Text with EEA relevance), [2008] OJ L164/19.

called upon to develop a marine strategy for their marine waters, notably including an assessment of the current environmental status of national marine waters, the determination of what GES means for national marine waters, etc. Among the qualitative descriptors for determining good environmental status set out in Annex I of the Directive, mention is made of the introduction of energy, including underwater noise, which should be at levels that do not adversely affect the marine environment.

The Directive came into force on 15 July 2008, and transposition of its requirements into the legal systems of the EU Members had to be effected by 15 July 2010 at the latest.

In addition to the above, the Environmental Impact Assessment (EIA) Directive, which is briefly described below, is of interest to the question of underwater noise from another standpoint.

8.7.2.2 Monitoring impacts of individual projects

The Environmental Impact Assessment Directive (EIA) (Directive 2011/92/EU[90]) is not proper to the maritime sphere. The Directive acknowledges the environmental effects of projects belonging to certain types and the need for those projects to be subject to a systematic environmental assessment; this includes, amongst others, an estimate of expected noise resulting from the operation of the proposed project (e.g. pipelines for the transportation of oil).

"Projects" are defined as the execution of construction works or of other installations or schemes, as well as other interventions in the natural surroundings and landscape, including those involving the extraction of mineral resources. Member States of the EU are required to adopt measures to ensure that projects likely to have significant effects on the environment by virtue of their nature, size or location, are subject to a requirement for development consent and an assessment regarding their environmental effects. In this context, on the basis of the significance of the environmental effects of projects, Member States may set out thresholds or criteria for the purpose of determining which projects should be subject to assessment. According to the Directive, the effects of a project on the environment should be assessed so as to take into account concerns to protect human health, to contribute to means of a better environment to the quality of life, to ensure maintenance of the diversity of species and to maintain the reproductive capacity of the ecosystem as a basic resource for life.[91] In other words, the Directive has harmonised the principles for the environmental impact assessment of projects by setting out minimum requirements with regard to the types of projects to be assessed, the main obligations of the developers,[92] the content of the assessment and participation of the competent authorities and the public. Among the types of projects subject to an environmental impact

---

90 European Parliament and Council (EU) Directive 2011/92 on the assessment of the effects of certain public and private projects on the environment (codification) (Text with EEA relevance) [2012] L 26/1.

91 See Recital 14 of the Directive.

92 According to the instrument, a developer is an applicant for authorisation for a private project or the public authority which initiates a project.

OTHER SOURCES OF MARINE POLLUTION

assessment, mention should be made of the extraction of petroleum and natural gas for commercial purposes, pipelines of specified dimensions for the transport of gas, oil and chemicals, ports for inland waterway traffic which permit the passage of certain vessels, trading ports, piers for loading and unloading connected to land and outside ports, etc.

It is noted that Directive 2014/52/EU[93] amended Directive 2011/92/EU with a view to improving environmental protection, energy efficiency and sustainable growth. The instrument also simplified and harmonised relevant procedures.

BIBLIOGRAPHY

DNV GL Technical & Regulatory news No. 20/2016, 'Update from the Marine Environmental Protection Committee' (MEPC.70)

EMSA, Best Practice Guidance Document on the Inventory of Hazardous Materials (2016)

European Commission Communication to the European Parliament, the Council, the European Economic and Social Committee and the Committee of the Regions, EU Strategy for Better Ship Dismantling, Brussels 19.11.2008, COM(2008)767final

European Commission, EC Green Paper on Better Ship Dismantling, Brussels 22.5.2007, COM(2007)269final

European Commission Implementing Decision (EU) 2016/2323 of 19 December 2016 establishing the European list of ship recycling facilities pursuant to Regulation (EU) 1257/2013 of the European Parliament and of the Council on ship recycling (Text with EEA relevance) [2016] OJ L 345/119

European Commission Regulation 536/2008 giving effect to Article 6(3) and Article 7 of Regulation (EC) 782/2003 of the European Parliament and of the Council on the prohibition of organotin compounds on ships and amending that Regulation [2008] L 156/10

European Parliament and Council (EC) Directive 2008/56 establishing a framework for Community action in the field of marine environmental policy (Marine Strategy Framework Directive) (Text with EEA relevance) [2008] OJ L164/19

European Parliament and Council (EU) Directive 2011/92 on the assessment of the effects of certain public and private projects on the environment (codification) (Text with EEA relevance) [2012] L 26/1

European Parliament and Council (EU) Directive 2014/52 amending Directive 2011/92/EU on the assessment of the effects of certain public and private projects on the environment (Text with EEA relevance) [2014] L 124/1

European Parliament and Council Regulation 782/2003 on the prohibition of organotin compounds on ships [2003] L 115/1

GARD, Insight 155 dating to 1st August 1999 ('More on Unwanted Aquatic Organisms in Ballast Water – All Ships Are Now Potential Polluters')

GARD, Insight dating to 10 July 2017 ('Ballast Water Management – Are You Ready for 8 September 2017'?)

IMO MEPC.1/Circ.674, 31 July 2009, Guidance Document for Minimizing the Risk of Ship Strikes with Cetaceans

---

93 European Parliament and Council (EU) Directive 2014/52 amending Directive 2011/92/EU on the assessment of the effects of certain public and private projects on the environment (Text with EEA relevance) [2014] L 124/1.

IMO MEPC 69/10/3, 12 February 2016, 'Identification and Protection of Special Areas and PSSAs – Information on Recent Outcomes Regarding Ship Strikes to Cetaceans' (Submitted by the International Whaling Commission)

IMO MEPC.1/Circ.833, 7 April 2014, 'Guidelines for the Reduction of Underwater Noise from Commercial Shipping to Address Adverse Impacts on Marine Life'

Laursen W., Noise Control at Sea and in Port, Maritime Executive, 22.3.2017

Lloyd's Register Marine, National Ballast Water Management Requirements, January 2014

MEPC.207(62) adopted on 15 July 2011 '2011 Guidelines for the Control and Management of Ships' Biofouling to Minimize the Transfer of Invasive Aquatic Species'

Pughiuc, Dandu, 'Ballast Water Management – An Overview of the Regulatory Process' p. 17, in N. Bellefontaine, F. Haag, O. Lindén and J. Matheickal (eds), GEF-UNDP-IMO GloBallast Partnerships Programme and the Global Industry Alliance 'Emerging Ballast Water Management Systems' Proceedings of the IMO-WMU Research and Development Forum, 26–29 January 2010, Malmö, Sweden

Regulation (EU) 1257/2013 of the European Parliament and of the Council of 20 November 2013 on ship recycling and amending Regulation (EC) 1013/2006 and Directive 2009/16/EC (Text with EEA relevance) [2013] OJ L330/1

WWF International, 'Silent Invasion – The Spread of Invasive Marine Species Via Ships' Ballast Water' (Gland, 2009)

CHAPTER 9

Preparedness, response, and cooperation in the context of marine pollution

TABLE OF CONTENTS

Section 1	Relevance of a coordinated framework and of intervention rights on the high seas to marine pollution control	234
9.1	The impact of landmark accidents on the legal framework governing cooperation and intervention	234
9.2	The position of the United Nations Convention on the Law of the Sea	235
9.3	The bodies involved	237
	9.3.1 The International Maritime Organisation	237
	9.3.2 The United Nations Environment Programme	238
	9.3.3 The European Maritime Safety Agency	238
	9.3.4 Other	239
9.4	Glossary	239
Section 2	The international framework on marine pollution preparedness, response and cooperation	242
9.5	The OPRC Convention	242
	9.5.1 Selected highlights	242
9.6	The OPRC-HNS Protocol	244
	9.6.1 Selected highlights	245
9.7	Spill response contracts	246
9.8	Challenges for preparedness and response	247
Section 3	Regional framework	248
9.9	Regional framework	248
9.10	Selected highlight: REMPEC (Regional Marine Pollution Emergency Response Centre for the Mediterranean Sea)	249
Section 4	Managerial aspects of response	251
9.11	Breaking down oil spill management	251
9.12	Challenges	254

SECTION 1: RELEVANCE OF A COORDINATED FRAMEWORK AND OF INTERVENTION RIGHTS ON THE HIGH SEAS TO MARINE POLLUTION CONTROL

Marine pollution control cannot be fully achieved in all instances by States acting alone. The cross-border nature of marine pollution and/or the complexity of polluting incidents, including from the standpoint of the stakeholders and the national interests involved, call for frameworks of cooperation.

It is clear that States have the duty under MARPOL to cooperate in the detection of infringements and the enforcement of marine pollution prevention regulations. In that regard, they are required to use measures of detection and environmental monitoring, as well as procedures for reporting and collection of evidence.[1]

Against this background, there are circumstances where the coastal State may be led to intervene beyond its usual scope of action, i.e. on the high seas, in order to protect its interests from marine pollution.

In the first case, the issue is coordination and mutual assistance; in the last case, the discussion is about the right of intervention of coastal States on the high seas. Before addressing these and other aspects such as preparedness and response, it may be of interest to take a look at the impact of landmark accidents on the development of regulations.

9.1 The impact of landmark accidents on the legal framework governing cooperation and intervention

The *Torrey Canyon* accident, often referred to as the United Kingdom's worst environmental accident, took place off the southwest coast of England in 1967, and involved a cargo of approximately 119,000 tonnes of crude oil. The casualty pointed to numerous critical questions which prompted reflection on polluting incidents and the appropriate ways to respond to them. The accident also triggered the adoption of important international legislation, including the adoption of MARPOL. Some of the questions raised in the aftermath of the *Torrey Canyon* included spill mitigation methods (e.g. slick burning, aerial bombardment, use of dispersants and detergents, etc.), inadequacy of financial compensation regimes, and organisation of the response of coastal States to incidents.

It was also in this context that the 1969 Intervention Convention[2] was adopted (entry into force 6 May 1975). The Convention stated the right of coastal States to take measures on the high seas necessary to prevent, mitigate or eliminate grave and imminent danger to its coastline or related interests from pollution by oil, or the threat thereof after a maritime casualty. However, such action on the part of the coastal State was also subjected to limitations.[3] Furthermore, the regime flowing from the 1969 Intervention Convention was extended to

---

1 Article 6, MARPOL Convention.
2 International Convention Relating to Intervention on the High Seas in Cases of Oil Pollution Casualties.
3 See Article III of relevant convention.

substances other than oil by a 1973 instrument, amended since then. This was the Protocol relating to Intervention on the High Seas in Cases of Marine Pollution by Substances other than Oil (entry into force 1983).

Another major accident, the *Exxon Valdez*, which took place in Alaskan waters in 1989, pointed to the need to provide for an international framework for cooperation supporting preparedness and response to major oil spills, and contributed to the adoption by the international legislator of the International Convention on Oil Pollution, Preparedness, Response and Cooperation (OPRC Convention was adopted on 30 November 1990; entry into force 13 May 1995). In this context, preparedness, response and cooperation can be seen as providing additional layers of protection to States to that sought through instruments targeting prevention (e.g. MARPOL) or compensation (see graph 9.1 below). The OPRC Convention was followed by a text with similar aims in the area of chemical pollution, i.e. the OPRC-HNS Protocol (2000). Both instruments are discussed in greater detail below under paragraphs 9.5 and 9.6.[4]

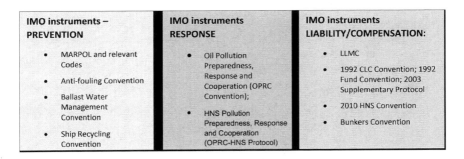

Graph 9.1 Pillars of IMO legislation, including preparedness, response and cooperation

9.2 The position of the United Nations Convention on the Law of the Sea

One of the first provisions of United Nations Convention on the Law of the Sea (UNCLOS III) (1982) under Part XII on marine environment protection and preservation provides for the duty of States Parties to the Convention to act individually or *jointly* in order to prevent, reduce and control marine environment pollution from any source.[5] In doing so, States must use the best practicable means at their disposal and in accordance with their capabilities;[6] States are also called

---

4 For a detailed description of the international instruments governing pollution preparedness, response and cooperation, see Gabino Gonzalez and Frédéric Hébert, 'Conventions Relating to Pollution Incident Preparedness, Response and Cooperation', in David J. Attard (General Ed), *The IMLI Manual on International Maritime Law* (Oxford University Press, Oxford, 2016), Vol. III, pp. 195–260. On the Intervention on the High Seas, see Augustin Blanco-Bazán, 'Intervention in the High Seas in Cases of Marine Pollution Casualties', in Attard (*id*), pp. 261–281.
5 Article 194 UNCLOS III
6 *Ibid.*

upon to harmonise their policies. Furthermore, in taking measures on marine pollution, States have the duty not to transfer, directly or indirectly, damage or hazards from one area to another or transform one type of pollution into another.[7]

A specific section (Section 2 of Part XII) is dedicated to global and regional cooperation, including in relation to notification of imminent or actual damage, contingency planning against pollution, etc.[8]

ARTICLE 197 ON COOPERATION ON A GLOBAL OR REGIONAL BASIS

"States shall cooperate on a global basis and, as appropriate, on a regional basis, directly or through competent international organizations, in formulating and elaborating international rules, standards and recommended practices and procedures consistent with this Convention, for the protection and preservation of the marine environment, taking into account characteristic regional features."

ARTICLE 198 ON NOTIFICATION OF IMMINENT OR ACTUAL DAMAGE

"When a State becomes aware of cases in which the marine environment is in imminent danger of being damaged or has been damaged by pollution, it shall immediately notify other States it deems likely to be affected by such damage, as well as the competent international organizations."

ARTICLE 199 ON CONTINGENCY PLANS AGAINST POLLUTION

"In the cases referred to in article 198, States in the area affected, in accordance with their capabilities, and the competent international organizations shall cooperate, to the extent possible, in eliminating the effects of pollution and preventing or minimizing the damage. To this end, States shall *jointly* develop and promote contingency plans for responding to pollution incidents in the marine environment."

A distinct section of Part XII with two articles is devoted to technical assistance to developing States.[9]

Furthermore, special mention is made by UNCLOS III of the duty of States bordering an enclosed or semi-enclosed sea to cooperate with each other; this duty of cooperation calls upon related States to coordinate the implementation of their rights and duties with respect to the protection and preservation of the marine environment.[10]

Shifting from cooperation to intervention, States are entitled under UNCLOS III to take and enforce measures beyond their territorial sea "proportionate to the actual or threatened damage to protect their coastline or related interests"

---

7 Article 195 UNCLOS III.
8 See Articles 197–201 of UNCLOS III.
9 Articles 202 and 203.
10 Article 123 UNCLOS III. It is noted that this provision is under Part IX of UNCLOS III which deals with enclosed or semi-enclosed seas.

from pollution or threat of pollution following upon a maritime casualty.[11] It is noted that the condition of grave and imminent danger, which features under the above-mentioned 1969 Intervention Convention, has not been included in UNCLOS III. As pointed out by commentators,[12] this is to some extent counterbalanced by a strict definition of maritime casualty. For the purposes of the intervention described in UNCLOS, maritime casualty is defined as "a collision of vessels, stranding or other incident of navigation, or other occurrence on board a vessel or external to it resulting in material damage or imminent threat of material damage to a vessel or cargo".[13]

Against this background, key stakeholders involved with preparedness, response and cooperation are identified below.

9.3 The bodies involved

9.3.1 The International Maritime Organisation

The International Maritime Organisation (IMO) was briefly presented in the introductory chapter of this book. In our context, the IMO can be viewed as an institutional facilitator of the cooperation required under MARPOL and other international instruments. For most part, environmental work at the IMO is conducted at the level of the Marine Environment Protection Committee (MEPC). During MEPC meetings, all aspects of marine pollution legislation are debated by the representatives of Member States; furthermore, a database of mandatory reports is maintained, and technical assistance is organised, on a regional or country basis.

In the above-mentioned (graph 9.1), IMO instruments targeting preparedness, response, and cooperation can be viewed in their overall context, and can be clearly distinguished from the other pillars of legislative work of the IMO governing prevention and liability/compensation.

Even though the IMO is not an operational organisation, it can be viewed as the body giving impetus to the international mechanisms on response to incidents involving pollution from oil and hazardous and noxious substances. Under the OPRC Convention and the OPRC-HNS Protocol the Parties designate the IMO to perform certain tasks, including in relation to information services, education and training, in the area of pollution preparedness and response, technical services (amongst others, this includes the analysis of information provided by the Parties and advice or information to States) and technical assistance (upon request of States faced with major polluting incidents).[14]

Furthermore, the IMO maintains under the 1973 Intervention Protocol a list of recognised regional centers of technical expertise (operational organisations) specialised in oil spill/HNS spill response. Even though in the majority of cases, the

---

11 Article 221(1) UNCLOS III.

12 See Philippe Boisson, *Safety at Sea – Policies, Regulations & International Law* (Bureau Veritas, Paris, 1999), p. 495.

13 See Article 221(2) UNCLOS III.

14 See Article 12(1) of OPRC Convention, and Article 10(1) of OPRC-HNS Protocol.

IMO is unlikely to be directly involved with the deployment of on-site assistance, it may be possible in some instances to have IMO expertise on the field for the purposes of facilitation or coordination. Last, but not least, if necessary, the IMO may engage in funding through the Marine Pollution Response Trust Fund.[15]

9.3.2 The United Nations Environment Programme

While the IMO is a specialised agency of the United Nations with technical expertise, the United Nations Environment Programme (UNEP) is a different forum of action. UNEP is a global environmental authority within the United Nations system aimed to promote the environmental dimension of sustainable development. More specifically, the mission of UNEP consists in providing "leadership and encouraging partnership in caring for the environment by inspiring, informing and enabling nations and peoples to improve their quality of life without compromising that of future generations".

UNEP was created following the United Nations Conference on the Human Environment, held in Stockholm in 1972. It was in this context that oceans had been identified a priority area of action.

Regional approaches to marine pollution and management were adopted by UNEP, referred to as regional sea programmes (RSP). A memorandum of understanding (MOU) between IMO and UNEP was signed on 9 November 1976 aimed at cooperation between the two institutions. As a result, the IMO and UNEP have contributed to a number of regional centers such as the Regional Marine Pollution Emergency Response Centre for the Mediterranean Sea (REMPEC), established by the Contracting Parties to the Barcelona Convention in 1976, etc.

9.3.3 The European Maritime Safety Agency

The European Maritime Safety Agency (EMSA) also has a role on preparedness, response and cooperation.

It may be recalled that EMSA is a decentralised agency of the European Union. It sits in Lisbon, Portugal, and can be viewed as the technical arm of the European Commission in the development and implementation of maritime policies on maritime safety, maritime security and protection of the marine environment at large. This means that EMSA provides technical and scientific assistance and advice to the European Commission; it also provides support to Member States in various ways, and ensures dissemination of best practice within the industry. Furthermore, EMSA is engaged in operational tasks in the area of marine pollution response, vessel monitoring, and long-range identification and tracking of vessels.

---

15 See Joint WMO/IOC Technical Commission for Oceanography and Marine Meteorology Expert Team on Marine Accident Emergency Support, World Meteorological Organization and Intergovernmental Oceanographic Commission (of UNESCO), *Coordination With Other Organizations – IMO Activities Relevant to the Work of the Expert Team on Marine Accident Emergency Support* (Submission by the International Maritime Organisation) (2007).

EMSA's creation was prompted by a number of maritime casualties which had adversely affected European waters. It is noted that EMSA does not directly participate in the legislative process of the European Union but its technical contribution is vital for the enforcement and the monitoring of implementation of EU maritime instruments.

Alongside maritime information capabilities (e.g. SafeSeaNet vessel tracking and monitoring system), as already mentioned, EMSA undertakes tasks relating to marine pollution preparedness, detection and response. An illustration of this capability is the establishment of a European network of stand-by oil spill response vessels, as well as CleanSeaNet, i.e. an oil spill monitoring and vessel detection service.

9.3.4 Other

The International Criminal Police Organisation (ICPO-INTERPOL) has an important role in the area of cooperation against environmental crime, including for MARPOL violations. In this context, INTERPOL is aimed at coordinated international police cooperation between the police forces of its Member States.

The AQUAPOL organisation, a joint venture of fluvial, inland waterway, port and maritime police agencies and institutions, provides a regional platform for cross-border cooperation in the area of law enforcement in waterborne transport in Europe. It was set up in 2003 and avails itself of a network of member organisations at the European level. It is a platform of exchange of intelligence and operational information as well as a platform of learning and exchange of best practice.

Selected key terms which help the understanding of this subject area are briefly defined below.

9.4 Glossary

BIMCO	The Baltic and International Maritime Council is an international shipping association providing expert knowledge to its members (i.e. shipowners, operators, managers, brokers and agents); it is known for its contribution to the development of standard maritime contracts. Based in Copenhagen. Established in 1905. BIMCO is also involved with educational/training services.
Booms	Floating barriers of varied sizes and forms (e.g. fence or curtain type) used as part of a response strategy in order to surround and prevent the spread of oil spilled at sea (containment); they also facilitate recovery. (See Table 9.3 below).
Contingency planning	In the context of marine pollution, contingency planning provides the necessary framework for the sound and effective management of response operations. Contingency planning is by definition proactive. It aims to identify the stakeholders involved with implementation, their roles and responsibilities, as well as to provide a risk assessment (correlating likelihood and consequences), possible response strategies, operational procedures and supporting data (e.g. contact details, etc). (also see graph 9.2 under paragraph 9.11) below.

(Continued)

(Continued)

European Maritime Safety Agency (EMSA)	European Union agency assisting in various ways the European Commission with the development, implementation, enforcement and monitoring of EU maritime legislation in the area of safety, security and marine environment protection. EMSA is also tasked with operational duties which relate to marine pollution preparedness, response and cooperation.
Hazardous and noxious substances (HNS)	Any substance other than oil which, if introduced into the marine environment, is likely to create hazards to human health, to harm living resources and marine life, to damage amenities or to interfere with other legitimate uses of the sea (definition for the purposes of the HNS-OPRC Protocol). It is noted that under another international legal instrument HNS include noxious liquid substances described in Annex II of MARPOL and the IBC Code,[1] dangerous goods described in the IMDG Code[2] and solid cargoes covered by the BC Code.[3]
HELCOM	Baltic Marine Environment Protection Commission, also known as Helsinki Commission. HELCOM is the governing body of the Helsinki Convention (Convention on the Protection of the Marine Environment of the Baltic Sea Area). HELCOM aims to protect the marine environment of the Baltic Sea from all sources of pollution through State cooperation.
International Salvage Union (ISU)	Global trade association representing the marine salvage industry. Based in London. It has consultative status at the IMO.
International Spill Control Organization (ISCO)	A not-for-profit London-based organisation with a consultative status at the IMO aimed at improving worldwide preparedness for response to oil and chemical spills.
International Tanker Owners Pollution Federation (ITOPF)	Private entity set up in 1968 following the *Torrey Canyon* oil spill. It provides spill response services, claims analysis and damage assessment, contingency planning, training and information. It has consultative status at the IMO.
Offshore unit	Any fixed or floating offshore installation or structure engaged in gas or oil exploration, exploitation or production activities, or loading or unloading of oil (definition according to the OPRC Convention).
Oil pollution emergency plan	Required by the OPRC Convention. It has to be present onboard a ship flying the flag of ratifying State. It is also required from operators of offshore units under the jurisdiction of a State Party and from various entities which present a risk of an oil pollution incident (e.g. sea ports, oil terminals, pipelines, and other oil handling facilities).
Oil pollution incident	According to the OPRC Convention, the term signifies an occurrence or series of occurrences with the same origin, which results or may result in a discharge of oil, i.e. petroleum in any form. Such incident poses or may pose a threat to the marine environment, or to the coastline, requiring emergency action or other immediate response.

Oil Pollution Preparedness, Response and Cooperation (OPRC) Convention (1990)	IMO Convention in force since 13 May 1995 with 112 Contracting Parties representing more than 75% of world tonnage (as at September 2017). The Convention sets out legal frameworks to be amplified by Parties focusing on the ability of States to prepare, respond and cooperate in the event of oil pollution incidents involving ships, offshore units, sea ports or other oil handling facilities.
OPRC-HNS Protocol (2000)	IMO instrument with Parties representing more than 50% of world tonnage (as at September 2017). The Protocol adopts the same approach on preparedness, response and cooperation as the OPRC Convention in the area of chemical pollution, i.e. marine pollution caused by hazardous and noxious substances.
OSPAR	OSPAR Convention is a regional (North East Atlantic region) instrument in force since 25 March 1998. (The abbreviation stems from the first letters of Oslo Convention and Paris Convention respectively on dumping and land-based marine pollution sources – conventions replaced by the OSPAR Convention). OSPAR is concerned with the prevention and elimination of pollution from land-based sources, by dumping or incineration, from offshore sources, assessment of the quality of the marine environment, and protection and conservation of the ecosystems and biological diversity of the area under its remit. With the participation of 15 Governments and the European Commission, the OSPAR Commission provides an implementation framework. The Commission is administered by a Secretariat based in London.
Regional sea programme (RSP)	A RSP may or may not be administered by the United Nations Environment Programme (UNEP), or even operate independently; it engages neighbouring countries in specific actions, including in the area of preparedness, response and cooperation.
Skimmers	Devices of varied types used in the frame of a response technique for the removal of oil from the water surface; they facilitate the transfer of the oil recovered to a collection point (e.g. storage tanks). (See Table 9.4 below).
Standard spill response contracts	They stem from BIMCO and the International Spill Control Organization (ISCO): RESPONSECON is designed for international use, and US RESPONSECON for use in the USA. They provide a contract template for the hire of spill response services and equipment. Intended to facilitate prompt clean-up operations while contractual negotiations on details are underway.
United Nations Environment Programme (UNEP)	United Nations agency created in the 1970s and headquartered in Nairobi, Kenya; it is an environmental authority assessing environmental conditions on the worldwide level, assisting developing countries, and promoting sustainable development and environmental policies within the United Nations system. UNEP and IMO cooperate. Some actions of UNEP present an interest to marine pollution preparedness, response and cooperation.

1 International Bulk Chemical Code
2 IMO Dangerous Goods Code
3 Code of Safe Practice for Solid Bulk Cargoes

SECTION 2: THE INTERNATIONAL FRAMEWORK ON MARINE POLLUTION PREPAREDNESS, RESPONSE AND COOPERATION

9.5 The OPRC Convention

As already mentioned, the OPRC Convention addresses preparedness, response and cooperation in the context of oil pollution. This is essentially a framework convention requiring actions from the Parties that have adhered to it. Being a framework convention, the instrument takes into account the need for flexibility at the national level.

Oil is defined as petroleum in any form, including crude oil, fuel oil, sludge oil, oil refuse and refined products. In this context, the Convention sets out a framework for the development of capacity on the national and regional level with a view to preparing for and responding to oil pollution incidents constituting a threat and necessitating emergency action.

Furthermore, the Convention constitutes a platform for the facilitation of international cooperation and mutual assistance in the area of preparedness and response.[16] The instrument encourages States to engage in developing the necessary capability so as to deal effectively with oil pollution emergencies.

9.5.1 Selected highlights

Table 9.1 Obligations in a nutshell (national and international level) under the OPRC Convention

Obligations at the national level	Obligations at the international level
Setting up a national response system; Providing for oil pollution emergency plans; Incident reporting; Developing and maintaining response capacity.	Informing neighbouring countries of oil spills that could affect them; Provide assistance, if required; Requesting that the Party facilitates the assistance received.

ARTICLE 3 ADDRESSES OIL POLLUTION EMERGENCY PLANS

(1) (a) Each Party shall require that ships entitled to fly its flag have on board a shipboard oil pollution emergency plan as required by and in accordance with the provisions adopted by the Organization for this purpose.

   (b) A ship required to have on board an oil pollution emergency plan in accordance with subparagraph (a) is subject, while in a port or at an offshore terminal under the jurisdiction of a Party, to inspection by

---

16 IMO-MOP Final Workshop, Miguel Palomares (IMO), 'IMO's Response to Current Environmental Challenges' (Madrid, 24 January 2008, Escuela Técnica Superior de Ingenieros Navales).

PREPAREDNESS, RESPONSE, AND COOPERATION

officers duly authorized by that Party, in accordance with the practices provided for in existing international agreements or its national legislation.

(2) Each Party shall require that operators of offshore units under its jurisdiction have oil pollution emergency plans, which are co-ordinated with the national system established in accordance with article 6 and approved in accordance with procedures established by the competent national authority.

(3) Each Party shall require that authorities or operators in charge of such sea ports and oil handling facilities under its jurisdiction as it deems appropriate have oil pollution emergency plans or similar arrangements which are co-ordinated with the national system established in accordance with article 6 and approved in accordance with procedures established by the competent national authority.

ARTICLE 4 ADDRESSES OIL POLLUTION REPORTING PROCEDURES

(1) Each Party shall:
   (a) require masters or other persons having charge of ships flying its flag and persons having charge of offshore units under its jurisdiction to report without delay any event on their ship or offshore unit involving a discharge or probable discharge of oil:
      (i) in the case of a ship, to the nearest coastal State;
      (ii) in the case of an offshore unit, to the coastal State to whose jurisdiction the unit is subject;
   (b) require masters or other persons having charge of ships flying its flag and persons having charge of offshore units under its jurisdiction to report without delay any observed event at sea involving a discharge of oil or the presence of oil:
      (i) in the case of a ship, to the nearest coastal State;
      (ii) in the case of an offshore unit, to the coastal State to whose jurisdiction the unit is subject;
   (c) require persons having charge of sea ports and oil handling facilities under its jurisdiction to report without delay any event involving a discharge or probable discharge of oil or the presence of oil to the competent national authority;
   (d) instruct its maritime inspection vessels or aircraft and other appropriate services or officials to report without delay any observed event at sea or at a sea port or oil handling facility involving a discharge of oil or the presence of oil to the competent national authority or, as the case may be, to the nearest coastal State;
   (e) request the pilots of civil aircraft to report without delay any observed event at sea involving a discharge of oil or the presence of oil to the nearest coastal State.

(2) Reports under paragraph (1)(a)(i) shall be made in accordance with the requirements developed by the Organization and based on the guidelines and

general principles adopted by the Organization. Reports under paragraph (1)(a)(ii), (b), (c) and (d) shall be made in accordance with the guidelines and general principles adopted by the Organization to the extent applicable.

ARTICLE 6 ON NATIONAL AND REGIONAL SYSTEMS FOR PRE-PAREDNESS AND RESPONSE

(1) Each Party shall establish a national system for responding promptly and effectively to oil pollution incidents. This system shall include as a minimum:
  (a) the designation of:
      (i) the competent national authority or authorities with responsibility for oil pollution preparedness and response;
      (ii) the national operational contact point or points, which shall be responsible for the receipt and transmission of oil pollution reports as referred to in article 4; and
      (iii) an authority which is entitled to act on behalf of the State to request assistance or to decide to render the assistance requested;
  (b) a national contingency plan for preparedness and response which includes the organizational relationship of the various bodies involved, whether public or private, taking into account guidelines developed by the Organization.
(2) In addition, each Party, within its capabilities either individually or through bilateral or multilateral co-operation and, as appropriate, in co-operation with the oil and shipping industries, port authorities and other relevant entities, shall establish:
  (a) a minimum level of pre-positioned oil spill combating equipment, commensurate with the risk involved, and programmes for its use;
  (b) a programme of exercises for oil pollution response organizations and training of relevant personnel;
  (c) detailed plans and communication capabilities for responding to an oil pollution incident. Such capabilities should be continuously available; and
  (d) a mechanism or arrangement to co-ordinate the response to an oil pollution incident with, if appropriate, the capabilities to mobilize the necessary resources [...].

9.6 The OPRC-HNS Protocol

The Protocol on Preparedness, Response and Cooperation to Pollution Incidents by Hazardous and Noxious Substances, 2000 (OPRC-HNS Protocol) (entry into force 14 June 2007) follows the principles of the above-mentioned OPRC Convention in relation to HNS spills.[17] Amongst others, it seeks to provide a platform for cooperation and mutual assistance through preparedness and response in view

---

17 See IMO, *Manual on Chemical Pollution – Section 3: Legal and Administrative Aspects of HNS Incidents* (2015 edition).

PREPAREDNESS, RESPONSE, AND COOPERATION

of combating incidents or threats of marine pollution involving hazardous and noxious substances which require emergency action or an immediate response. It may be relevant to note that only Parties to the OPRC Convention can accede to the Protocol.

As its names suggests, the Protocol is an instrument on preparedness, response and cooperation in the area of chemical pollution, which should not be confused with HNS Convention 2010 which governs liability and compensation. In this respect, it is noted that hazardous and noxious substances are defined differently in each of the above-mentioned instruments (i.e. in the OPRC-HNS Protocol 2000 and in the HNS Convention 2010) (on the definition of HNS under the Protocol, see the Glossary above paragraph 9.4).

It may be appreciated that this is an area which involves a wide range of cargoes (e.g. flammable liquids, corrosive materials, oil derivatives, solid bulk material presenting chemical hazards, etc.), of types of shipments (e.g. bulk, packaged goods) and of ship types. It is estimated that one or two major HNS accidents can be expected each year.[18]

The Protocol provides a global framework for cooperation in combating major incidents of chemical pollution. It generates duties for State Parties, ships, and entities in charge of seaports and facilities handling HNS.

9.6.1 Selected highlights

States Parties to the Protocol are held to require a Pollution Incident Emergency Plan from ships flying their flag and entities under their jurisdiction in charge of seaports and facilities handling HNS (see Article 3 below). Furthermore, each Party is held to establish a national system for responding in a prompt and effective manner to pollution incidents (see Article 4 below).

ARTICLE 3 ON EMERGENCY PLANS AND REPORTING

1. Each Party shall require that ships entitled to fly its flag have on board a Pollution Incident Emergency Plan and shall require masters or other persons having charge of such ships to follow reporting procedures to the extent required. Both planning requirements and reporting procedures shall be in accordance with applicable provisions of the conventions developed within the Organisation which have entered into force for that Party. On-board Pollution Incident Emergency Plans for offshore units, including Floating Production, Storage and Offloading Facilities and Floating Storage Units, should be dealt with under national provisions and/or company environmental management systems, and are excluded from the application of this article.

2. Each Party shall require that authorities or operators in charge of sea ports and hazardous and noxious substances handling facilities under its juris-

---

18 See IMO, *Manual on Chemical Pollution – Section 1: Problem Assessment and Response Arrangements* (1999 edition).

diction as it deems appropriate have Pollution Incident Emergency Plans or similar arrangements for hazardous and noxious substances that it deems appropriate which are co-ordinated with the national system established in accordance with article 4, and approved in accordance with procedures established by the competent national authority.

ARTICLE 4 ON NATIONAL AND REGIONAL SYSTEMS FOR PREPAREDNESS AND RESPONSE

1. Each Party shall establish a national system for responding promptly and effectively to pollution incidents. This system shall include as a minimum:
    (a) the designation of:
        (i) the competent national authority or authorities with responsibility for preparedness for and response to pollution incidents;
        (ii) the national operational contact point or points; and
        (iii) an authority which is entitled to act on behalf of the State to request assistance or to decide to render the assistance requested.
    (b) a national contingency plan for preparedness and response which includes the organizational relationship of the various bodies involved, whether public or private, taking into account guidelines developed by the Organization.
2. In addition, each Party within its capabilities either individually or through bilateral or multilateral co-operation and, as appropriate, in co-operation with the shipping industries and industries dealing with hazardous and noxious substances, port authorities and other relevant entities, shall establish:
    (a) a minimum level of pre-positioned equipment for responding to pollution incidents commensurate with the risk involved, and programmes for its use;
    (b) a programme of exercises for pollution incident response organizations and training of relevant personnel;
    (c) detailed plans and communication capabilities for responding to a pollution incident. Such capabilities should be continuously available; and
    (d) a mechanism or arrangement to co-ordinate the response to a pollution incident with, if appropriate, the capabilities to mobilize the necessary resources.

Last, but not least, it should not be forgotten that the Protocol also provides for a platform for cooperative arrangements with other States that have adhered to it. This means the possibility of providing or benefiting from assistance to other States in case of chemical pollution emergency, and the possibility of mechanisms for reimbursement.

9.7 Spill response contracts

Spill response contracts do not constitute an item directly addressed in the OPRC Convention or the OPRC-HNS Protocol. This is not surprising as international regulations on the matter have provided a framework for action to be undertaken by States. However, spill response contracts are relevant to the discussion.[19] In the absence of clarity on contractual aspects, delayed clean-up arrangements, including mobilisation of personnel and equipment following an oil or chemical spill incident, may be prejudicial to the marine environment and public interest.

With this in mind, it has been recognised that until the BIMCO/ISCO (International Spill Control Organization) spill response contracts, there was no single standard contract for the hire of spill response services and equipment. RESPONSECON (for use outside the USA) and US RESPONSECON (for use only in the USA) were drafted by BIMCO and ISCO. The International Group of P&I Clubs, International Salvage Union (ISU), International Tanker Owners Pollution Federation (ITOPF) and the Spill Control Association of America (SCAA) have contributed to the undertaking.

These legal forms aim to provide a framework agreement on essential contractual aspects that would avoid delays. Interestingly, RESPONSECON and US RESPONSECON are not limited to shipping incidents or shipping stakeholders (i.e. they may be of interest to oil companies, pipeline operators, etc.). Based, in principle, on the contractor's provision of equipment and personnel, these framework agreements seek to facilitate signatures and services while rates and other details are being discussed; at the same time, they provide a way out in case of failure of discussions.

Viewed from a technical standpoint, standard clauses set out in the forms are complemented by annexes where detailed descriptions should be inserted on the required services and rates of personnel and equipment.

These recently adopted legal forms are reasonably expected to facilitate the prompt undertaking of spill response.

9.8 Challenges for preparedness and response

Due to their nature – oil spills generally being visible, and related technology being well developed – marine oil spills are relatively well understood from the standpoint of preparedness and response. Marine chemical spills response may be more challenging.

Challenges in this area may reflect more general concerns such as the quality of the legislation implementing international requirements and the ensuing measures. Challenges may also be proper to this area: an illustration would be poor contingency planning at the national level, difficulty in ensuring cooperation among the numerous stakeholders involved with response, delayed action due to the contractual framework, etc.

A first question is obviously the failure of certain States to adhere to the international system on preparedness, response and cooperation; this failure would be evidenced by the non-ratification of the OPRC Convention and/or the

---

19 See BIMCO/Donald Chard, 'New Contracts Speed Up Spill Response' (14 September 2017); BIMCO/ISCO, 'RESPONSECON, International Spill Response Contract (for use outside the USA)', (Explanatory Notes, document date unavailable); BIMCO/ISCO, 'US RESPONSECON, US Spill Response Contract (for use only in the USA)' (Explanatory Notes, document date unavailable).

OPRC-HNS Protocol. Arguably, in these cases the States concerned have provisions of domestic (rather than international) origin governing relevant situations, which may depart from the OPRC approach, thus contributing to nonuniformity.

As noted above, another issue is the quality of the implementation process of States Parties to the IMO instruments. For example, the relevant legislative framework is not robust enough to support implementation in practice; or even though domestic legislation introducing into the national legal system the international instruments is formally in good order, in practice there is poor implementation. Poor implementation may be attributed to lack of willingness to ensure that standards are met, limited resources (e.g. to ensure the capabilities required by the instruments on the level of equipment required for preparedness and/or response) or weak enforcement mechanisms at large.

Limited resources and/or expertise, a challenge which is of greater interest to developing States, is a multifaceted question. Limited resources or expertise may relate to access to training, to the use of means of mechanical containment and recovery, sensitivity maps, trajectory modeling, aerial equipment, storage areas, waste disposal areas, etc.

As already mentioned, when the contractual framework is not clear, delays are likely to be experienced with negative impact on the effectiveness of response.

As it will be briefly seen below, regional frameworks on the matter have the potential to boost the effectiveness of preparedness, response and cooperation, and contribute to remedying to some of the challenges raised above.

SECTION 3: REGIONAL FRAMEWORK

9.9 Regional framework

Regional framework is highly important in this area as, amongst others, it facilitates implementation of international conventions. That said, this is a most diverse area.

In an attempt to simplify the description of the regional framework governing preparedness, response and cooperation, the following layers can be identified[20] – the last ones are not clear-cut and they may interphase at some stage:

- Regional agreements signed by States in relation to a particular sea area in order to combat in a proactive manner marine environment pollution (e.g. in the framework of a regional convention such as the Helsinki Convention (HELCOM being the governing body of the Convention)[21] covering the Baltic Sea area or the Barcelona Convention on the protection of the Mediterranean Sea, etc.);

---

20 For a detailed description of the regional framework, see Gonzalez and Hébert, *supra* note 4. Also see, Elizabeth Maruma Mrema, 'Regional Seas Programmes: The Role Played by UNEP in its Development and Governance', in David J. Attard (General Ed), *The IMLI Manual on International Maritime Law* (Oxford University Press, Oxford, 2016, Vol. III, pp. 345–372).

21 Convention on the Protection of the Marine Environment of the Baltic Sea Area, 1992 (Helsinki Convention).

PREPAREDNESS, RESPONSE, AND COOPERATION

- Bilateral agreements between neighbouring countries (e.g. France and the UK; Finland and Russia, etc.). It may be noted on this point that the international framework, i.e. the OPRC Convention and the OPRC-HNS Protocol, call upon States ("shall endeavour") to cooperate at a bilateral or multilateral level;[22]
- Trilateral agreements;
- Mutilateral agreements;
- Regional sea programmes administered by UNEP. For example, in relation to the Mediterranean Sea, the Mediterranean Action Plan (MAP) may be noted as well as the Regional Marine Pollution Emergency Response Centre for the Mediterranean Sea (REMPEC), etc.
- Non-UNEP administered regional sea programmes: for example, in relation to the Black Sea under the 1992 Bucharest Convention;[23] also, amongst others, in relation to the so-called ROPME sea area covering the marine environment and coastal areas of Bahrain, Islamic Republic of Iran, Iraq, Kuwait, Oman, Qatar, Saudi Arabia and the United Arab Emirates;[24]
- Independent Regional Sea Programmes: for example, in relation to the Arctic Region, the Baltic Sea (HELCOM), North East Atlantic Region (OSPAR), etc.

In light of the vastness and diversity of regional frameworks, we have narrowed down the focus on a specific example concerning regional cooperation in the field of marine pollution prevention, preparedness and response in the Mediterranean Sea, where the interphase between the various institutional and legal frameworks are briefly identified.

9.10 Selected highlight: REMPEC (Regional Marine Pollution Emergency Response Centre for the Mediterranean Sea)

Administered by the IMO in cooperation with UNEP/MAP, REMPEC is involved with the prevention and reduction of pollution from ships and sea-based sources in case of emergency. REMPEC is also engaged in assisting Mediterranean countries in adopting an appropriate legal framework for the transposition in national legal systems of MARPOL requirements on illicit discharges. It may be relevant to note that according to MAP/REMPEC data, the total number of reported[25] accidents in

---

22 See Article 10 of OPRC Convention, and Article 8 of OPRC-HNS Protocol.

23 Convention on the Protection of the Black Sea against Pollution, 1992 (Bucharest Convention).

24 An illustration of this framework in the area under discussion is the adoption of a Protocol addressing regional cooperation in combating pollution by oil and other harmful substances in cases of emergency. The Marine Emergency Mutual Aid Centre (MEMAC) that operates within the framework of ROPME is also to be noted.

25 Accidents reported to REMPEC that caused or were likely to cause pollution of the Mediterranean Sea by oil and HNS.

249

the Mediterranean between August 1977 and December 2010 was 659; 545 accidents involved oil and 114 HNS other than oil.[26] In this context, the mission of REMPEC is to assist the Contracting Parties in meeting their obligations under the above-mentioned Barcelona Convention[27] on the protection of the Mediterranean Sea (entry into force 1978), the 2002 Prevention and Emergency Protocol[28] (entry into force 17 March 2004) to the Barcelona Convention, and the Regional Strategy for Prevention of and Response to Marine Pollution from Ships (2016–2021).

The 2002 Protocol sets out the main principles of cooperation of Contracting Parties in relation to threats to the marine environment and relevant coasts from accidental releases or by accumulations of small, operational discharges of oil or other harmful substances. It is noted that the Protocol also covers marine pollution from sea-based sources. Furthermore, it takes into account the OPRC Convention. According to Article 12 of the 2002 Prevention and Emergency Protocol

"1. Any Party requiring assistance to deal with a pollution incident may call for assistance from other Parties, either directly or through the Regional Centre, starting with the Parties which appear likely to be affected by the pollution. This assistance may comprise, in particular, expert advice and the supply to, or placing at the disposal of the Party concerned of the required specialised personnel, products, equipment and nautical facilities. Parties so requested shall use their best endeavours to render this assistance.

2. Where the Parties engaged in an operation to combat pollution cannot agree on the organization of the operation, the Regional Centre may, with the approval of all the Parties involved, coordinate the activity of the facilities put into operation by these Parties.

3. In accordance with applicable international agreements, each Party shall take the necessary legal and administrative measures to facilitate:

   (a) the arrival and utilization in and departure from its territory of ships, aircraft and other modes of transport engaged in responding to a pollution incident or transporting personnel, cargoes, materials and equipment required to deal with such an incident; and

   (b) the expeditious movement into, through and out of its territory of the personnel, cargoes, materials and equipment, referred to in subparagraph (a)."

The above-mentioned regional strategy aims to prevent marine pollution from ships and to enhance the level of preparedness to major incidents in the Mediterranean. The strategy also lists priority issues in the implementation of the 2002 Prevention and Emergency Protocol.

Some illustrations of REMPEC's activities are the following:

- enhancement of the capacities of coastal States in order to prevent marine pollution from ships;

---

26 IMO/UNEP 2011, Regional Information System; Part C2: Statistical Analysis Alert and Accidents Database, REMPEC, February 2011. Available at www.rempec.org (last visit 14 September 2017).

27 Articles 4(1), 6 and 9 of the Barcelona Convention (Convention for the Protection of the Mediterranean Sea against Pollution, 1976, as amended).

28 Protocol concerning Co-operation in Preventing Pollution from Ships and, in Cases of Emergency, Combating Pollution of the Mediterranean Sea.

PREPAREDNESS, RESPONSE, AND COOPERATION

- development of regional cooperation in the area of marine pollution prevention;
- assistance to coastal States of the Mediterranean where they request so in developing their own capabilities;
- exchange of information on best practice;
- facilitating assistance to coastal States in cases of emergency.

Contracting Parties to the Barcelona Convention are the following: Albania, Algeria, Bosnia Herzegovina, Croatia, Cyprus, Egypt, European Union, France, Greece, Israel, Italy, Lebanon, Libya, Malta, Monaco, Montenegro, Morocco, Slovenia, Spain, Syria, Tunisia, and Turkey. It is noteworthy that not all the State Parties have ratified the 2002 Protocol.

With the fundamentals of the institutional and legal framework in mind, let us now examine some selected managerial aspects on response.

SECTION 4: MANAGERIAL ASPECTS OF RESPONSE

9.11 Breaking down oil spill management

Marine spill management is a demanding process, especially in the event of major and/or cross border spills. Oil spill response and chemical spill response, i.e. response to spills caused by hazardous and noxious substances (HNS),[29] share common features (e.g. contingency planning, risk assessment, etc.) but also point to numerous differences. The differences pertain, amongst others, to response options[30] and management,[31] and they are triggered by the nature and behavior of the substances involved. Furthermore, under the oversight of the State or the entity in control of response strategy, clean-up operations are conducted by spill responders contracted for the purpose. Distinct salvage operations may also be needed, and they are likely to be conducted in parallel with response operations. It may be recalled on this point that standard contract agreements have been established by the industry (see above paragraph 9.7).

The brief discussion which follows is held with oil spill management in mind.

A robust Incident Management System (IMS) where command, control and objectives are clearly and proactively determined, is central to effective oil spill management.[32] It should not be forgotten that, in practice, oil spill management takes place in parallel with enforcement actions undertaken by the competent authorities – enforcement actions typically include, amongst others,

---

29 On the definition of HNS see above para. 9.4 (Glossary).

30 Response will have to consider, amongst others, the physical properties of the chemical, i.e. whether the substance involved is an evaporator, gas, dissolver or sinker. See *infra*, note 31.

31 ITOPF (International Tanker Owners Pollution Federation), Response to Marine Chemical Incidents, Technical Information Paper No. 17.

32 See IPIECA-IOGP (International Association of Oil and Gas Producers), Oil Spill Preparedness and Response: An Introduction, London 2015.

251

investigations, collection of evidence (e.g. documentary evidence through documentation aboard, real evidence (e.g. bypass pipes)), and, if appropriate, prosecution. In addition to the State that has suffered from the slick, the flag State and other States may also be involved.

Response revolves around contingency planning (see glossary above under paragraph 9.4). In graph 9.2 below the components of a well-designed contingency plan are clearly identified.

A brief description of the stages commonly involved in the response process includes the following:[33]

When a spill occurs, competent authorities are notified of the spill and consider whether they should follow up or not. It is relevant to note that spill detection at sea may result from various means, including satellite monitoring, aircrafts, patrol boats, coastal stations or other vessels. Spills may also be the obvious result of collisions or other accidents. Information on the spill may result from witnesses (e.g. passengers), from the polluting vessel, other vessels, or from the sight of the spill ashore or in port.

That said, the entities involved will have to be determined. It may be appreciated that the contingency plan is central to this aspect.

Furthermore, the incident will have to be characterised. This will be done in relation to numerous aspects, including its location, extent, impact, etc. The severity of the incident has to be assessed – a task that will have to take into count many factors, including the polluting substance (for example, is it heavy fuel oil?), the size of the spill, weather and sea conditions (e.g. currents), environmental resources potentially at risk, etc.

The oil spill framework is based on an internationally recognised planning approach referred to as tiered preparedness and response; the applicable tier will have to be determined in order to respond in an appropriate manner. Thus, the deployment of unnecessary resources will be avoided (see Table 9.2 below). It is noteworthy that tiered capabilities allow for escalation to response according to changing circumstances, and operate in a cumulative manner.

Consideration of appropriate response strategy will take into account, amongst others, legal constraints, which may vary from one country to another, applicable contingency plans, material circumstances and risk factors (for example, does the polluting incident involve pollution at sea, pollution of the shoreline, or sensitive areas?).

Appropriate response strategy will notably include decisions on response options: e.g. use of booms, dispersants, *in situ* burning of oil, etc. Tables 9.3 and 9.4 below depict in a brief and generic manner the techniques available for response to oil floating at sea and to oil near and on the shoreline. This aspect requires technical expertise and is subject to legal constraints. Possible advantages and disadvantages are considered by experts, including the potential of natural processes. Decisions should be balanced against possible harms – the aim

---

33 See, amongst others, IOTPF, Leadership, Command and Management of Marine Oil Spills, Technical Information Paper No. 10.

Risk assessment

Determine the likelihood of a spill occurring

- Number and type of vessel calls or vessels passing
- Type and volume of oil carried
- Expected frequency and size of spills
- Identify areas with a high risk of spills

Determine the probable consequences

- Location of sensitive resources
- Probable spill movement
- Effects of oil on resources

Determine likely spill scenarios

Gauge the benefits of developing a contingency plan

- Determine existing spill response arrangements
- Determine whether the proposed contingency arrangements serve to reduce the consequences of a spill
- Decide to what extent a contingency plan is required

Strategic policy

Plan overview

- Identify the lead organisations
- Outline the regulatory framework and jurisdiction
- Define the geographical area of the plan
- Define the interaction with other plans – scaling of tiered response
- Outline the role of the shipowner

Response techniques

- State the preferred response techniques to address floating oil and any restrictions on their use
- Determine the importance of and ability to protect sensitive resources identified in the risk assessment, accounting for seasonal variation
- Determine the appropriate clean-up techniques for the shoreline types within the plan area
- Outline response to oiled wildlife

Response resources

- Ensure suitable resources are available to address the risk, either purchased or contracted-in
- Allocate stockpile locations
- Identify suppliers of materials and services likely to be required
- Determine preferred waste storage, treatment and disposal options

Leadership, command and management

- Define the key response functions
- Outline the divisions of responsibility
- Ensure coordination of all the organisations involved
- Define the responsibility for decisions
- Decide command centre and forward operational base locations
- Outline the involvement of third parties in the response
- Allow for media and public relations
- Ensure accurate record keeping

Training and review procedures

- Outline timetable for training and exercises
- Define the procedure for regular review and update of the plan

Operational procedures

Notification

- Establish notification routes
- Outline the details needed to determine the incident circumstances

Evaluation

- Source details of the oil, wind and currents – slick trajectory modelling
- Establish the threat to resources
- Obtain additional information from aerial, boat and foot surveys

Initiation

- Initiate the response
- Identify response team members, their responsibilities and contact details
- Notify or liaise with other organisations, including other plan holders
- Make the response decisions required in the light of threats

Mobilisation

- Determine availability of resources and outline mobilisation procedures
- Ensure resources are deployed in accordance with strategic policy
- Maintain activity & cost records

Clean-up support

- Ensure sufficient logistic support
- Ensure integrated communications for all parts of the response
- Determine optimum waste treatment routes

Progress review

- Ensure all aspects of the response are continuously re-evaluated
- Highlight response aspects requiring modification – scale up or down

Termination

- Determine the criteria for termination and signing-off work sites
- Demobilise, clean, repair and repatriate resources
- Restore temporary waste sites

Plan review

- Establish a review of the response

Information Directory

Operational references

- Contact details and remit of relevant government agencies and other response organisations
- Inventory of available resources and contact details of operators
- Contact details of third party suppliers of materials and services
- Sensitive area maps
- Restrictions on dispersant use

Sample documents

- Example equipment charter and hire agreements
- Sample pro-forma daily aerial, at-sea and shoreline progress reports
- Example forms for recording expenditure

Supplementary information

- List of approved response products
- Guidelines for observation and recording oil at-sea and on shore
- Guidelines for use of preferred response techniques, including booming plans
- Guidelines for sampling and for monitoring contamination levels
- Sources of funding and compensation
- Information necessary to expedite cost recovery
- Legislation stating statutory powers of the plan holder

Graph 9.2 Examples of the four-stage components required for a comprehensive and well-designed contingency plan

Source: Reproduced with the permission of the International Tanker Owners Pollution Federation Ltd. (ITOPF, Technical Information Paper No. 16, Contingency Planning for Marine Oil Spills)

Table 9.2 Tiered response and cooperation system in a nutshell

Tier 1	Geographical scope: local
	Capability adapted to local or small spill and/or providing of initial response
	E.g. leaking valve (operational accident) at a fixed location
Tier 2	Geographical scope: regional or national
	Regional capability; it supplements Tier 1 response; it commonly involves a wider range of equipment
	E.g. cross-border spill
Tier 3	Geographical scope: international
	Capabilities adapted to remote spills; capabilities which further supplement tiers 1 and 2. Tier 3 provides enhanced/global capability required due to factors such as scale of the oil spill, impact, etc.
	E.g. damaged cargo tanks of an oil tanker releasing oil at sea

being to minimise adverse effects on humans and the environment; this approach whereby the response community endeavours to ensure the least possible impact of oil spills on people and the environment should be integrated in contingency planning, and is referred to as Net Environmental Benefit Analysis (NEBA). The NEBA process provides an answer to the question as to which tools will minimise the impact of oil spills.

Monitoring of clean-up activities (e.g. via aerial observation) will assist the effectiveness of the process and allow reassessment, and possible readjustment, of relevant actions. Monitoring will also be critical for terminating the operations.

There are additional aspects that need to be addressed during response, notably including waste management,[34] post-spill monitoring, and reporting.

Waste management is a component of contingency planning and response strategy. It is necessary due to the large quantities of oily waste and associated waste that are generally accumulated during response. Such quantities of waste may exceed the capacities of infrastructure locally available, thus require actions in order to avoid adverse impacts on public health and/or the environment.

Lessons learnt may point to the improvement of procedures, and, if appropriate, necessitate the update of contingency planning.

9.12 Challenges

In the context described above, selected points which deserve special focus from a managerial standpoint would be the following:

- Whether of civilian (e.g. State authority or agency) or military type (e.g. national coastguard), the entities which will interact with clean-up services and/or salvors and other stakeholders involved with response need to be clearly identified. Their effective interphase, including with external

---

34 IPIECA/IOGP Oil Spill Waste Minimization and Management – Good Practice Guidelines for Incident Management and Emergency Response Personnel (April 2014).

Table 9.3 Summary of the primary techniques available for response to oil floating at sea

Technique	When suitable	Resources	Benefits	Limitations
Aerial surveillance and monitoring	Necessary in many responses but may be sole activity required if oil is moving away from the shore or is dissipating naturally.	Aircraft – fixed or rotary wing. Remote sensing equipment for advanced surveillance techniques.	Provides the most rapid and straightforward method of obtaining an overview of oil position, volume and movement as well as the extent of shoreline contamination.	Twin-engine aircraft required for flying over open water. Experienced observers needed for maximum benefit. Specialised remote sensing equipment may enable surveillance at night or in fog, heavy rain, snow etc.
Containment and recovery	Recovery of floating oil in calm conditions. Best results achieved in large slicks of freshly spilt oil.	Specialised equipment – booms, skimmers, vessels with sufficient and suitable storage and offloading pumps.	In ideal circumstances, a single, suitably equipped vessel can recover a significant amount of oil. Removes pollutant from the sea.	Equipment cannot be deployed in rough weather. Efficiency of skimmers and pumps decreases as oil viscosity rises and as oil spreads and fragments. Often limited by storage availability. Rarely more than 10% of spilt oil recovered.
Dispersants	Floating slicks of oil amenable to dispersion.	Spraying equipment mounted on suitable aircraft or vessels. Stocks of appropriate dispersant.	Can rapidly remove large amounts of oil from the water surface. Can be applied in rougher conditions than would allow containment and recovery.	Efficiency decreases as oil viscosity rises. Largely ineffective on oils with viscosity greater than 5,000–10,000 cSt. Limitations on use close to shore or near coral reefs and mariculture facilities.
***In situ* burning of oil**	Floating slicks of freshly spilt oil.	Fire resistant booms, towing vessels, ignition source.	Can rapidly remove large amounts of oil from the water surface.	Minimum thickness of oil required to sustain a burn. Large quantities of smoke produced. Resultant highly viscous residue may sink to the seabed. Weathered oil difficult to burn.

Source: Reproduced with the permission of the International Tanker Owners Pollution Federation Ltd.(ITOPF, Technical Information Paper No. 10, Leadership, Command and Management of Marine Oil Spills)

Table 9.4 Summary of the main techniques available for response to oil near and on the shoreline

Technique	When suitable	Resources	Benefits	Limitations
Protective booming	In calm water and low currents when floating oil poses a threat to sensitive resources.	Boom, anchors, vessels to deploy, maintain and retrieve boom.	Can deflect oil from sensitive resources.	Will have limited or no effectiveness in currents over ~0.5m/s. Skimmers required to recover contained oil. Requires pre-planning to be most effective.
Use of pumps and skimmers	Recovery of bulk oil in calm water with access from shoreline or shallow draft vessels. Large pools of oil on the shoreline.	Skimmers, pumps, vacuum trucks, temporary storage.	Can recover floating or pooled bulk oil relatively quickly.	Coherent patches of oil required for technique to work effectively. Limited by weather conditions and available storage. Equipment can become blocked by debris.
Mechanical collection	Slicks of high viscosity oil close to the shore or accessible by vessels. Thick patches of oil on the shoreline.	Excavators, bulldozers, shore or vessel-based cranes with grabs, storage containers.	Allows recovery of highly viscous oil and recovery of oil stranded on the shoreline.	Can recover a high proportion of water or clean shoreline substrate. Recovery of oil can be slow. Heavy machinery can damage sensitive areas.
Manual collection	Oil stranded on the shoreline. Applicable to recovery of bulk oil and low-level contamination.	Access to labour force, personal protective equipment, hand tools, buckets, temporary storage.	Highly selective recovery of oil on many shoreline types.	Can be labour intensive and slow. Requires careful supervision to be most effective and to minimise trampling of sensitive shorelines.
Flushing	Light to moderately contaminated shoreline sediment and oil in sensitive areas.	Pumps, hoses, lances, means of recovery of released oil, e.g. sorbent, skimmers.	Recovery of buried oil without removal of sediment. Removal of oil from sensitive areas with minimal disturbance.	Can produce large amounts of sheen. Care needs to be taken not to undermine root structures on sensitive vegetated shorelines. Otherwise few disadvantages.
Surf washing	Light to moderately contaminated shoreline sediment on exposed shorelines.	Bulldozers, excavators.	Uses natural energy of the surf-zone to clean sediment. Negates removal of sediment from site.	Can produce large amounts of sheen and cause a temporary imbalance of substrate size. Otherwise few disadvantages.

Pressure washing	Light contamination of hard structures e.g. seawalls, rocks.	Pressure washer (preferably adapted for use with seawater), pumps, means of recovery of released oil.	Generally effective for removal of light contamination. Minimal training required to operate.	An aggressive technique that can damage underlying surfaces. High temperatures may affect marine biota.
Pebble washing	Lightly contaminated pebbles and cobbles.	Concrete mixer or other mixing facilities, hot water baths, front loader, storage tanks.	Allows washing of cobbles at, or close to, the affected shoreline. Negates the need to remove sediment from site.	Can be a slow process. Can generate large amounts of oily liquid. "Fines" (fine clays and sand) can accumulate requiring disposal. Where possible, surf washing is a better method for cleaning this type of substrate.
Ploughing/ harrowing	Light contamination of sand or shingle beaches.	Tractor and towed plough or harrow.	Breaks up and exposes oiled sediment to washing on subsequent tides. Useful when surf washing is impractical.	Reworking shoreline material can have an impact on sediment dwelling species. Produces sheen.
Sand sieving	Recovery of tarballs and small nodules of oiled sand on sand beaches.	Tractor towed or self-propelled beach cleaning machine, large mesh and excavators, hand sieves.	Driven machines can be an effective way of collecting tarballs over a large area. Minimises collection of clean substrate.	Hand sieving is slow and labour intensive. Small tarballs may fall through mesh. Agglomerates of fresh, lower viscosity oils may break-up and fall through vibrating screens.
Wiping	Light to moderately contaminated rocky or cobble areas with restricted access.	Rags, waste sacks.	Allows cleaning when other techniques cannot be used.	Labour intensive and slow. Requires close supervision to minimise secondary contamination.
Natural cleaning	On exposed shorelines. On sensitive shorelines where other techniques would cause additional damage. Where safety concerns prohibit cleanup.	None. Surveys of the shoreline will allow the progress to be determined.	Allows removal of oil with little human effort. Minimises damage to sensitive areas.	Where possible, removal of bulk oil may be necessary to prevent contamination of nearby areas. Cleaning can be protracted on low-energy shorelines. Most effective during winter storms. May occur too slowly for tourist areas.

Source: Reproduced with the permission of the International Tanker Owners Pollution Federation Ltd. (ITOPF, Technical Information Paper No. 10, Leadership, Command and Management of Marine Oil Spills)

stakeholders, also needs to be addressed. Furthermore, it is important to clarify the chain of command and reporting.

- There must be a clear understanding of the role of the shipowner and of the entities involved under applicable contingency plans. The powers of each entity in relation to operations, planning, logistics and contracting need to be clearly set out.
- A key factor for successful operations is leadership. Leadership is relevant to overall and specific activities, and requires the ability to command, work under pressure, understand complex and/or technical situations, communicate effectively, motivate others, and identify limitations on the level of options and operations.
- The exposure of polluting incidents to media coverage, social media, etc. raises challenges which need to be handled by professionals. The information spreads rapidly and the quality of the messages to be conveyed to the public is important. Transparency, avoidance of wrong or misleading statements, etc. can support the work undertaken instead of raising hurdles to it.[35]
- Volunteers may provide under conditions a useful contribution to clean-up activities. They may have knowledge of local conditions and/or provide bridges of communication with local communities. However, they may raise various challenges, including on the level of their safety, training, and cover (e.g. insurance).

BIBLIOGRAPHY

Augustin Blanco-Bazán, 'Intervention in the High Seas in Cases of Marine Pollution Casualties' in David J. Attard (General Ed), *The IMLI Manual on International Maritime Law* (Oxford University Press, Oxford, 2016), Vol. III

BIMCO/ISCO, 'RESPONSECON, International Spill Response Contract (for use outside the USA)' (Explanatory Notes, document date unavailable)

BIMCO/ISCO, 'US RESPONSECON, US Spill Response Contract (for use only in the USA)' (Explanatory Notes, document date unavailable)

BIMCO/Donald Chard, 'New Contracts Speed Up Spill Response' (14 September 2017)

Boisson, Philippe, *Safety at Sea – Policies, Regulations & International Law* (Bureau Veritas, Paris, 1999)

Chilvers, B.L., Low, S.W., Pearson, H.S., Finlayson, G.R., White, B.J., and Morgan, K.J., 'Oil Spill Response and Public/Media Perception' (Interspill 2015 White Papers) (available on the internet)

Davies, Ged (Environmental Agency Wales), 'Integration of Waste Legislation into Response Planning and Operations (Interspill 2006)

---

35 On the analysis of media coverage involving an incident in New Zealand (container ship *Rena* grounding in 2011), see B.L. Chilvers, S.W. Low, H.S. Pearson, G.R. Finlayson, B.J. White and K.J. Morgan, 'Oil Spill Response and Public/Media Perception' (Interspill 2015 White Papers) (available on the internet).

Gonzalez, Gabino, and Hébert, Frédéric, 'Conventions Relating to Pollution Incident Preparedness, Response and Cooperation' in David J. Attard (General Ed), *The IMLI Manual on International Maritime Law* (Oxford University Press, Oxford, 2016), Vol. III

IMO/UNEP 2011, 'Regional Information System; Part C2: Statistical Analysis Alert and Accidents Database, REMPEC, February 2011' <www.rempec.org> last visit 14 September 2017

IMO, *Manual on Chemical Pollution-Section 3: Legal and Administrative Aspects of HNS Incidents* (IMO, London, 2015)

IMO, *Manual on Chemical Pollution – Section 1: Problem Assessment and Response Arrangements* (IMO, London, 1999 Edition)

IMO-MOP Final Workshop, Miguel Palomares (IMO), 'IMO's Response to Current Environmental Challenges' (Madrid, 24 January 2008, Escuela Técnica Superior de Ingenieros Navales)

IOTPF, Leadership, Command and Management of Marine Oil Spills (Technical Information Paper No. 10)

IPIECA -IOGP (International Association of Oil and Gas Producers), *Oil Spill Preparedness and Response: An Introduction* (IPIECA -IOGP, London, 2015)

IPIECA/IOGP Oil Spill Waste Minimization and Management – Good Practice Guidelines for Incident Management and Emergency Response Personnel (April 2014)

ITOPF (International Tanker Owners Pollution Federation), Response to Marine Chemical Incidents, Technical Information Paper No. 17

ITOPF, Contingency Planning for Marine Oil Spills (Technical Information Paper No. 16)

Joint WMO/IOC Technical Commission for Oceanography and Marine Meteorology Expert Team on Marine Accident Emergency Support, World Meteorological Organization and Intergovernmental Oceanographic Commission (of UNESCO), *Coordination With Other Organizations – IMO Activities relevant to the work of the Expert Team on Marine Accident Emergency Support* (Submission by the International Maritime Organisation) (2007)

Laruelle, Franck, and Beer, Nicola (ITOPF), 'The ITOPF Perspective on Current Challenges in Responding to an Oil Spill in the Arctic' (Interspill 2015)

Mrema, Elizabeth Maruma, 'Regional Seas Programmes: The Role Played by UNEP in Its Development and Governance' in David J. Attard (General Ed), *The IMLI Manual on International Maritime Law* (Oxford University Press, Oxford, 2016), Vol. III

O'Hagan, Colleen and Tucker, Andrew /ITOPF, 'Responding to Containership Incidents' (Interspill 2012)

CHAPTER 10

The contribution of the human element to marine pollution control

TABLE OF CONTENTS

Section 1	The importance of the human element and its relevance to marine pollution control	262
10.1	Identifying the human element: setting the scene	262
10.2	Key terms/definitions	266
Section 2	The regulatory framework and related developments	268
10.3	Legislative background and discussion	268
	10.3.1 ILO MLC 2006	268
	10.3.2 STCW 2010	274
	10.3.2.1 STCW 2010 from the standpoint of its contribution to marine pollution control	279
	10.3.3 The International Safety Management Code	279
	10.3.3.1 Overview	279
	10.3.3.2 Selected highlights	282
	10.3.3.3 The ISM Code and the marine environment	284
10.4	Areas of special interest (e.g. amendments underway, interface with other areas, etc.)	285
	10.4.1 Fatigue	285
	10.4.2 Criminalisation of seafarers	286
Section 3	Key management issues	290
10.5	Procedures/operations and relevant documentation	290
	10.5.1 Non-exhaustive list of documents generally required by international regulations which relate to the human element to be carried onboard	290
	10.5.2 Selective question: the complaint's procedure under ILO MLC 2006	290

261

SECTION 1: THE IMPORTANCE OF THE HUMAN ELEMENT AND ITS RELEVANCE TO MARINE POLLUTION CONTROL

10.1 Identifying the human element: setting the scene

It is estimated that between 1.2 and 1.5 million seafarers are currently employed at sea; there are several million non-seafarers who work in activities and companies directly and indirectly related to oceans and seas worldwide. So apart from those actively serving aboard ships, we need also to consider those serving in the shipping companies ashore, those legislating, as well as those enforcing the laws, including in flag State administrations, port State control and classification societies. Also, other groups would include naval architects, underwriters, marine and cargo surveyors, crew trainers and examiners, crewing agents and many others. Whilst the seafarers tend to be in the spotlight of a maritime accident, it is this whole group that constitutes the human factor that this chapter will discuss.

It is accepted by the maritime industry that over 80% of marine accidents are caused by the human factor. Identifying the dominant factor in accidents has been of interest to numerous stakeholders. Existing findings currently point to the crucial role of the human contribution under its multiple facets to maritime accidents which impact on safety and/or the marine environment (e.g. *Exxon Valdez* (1989), *Erika* (1999), *Prestige* (2002), etc.). Not only is the human factor associated with the success of any shipping activity, including marine pollution prevention and/or mitigation; the human factor is also related to failures affecting maritime safety and the marine environment.

So we need to ask: in what ways is marine pollution prevention and control impacted by the so-called human element? What is the significance of the human element, and its practical impact?

Some examples of failures (in random order) in the maritime context which revolve around the human factor can be found below. The failures in question may interphase with each other.

- human error on the level of operations, including maintenance, repair, etc.;
- complacency/poor risk assessment;
- task omission;
- handling mistakes on the level of the engine;
- watchkeeping-related failures;
- miscommunication aboard, and/or between the vessel and the shore, while the vessel is under pilotage, etc.;
- wrong execution of tasks due to stress, lack of competence and/or experience, lack of training or inadequate training, and/or fatigue;
- poor management aboard and/or ashore;
- other.

In spite of current and recent discussions at various levels, from academia to industry *fora*, on increasing ship automation, the role of humans aboard and ashore will always remain a contributing factor to ship's operation and

THE CONTRIBUTION OF THE HUMAN ELEMENT

the regulatory framework on maritime safety and marine pollution prevention takes this into consideration. Interestingly, the technical understanding and addressing of safety and marine pollution-related matters had taken place long before the taking into account of the role of the human element. The human perspective appears nowadays to be in the spotlight by international regulators, port State control officers, national administrations, managers and judges (in the latter case, for example, in the context of legal proceedings following casualties).

For example:

- Was the crew member medically fit and qualified under applicable standards to perform the tasks concerned?
- Was the crew member involved in an accident certificated in good order, as required by international and domestic law?
- Were the training requirements (e.g. refresher courses) valid?
- Was the required handover and familiarisation procedure carried out before the master took over command of the ship?
- Was there a clear and unambiguous quality of communication among crew members as well as between the ship and the personnel ashore?
- Did the senior management involved properly support the ship's needs? For example, in a pollution incident caused by an unacceptable tolerance of technical problems, did the management neglect to carry out the ship's request for repairs?
- Are there any cultural barriers to a sound safety and marine pollution prevention culture?
- What were the corrective actions taken following problematic port State control findings?
- Were near-misses appropriately reported and addressed in order to avoid recurrence or transforming into accidents?
- Beyond and in addition to legal and technical requirements, does the personnel aboard and ashore adhere to well-embedded principles within the company which function as a safety valve against failures?
- Are existing policy and procedure requirements viewed by most people within the company as a mere documentation exercise and, consequently, regarded as a waste of time?
- Was there a fatigue issue? Did the working (e.g. hours of work) and living conditions aboard have an impact on the ability of the crew to deal with a specific problem?

These are only some of the questions which may arise in the context where the human element is in the spotlight. Self-assessment actions, in addition to prescriptive requirements, may complement the picture.

The International Safety Management (ISM) Code, which is a mandatory tool on the basis of which self-assessment is conducted, is highly relevant, and this will be discussed under paragraph 10.3.3.

Experts see in the ship an environment where the boundaries between work, personal and social life are not clear-cut. This may generate challenges potentially impacting on safety and marine pollution prevention. One may think, for example, of the risk of fatigue and/or stress due to hours of work/rest violations. Multicultural crews are also part of the picture, as their contribution to shipping is vital. Multicultural and/or multilingual crews put a spotlight on the question of communication, especially in the context of emergencies. They also bring forward the challenge of managing cultural differences which may adversely impact on effective communication and, consequently, on safety and marine pollution prevention. However, this aspect may also be of interest to crews of the same nationality.

In a project undertaken on behalf of the European Commission, it was pointed out that the vast majority of the international merchant fleet was by far multilingual and multiethnic in terms of crew composition.[1] The need for clear communication between the vessel and shore stations in coastal waters and under port pilotage, as well as in areas of traffic congestion or during manoeuvering difficulties, was pointed out by the same study. As noted, problems of communication may lead to dangers to the ship, to the people onboard and to the environment. Despite an external environment geared towards regulation and standardisation, humans (e.g. crew members and/or managers ashore regardless of ethnic origin or nationality) may make different sense of the same information, thus end up with different interpretations. The latter may be based on personal needs, past experience (one may think, for example, of the impact of a near-miss on the behavior of a master or officer in charge of a navigation watch), or other factors.[2] Each person has its own mental filters through which messages received pass. As noted by organisational psychologists, people "use the signals from the others to construct meaning for themselves based on what they already know, expect, and are able to attend to".[3] In the box below you can see a few examples of poor communication with adverse consequences.

---

1 The MARCOM Project, Final Report, Vol. 1 on the Impact of Multicultural and Multilingual Crews on MARitime COMmunication (Contract No. WA-96-AM-1181 – A Transport RTD Programme DG VII). The project was coordinated by The Seafarers International Research Centre (SIRC) with the following partners, namely: World Maritime University, Institut für Sicherheitstechnik/Verkehressicherheit e.V, Centre for Language and Communication Research (School of English Studies, Communication and Philosophy, Cardiff University) and Escuela Superior de la Marina Civil de Bilbao. The project's overall objective was the improvement of communication among multicultural and multilingual crews. It also aimed at recommending improvements in communication skills on the bridge through the assessment of the value of a single working language which could be used in all circumstances, the conduct of a linguistic analysis of ship-to-ship and ship-to-shore communications, the drafting of guidance on the use of language in emergencies and accident prevention, analysis of the incidence and causes of cross-cultural tensions on board and their current management, and the evaluation of present standards of teaching communication skills in maritime colleges, including the production of a syllabus that responds to new regulation and current thinking.

2 See an interesting guide authored by Dik Gregory and Paul Shanahan for the UK Maritime and Coast Guard Agency (MCA) entitled *The Human Element: A Guide to Human Behaviour in the Shipping Industry* (Crown Copyright 2010). The Guide was supported by BP Shipping, Teekay Marine Services and the Standard P&I Club.

3 *Ibid.*, p. 79.

THE CONTRIBUTION OF THE HUMAN ELEMENT

Poor master/pilot exchange disregarding the roles and responsibilities of the members of the bridge team. Poor overall internal communication rendering bridge communication ineffective. (See MAIB Safety Digest 2/2015, Case 3, 'Blind Pilotage', p. 11)

Cumulative fatigue and lone watchkeeping. Insufficient manning. (See MAIB Safety Digest 3/2007, Case 8, "Same Old Story…", p. 24)

The Roll on/Roll off passenger and freight ferry *Herald of Free Enterprise* capsized on 6 March 1987 because she went to sea with her inner and outer bow doors open (the crew member in charge of this duty had fallen asleep in his cabin, and this failure had not been noticed). According to the investigation, this was only the immediate cause of the accident; among others, the failure of the shore management to give proper and clear directions was considered to be a contributory cause to the accident, which had resulted in the loss of 193 lives.[4]

Appropriate management of the human factor may have a positive impact on the quality of shipping practice, including for the purpose of fostering marine environment protection. As it can be seen below, communication failures may be prevented in a number of ways.[5]

- improvement of critical skills through education, appropriate training, leadership skills and experience. By developing a critical attitude towards the messages received, people, including maritime practitioners, can better assess and use the information and messages they receive;
- improvement of the use of a common language;
- through training in standard marine communication phrases (SMCP). SMCP were adopted in 2001 via IMO Resolution A.918(22). They are aimed at facilitating communication and at avoiding misunderstanding through the use of standard phrases in routine and emergency situations;
- addressing equipment relating to communications (for example, communication may be adversely impacted from the operations being conducted in a noisy environment);
- appropriate recruitment and selection policies and practices;
- improvement of education, task training to defined performance standards, refresher training, and, as already mentioned, critical skills so as to identify what is important to communicate and when;
- ensuring that the documentation used aboard, including manuals, is well written and/or translated, and that it can be easily used and understood;
- improvement of team task skills and knowledge (e.g. through team training);
- improvement of social skills aimed at enabling the personnel to overcome personal incompatibilities, and improve performance;
- addressing cultural awareness and diversity through training;
- addressing excessive workload.

---

4   Department of Transport (UK), The Merchant Shipping Act 1894, MV Herald of Free Enterprise, Report of Court No. 8074, Formal Investigation (Crown Copyright 1987).

5   Based on *The Human Element: A Guide to Human Behaviour in the Shipping Industry, id.*

There are intergovernmental organisations (e.g. IMO, ILO), non-governmental organisations (NGOs), trade and labour unions (e.g. the International Transport Workers' Federation (ITF)) whose action is relevant to the protection of workers at sea.

Recent developments are to be noted. They range from the amendments of the legal regime concerning training, certification and watchkeeping of seafarers in 2010 (the so-called Manila amendments to the STCW Convention) to the adoption of the ILO Maritime Labour Convention (MLC) 2006, a landmark instrument in the area of social protection of seafarers.

Through its maritime conventions on safety, marine pollution prevention and addressing, training, certification and watchkeeping, the work of the IMO is central to the addressing of the human element. In addition to IMO conventions, a number of codes, resolutions, circulars and other acts adopted by the same organisation, touched upon in the introductory chapter, shape the legal regime of seafarers on the international level.

The ILO, a specialised agency of the United Nations sitting in Geneva, is concerned with the protection of seafarers from the standpoint of its remit. The latter deals with decent living and working conditions of seafarers. In 2006, a landmark global instrument was adopted with a view to ensuring an updated legal regime on seafarers' protection – contrary to past instruments which were adopted since the 1920s in a piecemeal manner and which had failed to be universally implemented. This resulted in the ILO MLC (Maritime Labour Convention) 2006, mention of which will be made below. The Convention currently covers more than 90% of the world tonnage.

10.2 Key terms/definitions

Communication	Communication means conveying an idea, a statement, a feeling. This is a process between the sender of a message and the receiver. Communication may be oral, written or take some other form. Not only communication is important for individuals but also for organisations (one may think of communication between levels, departments, employees). Problems in communication have the potential to result in adverse consequences such as negative working atmosphere, near-misses, incidents, contract violations, law infringements, etc. A number of maritime casualties may be attributed to poor communication.
Culture	Culture impacts on the behavior of a person. As a result, there are cultural factors which may interplay with maritime safety and marine pollution prevention, and which should be addressed. There is no single definition of culture. It may be understood as the body of "norms and expectations about behavior that color and in turn take shape from the environment".[1]

Fatigue	Fatigue may result from various factors, including a combination of factors; for example, prolonged mental or physical exertion, stress, the environment (think of noise or harsh weather conditions), etc. It may result in "the degradation of human performance, the slowing down of physical and mental reflexes and/or the impairment of the ability to make rational judgments".[3] Amongst others, regulations on hours of work/rest and standards on accommodation and recreational facilities aim at addressing fatigue.
Human element	There is no single definition of the human element in shipping. The question of human element can be understood as a multifaceted issue which impacts on numerous aspects of shipping, including marine environment protection and maritime safety; the human element involves the entire spectrum of activities conducted by humans who need to cooperate effectively in shipping – from ships' crews to shore-based management, from regulators to classification societies, and from shipyards to other relevant stakeholders.
ISM Code	This is the International Safety Management Code adopted in 1993 by the IMO (Resolution A.741(18)). It was incorporated into SOLAS Convention in 1994 as a new chapter (Chapter IX). It entered into force on 1 July 1998; since then, the ISM Code has been amended a number of times. The Code represents an important contribution to maritime safety and marine environment protection. This is a mandatory instrument introducing elements of self-regulation. It sets out an integrated, including managerial, approach to maritime safety and marine environment protection. It is aimed at ensuring maritime safety, at protecting human life, and at avoiding damage to the environment and to property.
Manila amendments (2010)	They refer to the amendments adopted in 2010 by the IMO (in a diplomatic conference held in Manila) to the STCW Convention and the STCW Code. They represent an important development in the international law governing training, certification and watchkeeping of officers and ratings. As a result, the STCW 1995 (major amendments of the initial instrument adopted in 1978) is now referred to as the STCW 2010.
Maritime Labour Convention (MLC) Code	This is the Code adopted in the framework of ILO MLC 2006, a landmark maritime labour convention adopted in 2006 by the ILO which consolidated and, on some points, reshaped previously adopted – by the same organisation – maritime labour standards. The MLC Code contains the details needed for the implementation of the requirements set out by ILO MLC 2006. The Code is integrated within the instrument and it consists of two parts: Part A, which is mandatory (regulations and standards), and Part B, which is recommendatory (guidelines). The Code addresses a wide range of items: minimum requirements for seafarers to work on a ship; conditions of employment; accommodation, recreational facilities, food and catering; health protection, medical care, welfare and social security protection; compliance and enforcement.

(Continued)

(Continued)

Near-miss	An occurrence that could have resulted in loss, such as human injury, environmental damage, etc. A fortuitous break in the chain of events/ conditions prevented the loss; for example, a collision that was narrowly avoided. As noted in IMO's Guidance on Near-Miss Reporting, "learning the lessons from near-misses should help to improve safety performance since near-misses can share the same underlying causes as losses".[2]
Safety management system	A key concept under the ISM Code, the safety management system signifies a structured and documented system. Through its use, the company personnel should be able to implement effectively the company safety and environmental protection policy. A safety management system includes a number of functional requirements which are set out by the ISM Code (e.g. instructions and procedures to ensure protection of the environment).
Standard	In broad terms, the term may signify a requirement (e.g. labour standard, technical standard, etc.) or a "target" of normative nature to be achieved by the entities concerned. Standards may be national or international. They are commonly backed by an enforcement mechanism verifying compliance.
STCW Code	This is the Code adopted in the framework of the STCW Convention, as amended, which contains technical standards in relation to the scope of operation of the said Convention. The Code was adopted in 1995 and was notably amended in 2010. It consists of two parts, i.e. Part A, which is mandatory, and Part B, with recommended guidance. The STCW Convention operates through references to the Code.
Training	Depending on the context, this term may have a different meaning. In the context of the STCW Convention, as amended, the term can be found in relation to "basic" or "advanced" training (e.g. special training requirements for personnel on certain types of ships). Other distinction includes, amongst others, "refresher" and "updating" training. Regulation 1.3 of ILO MLC 2006 pertains to training and qualifications. It is aimed at ensuring that seafarers are trained or qualified to carry out their duties on board ship.

1 Edward A. Dauer, 'The Role of Culture in Legal Risk Management' [2006] in A Proactive Approach, Series Scandinavian Studies in Law, Vol. 49, p. 98 (pp. 93–108).
2 IMO Guidance on Near-Miss Reporting, MSC-MEPC.7/Circ.7.
3 See IMO Resolution A.772(18) adopted on 4 November 1993 on 'Fatigue Factors in Manning and Safety'.

SECTION 2: THE REGULATORY FRAMEWORK AND RELATED DEVELOPMENTS

10.3 Legislative background and discussion

10.3.1 ILO MLC 2006

It is the right of every seafarer to enjoy a safe and secure workplace that complies with applicable standards, as well as to live and work aboard under decent conditions. This and other related rights which are relevant to safety and marine environment protection can be found in ILO MLC 2006, one of the pillars of international quality shipping legislation. A seafarer who is impaired by fatigue, who does not enjoy appropriate conditions of life and work aboard, or whose contractual or statutory rights are breached, may reasonably be expected to have a greater difficulty in identifying or ensuring marine environment protection.

ILO MLC 2006 provides a legal framework on seafarers' rights through minimum standards. With the risk of stating the obvious, minimum standards signify standard levels of protection which operate as a minimum. States that adhere to them may provide for higher levels of protection, but they do not have the right to provide for lower levels (even though, in practice, it may be observed that a State, member of the ILO, is actually in breach of its obligations under the Convention). Being an international instrument, the Convention does not operate directly in national systems. States must have ratified the Convention or proceeded with other actions which produce a similar effect in their legal system. ILO MLC 2006 was adopted on 23 February 2006 by the ILO, a specialised agency of the United Nations involved with the protection of labour (maritime and other forms of labour) through international standards. It is noted at this point that the ILO was created in 1919 and sits in Geneva. Its uncommon institutional structure, referred to as "tripartite", comprises on an equal footing of representation Member States, employers' and employees' organisations. The adoption of ILO MLC 2006, which has brought together the vast majority of maritime labour standards within a single instrument,[6] can be viewed as a landmark development in the contribution of the ILO to decent working and living conditions of seafarers. This aspect is also relevant to maritime safety and marine pollution prevention. It is clear that even though the focus of the instrument is placed on working and living conditions (e.g. contract of engagement, hours of work/rest, food and catering, social protection, accommodation, repatriation, etc.), conditions that are in line with the standards set out by the Convention have the potential of an overall contribution to safe and environmentally friendly shipping.

That said, prior to the adoption and entry into force of the Convention at the international level on 20 August 2013, international maritime labour standards were generally considered to lack the necessary impetus that would ensure uniformity and adequate protection. This was the result of numerous factors, including, amongst

---

6   The ILO MLC has grouped the vast majority of ILO labour standards that were expressed in the form of binding and non-binding instruments, i.e. conventions and recommendations. However, four instruments have not been included. These are the Seafarers' Identity Document Conventions, adopted in 1958 and in 2003, (Nos. 108 and 185), the Seafarers' Pensions Convention, 1946 (No. 71), and the Minimum Age (Trimmers and Stockers) Convention, 1921 (No. 15). Eight years after the adoption of the Convention two important amendments to the ILO MLC 2006 were adopted, which entered into force in 2017. These are regulation 2.5 on repatriation and regulation 4.2 on shipowner's liability. The first amendment sets out a financial security to be provided by the shipowner in varied forms with a view to assisting seafarers in the event of their abandonment. The amendment enumerates the cases where a seafarer is to be considered abandoned (e.g. amongst others, when there is failure to cover repatriation cost). The other amendment sets out a financial security to be ensured by the shipowner in relation to contractual claims. The term "contractual claim" here means "any claim which relates to death or long-term disability of seafarers due to an occupational injury, illness or hazard as set out in national law, the seafarers' employment agreement or collective agreement" (See Standard A4.2.2, para. 1).

others, the existence of more than 60 distinct ILO instruments (conventions and recommendations) in the area of maritime labour standards adopted in a fragmented manner throughout the years; their focus was rather unclear, and the technical language used appeared in some regards to be inconsistent or not apt to facilitate proper implementation.[7] More importantly perhaps, the context in which shipping was conducted had changed, and this aspect required to be reflected in the international legal regime, i.e. modern employment practice. Adopted with no vote against, ILO MLC 2006 succeeded in achieving the consensus required for its entry into force – as at February 2018, 84 member States have ratified the Convention, representing about 91% of world tonnage. Regional port State control includes ILO MLC 2006 among the instruments under which port State control is conducted alongside SOLAS, MARPOL and STCW. In some cases, detentions may be conducted on the grounds of deficiencies pertaining to ILO MLC 2006 – which was impossible or, in any case, uncommon under the "previous" regime.

Key terms relating to the legal framework introduced by ILO MLC 2006 are explained below. Furthermore, in figure 10.1 the main areas addressed by MLC 2006 can be identified.

Ship	It does not include ships navigating exclusively in inlands waters or waters within, or closely adjacent to, sheltered waters or areas where port regulation apply. It is noted that the Convention is intended to apply to the vast majority of ships regardless of their ownership status (private or public) ordinarily engaged in commercial activities. Ships engaged in fishing or in similar pursuits and ships of traditional build such as dhows and junks, warships or naval auxiliaries are not included in the definition of ship for the purposes of the Convention. There are provisions which address the issue in the event of doubt.[1]
Seafarer	Any person employed or engaged or working in any capacity on board a ship to which the Convention applies is considered to be a seafarer. This is a broad definition which also includes persons that are not engaged in navigational/ operational tasks (e.g. casino, beauty or hotel personnel). There are provisions which address the issue in the event of doubt.[2]
Shipowner	This is the owner of the ship or another organisation or person, such as the manager, agent or bareboat charterer, who has assumed the responsibility for the operation of the ship from the owner and who, on assuming such responsibility, has agreed to take over the duties and responsibilities imposed on shipowners in accordance with this Convention; this is regardless of whether any other organisation or persons fulfill certain of the duties or responsibilities of the shipowner.
ILO MLC Code	The Code is integrated within the Maritime Labour Convention. It complements other parts of the Convention by setting out necessary details for the implementation of Regulations. The Code contains a mandatory part referred to as "Standards" and a part of recommendatory nature called "Guidelines".

---

7   See I. Christodoulou-Varotsi and D. Pentsov, *Maritime Work Law Fundamentals: Responsible Shipowners, Reliable Seafarers* (Springer, Heidelberg, 2008); also see I. Christodoulou-Varotsi, 'Critical Review of the Consolidated Maritime Labour Convention (2006) of the International Labour Organization: Limitations and Perspectives', 1 October, Journal of Maritime Law & Commerce.

ILO MLC Regulations	The provisions in ILO MLC 2006 referred to as Regulations set out a general purpose. For example, the purpose of Regulation 1.1 on Minimum Age is "to ensure that no under-age persons work on a ship". Under the same Regulation some additional points are set out in very general terms (e.g. no person below the minimum age shall be employed or engaged or work on a ship). The Standard which follows spells out more specific requirements, such as that "the employment, engagement or work on board a ship of any person under the age of 16 shall be prohibited".
ILO MLC Standard	ILO MLC Standards are the binding part of the Code – this is Part A. They are obligatory requirements which set out a minimum standard of protection. They specify the general aim of Regulations. Their implementation is supported by recommendatory guidance.
ILO MLC Guidance	ILO MLC Guidance is the recommendatory part of the Code which supports proper implementation of Part A (Standards). For example, according to relevant Guidance on Minimum Age, when regulating working and living conditions, Member States *should* give special attention to young persons' needs aged under 18.
Maritime Labour Certificate (MLC)	It is issued by or under the authority of the flag State (which may empower in that regard a recognised organisation – the latter often being a ship classification society). A Declaration of Maritime Labour Compliance (DMLC) (see below) is attached to the MLC. The MLC provides evidence at first glance (*prima facie*) that the ship has been inspected in good order by the flag State and that the requirements of the Convention have been met to the extent certified.
Substantial equivalence	This is a legal device which allows ILO MLC 2006 a certain flexibility on the implementation level by Member States – it should be noted that the principle was also provided in the regime governing maritime labour standards prior to ILO MLC 2006. Substantial equivalence signifies that in some circumstances when a domestic provision implements the Convention differently than the manner set out by a standard, the provision will be, nevertheless, considered as acceptable, from the standpoint of compliance, on the grounds of being substantially equivalent. It is noted that the Convention provides for this tool, which introduces an element of flexibility, under conditions.[3] For example: a Member States is held under the Convention to post a shipboard working arrangements table which shall contain for every position at a minimum the schedule of service at sea and service in port, and the maximum hours of work or minimum hours of rest, as required under national provisions. The said table "shall be established in a standardized format in the working language or languages of the ship and in English".[4] Compliance by a Member State through substantial equivalence on this point could possibly mean that the flag State accepts in addition to the relevant table under the format published by the IMO/ILO, a format recognisably similar to the said format. In such a case, the possibility of using substantial equivalence would have to be mentioned by the flag State in Part I of the declaration of maritime labour compliance.

(Continued)

(Continued)

Declaration of Maritime Labour Compliance	It is attached to the Maritime Labour Certificate. Together, they constitute, in principle, *prima facie* evidence that the ship has been inspected in relation to the requirements of the Convention, and to the extent so certified, the ship has been found compliant. With the risk of stating the obvious, the Declaration has a different function than the Certificate. The Declaration has two parts. The first part is standard and is drawn by the flag State. In practice, this is where, amongst others, the flag State declares that the provisions of the Convention are fully embodied in national law. Relevant national provisions are also referenced here (for example, "National Law 'X' sets out the requirements on on-board recreational facilities"). Substantial equivalences and exemptions granted are also mentioned here. The second part is ship specific. It is filled out by the shipowner. This is where the shipowner demonstrates the measures taken with a view to ensuring ongoing compliance.
Flag State	It is held to ensure implementation of its obligations under the instrument on ships flying its flag. This notably means the duty of the flag State to adopt an effective system for the inspection and certification of maritime labour conditions. The flag State issues relevant certification. It may empower, as appropriate, recognised organisations with a view to conducting inspections and/or issuing certificates.
Port State	Port States have the duty to inspect foreign flagged vessels in light, amongst others, of the Convention. They aim at reviewing compliance with the requirements of the instrument. Port States' inspection is limited, in principle, to the review of the MLC and the DMLC. There may be circumstances entitling port States under the instrument to go beyond the visual review of relevant certificates, and conduct a more detailed inspection.
Labour supplying countries	They are also involved, in the manner set out by the Convention, with the protection of seafarers who are their nationals, resident or are otherwise domiciled in their territory. They have obligations under the Convention in relation to the recruitment and placement of seafarers as well as their social security protection.
Recruitment and placement services	They may be public or private, and they are involved with the recruitment of seafarers on behalf of shipowners or with the placement of seafarers with shipowners. In practice, they are commonly referred to as manning or crewing agencies. It is noted that ILO MLC 2006 uses the generic term "recruitment and placement services".

1 See Article II, para. 5 of ILO MLC 2006.
2 See Article II, para. 3 of ILO MLC 2006.
3 See Article VI of ILO MLC 2006.
4 See Standard A2.3 (Hours of work and hours of rest), para. 11 of ILO MLC 2006.

Some of the key features of ILO MLC 2006 are the following:

- The structure of the instrument is designed so as to support implementation and enforcement: e.g. mandatory provisions (standards) are clearly separated from provisions of a recommendatory nature (guidance); another illustration of this would be the existence of a part specifically

THE CONTRIBUTION OF THE HUMAN ELEMENT

dealing with implementation and enforcement. More specifically, Title 5 groups the provisions which are of interest to practical matters such as inspections, certification, deficiencies, detentions, complaints, etc.

- Incorporation of the principle of "no favourable treatment"; this means that the vessels flying the flag of a non-ratifying country do not benefit from an exemption or a more favourable treatment in comparison with vessels flying the flag of a ratifying country. As a result, vessels flying the flag of a non-ratifying country will be required to demonstrate compliance.
- Involvement of more than one entity in order to ensure or facilitate proper implementation. The flag State, the port State, labour-supplying countries, recruitment and placement services (e.g. manning agents), recognised organisations, shipowners (or entities assimilated to the shipowner for the purposes of the Convention), and seafarers have a role to play under the Convention.
- Enhancement of certain aspects such as the complaints' procedure; complaints can be submitted by seafarers alleging a breach of the requirements of the Convention to the department head, the master or to an authorised port officer ashore. A complaint has the potential to cause, under conditions, the detention of the ship.
- ILO MLC 2006 documentation is aimed at ensuring a level playing field by working to the advantage of ships whose documentation is in good order (e.g. by avoiding unnecessary delays). As already noted, a Maritime Labour Certificate, complemented by a Declaration of Maritime Labour Compliance, constitutes at first glance evidence that the ship has been inspected in good order by the flag State and ILO MLC 2006 requirements on working and living conditions aboard "have been met to the extent so certified".[8] While the Convention is primarily intended to apply to nearly all ships, it should be noted that certification is not required for ships less than 500 GT that are not engaged on international voyages or are not engaged on voyages between foreign ports.

The areas that must be inspected and certified by the flag State are set out in Appendix A5-I of the Convention, namely:
- minimum age;
- medical certification;
- qualification of seafarers;
- seafarers' employment agreements;
- use of any licensed or certified or regulated private recruitment and placement service;
- hours of work or rest;
- manning levels for the ship;
- accommodation;

---

8 See regulation 5.1.1, para. 4 of ILO MLC 2006.

- on-board recreational facilities;
- food and catering;
- health and safety and accident prevention;
- on-board medical care;
- on-board complaint procedures;
- payment of wages;
- financial security for repatriation;[9]
- financial security relating to shipowners' liability.[10]

A good picture on the challenges stemming from the implementation and enforcement of ILO MLC 2006 can be found in regional Port State Control findings.[11] In addition to ILO MLC 2006, the human element also falls in the scope of STCW 2010.

10.3.2 STCW 2010

It is clearly evident from accident-related findings that properly qualified, certificated and trained crews are better prepared to contribute to maritime safety and marine environment protection. Furthermore, proper compliance to regulated hours of work/rest is also critical to safe and environmentally friendly shipping, due to the fatigue factor which represents a true risk in an industry requiring constant alertness and concentration.[12] Being one of the pillars of international shipping legislation and involving numerous stakeholders such as flag administrations, shipping companies, seafarers and training institutions, the STCW Convention was originally adopted by the IMO in 1978, and entered into force in 1984. The STCW operates in parallel with the other pillars of international quality legislation, i.e. SOLAS, MARPOL and ILO MLC 2006. The instrument takes a different perspective than ILO MLC 2006, whose focus is placed on social protection. For example, minimum hours of rest are addressed by the STCW Convention from the standpoint of safety, whereas the MLC is interested in the social dimension of the issues dealt with which go beyond IMO's remit.[13]

The STCW Convention sets out a number of legal duties articulated in articles.

---

9 This mention was introduced by an amendment to ILO MLC 2006 adopted by the ILO Special Tripartite Committee on 11 April 2014, i.e. Amendments to the Code implementing Regulation 2.5 – Repatriation of the MLC, 2006 (and appendices).

10 This mention was introduced by an amendment to ILO MLC 2006 adopted by the ILO Special Tripartite Committee on 11 April 2014, i.e. Amendments to the Code implementing Regulation 4.2 – Shipowners' liability of the MLC, 2006 (and appendices).

11 See, for example, Paris MOU Annual Report 2016, etc.

12 On the problem of fatigue in the shipping industry, the following video is to be noted: Economic and Social Research Council, and Cardiff University, Fatigue at Sea – The Cardiff University Research Programme (2011).

13 See a brief comparison of STCW 2010 with ILO MLC 2006 in Oil Companies International Marine Forum (OCIMF) (January 2012) Recommendations Relating to the Application of Requirements Governing Seafarers' Hours of Work and Rest.

Figure 10.1 ILO MLC 2006 overall presentation

Articles	Generic provisions (e.g. definitions, scope of application, etc.)				
Titles	Regulations and the Code (Standards and Guidance) which supports the implementation of Regulations				
	TITLE 1 **Minimum requirements for seafarers to work on a ship**	**TITLE 2** **Conditions of employment**	**TITLE 3** **Accommodation, recreational facilities, food and catering**	**TITLE 4** **Health protection, medical care, welfare and social security protection**	**TITLE 5** **Compliance and enforcement**
	Minimum age Regulation 1.1 – Purpose: To ensure that no under-age persons work on a ship Standard & Guideline	Seafarers' employment agreements Regulation 2.1 on SEA – Purpose: To ensure that seafarers have a fair employment agreement	Accommodation and recreational facilities Regulation 3.1 – Purpose: To ensure that seafarers have decent accommodation and recreational facilities on board	Medical care on board ship and ashore Regulation 4.1 – Purpose: To protect the health of seafarers and ensure their prompt access to medical care on board ship and ashore	Flag State responsibilities Regulation 5.1 – Purpose: To ensure that each Member implements its responsibilities under this Convention with respect to ships that fly its flag
	Medical certificates Regulation 1.2 – Purpose: To ensure that all seafarers are medically fit to perform their duties at sea Standard & Guideline	Wages Regulation 2.2 – Purpose: To ensure that seafarers are paid for their services	Food and catering Regulation 3.2 – Purpose: To ensure that seafarers have access to good quality food and drinking water provided under regulated hygienic conditions	Shipowners' liability Regulation 4.2 – Purpose: To ensure that seafarers are protected from the financial consequences of sickness, injury or death occurring in connection with their employment	Port State responsibilities Regulation 5.2 – Purpose: To enable each member to implement its responsibilities under this Convention regarding international cooperation in the implementation and enforcement of the Convention standards on foreign ships
	Training and qualifications Regulation 1.3 – Purpose: To ensure that seafarers are trained or qualified to carry out their duties on board ship Standard & Guideline	Hours of work and hours of rest Regulation 2.3 – Purpose: To ensure that seafarers have regulated hours of work or hours of rest		Health and safety protection and accident prevention Regulation 4.3 – Purpose: To ensure that seafarers' work environment on board ships promotes occupational safety and health	Labour-supplying responsibilities Regulation 5.3 – Purpose: To ensure that each Member implements its responsibilities under this Convention as pertaining to seafarer

(Continued)

Figure 10.1 (Continued)

recruitment and placement
and the social protection of its
seafarers

Recruitment and placement
Regulation 1.4 – Purpose:
To ensure that seafarers have
access to an efficient and well-
regulated seafarer recruitment
and placement system
Standard & Guideline

Entitlement to leave
Regulation 2.4 – Purpose: To ensure
that seafarers have adequate leave

Access to shore-based welfare
facilities
Regulation 4.4 – Purpose: To
ensure that seafarers working
on board a ship have access
to shore-based facilities and
services to secure their health
and well-being

Repatriation
Regulation 2.5 – Purpose: To ensure
that seafarers are able to return home

Social security
Regulation 4.5 – Purpose:
To ensure that measures are
taken with a view to providing
seafarers with access to social
security protection

Seafarers' compensation for the ship's
loss or foundering
Regulation 2.6 – Purpose: To ensure
that seafarers are compensated when a
ship is lost or has foundered
Manning levels
Regulation 2.7 – Purpose: To ensure
that seafarers work on board ships
with sufficient personnel for the safe,
efficient and secure operation of the ship
Career and skill development and
opportunities for seafarers' employment
Regulation 2.8 – Purpose: To promote
career and skill development and
employment opportunities for seafarers

For example, in Article I on the general obligations under the Convention, it is mentioned in paragraph 2 that the Parties, i.e. States, undertake to adopt all laws, decrees, orders and regulations and to take all other steps necessary to give the Convention full and complete effect, in order to ensure that seafarers aboard are qualified and fit for their duties from the standpoint of maritime safety and marine pollution prevention.

In Regulations, which are annexed to the Convention and which are structured over a number of chapters, one may find the technical details on how legal responsibilities should be met. For example, in Regulation I/6 on training and assessment, it is mentioned that each Party has the duty to ensure that training and assessment of seafarers in virtue of the Convention are administered, supervised and monitored in line with the STCW Code (more specifically, in line with section A-I/6).

In addition to the Articles and the Regulations, there is, as already mentioned, a Code. The Code interplays with the instrument through references to it (such as the one just mentioned). The Code contains the technical standards necessary for the operation of the Convention. Some illustrations are provided below.

In the Code one may find a number of sections and tables. Tables are structured over four directions (see below). An example of the structure used follows below (short extract from Table A-II/5 in relation to the function required from able seafarers deck on controlling the operation of the ship and care for persons on board at the support level). Our comments are marked in smaller font in inner boxes.

Note: Function means areas for which standards are defined by the Convention. Amongst others, controlling the operation of the ship and care of the persons aboard (deck and engine) is a functional area. It should be noted that shipboard tasks are also classified by defined level of responsibility, i.e. management level, operational level and support level applying respectively to senior officers, junior officers, and ratings.[14]

Column 1	*Column 2*	*Column 3*	*Column 4*
Competence Our note: Competence of being able to do something. Competence represents practical units of ability that can readily be assessed.[1] Standards of competence are the minimum standards of knowledge and	Knowledge, understanding and proficiency Our note: This is about minimum knowledge.	Methods for demonstrating competence Our note: For evidence purposes.	Criteria for evaluating competence

(Continued)

14 The levels (management, operational, support) are defined in Chapter I of STCW 2010 on Standards regarding general provisions (see Section A-I/1).

(Continued)

Column 1	Column 2	Column 3	Column 4
understanding required for certification. For a formal definition of standards of competence, see Section A-I/1 of the STCW Code.			
Apply precautions and contribute to the prevention of pollution of the marine environment	*Knowledge of the precautions to be taken to prevent pollution of the marine environment Knowledge of the use and operation of anti-pollution equipment Knowledge of the approved methods for disposal of marine pollutants*	*Assessment of evidence obtained from one or more the following:* 1. *approved in-service experience* 2. *practical training* 3. *examination* 4. *approved training ship experience*	*Procedures designed to safeguard the marine environment are observed at all times*

1 See ISF (2011) Guidelines on the IMO STCW Convention – Including the 2010 Manila Amendments (3rd edition), p. 37.

The instrument underwent major amendments, notably including, in 1995 (STCW-95) and in 2010 ("Manila amendments", entry into force 1 January 2012 with transitional arrangements until 1 January 2017). The Manila amendments improved the text and harmonised it with other instruments, including ILO MLC 2006. The STCW Convention is a highly important instrument from the standpoint of the human element, including on the level of maritime safety and marine pollution prevention, as it notably addresses:

- competence (uniform standards of competence);
- training (e.g. basic, advanced, refresher);
- certification;
- watchkeeping arrangements;
- hours of work and rest;
- record books in relation to the items addressed; and
- prevention of fatigue of officers and ratings.

The Convention does not apply to seafarers serving on warships, naval auxiliaries, or other government ship used for non-commercial purposes, fishing vessels, pleasure yachts not engaged in trade, and wooden ships of primitive build.

10.3.2.1 STCW 2010 from the standpoint of its contribution to marine pollution control

STCW 2010 includes numerous provisions which are of interest to the protection of the marine environment. Even though the focus of the Convention, including the Code, is not marine pollution control, it can be said that the instrument contributes in at least three manners to marine pollution prevention and control. Firstly, in a general manner by ensuring that officers and ratings have the skills and formal recognition of the skills needed for proper task performance aboard. Secondly, through continued improvement of their skills (e.g. refresher training). Thirdly, through appropriate watchkeeping arrangements, including hours or rest/work.

In addition to the above, STCW 2010 is of interest to marine pollution prevention in a more focused manner. This is in the context where the Convention provides for specific competences which relate to marine pollution prevention. An illustration was given in the table above in relation to the function on controlling the operation of the ship and care for persons on board at the support level for able seafarers deck, which includes the competence of applying precautions and contributing to the prevention of pollution of the marine environment. The same requirement on competence ("apply precautions and contribute to the prevention of pollution of the marine environment") can be found, for example, in relation to the function on controlling the operation of the ship and care for persons on board at the support level, with regard to able seafarers engine (see Table A-III/5 of the STCW Code). Some additional selective examples are set out below (figures 10.2 and 10.3). Readers are encouraged to place the extracts in their overall context by having access to the instrument.

In addition to the above, the human element should also be addressed from the standpoint of the International Safety Management Code.

10.3.3 The International Safety Management Code

10.3.3.1 Overview

Adopted in 1993 through IMO Assembly Resolution A.741(18) and integrated as an additional chapter within SOLAS (Chapter IX) in 1994, the International Safety Management (ISM) Code represents a major development in shipping regulatory framework and management with a clear impact on safety and marine environment protection. The Code is aimed at ensuring "safety at sea, prevention of human injury or loss of life, and avoidance of damage to the environment, in particular to the marine environment and to property". As mentioned in previous chapters, the adoption of the Code was prompted by a number of casualties which had drawn public attention to the problem of poorly maintained ships that endanger humans, property and the environment (see, for example, the *Herald of Free Enterprise* in 1987). While numerous conventions were adopted since the creation of the IMO on specific items, it appeared that there was room for improvements in relation to a global approach to the challenge of safe and environmentally friendly shipping; this would especially be the case from the standpoint of internal management

Column 1	Column 2	Column 3	Column 4
Competence	*Knowledge, understanding and proficiency*	*Methods for demonstrating competence*	*Criteria for evaluating competence*
Monitor and control compliance with legislative requirements and measures to ensure safety of life at sea, security and the protection of the marine environment	Knowledge of international maritime law embodied in international agreements and conventions Regard shall be paid especially to the following subjects: .1 certificates and other documents required to be carried on board ships by international conventions, how they may be obtained and their period of validity .2 responsibilities under the relevant requirements of the International Convention on Load Lines, 1966, as amended .3 responsibilities under the relevant requirements of the International Convention for the Safety of Life at Sea, 1974, as amended .4 responsibilities under the International Convention for the Prevention of Pollution from Ships, as amended .5 maritime declarations of health and the requirements of the International Health Regulations .6 responsibilities under international instruments affecting the safety of the ship, passengers, crew and cargo .7 methods and aids to prevent pollution of the marine environment by ships .8 national legislation for implementing international agreements and conventions	Examination and assessment of evidence obtained from one or more of the following: .1 approved in-service experience .2 approved training ship experience .3 approved simulator training, where appropriate	Procedures for monitoring operations and maintenance comply with legislative requirements Potential non-compliance is promptly and fully identified Planned renewal and extension of certificates ensures continued validity of surveyed items and equipment

Figure 10.2 Extract from Table A-II/2 on the specification of minimum standard of competence for masters and chief mates on ships of 500 gross tonnage or more

Function: Controlling the operation of the ship and care for persons on board at the management level

Function:

Column 1	Column 2	Column 3	Column 4
Competence	Knowledge, understanding and proficiency	Methods for demonstrating competence	Criteria for evaluating competence
Take precautions to prevent pollution of the environment	Understanding of procedures to prevent pollution of the atmosphere and the environment	Examination and assessment of evidence obtained from one or more of the following: .1 approved in-service experience .2 approved training ship experience .3 approved simulator training .4 approved training programme	Operations are conducted in accordance with accepted principles and procedures to prevent pollution of the environment
Monitor and control compliance with legislative requirements	Knowledge and understanding of relevant provisions of the International Convention for the Prevention of Pollution from Ships (MARPOL) and other relevant IMO instruments, industry guidelines and port regulations as commonly applied Proficiency in the use of the IBC Code and related documents	Examination and assessment of evidence obtained from one or more of the following: .1 approved in-service experience .2 approved training ship experience .3 approved simulator training .4 approved training programme	The handling of cargoes complies with relevant IMO instruments and established industrial standards and codes of safe working practice

Figure 10.3 Extracts from Table A-V/1–1–3 on specification of minimum standard of competence in advanced training for chemical tanker cargo operations

on ship/company level with the focus placed on all humans involved in different capacities, i.e. seafarers, officers, managers ashore – including senior management.

As already mentioned, the Code came into force on 1 July 1998. Its scope of application was progressively extended so as to cover the vast majority of ships. The legal rationale underpinning the Code is self-regulation. Contrary to prescriptive standards which are imposed from outside, i.e. from regulators, and which prescribe what shall or what shall not be done (see, for example, the control of oil or garbage discharges under MARPOL where there is a prohibition to illegally discharge at sea), a self-regulation approach is based on mandatory rules and is supported by internal action. Internal action entails that a specified performance target may be achieved via measures selected fit for the purpose by the entity which is required to ensure compliance, and which will be held responsible in case of failure. From this standpoint, the implementation of the ISM gives rise to tailor-made approaches, taking into account the diversity of the subject matter (types of ships, tonnage, trade and areas involved, etc.). Also, from this angle, it can easily be understood why the ISM Code, which is in nature a generic text, is rather limited in length. It is confined to setting targets rather than setting out in a detailed manner the way through which targets must be achieved.

The Code endeavours to promote a safety culture where the embedded values shared by officers and ratings at sea and personnel ashore would be at such level so as to clearly support the commitment for safe and environmentally responsible shipping. At its simplest, safety culture implies something more than a formal compliance to regulations. As to whether the Code also achieves a just culture, i.e. a culture that is neither focused on blame nor on complacency, this is a more difficult question to be answered in a general manner.

With this background information in mind, it should be noted that, since its adoption, the text has undergone a number of amendments:

- Resolution MSC.104(73) adopted in 2000 (in force since 1 July 2002)
- Resolution MSC.179(79) adopted in 2004 (in force since 1 July 2006)
- Resolution MSC.195(80) adopted in 2005 (in force since 1 January 2009)
- Resolution MSC.273(85) adopted in 2008 (in force since 1 July 2010)
- Resolution MSC.353(92), adopted on 21 June 2013 (in force since 1 January 2015)

In addition to the amendments above, the Revised Guidelines on the Implementation of the International Safety (ISM) Code by Administrations[15] and the Revised Guidelines for the Operational Implementation of the ISM Code by Companies[16] are to be noted.

10.3.3.2 Selected highlights

The Code has a broad ambition. It seeks to achieve its goals through a first part on implementation-related aspects and a second part on certification and verification. In this context, as already mentioned, the Code is aimed at ensuring safety at sea, prevention of human injury or loss of life, and avoidance of damage to the environment, including the marine environment, and to property. It is primarily designed to create obligations for the company, i.e. the owner of the ship or any other entity (e.g. ship manager) "who has assumed the responsibility for operation of the ship from the shipowner and who, on assuming such responsibility, has agreed to take over all duties and responsibilities by the Code".[17]

---

15 IMO Resolution A.1071(28) adopted on 4 December 2013.
16 IMO MSC-MEPC.7/Circ.8, 28 Junes 2013.
17 See para. 1.1.2 of ISM Code.

The Code sets out the obligation for companies to have a Safety Management System (SMS) in place, aimed at ensuring compliance – on the one hand, compliance with mandatory regulations and, on the other hand, compliance with recommended standards. The SMS must be "a structured and documented system enabling Company personnel to implement effectively the Company safety and environmental protection policy".[18] The Safety Management System to be implemented by the company should satisfy a number of criteria, referred to by the Code as "functional requirements".

The functional requirements for a Safety Management System according to the ISM Code are the following, namely:[19]

- a safety policy;
- en environmental protection policy;
- instructions and procedures in line with international and flag State's legislation
  - on safe operation of ships;
  - on the protection of the environment;
- in relation to the personnel aboard and ashore: defined levels of authority and lines of communication between them;
- additional procedures in relation to the following:
  - accident reporting;
  - non-conformities (with the provisions of the Code) reporting;
  - preparation for and response to emergencies;
  - internal audits and management reviews.

In addition to the above, the Code sets out the role of one or more designated person (in practice, commonly referred to as the Designated Person Ashore or DPA), with defined responsibility and authority, i.e. monitoring the safety and pollution-prevention aspects of the operation of each ship and ensuring adequate resources and shore-based support. The DPA should function as a link between those aboard and those ashore, especially at the level of senior management.[20] Furthermore, the role of the master is enhanced. His/her responsibility should be clearly defined and documented by the company in relation to items such as the implementation of safety and environmental protection policy of the company, issuance of appropriate orders and instructions, verification of whether specified requirements are observed, etc.[21] In addition to the above, the company should ensure a number of items, including in relation to resources and personnel.[22] Concerning the human element, which is the focus of this chapter, the company should notably satisfy certain prerequisites on the level of manning. More specifically, it should make sure that each ship is manned with qualified,

---

18 See para. 1.1.4 of ISM Code.
19 See para. 1.4 of ISM Code.
20 See para. 4 of the ISM Code.
21 See para. 5 of the ISM Code.
22 See para. 6 of the ISM Code.

certificated and medically fit seafarers in accordance with applicable regulations and is appropriately manned in order to encompass all aspects of maintaining safe operations on board.[23] The Code also pertains to emergency preparedness, reports and analysis of non-conformities, accidents and hazardous occurrences, ship and equipment maintenance, documentation, company verification, review and evaluation.

In the second part of the Code, which deals, as already mentioned, with certification and verification, the Code spells out, amongst others, the document of compliance (DOC) and the safety management certificate (SMC). The DOC is issued to the company (the interim document of compliance is also to be noted) complying with the requirements of the Code. Its maximum duration is five years. The said document is issued by the flag State, by an organisation empowered by the flag State to do so (in practice, commonly a classification society) or "at the request of the Administration, by another Contracting Government to the Convention".[24] A copy should be placed on board. The function of the DOC is to provide evidence that the company is capable of meeting the requirements of the instrument. The conditions of its withdrawal are also set out in the instrument.

The SMC is issued to the ship. Its maximum duration is five years. It is issued following verification that the company and its shipboard management operate in line with the approved safety management system. The function of the certificate is to provide evidence that the ship is ISM Code-compliant.[25] An intermediate verification is also spelled out, as well as, amongst others, the conditions of its withdrawal.

10.3.3.3 The ISM Code and the marine environment

By integrating the marine environment component in the overall system and on the same footing as safety and protection the human element, the Code becomes pivotal in marine pollution control. On the one hand, marine environment protection features among the Code's objectives.[26] On the other hand, this is also a functional requirement set out by the Code alongside safety and critical procedures and instructions (e.g. emergencies), as a safety management system has to include an environmental protection policy. Relevant policy is expected to describe how the objectives on environmental protection will be achieved. Furthermore, major non-conformities, for example, would not only include identifiable deviations posing serious threats to safety; they would also comprise serious threats to the environment. The designated person's role also involves monitoring pollution prevention aspects, including, making sure that there are adequate resources. The master's responsibility with regard to the implementation of environmental protection policies is also set out – a responsibility which should be defined and documented by the company. Furthermore, according to the Code, the master is

---

23 See para. 6.2 of the ISM Code.
24 See para. 13.2 of the ISM Code.
25 See para. 13.7 of the ISM Code.
26 See para. 1.2.1 of the ISM Code.

given the overriding authority to make decisions with respect to pollution prevention. Appropriate procedures should exist so that new personnel and personnel assigned to new tasks related to protection of the environment are given proper familiarisation with their duties.[27] Shipboard operations concerning the protection of the environment call for the adoption of appropriate procedures, plans and instructions by the company. Internal audits conducted by the company comprise, amongst others, verifying whether pollution-prevention activities comply with the Safety Management System.

A number of key questions are touched upon below in relation to resources and personnel under the ISM Code which can be critical in assessing, amongst others, the ability of the personnel to deal with marine environment protection. These questions may be part of a wider agenda raised, for example, during Port State Control inspections.

- What is the degree of familiarisation of crew members with the environmental protection policy of the company? Have crew members received necessary or required familiarisation and training, including in relation to marine environment protection?
- To what extent is the crew familiar with their duties and responsibilities as spelled out in the Safety Management System, including in relation to safety and marine environment protection?
- Does the number of personnel satisfy the requirements of the minimum safe manning certificate (SOLAS)?
- Is STCW-related certification in good order? Are STCW standards on hours of work and rest met? As already mentioned, working in the maritime transport industry requires continued alertness and concentration, including in relation to marine environment-related items, which is likely to be negatively impaired in case, for example, of fatigue.
- Are the personnel in a position to communicate effectively in the working language of the ship?
- Is the master's authority and responsibility clearly identified? Is it documented and understood?
- Does the designated person ashore assume its role effectively? How does he/she interphase with the personnel ashore and aboard in relation to marine pollution control-related failures? Is corrective action taken whenever and wherever required?

10.4 Areas of special interest (e.g. amendments underway, interface with other areas, etc.)

10.4.1 Fatigue

Fatigue was mentioned a few times above, including its definition, and its addressing in a number of instruments such as the STCW 2010 and ILO MLC 2006. Determined to be geared towards the human element (and not just adopt a

---

27 See para. 6.3 of the ISM Code.

technical approach to the maritime agenda) IMO legislation could not disregard the problem of fatigue. In Resolution A.947(23) adopted on 27 November 2003 on "Human Element Vision, Principles and Goals for the Organization" the IMO puts anew a spotlight on the importance of the human element in shipping legislation by introducing a number of goals to be taken into consideration by regulators (e.g. proper consideration of human element issues in the development of IMO regulations, review of selected IMO instruments from a human element perspective, promotion through human element principles of heightened marine environment awareness, etc.). The IMO also acknowledges that human element issues are given high priority on its legislative agenda because of the prominent role of the human element in the prevention of maritime casualties. Furthermore, the ILO points out the need for increased focus on the human element in the safe operation of ships, and the need to achieve, amongst others, high standards of environmental protection.

Fatigue-related items also pertain to manning of ships with qualified and medically fit personnel, familiarisation and training for shipboard personnel and providing for necessary support to ensure that the shipmaster's duties can be adequately performed. Adopted on 4 November 1993, IMO Resolution A.772(18) on Fatigue Factors in Manning and Safety provides a general description of fatigue. Introduced by factors such as prolonged periods of mental or physical activity, inadequate rest, adverse environment, etc., fatigue entails, according to the Resolution, the degradation of human performance by slowing down reflexes and/or by impairing the ability to make rational judgments. In addition to the description of fatigue, Resolution A.772(18) is also aimed at identifying and classifying fatigue factors at the level of ship operations. The objective of the instrument is to enhance awareness and encourage the Parties concerned to take into consideration relevant factors when making operational decisions. There are also IMO circulars which address fatigue, which are not discussed here.[28]

10.4.2 Criminalisation of seafarers

As a result of the highly regulated environment in which the shipping industry operates, the diversity of jurisdictions that seafarers are confronted with, and the exposure of those working at sea to the media in case of major accidents, the question of the criminalisation of seafarers nowadays attracts special attention. A related aspect is the exposure of seafarers to criminal liabilities in the event, amongst others, of failure to deter and/or confine marine pollution and/or collaborate, as appropriate, with local authorities (in the latter case, there are offences relating to the administration of justice). Additional legal requirements on the protection of the environment which were recently adopted or which are currently underway have the potential to further expose seafarers to the risk of litigation (e.g. ballast water management, use of compliant fuels, etc.).

---

28 See MSC/Circ.1014 of 12 June 2001 containing Guidance on Fatigue Mitigation and Management.

It is generally recognised that seafarers involved with legal proceedings in foreign jurisdictions, amongst others as a result of marine pollution casualties, tend to be psychologically vulnerable. Being needed as witnesses or charged with criminal offences, seafarers often have no knowledge of the local language or legal system. Away from home, their freedom is restricted under stressful circumstances. Deprivation of freedom may last for months or years.

Depending on the legal system involved, there are varied circumstances where the personnel of a ship may be exposed to liabilities, including criminal liability.

One may think, for example, of a ship whose certification and risk profile are formally in good order but which has been subjected to limited repairs and/ or substantially poor safety management oversight by the owners and/or ship managers (e.g. a safety management system under the ISM Code which has failed to introduce a safety/marine environment protection culture). In the same example one may assume that key stakeholders such as the classification society involved with the surveys and audits or the ship management company concerned have not objected to repairs of this scale and/or adhered to poor overall management. During harsh weather conditions, an accident takes place, resulting in the sinking of the ship and in large-scale pollution. In our example, there is probably more than one causal factor to the accident, and the crew aboard has probably not directly triggered the accident. Let us also assume that the master, the officers and the crew demonstrate good seamanship during the casualty, even though they fail to prevent the environmental disaster. This hypothetical context should suggest a different perspective on the involvement (and potentially on the liabilities) of the crew than in the context, for example, of deliberate discharges of oily waste at sea committed with intent or recklessly – to which civil society is naturally inclined to show less sympathy. It appears, however, that public opinion may not always make a clear and fair distinction between these circumstances. As a result, in presence of major pollution casualties it is sometimes recognised that moral pressure may be exercised on the judiciary by the local society, entailing the risk of unfair treatment of seafarers. This may be done with a view to reassuring those who have suffered from marine pollution. Such approaches are expected to convey the message that by punishing in an exemplary manner the crew, this expectation is fulfilled. To name but a few of the incidents which have pointed to challenges on criminalisation of seafarers under very different circumstances, the following can be mentioned: the *Nissos Amorgos* (1997), the *Erika* (1999), the *Prestige* (2002), the *Tasman Spirit* (2003), and the *Hebei Spirit* (2007). In the case of the *Prestige* legal proceedings against the Master displaced attention from possible failures of certain institutional stakeholders in relation to the prompt granting of a place of refuge. There have been cases suggesting that the treatment of the crew had disregarded a number of rights granted to them under international instruments.

There are numerous instruments involved at the international level. Some of them are binding in relation to the ratifying States concerned. Others provide guidance. In the first category, there is the United Nations Convention on the Law of the Sea (UNCLOS III), adopted in 1982, which provides, as already mentioned in previous chapters, the framework of reference on international law of navigational freedoms and international management of oceanic resources. Article 230 of UNCLOS III is relevant.

> According to Article 230 on Monetary penalties and the observance of recognised rights of the accused:
>
> 1. Monetary penalties only may be imposed with respect to violations of national laws and regulations or applicable international rules and standards for the prevention, reduction and control of pollution of the marine environment, committed by foreign vessels beyond the territorial sea.
> 2. Monetary penalties only may be imposed with respect to violations of national laws and regulations or applicable international rules and standards for the prevention, reduction and control of pollution of the marine environment committed by foreign vessels in the territorial sea, except in the case of a willful and serious act of pollution in the territorial sea.
> 3. In the conduct of proceedings in respect of such violations committed by a foreign vessel which may result in the imposition of penalties, recognised rights of the accused shall be observed.

Article 230 can be correlated with Article 218 of the same instrument, which sets out port State jurisdiction to bring legal proceedings in relation to marine pollution offences committed on the high seas.

More specifically, according to Article 218:

> (1) When a vessel is voluntarily within a port or at an off-shore terminal of a State, that State may undertake investigations and, where the evidence so warrants, institute proceedings in respect of any discharge from that vessel outside the internal waters, territorial sea or exclusive economic zone of that State in violation of applicable international rules and standards established through the competent international organization or general diplomatic conference.

Furthermore, Article 4 of MARPOL, which prohibits violations of its provisions, is of interest to the discussion. Sanctions shall be established under the law of the flag State "wherever the violation occurs". If the flag State administration is informed of such violation and is satisfied that sufficient evidence is available, it shall cause legal proceedings to be taken as soon as possible in accordance with its law. The same provision also deals with violations of MARPOL within the jurisdiction of any Party to the Convention. Such violations are prohibited and sanctions shall be imposed under the law of that Party. Amongst others, Article 4 sets out in paragraph 4 that "The penalties specified under the law of a Party pursuant to the present article shall be adequate in severity to discourage violations of the present Convention and shall be equally severe irrespective of where the violations occur."

In addition to the above, the European Convention on Human Rights (ECHR), which is about the protection of human rights and fundamental freedoms, and

THE CONTRIBUTION OF THE HUMAN ELEMENT

is primarily of European interest, may also come into play. The instrument was adopted by the Council of Europe on 4 November 1950 and has been in force since 3 September 1953. The text seeks, amongst others, to make effective the traditions of civil liberty. To name but a few of the rights enshrined in the Convention, one may mention the right to life, prohibition of torture, prohibition of slavery and forced labour, the right to liberty and security, the right to a fair trial, etc. It should be noted that the Council of Europe currently comprises 47 Member States. The European Court of Human Rights, an international court set up in 1959 which sits in Strasburg, France, implements the Convention (in broad terms, its involvement is subject to conditions, including the claim not being remedied on the domestic level). The text contributes significantly to the discussion on the criminalisation of seafarers.

The right to a fair trial, including legal representation,[29] which, as a right, must be practical and effective is set out in the Convention. It should be noted that the exact "weight" given to the right to legal representation varies from one jurisdiction to another. Furthermore, the European Convention on Human Rights sets out the right to interpretation and translation.[30] The right to legal representation is also enshrined in other legal instruments which involve a different geographical scope, such as the American Convention on Human Rights, the African Charter on Human and Peoples' Rights, etc. The right to free legal assistance, is, however, subject to some limitations under the ECHR. Furthermore, the right of seafarers to communicate freely and confidentially with their lawyer has been interpreted as being part of the practical and effective nature of the right to legal representation[31] – features that the ECHR seeks to ensure.

Among existing texts of a recommendatory nature, the 2006 Guidelines on the Fair Treatment of Seafarers in the Event of a Maritime Accident[32] is worth a mention. In the event of a maritime accident, it is recommended that the Guidelines be followed in all instances where seafarers may be detained by public authorities. Seafarers are defined in a generic manner so as to include anyone employed, engaged or working in any capacity aboard a ship. The Guidelines, which do not apply to warships or naval auxiliaries, are not designed to constitute an interference with domestic regulations or international instruments on seafarers' human rights. According to the Guidelines, seafarers are entitled to protection against coercion and intimidation during or after any investigation into a maritime accident. The Guidelines are aimed at the fair treatment of seafarers following a maritime accident and during any investigation and detention by public authorities. Furthermore, the Guidelines are intended for all key stakeholders involved, namely: the port/coastal State (for example, by recommending that investigations on the cause of the maritime accident be

---

29 Article 6(3).

30 Article 6(1)(3).

31 See Seafarers Rights International (SRI) Survey – Seafarers and the Criminal Law, May 2013, p. 48.

32 IMO Resolution 987(24), 1 December 2005.

conducted in a fair and expeditious manner), the flag State (amongst others, it is encouraged to assist seafarers in order to secure fair treatment), the seafarer State (e.g. through the monitoring of mental and physical well-being and treatment of seafarers of its nationality involved in a maritime accident and in associated proceedings), shipowners (they are recommended, for example, to use all reasonable means to preserve evidence with a view to minimising the need for the physical presence of seafarers) and seafarers. In the last case, it is notably provided that seafarers should "take steps to ensure that they fully understand their right not to self-incriminate, and that they fully understand that when statements are made to port, coastal or flag State investigators, these may potentially be used in a future criminal prosecution". This provision suggests the difficulties which characterise the legal position of seafarers and the somewhat delicate balance between collaboration with justice and protection of one's legal position.

SECTION 3: KEY MANAGEMENT ISSUES

10.5 Procedures/operations and relevant documentation

10.5.1 Non-exhaustive list of documents generally required by international regulations which relate to the human element to be carried onboard[33]

SOLAS	• Minimum Safe Manning Document
	• Safety Management Certificate (ISM Code)
	• Document of Compliance (ISM Code)
	• Various training manuals
STCW	• Certificates for masters, officers and ratings
	• Records of hours of rest
ILO MLC 2006	• Maritime Labour Certificate (MLC)
	• Declaration of Maritime Labour Compliance (Parts I & II)

10.5.2 Selective question: the complaints procedure under ILO MLC 2006

In what ways may a complaints procedure impact on marine environment protection?

The complaints procedure under ILO MLC 2006 is intended to remedy problems expressed by seafarers which fall within the scope of the Convention, i.e. which pertain to the working and living conditions aboard. If, for example, there is a complaint that hours of work or rest are violated, it is sensible to assume that this anomaly may jeopardise the ability of the crew to be on alert, and prospectively prevent or address casualties, including casualties which may impact on the marine environment.

---

33 Detailed lists are commonly provided by ship classification societies. Also see IMO List of Certificates and Documents Required to be Carried on Board Ships 2017 (FAL.2/Circ.131,19 July 2017).

THE CONTRIBUTION OF THE HUMAN ELEMENT

The procedure in question may go in two directions: it may be conducted aboard or ashore. The procedures may interact at some stage. Complaint procedures can be found under Title V, which deals with compliance and enforcement.[34] As pointed out below, it is noteworthy that the complaint procedure may potentially lead to a more detailed inspection of the ship and/or to detention. Moreover, the requirements relating to the on-board complaint procedures are among the items for inspection and certification set out in Annex A5-I of the Convention.

More specifically, regulation 5.1.5 of ILO MLC 2006 deals with the on-board complaint procedure (please see below Figure 10.4). Ships flying the flag of a ratifying country must have on-board procedures for "the fair, effective and expeditious handling of seafarer complaints alleging breaches of the requirement of this Convention (including seafarers' rights)". Filing a complaint, according to the instrument, must not result in the victimisation of the seafarer concerned, and appropriate measures must be taken by national regulators in that regard ("Each Member shall prohibit and penalize any kind of victimization ..."). Victimisation means, according to the text, any adverse action taken with respect to the seafarer who lodged a complaint that "is not manifestly vexatious or maliciously made".[35] That said, the provisions on on-board complaint procedures do not cancel the seafarer's right to seek redress through other legal means.

Standard A5.1.5 spells out relevant details of the on-board complaint procedure. Member States are held to provide in their legal system for on-board complaint procedures. While complaints must be addressed "at the lowest level possible",[36] this does not put aside the right of seafarers to lodge a complaint directly before the master and, where considered necessary, before appropriate external authorities. A copy of the on-board complaint procedure applicable on the ship must be provided to seafarers. The information that must be made available in relevant document is set out by Standard A5.1.5. Additional aspects are addressed in Guidelines B5.1.5, such as the recommendation that Member States establish a model for fair, expeditious and well-documented on-board complaint-handling procedures for the ships flying their flag.

The onshore seafarer complaint-handling procedure is spelled out in regulation 5.2.2. When a ship calls at a port breach and there is alleged of the MLC, including seafarers' rights, seafarers are entitled to report such a complaint "in order to facilitate a prompt and practical means of redress".[37] The authorised officer has the duty to undertake an initial investigation.[38] Firstly, the authorised officer may consider whether the on-board complaint procedure has been explored. The next thing to note is that a more detailed inspection may be triggered by a complaint.[39]

---

34 On the complaint procedures, notably see the ILO MLC 2006, regulations 5.1.5 and 5.2.2 as well ILO (2009) Guidelines for Port State Control Officers Carrying Out Inspections Under the Maritime Labour Convention, 2006 (available at the website of the ILO).

35 See Standard A5.1.5, para. 3.

36 *Ibid.*, para. 2.

37 See relevant regulation.

38 See Standard A5.2.2, para. 1.

39 See Standard A5.2.2, para. 2.

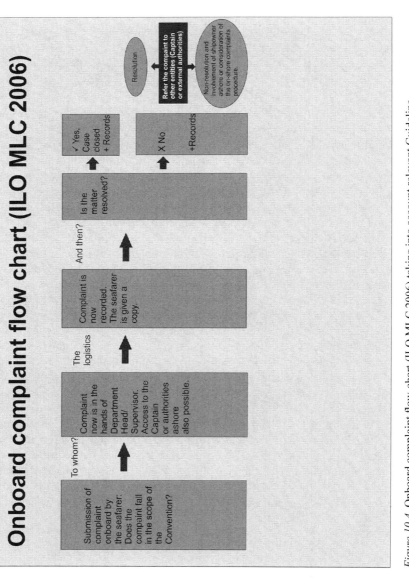

Figure 10.4 Onboard complaint flow-chart (ILO MLC 2006) taking into account relevant Guideline.

The resolution of the complaint at the level of the ship is sought by the author-ised officer, "where appropriate". For obvious reasons, the confidentiality of the complaint must be safeguarded.

An interphase with inspections in port is provided by the instrument:[40] if a non-conformity grasped by paragraph 6 of Standard A5.2.1 is revealed following an investigation or a more detailed inspection, "the provisions of that paragraph shall be applied". It should be recalled on this point that relevant provision[41] sets out the right of the port State to prevent the ship from sailing – until appropriate action is taken – in the context where following a more detailed inspection the ship is not ILO MLC 2006 compliant and:

- the conditions on board are clearly hazardous to the safety, health or secu-rity of seafarers; or
- the non-conformity constitutes a serious or repeated breach of the require-ments of the instrument, including seafarers' rights.

Where the provisions of paragraph 4 of Standard A5.2.2 do not apply, in presence of a complaint that has not been resolved on the level of the vessel, the flag State shall be forthwith notified. A prescribed deadline, advice and a corrective plan of action will be sought.[42] If the complaint continues to remain unresolved despite the actions taken at the level just described, additional actions may be taken by the port State involving the Director-General of the ILO and shipowners' and seafarers' organisations in the port State.[43]

Additional aspects are addressed in the recommendatory part under Guideline B5.2.2. Amongst others, it is spelled out that in the presence of a seafarer's com-plaint which is of a general nature, i.e. it concerns all seafarers aboard (in contrast to complaints which are of interest to a category of seafarers or even only to indi-vidual seafarers), "consideration should be given to undertaking a more detailed inspection in accordance with Standard A5.2.1".[44]

BIBLIOGRAPHY

Allen, P., Wadsworth, E., and Smith, A., 'Seafarers' Fatigue: A Review of the Recent Lit-erature' [2008] International Maritime Health 59(1–4), 81

Anderson, P., *ISM Code – A Practical Guide to the Legal and Insurance Implications* (3rd edition, Lloyd's Practical Shipping Guides, Informa Law from Routledge, 2015)

Bailey, N., Ellis, N., and Sampson, H., *Safety and Perceptions of Risk: A Comparison Between Respondent Perceptions and Recorded Accident Data* (Lloyd's Register Edu-cational Trust – SIRC, Cardiff University, October 2010)

---

40 See para. 4 of Standard A5.2.2 which refers to non-conformities falling within the scope of para. 6 of Standard A5.2.1.

41 I.e. para. 6 of Standard A5.2.1

42 See Standard A5.2.2, para. 5.

43 See para. 6 of Standard A5.2.2

44 See Guideline B5.2.2, para. 2.

Batalden, B.-M., and Kristoffer Sydnes, A., 'Maritime Safety and the ISM Code: A Study of Investigated Casualties and Incidents' [2014] WMU Journal of Maritime Affairs, September, 3–25.

Boisson, P., *Safety at Sea – Policies, Regulations & International Law* (Bureau Veritas, Paris, 1999) (see pp. 287–304)

Christodoulou-Varotsi, I., 'Critical Review of the Consolidated Maritime Labour Convention (2006) of the International Labour Organisation: Limitations and Perspectives' [2012] Journal of Maritime Law & Commerce, 1 October.

Christodoulou-Varotsi, I., & Pentsov, D., *Maritime Work Law Fundamentals: Responsible Shipowners, Reliable Seafarers* (Springer, Heidelberg, 2008)

Dauer, E.A. in Wahlgren, P. (ed), 'The Role of Culture in Legal Risk, Scandinavian Studies in Law' [2006] Vol. 49, Stockholm Institute for Scandinavian Law 1957–2010, pp. 93–108

European Commission – Sulpice G., *Study on EU Seafarers Employment-Final Report* (20 May 2011)

Gregory, D., and Shanahan, P., *The Human Element: A Guide to Human Behaviour in the Shipping Industry*, authored for Maritime & Coastguard Agency (MCA) (UK) [2010] (Crown Copyright)

Heijari, J., and Tapaninen, U. (eds), *Efficiency of the ISM Code in Finnish Shipping Companies* (Center of Maritime Studies, University of Turku, Turku, 2010)

ICS, *Implementing an Effective Safety Culture – Basic Advice for Shipping Companies and Seafarers* (2013)

ICS/ISF, *Guidelines on the Application of the IMO International Safety Management (ISM) Code* (Marisec Publications, London 2010)

ILO, *Guidelines for Port State Control Officers Carrying Out Inspections Under the International Maritime Labour Convention 2006* (2009)

ILO, International Labour Standards Department, *Maritime Labour Convention, 2006 (MLC, 2006)*, Frequently Asked Questions [2014] 3rd revised edition (available on the internet, www.ilo.org/mlc)

ILO, *Guidelines for Flag State Inspections Under the Maritime Labour Convention 2006* (2009)

IMO, *Guidance on Fatigue Mitigation and Management* (MSC/Circ. 1014 12 June 2001)

IMO, *ISM Code – International Safety Management Code with Guidelines for Its Implementation* (2014)

IMO, *STCW Including 2010 Manila Amendments* (2011 edition)

ISF, *Guidelines on the IMO STCW Convention Including the 2010 Manila Amendments* (Marisec Publications, London, 2011)

ITF, *STCW A Guide for Seafarers – Taking Into Account the 2010 Manila Amendments* (document date unavailable)

Lavelle, J. (ed), *The Maritime Labour Convention 2006: International Labour Law Redefined* [2013] Informa Law

Mandaraka-Sheppard, A., *Modern Maritime Law* (Vol. 2) (3rd edition, Informa Law, Routledge, 2013)

McConnel, M., Devlin, D., and Doumbia-Henry, C., *The Maritime Labour Convention 2006 – A Legal Primer to an Emerging International Regime* (Martinus Nijhoff, 2011)

Murray, O., 'Fair Treatment of Seafarers' [2012] International Law and Practice 18, 150–164

SKULD Guide, *How to Prevent and Mitigate Fatigue* (document date unavailable)

Sollien, K., Jensen, T.E., and Schøyen, H., 'Designated Person Ashore – How Do They Perceive Their Role in the Organization and to Which Extent Are They Legally Exposed in Case of an Accident?' [2014] Journal of Maritime Research XI(III), 3–12

CHAPTER 11

Legal aspects of marine pollution from ships

TABLE OF CONTENTS

Section 1	The basics governing the legal framework on marine pollution damage	296
11.1	About damages/losses and claims	297
	11.1.1 The involvement of the International Oil Pollution Compensation Funds	298
	11.1.1.1 Handling of claims by the IOPC Funds	299
	11.1.2 The involvement of Protection and Indemnity Clubs	300
	11.1.3 The involvement of salvors	301
11.2	Glossary	303
11.3	Types of liability in a nutshell	305
	11.3.1 Civil liability	305
	11.3.2 Criminal liability	306
	11.3.2.1 EU Directive 2005/35, as amended	309
Section 2	Limitation of liability of the polluter	310
11.4	The concept of limitation of liability in a nutshell	310
11.5	Global limitation of liability for maritime claims: the Convention on Limitation of Liability for Maritime Claims Convention (1976), as amended	311
	11.5.1 European Union Directive 2009/20/EC	313
11.6	Limitation of liability for oil pollution damage: the 1992 Civil Liability Convention, the 1992 Fund Convention and the 2003 Supplementary Fund Protocol	315
	11.6.1 The Small Tanker Oil Pollution Indemnification Agreement 2006 and the Tanker Oil Pollution Indemnification Agreement 2006	325
11.7	Limitation of liability for pollution from bunkers: the 2001 Bunker Pollution Convention	326
11.8	Limitation of liability for pollution from chemicals: the 2010 HNS Convention	327
11.9	Liability of the shipowner in the context of wreck removal: the 2007 Nairobi Convention	329

SECTION 1: THE BASICS GOVERNING THE LEGAL FRAMEWORK ON MARINE POLLUTION DAMAGE

Up to the early 1970s marine pollution from shipping was far from being regulated. Public outcry following major oil spills had triggered the adoption of regulations, and required the increase of protection to victims. Important legal questions were raised in the aftermath of casualties, like the possible compensation of moral damage sustained by a local population in case of polluting incident, the quantification of losses for compensation purposes or the legal limits to compensation, especially in relation to the unowned natural environment. The international regime currently in place principally revolves around the principle according to which the polluter must pay, and it is shaped in practice by a legal device which is referred to as limitation of liability. International, regional and domestic regulations on marine pollution from ships are generally centered on strict liability, i.e. a form of liability which does not require proving the fault or negligence of the polluter. Particularly interesting and relevant to future regulations is the growing weight of societal expectations on the matter, in the wider context of the discussion on environmental sustainability.

States are well placed under international law to provide for action in the area of marine pollution prevention and management. As already pointed out in the introductory chapter which discussed the United Nations Convention on the Law of the Sea (UNCLOS III), this duty includes the adoption of appropriate regulations as well as the existence of a legal machinery capable of addressing the consequences of polluting incidents. The same instrument explicitly compels ratifying States to ensure availability of recourse for prompt and adequate compensation or other relief in respect of damage caused by pollution of the marine environment by natural or legal persons under their jurisdiction.[1]

Not only marine pollution is a challenge for regulators, and an adverse occurrence for the environment, marine pollution also generates adverse consequences to polluters, including consequences on the level of their civil, including financial, liability.[2] This aspect is additional to possible criminal repercussions whose aim is the punishment of the perpetrator, and deterrence of similar acts in the future.[3] The civil law sphere which relates to compensation commonly involves mutual associations of shipowners and charterers commonly known as Protection and Indemnity (P&I) Clubs which specialise in the cover of third party liability

---

1 See Article 235, para. 2 of UNCLOS III.

2 Michael Tsimplis, 'Marine Pollution from Shipping Activities', in Yvonne Baatz (ed), *Maritime Law* (3rd edition, Informa Law, Routledge, 2014, pp. 368–427).

3 A detailed presentation of the legal aspects of marine pollution can be found in Colin de la Rue and Charles B. Anderson, *Shipping and the Environment* (2nd edition, LLP, 2009).

from the operation of ships. As it will be seen below, shipowners are required to ensure cover evidenced by appropriate certification for their prospective liability from pollution; this obligation stems from applicable international instruments governing oil pollution from tankers, bunker oil pollution, and wreck removal (in relation to hazardous and noxious substances (HNS), it is noted that relevant international convention is not in force but an obligation to ensure appropriate cover may exist under domestic law). The said cover is provided by insurers or other entities (financial institutions), and gives access to proceedings directly against the insurer (e.g. P&I club) or other guarantor.[4] That said, in some cases legal proceedings may reach the level of international bodies entrusted with compensation – mention will be made in the process of the International Oil Pollution Compensation Funds (IOPCF).

11.1 About damages/losses and claims

Marine pollution from ships may stem from oil carried on tankers or bunker fuel carried from any type of ship as well as from other substances such as chemicals. Marine pollution generates various types of losses, damages and expenses eligible for compensation by the polluter and/or his insurers. The liability to pay compensation is governed by the law of the jurisdiction where the pollution is suffered. While international conventions on the matter establish uniform law, oil spills falling outside the scope of relevant conventions are governed by applicable national laws which may be different to the international system. An example of a domestic regime departing from the international system is the Oil Pollution Act 1990 in the USA, which was discussed in a previous chapter. As it will be seen below, the international regime governing marine pollution compensation is based on the principle of limitation of financial liability of the polluter, and it can be described as two-fold: on the one hand, it is centered on general ship-sourced damage through a system on limitation of liability (Convention on Limitation of Liability for Maritime Claims (LLMC), as amended) which runs in parallel with international specialised instruments (e.g. Civil Liability Convention (CLC), etc.); on the other hand, it sets out limits on financial liability based on the nature of the substance which caused pollution (e.g. CLC in relation to oil; the International Convention on Liability and Compensation for Damage in Connection with the Carriage of Hazardous and Noxious Substances by Sea (HNS Convention) sets limits in relation to chemical pollution, etc.).

The graph below is largely based on the international legal regime governing marine oil pollution, an area which will be examined as the chapter progresses; the graph may be of interest on a more general level of discussion as it shows in a simplified manner the breadth of losses, damages and expenses that may be

---

4   See Article VII para. 8 of 1992 CLC Convention; Article 7(10) of the 2001 Bunker Pollution Convention; Article 12(10) of 2007 Nairobi Wreck Removal Convention; Article 12(8) of the 2010 HNS Convention.

generated from marine pollution, and may be generally eligible for compensation. The graph does not showcase the criminal/penal ramifications of marine pollution.

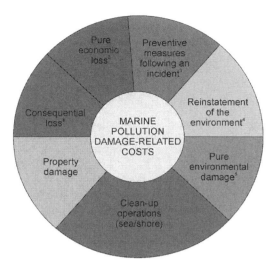

Graph 11.1 Marine pollution damage-related costs generally eligible for compensation

Notes:
1. E.g. Loss of income by fishermen as a result of their nets becoming oiled.
2. E.g. Nets of fishermen giving rise to loss of earnings without their nets being oiled as they are prevented from fishing due to oil pollution.
3. E.g. Measures to prevent the escape of oil from a ship or collection of the oil spilt at sea.
4. E.g. Accelerating natural recovery.
5. E.g. Not convered by 1992 CLC. It may be subject to restrictive conditions which differ from national system to national system.

In prelude to the main discussion, an overview of the stakeholders involved would be useful at this point.

11.1.1 *The involvement of the International Oil Pollution Compensation Funds*

Triggered by major accidents such as the *Erika* (1999) and the *Prestige* (2002), the 1992 Fund and the Supplementary Fund are the intergovernmental organisations which constitute the IOPC Funds. They sit in London and are involved with the financial compensation in Member States for oil pollution damage caused by spills of persistent oil from tankers. The Funds are financed by levies on oil receivers of certain types of oil transported by sea in Member States. The work of the IOPC Funds is intertwined with the international (i.e. IMO) legal regime governing oil pollution, which consists of the 1992 Civil Liability

Convention (CLC) and the 1992 Fund Convention. The predecessors of the 1992 CLC and 1992 Fund Convention were the 1969 CLC and the 1991 Fund Convention. In the interest of clarity, it is noted that following the adoption of the 2003 Supplementary Fund Protocol (entry into force of the last instrument in 2005), a Supplementary Fund was established which is administered by the Secretariat of the 1992 Fund.

It should be noted from the outset that the above-mentioned conventions represent tiers, i.e. levels, of compensation, which come into play when certain conditions are met (this aspect will be discussed under para. 11.6). Up to this stage, the IOPC Funds have been involved with 149 incidents around the world.[5] Mention should be made of the *Alfa I*, which took place in Greece in 2012; this was the first incident involving a Member State Party to the 2003 Supplementary Fund. Greek tanker *Alfa I* had collided with a submerged wreck in Elefsis Bay. The tanker was reported to carry intermediate fuel oil (IFO), heavy fuel oil (HFO), and marine gas oil (MGO). An estimated amount of 100 tonnes or 330 mt of oil was spilt at sea. Relevant proceedings are currently pending.[6]

11.1.1.1 Handling of claims by the IOPC Funds

Compensation by the IOPC Funds is available when the claims presented to the Funds satisfy certain conditions. Claims for compensation may stem from anyone who has suffered pollution damage in a Member State, i.e. a State that is party to the 1992 CLC and the 1992 Fund Convention.[7] The criteria on admissibility of claims are discussed in a practical guide published by the IOPC Funds, the Claims Manual (last edition dating to October 2016). Amongst others, the criteria include the type of incident involved, which should be an incident caused by a spill of persistent mineral oil (e.g. crude oil, fuel oil, etc.) carried by a ship constructed or adapted to carry oil in bulk as cargo. The next direction concerns the types of damage covered. As it will be seen below in the main discussion on the CLC and Fund Conventions, the definition of pollution damage is essential. Admissibility of claims under the IOPC Fund's policy, includes, amongst others, criteria on certain features of the expense, loss or damage (e.g. expense actually incurred; expense relating to measures considered reasonable and justifiable; expense, loss or damage caused by contamination resulting from the spill; compensation being dependent on a quantifiable economic loss, etc.). The information that should be contained in the claims and time limits are also explained in the Manual.

---

5 The description of the incidents, including details on possible compensation, can be found on the website of the IOPC Funds.

6 A detailed presentation of the accident, including compensation aspects and clean-up operations, can be found on the website of the IOPC Funds.

7 According to the IOPC Funds Claims Manual, in case of damage caused in a State that is only party to 1992 CLC, the claim can only be made against the shipowner and his insurer; in the context of claims for damage in States that are party to the 1992 CLC and the 1992 Fund Convention, claims for damage may be made against this shipowner and his insurer and the Fund.

The involvement of Protection and Indemnity Clubs, including their inter-phase with the IOPC Funds during compensation proceedings, is vital. In the same vein, it is noted that the International Group (IG) of P&I Clubs signed a memorandum of understanding with the IOPC Funds in April 2006 (replacing older memoranda) setting out the agreed understandings between the two Parties in relation, amongst others, to compensation payments and recourse procedures following voluntary industry compensation schemes referred to as STOPIA and TOPIA (2006) (the schemes are defined in the glossary and discussed below under paragraph 11.6.1).

11.1.2 The involvement of Protection and Indemnity Clubs

P&I clubs are mutual associations of shipowners and charterers which provide insurance cover for risks stemming from the management and operation of the ships of their members. Being mutual associations, P&I clubs are under the con-trol of their members, who contribute financially, on the basis of vessel tonnage, through "calls". The vast majority of the world merchant tonnage is nowadays entered with one of the 13 P&I clubs that constitute the International Group of P&I Clubs. The International Group Agreement and the Pooling Agreement pro-vide for the terms that the 13 P&I Clubs are subject to.

P&I Clubs specialise in the cover of third party liabilities. A third party is anyone other than the shipowner who has a claim against the vessel. P&I Clubs commonly cover risks relating to cargo (e.g. loss or damage to cargo), to the crew (e.g. repatriation, medical expenses, etc.), collisions, fixed and floating objects (e.g. damage to docks, etc.), wreck removal, liabilities in respect of oil pollution, etc. Furthermore, the Clubs' rules contain a "pay to be paid" rule, according to which a member can only be reimbursed for claims it has actually paid. This means that the owner is responsible for payments. In practice, the Club will take over claims handling. The "pay to be paid" rule may generate frictions with the right of direct action against the insurer. It may be relevant to note on this point that under English law there is no direct action against the insurer. In *Shipowners' Mutual v Containerships Denizclik* (2015)[8] English judges dealt with an anti-suit injunction restraining direct action in Turkey against a P&I Club, and addressed the challenges faced by P&I Clubs in the context where certain jurisdictions pro-vide for direct action against insurers, thus providing a tool for putting aside the "pay to be paid" rule.

It should be clear that, as their name suggests, P&I clubs are not confined to the role of a robust insurer with the possibility to provide the security needed for the release of the offending ship. They also provide assistance, including legal assistance and expertise, to their members; they deal with the response/minimi-sation of the risk, gather and preserve evidence, and develop a strategy in relation to liability. They also act as a central point of contact for the management of

---

8 [2015] 1 Lloyd's Rep 567. It is noted that the decision was appealed in 2016. The anti-suit injunction was maintained and permission to appeal to the Supreme Court was refused.

occurrences that fall in their scope of activities. In this respect, they are assisted by P&I correspondents and local surveyors.

There is close cooperation for the handling of oil pollution claims between the 1992 Fund and P&I clubs in their capacity as the insurer of the shipowner. In the interest of clarity, it should be recalled at this point that in case of damage caused in a State that is only party to 1992 CLC, claims can only be made against the shipowner and his insurer; in the context of claims for damage in States that are party to 1992 CLC and 1992 Fund Convention, claims for damage may be made against the shipowner and his insurer and the Fund.

11.1.3 The involvement of salvors

Involved with marine casualty response, pollution defence, wreck removal, cargo recovery, towage and many other activities, salvors are key contributors to the protection of the marine environment. In addition to life salvage, the energy of salvors was primarily geared towards salvaging endangered property at sea. Triggered by the *Amoco Cadiz* accident, the 1989 Salvage Convention (entry into force 14 July 1996), was adopted in order to provide an international framework to salvage operations. The Convention defines salvage operations as the act or activity undertaken to assist a vessel or any other property in danger in navigable waters or in any other waters whatsoever.

Against this background, a shift can be observed in recent years from what can be viewed as property salvage to actions presenting an interest to the environment. One can easily think of situations where the oil laden on a tanker may exceed the value of the vessel as such, and where the escape or discharge of a potentially harmful cargo at sea following a casualty may be detrimental to humans and the environment. In this context, the involvement of salvors is central to preventing and/or limiting marine pollution, and it gives rise to a number of legal questions, mainly centered on their award.

The departing point is the legal regime governing salvage under the Salvage Convention and generally under standard contracts such as Lloyd's Open Form (LOF), which, despite a certain decline at present, constitutes, at least in some parts of the world, the most commonly used salvage contract.[9] The said regime is based on the principle "no cure, no pay". In broad terms, the salvage contract is concluded between the shipowner/master, the cargo interests, and the owners of all property on board. As noted by an authoritative commentator, "though the liability to pay salvage may be under contract, the nature and quantification of the claim are not recoverable by way of contract".[10] LOF is designed to be signed immediately with

---

9 Subject to English law and considered as a trusted instrument, LOF was initially published in 1908. Eleven versions (revisions) of LOF are noted, with the most recent dating to 2011 (LOF 2011). LOF adheres to the principle of "no cure, no pay" (LOF 1980 had departed from this principle). Interestingly LOF 1990 had incorporated the Salvage Convention before its entry into force. LOF 2011 incorporates Lloyd's Standard Salvage and Arbitration Clauses (LSSA), the Lloyd's Procedural Rules and, when this option is activated, the SCOPIC clause.

10 Susan Hodges, *Law of Marine Insurance* (Cavendish Publishing Limited, 1996, p. 429).

no negotiation of its terms; remuneration will be determined at a subsequent stage through arbitration in London.

Article 13 of the Convention, which comes into play when salvage produces a "useful result", sets out a number of criteria for the award of the salvor. The criteria in question should assist the adjudicators, arbitrators and judges in the determination of the award. They include, amongst others, the salved value of the property (vessel and other), the skills and efforts of salvors in preventing or minimising environmental damage,[11] the degree of success achieved by the salvor, etc.

A different kind of reward is spelt out in Article 14 of the Convention. This provision reflected an encouragement of salvors to provide assistance to ships threatening the environment. Failure to salve would not deprive salvors in this case from remuneration. Article 14 can be found below.

ARTICLE 14 OF THE 1989 SALVAGE CONVENTION

1. If the salvor has carried out salvage operations in respect of a vessel which by itself or its cargo threatened damage to the environment and has failed to earn a reward under article 13 at least equivalent to the special compensation assessable in accordance with this article, he shall be entitled to special compensation from the owner of that vessel equivalent to his expenses as herein defined.

2. If, in the circumstances set out in paragraph 1, the salvor by his salvage operations has prevented or minimised damage to the environment, the special compensation payable by the owner to the salvor under paragraph 1 may be increased up to a maximum of 30% of the expenses incurred by the salvor. However, the tribunal, if it deems it fair and just to do so and bearing in mind the relevant criteria set out in article 13, paragraph 1, may increase such special compensation further, but in no event shall the total increase be more than 100% of the expenses incurred by the salvor.

3. Salvor's expenses for the purpose of paragraphs 1 and 2 means the out-of-pocket expenses reasonably incurred by the salvor in the salvage operation and a fair rate for equipment and personnel actually and reasonably used in the salvage operation, taking into consideration the criteria set out in article 13, paragraph 1 (h), (i) and (j).

4. The total special compensation under this article shall be paid only if and to the extent that such compensation is greater than any reward recoverable by the salvor under article 13.

5. If the salvor has been negligent and has thereby failed to prevent or minimize damage to the environment, he may be deprived of the whole or part of any special compensation due under this article.

6. Nothing in this article shall affect any right of recourse on the part of the owner of the vessel.

---

11 Article 13(1)(b).

As a result of problems concerning the implementation of the special compensation set out in Article 14, the industry sought to find a more straightforward tool. It was in this context that the SCOPIC clause was adopted in 1999 seeking a remuneration that would be easy to make. SCOPIC revolves around fixed tariffs and a bonus. It is noteworthy that it puts aside the compensation flowing from Article 14. The salvor will use Article 13 until he chooses to invoke in writing the SCOPIC clause. SCOPIC remuneration is paid out by the shipowner, and only to the extent it goes beyond the reward stemming from Article 13 of the Salvage Convention. Technically speaking, SCOPIC 2011 is a set of sub-clauses operating as an addendum to Lloyd's Open Form. One of the advantages of the SCOPIC clause is that it is not conditional on a threat of damage to the environment. Furthermore, it is not dependent on a particular sea area (e.g. territorial waters).

Against this background which focuses on the basics, some selected terms mentioned in the main discussion are defined below.

11.2 Glossary

HNS (hazardous and noxious substances)	A substance is classed as HNS if it is included in one or more lists of IMO Conventions and Codes designed to ensure maritime safety and prevention of pollution.
Incident	Occurrence or series of occurrences with the same origin causing pollution damage or creating a grave or imminent threat of causing such damage (1992 CLC).
IOPCF (International Oil Pollution Compensation Funds)	It consists of the 1992 Fund, set up under the 1992 Fund Convention, and the 2003 Supplementary Fund. Intergovernmental organisations headquartered in London, sharing a secretariat. Involved (under conditions) with the financial compensation in Member States for oil pollution damage caused by spills of persistent oil from tankers.
Limitation of liability (in the context of pollution damage)	Legal device ensuring a ceiling, i.e. a financial limit that is known in advance, to the liability of the polluter to compensate. This is a form of civil (as opposed to penal) liability, and it stems from general (e.g. LLMC 1976, as amended), or specialised legal instruments applicable with variations on the international (1992 CLC, 1992 Fund Convention, 2003 Supplementary Fund Protocol, 2001 Bunkers Convention, 2010 HNS Convention, etc.) and/or domestic level (for example, limitation of liability under the Oil Pollution Act 1990 (OPA) in the USA initially caps exposure but through broad exceptions it may lead to unlimited liability).
Lloyd's Open Form (LOF)	Salvage standard agreement used for more than 100 years (the most recent dating to 2011 (LOF 2011)). Designed to be readily used in the context of a maritime casualty necessitating salvage on the basis of "No cure, no pay" principle, thus rewarding success but not the efforts. Remuneration of the salvor is based on arbitration in London administered by the Lloyd's Salvage Arbitration Branch.

(Continued)

Oil	Oil is defined by the 1992 CLC as any persistent hydrocarbon mineral oil. This notably includes crude oil, fuel oil, heavy diesel oil and lubricating oil, whether carried on board a ship as cargo or in the bunkers of such ship.
OPOL (Offshore Pollution Liability Agreement)	Voluntary oil pollution compensation scheme involving offshore operators active in exploration and production on the UK continental shelf and in other offshore areas in northwest Europe. In the scope of the scheme fall offshore facilities from which there is a risk of oil discharge causing pollution damage.
Pollution damage	The term means the loss or damage outside the ship caused by contamination resulting from the escape or discharge of oil from the ship (definition based on 1992 Civil Liability Convention (CLC)). It is noted that according to the same text, pollution damage also includes costs of preventive measures following the incident.
Protection and Indemnity (P&I) Club	Mutual associations of shipowners and charterers specialised in covering third party liabilities stemming from the operation of the ship (e.g. oil pollution, crew repatriation, wreck removal, etc.). They also provide legal and other expertise to their members in relation to risk exposure and claims-handling strategy.
Salvage operations	Activities undertaken to assist a ship or any other property endangered in navigable or other waters.
SCOPIC clause	SCOPIC clause is relevant to the calculation of the remuneration of the salvor for salvage operations regardless of environmental considerations; it puts aside the compensation flowing from Article 14 of the Salvage Convention which was adopted with a view to ensuring the cover of the expenses of the salvor in case of assistance to ships in need of salvage threating the environment. SCOPIC remuneration is paid by the shipowner, and only to the extent it goes beyond the reward stemming from Article 13 of the Salvage Convention, which is a provision setting out criteria for the calculation of the award of the salvor, and which includes a criterion on the skills and efforts of the salvor in preventing or minimising environmental damage. Technically speaking, SCOPIC 2011 is a set of sub-clauses operating as an addendum to Lloyd's Open Form.
STOPIA (Small Tanker Oil Pollution Indemnification Agreement) 2006 & TOPIA (Tanker Oil Pollution Indemnification Agreement) 2006	Voluntary schemes introduced by the International Group of Protection and Indemnity Clubs set out for compensation purposes, and functioning as contractually binding private agreements between the 1992 Fund (STOPIA) or the Supplementary Fund (TOPIA) and participating shipowners (entry into force on 20 February 2006; amended in 2016, amendment effective on 20 February 2017). The schemes seek to strike a balance on the financing of compensation as it stems from the 1992 Fund and the Supplementary Fund between the shipping and the oil industry.

Supplementary Fund	It was established following the adoption of the 2003 Supplementary Fund Protocol. It works in the framework of the 2003 Supplementary Fund Protocol which provides additional compensation to that available under the 1992 Fund Convention for pollution damage in the States concerned (financial limits of liability up to 750 SDRs including sums available under the 1992 CLC and the 1992 Fund Convention).
Wreck	It means a sunken or stranded ship; it may also mean any part of a sunken or stranded ship, including any object that is or has been onboard such a ship. The meaning also comprises any object that is lost at sea from a ship and that is stranded, sunken or adrift at sea, or a ship that is about, or may reasonably be expected, to sink or to strand, where effective measures to assist the ship or any property in danger are not already being taken (Nairobi Convention, see paragraph 11.9 below)

11.3 Types of liability in a nutshell

Liability of the polluter is generally structured over civil and criminal liability. Each form of liability has a distinct role in the control of anti-environmental behaviour. That said, civil and criminal law provisions may be related. In a number of legal systems, the degree of severity of sanctions for pollution damage is intended to invalidate the potential benefits from violating the law. Furthermore, the polluter may be exposed to disciplinary or other consequences. It is noted that international regulations do not spell out any sanctions for polluters, as this is within the remit of the national legislator. Nor are international *fora* such as the IMO empowered to deal or are entrusted with any mechanisms aimed at compliance and/or enforcement.

11.3.1 Civil liability

The polluter has to pay ("polluter pays" principle). In practice, it does so through insurance mechanisms. Civil liability primarily aims at the compensation of the victims of pollution damage. It may also include preventive measures following the incident for minimising adverse consequences. This is an area where civil liability is generally strict, in the sense that it does not require proving the fault or negligence of the polluter.

It is not our intention to focus on a particular national legal system or to exhaust the question of liability, including civil liability, in case of marine pollution. Given the limited confines of the book, some indicative highlights have been selected.

In the accident of the oil tanker *Erika* (1999), which sank off the coast of Brittany (France) on 12 December 1999 following a structural failure[12] causing

---

12 See Chapter I on marine pollution from oil.

305

large-scale pollution, the highest court in France[13] had held the cargo owner to be liable on civil grounds despite protection provided under international rules.[14] As it will be seen below, in the same case criminal liability was also spelt out against the cargo owner and some other entities.

With the above in mind, a facet of civil liability is the concept of channeling of liability. It signifies that the statutory party will be exclusively liable for marine pollution damage, and that other potentially related Parties which may have contributed to the damage will be protected. In other terms, no claims shall be made against certain entities explicitly identified in international conventions; the "protected" entities may differ from one convention to another, and there may be variations at the level of domestic law. An illustration in the context of oil pollution damage governed by the 1992 CLC Convention would be the protection provided to servants or agents of the owner and the members of the crew,[15] or the protection provided to pilots or "any other person, who, without being a member of the crew, performs services for the ship".[16] Thus, in this context (1992 CLC Convention), liability is channeled to the owner.[17] This is not the case, for example, with the 2001 Bunker Pollution Convention which governs liability for bunker spills from ships other than tankers. The Bunker Convention, which is examined below under paragraph 11.7, channels liability to the owner, including the registered owner, bareboat charterer, manager and operator of the ship. Where more than one person is liable, the Bunker Convention provides joint and several liability.[18]

11.3.2 Criminal liability

With details set out by each national system, the criminal liability of the polluter is generally additional to civil liability. Criminal sanctions such as orders to clean up, fines, imprisonment, etc. express social disapproval. They have a different nature than the obligation to compensate or administrative sanctions (e.g. administrative fines). Their function is to punish the polluter and to support and strengthen regulatory compliance. They are normally designed to be sufficiently severe to dissuade potential polluters from infringements. Polluters may also be placed on probation for a number of years and/or be subjected to compulsory environmental compliance programmes.

In the case of the above-mentioned case involving the *Erika* (1999), not only criminal liability was recognised by French judges against the representative of the registered owner and the president of the management company, but also against the classification society and the cargo owner.[19] Criminal liability against

---

13 Judgment of the Cour de Cassation dating to 25 September 2012, no. 3439.
14 See 1992 CLC Article III para. 4.
15 Article III para. 4(a).
16 Article III para. 4(b).
17 Article III para. 1.
18 Article 3(1) and (2) of the Bunker Convention.
19 Judgment of the Tribunal de Grande Instance de Paris dating to 16 January 2008, 11ème chambre, 4ème section. Judgment appealed before the Court of Appeal, no. 08/02278, judgment dating to 30 March 2010. A discussion of the legal proceedings before French courts and their interphase with

the classification society and the cargo owner can be viewed as highly uncommon with no, or in any case unclear, foundation under international law.

That said, criminal prosecution may be preceded by enquiries such as those conducted by the Marine Accident Investigation Branch (MAIB) in the context of the UK or similar bodies in other countries. Depending on the State, criminal prosecution may also involve environmental agencies entrusted with enforcement and prosecution powers. Depending also on the facts of each case, prosecution is likely to be conducted against the owner (i.e. the company) and/or crew members – an aspect which is determined by national legal systems. For example, deliberate pollution from ships, intentional falsification of records with a view to covering up pollution and obstruction of justice (practices commonly associated with the use of what is referred to as the "magic pipe") are considered to be serious crimes under the law of the USA, and they generally lead to criminal prosecutions involving the company and crew members (commonly the chief engineer).

In the context of English law, the Merchant Shipping Act (MSA 1995), as amended,[20] addresses criminal liability for oil spills, relevant defences, and the duty of the owner or master to report spills.[21] Furthermore, under the powers given to the Secretary of State by section 85 of the MSA 1995, a statutory instrument[22] was issued setting out offences and penalties in the context of the International Safety Management (ISM) Code. These are offences likely to be committed by the company, the master or the designated person ashore, or by any person.

In the same legal system, the Environmental Offences Definitive Guideline issued by the Sentencing Council in 2014[23] determines the approach to be followed by courts when they sentence certain environmental offences including, in relation to unauthorised or harmful deposit, treatment or disposal of waste, illegal discharge to air, land and water, etc. The Guideline specifies offence ranges within which category ranges have been set out in conjunction with degrees of seriousness. It applies to all individual offenders aged 18 and older and organisations that are sentenced on or after 1 July 2014. This is regardless of the date of the offence.[24] Every court must, in sentencing an offender, follow any sentencing guideline which is relevant to the offender's case, and must, in exercising any other function relating to the sentencing of offenders, follow any sentencing guidelines relevant to the exercise of the function, unless the court is satisfied that this is contrary to the interests of justice to do so.

In addition to the above, it is clear that companies may be held liable on the grounds of acts committed by their employees.[25] Yet, prosecution and liability

---

the international legal regime can be found in José Juste-Ruiz, European Courts Go Beyond the IMO Conventions on Civil Liability for Oil Pollution damage (Insight dating to 5 April 2013, MEPIELAN Centre E-bulletin).

20 See sections 131, as amended by section 7 of the Merchant Shipping Maritime Security Act (MSMSA) 1997, section 132–134, section 136 and section 143 of the MSA 1995.

21 A. Mandaraka-Sheppard, *Modern Maritime Law, Volume 2, Managing Risks and Liabilities* (3rd edition, Informa Law, Routledge, 2013, p. 872).

22 See regulation 19, SI 1998/1561.

23 In accordance with section 120 of the Coroners and Justice Act 2009.

24 See p. 2.

25 In the context of English law, see, amongst others, *The Lady Gwendoline* [1965] 2 All ER 283 and *HMS Truculent v The Divina* [1951] 2 All ER 968.

may also operate the other way round, i.e. legal proceedings may be brought in some cases against certain individuals within the company (in addition to proceedings against the company) for offences committed by the company.

Directors and managers commonly represent the directing mind and will of a company and control the company's actions.[26] The question of the possibility to legally prosecute and hold criminally liable the directors, managers or other officers of the company whose consent, connivance or neglect has led to the polluting incident has been a question of growing concern. The question of personal director liability is not new, as it has drawn the attention of regulators in the context of criminal law[27] or general environmental law,[28] and has led, in some countries, to a statutory framework in place. In the latter case, in presence of specific regulatory offences, proceedings against individuals, additionally or alternatively to the proceedings targeting the corporate polluter, have been set out. Their aim is to render possible prosecution and punishment not only at the level of the corporate entity but also, where appropriate, at the level of those who control the entity and are found to be complicit in offences committed by companies.

Criminal actions against directors and other officers of the company raise a number of legal points, which go beyond the confines of this discussion, including at the level of the so-called corporate veil – the corporate veil being the expression of the separation of the company, as an artificial entity, from those who own and manage it;[29] another concern is the identification of control (held by an individual) that would be sufficient so as to found liability.

> In the context of English law, according to section 277 of the Merchant Shipping Act (MSA) 1995:
>
> (1) Where a body corporate is guilty of an offence under this Act or any instrument made under it, and that offence is proved to have been committed with the consent or connivance of, or to be attributable to any neglect on the part of, a director, manager, secretary or other similar officer of the body corporate or any person who was purporting to act in such a capacity, he as well as the body corporate shall be guilty of that offence and shall be liable to be proceeded against and punished accordingly.
>
> (2) Where the affairs of a body corporate are managed by its members, subsection (1) above shall apply in relation to the acts and defaults of a member in connection with his functions of management as if he were a director of the body corporate.

---

26 In the context of English law, see, amongst others, *H.L. Bolton (Engineering) v T.J. Graham & Sons Limited* [1956] 3 All ER 624 and *Tesco Supermarkets Ltd v Nattrass* [1972] AC 153 (HL).

27 See, for example, section 14 of the Bribery Act 2010.

28 See Neil Hawke, 'Corporate Environmental Crime: Why Shouldn't Directors Be Liable?' [1997] The London Journal of Canadian Studies 13, 12–24. A comparative discussion of directors' personal liability is held in Helen Anderson (ed), *Director's Personal Liability for Corporate Fault – A Comparative Analysis* (Wolters Kluwer Law & Business, 2008).

29 *Salomon v A. Salomon & Co. Ltd.* [1897] AC 22.

Against this background, it can be said that in the shipping context the International Safety Management (ISM) Code, which establishes a safety management system and is highly relevant to marine pollution, provides additional criteria for the legal assessment of the actions or omissions of the individuals within the company in case of polluting incidents.[30]

Shifting from the domestic level to the regional level, an interesting point concerns the impact of European Union law on the legislation of Member States in this area. The criminal competence of the European Union is to some extent controversial; that said, the EU has taken interest in the criminal framework of ship-source pollution, as suggested by the EU Directive 2005/35 briefly presented below.

11.3.2.1 EU Directive 2005/35, as amended

European Union Directive 2005/35[31] on ship-source pollution and on the introduction of penalties for infringements, as amended by Directive 2009/23/EC, was adopted in recognition of a certain weaknesses on the level of MARPOL, including discrepancies affecting implementation. Aimed to incorporate international standards for ship-source pollution into EU law, Directive 2005/35/EC also seeks to ensure that persons responsible for discharges are subject to adequate penalties. It may be recalled at this point that the question of sanctions of marine pollution has been left by the international legislator to the competency of national regulators.[32] That said, the advisability of EU legislative measures on the matter had been questioned through legal proceedings brought forward by a number of shipping stakeholders.

In the interest of clarity, it is noted that Council Framework Decision 2005/667/ JHA on the strengthening of the criminal law framework for the enforcement of the law against ship-source pollution[33] aimed at complementing the Directive by setting out detailed rules over criminal issues.[34] However, on 23 October 2007 the European Court of Justice annulled the above-mentioned Framework Decision and Directive 2009/123/EC had to be adopted in order to cover the legal vacuum created by this development.

---

30 On the impact of the ISM Code on limitation of liability, see Mandaraka-Sheppard, *supra* note 21, p. 113 *seq.*

31 European Parliament and Council (EC) Directive 2005/35 on ship-source pollution and on the introduction of penalties for infringements [2005] L 255/11. The Directive was amended by European Parliament and Council (EC) Directive 2009/123 (Text with EEA relevance) [2009] L 280/52. For a discussion of Directive 2005/35/EC and its interphase with the international regime on ship-source pollution, see Iliana Christodoulou-Varotsi, 'Recent Developments in the EC Legal Framework on Ship-Source Pollution: The Ambivalence of the EC's Penal Approach' [Fall 2006] Transportation Law Journal, Vol. 33, No. 3, pp. 371–386.

32 See MARPOL Article 4.

33 Council Framework Decision 2005/667/JHA [2005] OJ L255/164.

34 On another level of discussion, it is noteworthy that the Directive is based on the so-called first institutional pillar of the EU, which represents binding law based on the EC Treaty that is subject to the control of the European Parliament and the European Court of Justice; this is not the case of the Framework Decision, which is governed by the third pillar, based, strictly speaking, on the EU Treaty. The last one is a text principally of intergovernmental nature. See Christodoulou-Varotsi, *supra* note 8.

As already mentioned in other chapters, EU Directives are not directly applicable in the legal systems of Member States, and they have to be introduced internally through transposition/harmonisation measures. Furthermore, Member States' performance in light of the requirements of Directives, which includes formal and/or substantial failure to transpose or achieve the goals of the Directive, is subject to the control of the European Court of Justice.

With the above in mind, the added value of Directive 2005/35, as amended, is to reshape to some extent at the EU level the international requirement on illegal discharges of oil, and to contribute to a revisited legal framework governing criminal sanctions. As already mentioned, according to MARPOL, sanctions must be adequate in severity to discourage violations and equally severe despite where the violations occur.[35] The Directive does not prevent Member States from taking more stringent measures against ship-source pollution in conformity with international law. According to the Directive illicit ship-source discharges of polluting substances (i.e. oil and noxious liquid substances in bulk) constitute a criminal offence provided they have been committed with intent, recklessly or with serious negligence and result in deterioration in the quality of the water. However, less serious cases of illicit ship-source discharges of polluting substances that do not cause deterioration in the quality of water need not be regarded as criminal offences. Under the Directive, these discharges would be considered as minor cases.[36] Repeated minor cases may be considered as criminal offences.

It should be stressed that private operators fall in the scope of the Directive through national transposition measures. Let us now focus on limitation of liability of the polluter.

SECTION 2: LIMITATION OF LIABILITY OF THE POLLUTER

11.4 The concept of limitation of liability in a nutshell

Limitation of liability of the shipowner is about the existence of a statutory ceiling of financial exposure for specified maritime claims. This limit to financial liability comes into play upon certain conditions and regardless of the actual amount of claims brought against the shipowner. The device on limitation of liability presents an interest which goes beyond the confines of marine pollution claims. Limitation is far from being a new device; it is considered by some to have existed around the eleventh century.[37] Initially practised through the abandonment of the ship (and pending freight) by the shipowner to its claimants, in the process, the system shifted towards limitation on the basis of the size of the vessel, i.e. by reference to the ship's tonnage.

---

35 MARPOL Article 4.
36 See Recital 9 of Directive 2005/35.
37 See Norman A. Martínez Gutiérrez, 'Limitation of Liability for Maritime Claims', in David Joseph Attard (General Ed), *The IMLI Manual on International Maritime Law*, Volume II, *Shipping Law* (Oxford University Press, Oxford, 2016, pp. 551–575).

The typical answer to the question why limitation of the financial liability of the shipowner (and other entities technically assimilated to the shipowner) is needed can be found in the high level of risk exposure of the shipping business; supporters of this device would advocate that no wise business person would ever assume such undertakings in the absence of limited liability. Despite criticism of the advisability of having a system on limitation of liability, limited liability clearly constitutes the reference nowadays.

IMO conventions addressing liability are briefly described below. It is noted that the Basel Convention, which is also relevant to the discussion on liability but is not an IMO instrument, was touched upon in the chapter on marine pollution from wastes. Because of its special interest, the legal regime governing liability in Antarctica has been included in this chapter as an additional highlight. Furthermore, as of today, there are no international regulations dealing with liability from pollution caused by unmanned vessels.

11.5 Global limitation of liability for maritime claims: the Convention on Limitation of Liability for Maritime Claims Convention (1976), as amended

The Convention on Limitation of Liability for Maritime Claims (LLMC) is a text on global limitation of liability; it was adopted in 1976 (entry into force 1 December 1986), and replaced a previous instrument on the matter.[38] Revised by the 1996 Protocol, which raised financial limits by approximately 250% in comparison with those set by the 1976 Convention, limits were further increased in 2012 (effective June 2015) through the tacit acceptance procedure. At the present stage, the LLMC, as amended, represents 55.83% of total world tonnage.[39]

It is not our intention to exhaust the Convention, whose interest, as already mentioned, goes beyond the confines of marine pollution damage. Being a global liability instrument, LLMC covers a wide range of claims[40] brought by persons entitled to limit. The said persons are the shipowner (which includes, owners, charterers, managers and operators of ships), salvors, any person for whose act, neglect or default the shipowner or salvor is responsible, and insurers of liability.[41] In broad terms, claims subject to limitation under LLMC include claims in relation to loss of life, personal injury or loss of or damage to property, claims for loss resulting from delay in the carriage of goods by sea of cargo, passengers or their luggage, claims for loss resulting from the infringement of rights other than contractual rights, claims for wreck and cargo removal, and claims in respect of measures taken in order to avert or minimise loss.[42]

---

38 LLMC replaced the International Convention Relating to the Limitation of the Liability of Owners of Seagoing Ships (adopted in 1957, entry into force in 1968).

39 As at June 2017.

40 See Article 2(1).

41 See Article 1.

42 See Article 2.

Amongst the types of claims excepted from limitation of liability,[43] one may identify claims for oil pollution damage within the meaning of the 1969 CLC, as amended.[44] Against this background, it may be relevant to note that not all oil pollution damage claims are excluded from the LLMC. Arguably, the LLMC provides a right of limitation for pollution damage caused by bunker spills. In this respect, it is noted by commentators that claims stemming from bunker oil spills would continue to be subject to limitation under LLMC following the adoption of the Bunker Convention, which primarily deals with the matter, as they are not covered by the definition of pollution damage under the CLC (unless they pertain to bunker spills of a tanker).[45] As it will be seen below under paragraph 11.7, limitation of liability in relation to pollution from ships' bunkers is governed by a specific IMO instrument.

In the above context, LLMC is relevant, as the graph below suggests, to limitation of liability on the grounds of general ship-sourced damage. As mention was made above of the CLC and the Bunkers Convention, it is also noted in the same graph that LLMC runs in parallel with a number of international instruments on limitation.[46] (The voluntary schemes mentioned in the graph will be explained in paragraph 11.6.1.) Furthermore, States are allowed to reserve the right to exclude from LLMC regime claims for damage relating to chemical pollution; more specifically, this concerns claims within the meaning of the International Convention on Liability and Compensation for Damage in Connection with the Carriage of Hazardous and Noxious Substances by Sea (referred to as HNS), 1996, as amended.[47]

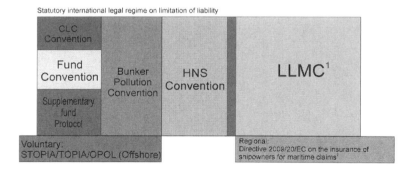

Graph 11.2 Limitation of liability in a nutshell (maritime sector)

Notes:
1. It applies to general ship-sourced damage (loss of life or personal injury and property claims) It runs in parallel with some international instruments.
2. Requires liability insurance covering the claims which fall in the scope of the LLMC up to the limits set out by the LLMC.

---

43 See Article 3.
44 Seer Article 3(b).
45 See Martínez Gutiérrez, *supra* note 37, p. 562.
46 See EMSA, EU *States Claims Management Guidelines – Claims arising due to marine pollution incidents* (2012) p. 16.
47 *Ibid.*, at. 20.

Like other international instruments dealing with limitation, the LLMC contains provisions on conduct which may bar limitation,[48] limits of liability (expressed in SDRs),[49] and on the constitution of a limitation fund. The regime set out by the Convention introduces a system which has been qualified by many as virtually unbreakable. Barring the right to limit liability would require investigating the actual state of mind of the person normally eligible to limit.

On a more technical note, and in contrast to other regimes, limitation of liability may operate even in the absence of the constitution of a limitation fund.[50] Some extracts from the provisions on the constitution and distribution of the fund are provided below:

ARTICLE 11: CONSTITUTION OF THE FUND

1. Any person alleged to be liable may constitute a fund with the Court or other competent authority in any State Party in which legal proceedings are instituted in respect of claims subject to limitation. The fund shall be constituted in the sum of such of the amounts set out in Articles 6 and 7 as are applicable to claims for which that person may be liable, together with interest thereon from the date of the occurrence giving rise to the liability until the date of the constitution of the fund. Any fund thus constituted shall be available only for the payment of claims in respect of which limitation of liability can be invoked.

2. A fund may be constituted, either by depositing the sum, or by producing a guarantee acceptable under the legislation of the State Party where the fund is constituted and considered to be adequate by the Court or other competent authority.

3. A fund constituted by one of the persons mentioned in paragraph 1(a), (b) or (c) or paragraph 2 of Article 9 or his insurer shall be deemed constituted by all persons mentioned in paragraph 1(a), (b) or (c) or paragraph 2, respectively.

ARTICLE 12: DISTRIBUTION OF THE FUND

1. Subject to the provisions of paragraphs 1, 2 and 3 of Article 6 and of Article 7, the fund shall be distributed among the claimants in proportion to their established claims against the fund [...].

Interestingly, the effectiveness of LLMC has been enhanced at the regional level through an EU instrument which requires liability insurance of the claims covered by the Convention.

11.5.1 European Union Directive 2009/20/EC

Directive 2009/20/EC[51] on the insurance of shipowners for maritime claims is part of a group of instruments adopted by the European Union which present

---

48 See Article 4.
49 See Articles 6, 7 and 8.
50 See Article 10(1).
51 European Parliament and Council (EC) Directive 2009/20 of 23 April 2009 on the insurance of shipowners for maritime claims (Text with EEA relevance), L 131/128, L 131/128, 28.5.2009.

an interest to the legal treatment of marine pollution (see Graph 11.3 below). Mention was made above of the Directive 2005/35/EC and Council Framework Decision 2005/667/JHA.

As the name of the Directive suggests, Directive 2009/20/EC lays down requirements relating to the obligation of shipowners to have their maritime claims insured. The Directive applies to ships of 300 gross tonnage or more. It may be relevant to note that the Directive operates without prejudice to the regimes in force in the European Union Member States concerned, and which are described in its annex. The regimes in question are the following: 1992 CLC, 1996 HNS, 2001 Bunker Oil Convention; and Nairobi Convention on the Removal of Wrecks, 2007, and EC Regulation 392/2009 on the liability of carriers of passengers by sea in the event of accidents.

The insurance in question is intended to cover maritime claims subject to limitation under the 1976 LLMC (Limitation of Liability for Maritime Claims), as amended by the 1996 Protocol. In the meaning of the Directive, "insurance means insurance with or without deductibles, and comprises, for example, indemnity insurance of the type currently provided by members of the International Group of P&I Clubs, and other effective forms of insurance (including proved self insurance) and financial security offering similar conditions of cover".[52] It is noted that the requirement on insurance involves not only ships flying the flag of a Member State, but also ships calling at EU ports or operating in Member States' territorial waters.[53]

In the graph below, a number of key EU instruments which present an interest to the legal regime governing certain aspects of marine pollution can be identified.

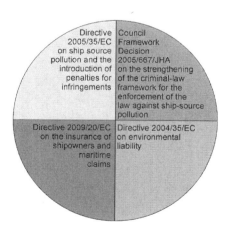

Graph 11.3 The European Union legal regime on marine pollution and environmental liability (as noted above, Council Framework Decision 2005/667/JHA was annuled)

---

52 See Article 3, para. (b).
53 See Article 4(1) and (2).

11.6 Limitation of liability for oil pollution damage: the 1992 Civil Liability Convention, the 1992 Fund Convention and the 2003 Supplementary Fund Protocol

Limitation of liability for marine oil pollution damage is shaped at the international level around the 1992 Civil Liability Convention (CLC), the 1992 Fund Convention and the 2003 Supplementary Fund Protocol. These IMO instruments are effective in a large number of States. In the interest of clarity, it should be noted that a State may have ratified one or all of these instruments. The implementation of the 1992 Fund Convention and of the Supplementary Fund Protocol involves the above-mentioned International Oil Pollution Compensation (IOPC) Funds.[54] The 1992 CLC, 1992 Fund and the 2003 Supplementary Fund Protocol constitute the "new" regime of reference, which provides higher levels of compensation in comparison with the old regime; in the last case, the instruments initially adopted on limitation of liability for marine oil pollution damage have either been denounced (this is the case of a large number of States in relation to the 1969 Civil Liability Convention) or have simply ceased to exist from a date onwards (this is the case of the 1971 Fund Convention, which ceased to be in force on 24 May 2002 and of the 1971 Fund, which ceased to exist from 31 December 2014). As at 2 June 2017, the 1992 CLC and 1992 Fund Convention have been respectively effective in 137 and 114 States.[55]

Furthermore, up to this stage, the vast majority of Parties (114 States) have adhered both to the 1992 CLC and the 1992 Fund Convention, and, consequently, are members of the 1992 Fund (e.g. Australia, Greece, Cyprus, the United Kingdom, etc.). There is a relatively small number of Parties to the 1992 CLC but which are not Parties to the 1992 Fund Convention, and therefore these Parties are not members of the 1992 Fund (e.g. Egypt, Jordan, Romania, etc.).

Thirty-four States are Parties to the 1969 CLC (as at 2 June 2017). Thirty-one States are Parties to the Supplementary Fund Protocol, and are consequently members of the Supplementary Fund (e.g. Australia, Greece, the United Kingdom, etc.).56

By becoming a Party to the 1992 CLC and the 1992 Fund Convention, in case of oil pollution damage caused by a tanker and *sustained* in a State Party, compensation is available regardless of the nationality of the tanker, the ownership of the oil or the place of the incident. Compensation is available to the stakeholders involved with clean-up operations or preventive measures (e.g. government and other authorities) as well as to private entities or individuals who have suffered damage as a result of the pollution.

The application of the 1992 CLC concerns oil pollution damage resulting from spills of persistent oil from tankers (see Glossary above). Owners of tankers are subjected to compulsory insurance, and must provide appropriate evidence

---

54 See IOPC Funds, *The International Regime for Compensation for Oil Pollution Damage, Explanatory note* (June 2017).

55 *Ibid.*, p. 1.

56 Reference as at 2 June 2017. *Ibid.*

through certification. Amongst others, compulsory insurance is required for tankers carrying more than 2,000 tonnes of persistent oil as cargo. Direct action against the insurer or other provider of financial security is provided for.

The owner of a tanker is strictly liable, i.e. no fault is needed for establishing liability. The Convention also states the circumstances under which the owner is exempted from liability.

> According to Article III, paragraph 2:
> No liability for pollution damage shall attach to the owner if he proves that the damage:
>
> (a) resulted from an act of war, hostilities, civil war, insurrection or a natural phenomenon of an exceptional, inevitable and irresistible character, or
> (b) was wholly caused by an act or omission done with intent to cause damage by a third party, or
> (c) was wholly caused by the negligence or other wrongful act of any Government or other authority responsible for the maintenance of lights or other navigational aids in the exercise of that function.
>
> Furthermore, the owner may be exonerated wholly or partially from his liability, if he:
>
> "proves that the pollution damage resulted wholly or partially either from an act or omission done with intent to cause damage by the person who suffered the damage or from the negligence of that person".
>
> (Article III, para. 3)

However, the benefit of limited liability may be lost. This is set out in Article V, paragraph 2:

> The owner shall not be entitled to limit his liability under this Convention if it is proved that the pollution damage resulted from his personal act or omission, committed with the intent to cause such damage, or recklessly and with knowledge that such damage would probably result.

Claims for compensation are made against the registered shipowner, not against other potentially related Parties (channeling of liability). This means that a number of persons are protected from claims. Protection is extended to the servants or agents of the owner or the members of the crew, the pilot, any charterer, manager or operator of the ship, the salvor, etc.[57]

Limits of liability are based on tonnage and have been expressed in Special Drawing Rights (SDR). Increased limits by more than 50% were provided by an amendment dating to 2000, and effective on 1 November 2003.

The 1992 Fund Convention represents the second tier of compensation. It was introduced in order to enhance protection by increasing the limits of financial liability; the text also seeks to strike the balance between the contribution of

---

57 Article III para. 4.

the shipping and the oil industry from the standpoint of financing. States that are Parties to the 1992 Fund Convention must have adhered to the 1992 CLC. The 1992 Fund Convention comes into play when full compensation under the 1992 CLC is not achieved. This includes the case where the shipowner benefits from an exemption under the 1992 CLC or when the shipowner's insurance cover fails or is inadequate or when the damage exceeds the shipowner's liability under the 1992 CLC. Financed by the oil industry, the 1992 Fund supports the implementation of the 1992 Fund Convention. While most claims tend to be settled out of court, legal proceedings on the grounds of the 1992 Fund Convention against the 1992 Fund may only be brought before the courts of a State Party to that Convention under the conditions stemming from the instrument (damage suffered in the territory, territorial sea or exclusive economic zone (EEZ) or equivalent area of that State).

A third tier of compensation has been introduced by the 2003 Supplementary Fund Protocol (entry into force on 3 March 2005). The purpose of the additional tier was to increase further the limits of liability for the compensation of pollution damage in the States Parties to the Protocol. As it can be seen below in Table 11.1, the total amount available for compensation is 750 million SDR, including the first and the second tiers. A Supplementary Fund has been set out for the purpose, which is administered by the 1992 Fund Secretariat. Any Party to the 1992 Fund may join the Supplementary Fund. As at present, 31 States are Parties to the Supplementary Fund Protocol.

In the graph below (Graph 11.4) the maximum limits of compensation under the 1992 CLC, the 1992 Fund Convention and the Supplementary Fund Protocol can be identified and compared. In the table which follows (Table 11.1) the main features of the three regimes are highlighted in a comparative manner.

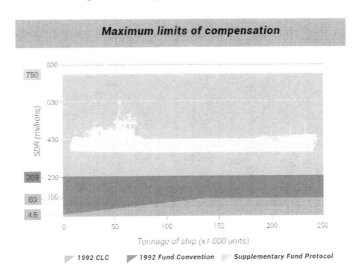

Graph 11.4 Maximum limits of compensation

Source: Reproduced with the permission of the International Oil Pollution Compensation Funds (www.iopcfunds.org)

Table 11.1 Simplified table of the main features of the 1992 CLC, the 1992 Fund Convention and the 2003 Supplementary Fund Protocol

	1992 Civil Liability Convention (CLC) with 2000 Amendments	*1992 Fund Convention with 2000 Amendments*	*2003 Supplementary Fund Protocol*
What type of oil pollution is covered?	Pollution damage caused by "*any persistent hydrocarbon mineral oil such as crude oil, fuel oil, heavy diesel oil and lubricating oil whether carried on board a ship as cargo or in the bunkers of such a ship*". • Ship means "*any sea-going vessel and seaborne craft of any type whatsoever constructed or adapted for the carriage of oil in bulk as cargo…*". • This includes a ship capable of carrying oil and other cargoes when the ship is actually carrying oil in bulk as cargo or during any voyage following such carriage (unless no oil residues remain on board).		
What type of pollution damage is compensation available for?	Pollution damage includes: • "*loss or damage caused outside the ship by contamination resulting from the escape or discharge of oil from the ship, wherever such escape or discharge may occur…*"; • costs of preventive measures taken after the incident to prevent or minimise pollution damage and further loss or damage caused by preventive measures. N.B. Compensation for "impairment of the environment other than loss of profit" is limited to the costs of "reasonable measures of reinstatement actually undertaken or to be undertaken".		
Geographical scope	Compensation is available – irrespective of where the incident itself occurred – in respect of pollution damage suffered in the territory, territorial sea, and exclusive economic zone (EEZ) or equivalent area of a Contracting State to the relevant legal instrument. Compensation is also available for preventive measures "wherever taken".		
Who is compensation available for?	For persons who suffer pollution damage in Contracting States to the 1992 CLC only, after the Convention has entered into force for the State concerned.	For persons who suffer pollution damage in contracting States to the 1992 CLC and the 1992 Fund Convention only, after the 1992 Fund Convention has entered into force for the State concerned.	For persons who suffer pollution damage in Contracting States to the 1992 CLC, the 1992 Fund Convention and the 2003 Supplementary Fund Protocol only, after the Protocol has entered into force for the State concerned.

Type of liability imposed	Strict liability of registered shipowner (or insurer) only, for pollution damage caused by oil that escaped or was discharged from his ship.	Liability of 1992 IOPC Fund where compensation provided under 1992 CLC is inadequate or unavailable because: • No liability for damage arises under the 1992 CLC; • The shipowner liable under the 1992 CLC is financially incapable of meeting his obligations in full or his insurance is insufficient to satisfy the claims for compensation;	Liability of Supplementary IOPC Fund for "established claims" only.
Who can be sued? Exemptions from liability	Shipowner or insurer only. Where pollution damage: • Resulted from an act of war, hostilities, civil war, insurrection or a natural phenomenon "*of an exceptional inevitable and irresistible character*";	• Because the damage exceeds the amount of the shipowner's limited liability under the 1992 CLC. 1992 IOPC Fund. Where pollution damage: • Resulted from an act of war, hostilities, civil war, or insurrection; • Was caused by oil which escaped from a warship or other State-owned ship being used for non-commercial activities;	Supplementary IOPC Fund. The Supplementary IOPC Fund is available for established claims only so no further exemptions or exclusions are applicable. Compensation may however be denied temporarily or permanently where a Contracting State has not fulfilled its reporting obligations under the Protocol.

(*Continued*)

Table 11.1 (Continued)

	1992 Civil Liability Convention (CLC) with 2000 Amendments	1992 Fund Convention with 2000 Amendments	2003 Supplementary Fund Protocol
	• Was wholly caused by an intentional act or omission of a third party; • Was wholly caused by the negligence or wrongful act of any Government or other authority responsible for maintaining lights or navigational aids. The insurer is entitled to use the same defences as the shipowner.	• Where the claimant cannot prove that the pollution damage resulted from an incident involving one or more ships. The 1992 Fund will however be obliged to compensate "mystery spills" where it is proved that the oil originated from a ship, but the ship cannot be identified.	
Defence of claimant's "contributory negligence"	Available to shipowner and insurer.	Available to the 1992 IOPC Fund. However, the Fund will not be discharged from liability in respect of preventive measures.	Not applicable.
Right of recourse against third Parties	Available to shipowner and insurer.	Not applicable.	Not applicable.
Monetary limit of liability	Based on ship's tonnage: • Less than 5,000 grt = 4,510,000 SDR; • Between 5,000 and 140,000 grt = 4,510,000 plus 631 SDR for each unit of additional tonnage; • More than 140,000 grt = maximum limit of 89,770,000 SDR. The shipowner's insurer will be entitled to the same limits as the shipowner.	In respect of any one incident, the maximum amount available from the 1992 IOPC Fund is 203 million SDR, inclusive of any compensation paid under the 1992 CLC. Where pollution damage is caused by a natural disaster, the maximum amount available is also 203 million SDR. Where three contributing Parties to the 1992 IOPC Fund receive 600 million tonnes or more of "contributing oil" during the preceding calendar year, limits are raised to 300,740,000 SDR.	In respect of any one incident, the maximum amount available from the Supplementary IOPC Fund is 750 million SDR. This amount is inclusive of any compensation actually paid under the 1992 CLC and the 1992 Fund Convention.

Loss of monetary limit of shipowner's liability	Where it is proved that the pollution damage resulted from an intentional or reckless act or omission of the shipowner. The insurer is nevertheless entitled to the shipowner's limits of liability.	Not applicable.	Not applicable.
Obligations to be fulfilled to benefit from limitation of liability	Constitution of a limitation fund by the shipowner for the total sum representing the limit of liability. The insurer is also entitled to constitute a limitation fund on the same conditions and having the same effect as if it were constituted by the shipowner.	Not applicable.	Not applicable.
Compulsory insurance required?	For ships, wherever registered, carrying more than 2,000 tonnes of oil in bulk as cargo only.	Not applicable.	Not applicable.
Insurance certification required?	Yes, for ships required to have compulsory insurance.	Not applicable.	Not applicable.
Direct action against the insurer for claimants?	Yes, up to the maximum amount of the shipowner's liability.	Not applicable.	Not applicable.
When will the insurer's liability be excluded?	• Where the shipowner's liability is excluded under the Convention; • Where the pollution damage resulted from the willful misconduct of the shipowner.	Not applicable.	Not applicable.
Jurisdiction	Exclusive jurisdiction of the Contracting State(s) where the pollution damage was suffered.	Exclusive jurisdiction of the Contracting State(s) where the pollution damage was suffered.	Exclusive jurisdiction of the Contracting State(s) where the pollution damage was suffered.

(*Continued*)

Table 11.1 (Continued)

	1992 Civil Liability Convention (CLC) with 2000 Amendments	1992 Fund Convention with 2000 Amendments	2003 Supplementary Fund Protocol
Time bar	Within three years from the date when the damage occurred; and in no case after six years from the date of the incident which caused the damage.	Within three years from the date when the damage occurred; and in no case after six years from the date of the incident which caused the damage.	Within three years from the date when the damage occurred; and in no case after six years from the date of the incident which caused the damage.
Contributions	Not applicable.	Annual contributions by oil importers who receive in any calendar year, total quantities of "contributing oil" exceeding 150,000 tonnes, which has been carried by sea to the ports or terminal installations in a Contracting State. If no person receives the requisite quantities of "contributing oil", no contributions need to be made.	Annual contributions by oil importers who receive in any calendar year, total quantities of "contributing oil" exceeding 150,000 tonnes, which has been carried by sea to the ports or terminal installations in a Contracting State. It is deemed by the Protocol that a minimum of 1 million tonnes of "Contributing oil" is received in each contracting State. Where the aggregate amount of "contributing oil" received is less than 1 million tonnes, the contracting State is liable to pay contributions for the difference between the amount of oil actually received in that State and 1 million tonnes.

Reporting requirements	Not applicable.	Contracting States must report to the 1992 IOPC Fund the name and address of any person that is liable to contribute to the Fund, including data on the relevant quantities of "contributing oil" received.	Contracting States must report to the Supplementary IOPC Fund the name and address of any person that is liable to contribute to the Fund, including data on the relevant quantities of "contributing oil" received. Reports made under the 1992 Fund Convention will be deemed made under the 2003 Supplementary Fund Protocol also.

Source: UNCTAD/DTL/TLB/2011/4, *Liability and Compensation for Ship Source Pollution: An Overview of the International Legal Framework for Oil Pollution Damage from Tankers* (http://unctad.org/ttl/legal)

In the simplified table above stemming from the United Nations Conference on Trade and Development (UNCTAD), the mean features of the 1992 CLC/Fund Convention and 2003 Supplementary Fund were identified. The table should be read in conjunction with the international conventions.

With the above in mind, an illustration of how the 1992 CLC and the 1992 Fund Convention have operated in practice is provided below. This is in the context of the accident of the *Prestige* (2002).[58]

> When the Bahamas flagged oil tanker *Prestige* (42,820 GT), laden with heavy fuel oil, sank off Galicia (Spain) on November 2002, it caused an estimated 63,200 tonnes spill, and triggered a large wave of claims and legal proceedings, which have not entirely crystallised up to present. The international legal framework was, once again, put to the test from the standpoint of its capacity to deal promptly and adequately with the financial consequences of a large-scale polluting incident. Hundreds of claims were made totaling 1,037 million euros. Claims stemming from private entities as well as from the Spanish, the French, and the Portuguese Governments, were the result of an exceptionally catastrophic casualty which had affected the coasts of respective countries. It should be noted from the outset that at the time of the casualty, the vessel was insured for oil pollution liability with a P&I Club, and that Spain, France and Portugal were Parties to the 1992 CLC and the 1992 Fund Convention. These aspects are fundamental for the understanding of proceedings.
>
> The CLC limit was 18.9 million SDR (which corresponded at that time to 22,777,986 Euros), an amount which was deposited by the owner with the criminal court in Spain in order to constitute the limitation fund required under the 1992 CLC. In the process, the incident also involved the 1992 Fund. With the CLC and the Fund limit put together, the ceiling reached 135 million SDR (171,520,703 euros). According to the IOPC Funds, the total compensation paid amounted to 120.8 million Euros.[59]
>
> The case involved proceedings and developments on numerous levels, including criminal and civil levels. These aspects were primarily addressed in the context of Spanish law.
>
> Concerning criminal proceedings in Spain, about 2,531 claims were made before the criminal court in Spain. Civil claims were submitted in the criminal proceedings (as required under Spanish law). The criminal court was therefore acting as a limitation court faced with compensation claims for losses sustained as a result of the spill.
>
> The judgment of the criminal court was issued on 13 November 2013. The master and the chief engineer of the *Prestige* and the civil servant involved with the decision on the controversial use of places of refuge in Spain were not held criminally liable for damage to the environment. However, the Greek master was convicted on the grounds of disobeying the Spanish authorities. In the context of Spanish law, criminal judges could declare civil liability in case of criminal offence. This was an obstacle to civil liability, which was technically put aside at this stage. It is noted

---

58 A detailed overview of legal proceedings and liability issues can be found in the fact sheet concerning the *Prestige* by the IOPC Funds. On the causes of the *Prestige*, see, amongst others, the report on the *Prestige* by the Bahamas Maritime Authority (2004).

59 It is noteworthy that STOPIA and TOPIA were not applicable then.

that the court had held that the limitation fund established by the P&I club was at the disposal of the club, which would decide about its distribution.

Following appeals against the judgment of the criminal court, the case reached the Supreme Court. In January 2016, the Supreme Court put aside the judgment of the criminal court and found the master to be guilty of a crime against the environment; these developments gave rise to an appeal lodged by the master. The court also examined civil liabilities. It recognised the applicability of the 1992 CLC, and examined liability in relation to the shipowner and the master in light of the channelling of liability (this concerned the registered owner), and the protection granted by the Convention to the master. Considering that there was recklessness and knowledge that the damage could occur, the court held that the shipowner and the master could not benefit respectively from limited liability or protection by virtue of the Convention. Strict liability of the 1992 Fund was recognised. The civil liability of the master was recognised by the court. Further proceedings were conducted, amongst others, in view of identifying losses.

Additional legal actions relating to the incident on a number of liability questions had taken place in France and in the USA involving the classification society of the ship. Not all aspects have crystallised up to this stage.

The conclusion one may draw from the above is that the international regime governing liability provides solutions to highly complex issues resulting from large-scale polluting incidents only to some extent. Furthermore, it is clear that there are factors that cannot be fully controlled. In practice, this means that depending on the features of each case and the national legal system involved, it has not been possible to eliminate entirely legal uncertainty on the matter.

In this context, private initiatives as the ones described below have sought to reshape the balance involving the financing of compensation.

11.6.1 The Small Tanker Oil Pollution Indemnification Agreement 2006 and the Tanker Oil Pollution Indemnification Agreement 2006

As already mentioned, the Small Tanker Oil Pollution Indemnification Agreement (STOPIA) 2006 and the Tanker Oil Pollution Indemnification Agreement (TOPIA) 2006 are voluntary schemes representing compensation packages (entry into force on 20 February 2006; amended in 2016, amendment effective on 20 February 2017). They were introduced by the International Group of Protection and Indemnity Clubs in an attempt to revisit the balance between the contribution of shipowners and the oil industry to the financing of compensation for oil pollution damage in the framework of the 1992 Fund Convention and the 2003 Supplementary Fund Protocol. It may be recalled at this point that under the 1992 Fund Convention and the Protocol, financing of compensation stems from the oil industry. Once the 1992 Fund and the Supplementary Fund have provided a compensation, they will be indemnified by the shipowner concerned, depending on the case, in accordance with the terms of STOPIA 2006 and TOPIA 2006 – the said schemes functioning as contractually binding private agreements.

11.7 Limitation of liability for pollution from bunkers: the 2001 Bunker Pollution Convention

The Bunkers Convention (International Convention on Civil Liability for Bunker Oil Pollution Damage) was adopted by the IMO in 2001 (entry into force on 21 November 2008). The instrument currently covers more than 92% of the world tonnage.

Let us note from the outset that the 1992 CLC and the 1992 Fund Convention are relevant to bunker pollution damage where the bunker oil escapes from a tanker. The adoption of an international text on pollution caused by bunker fuel became necessary in recognition, amongst others, of the gaps of the existing instruments on limitation of liability (bunker oil spills from non-tankers, including general cargo ships), the significant quantities of bunker fuel onboard ships other than tankers, and the harm that bunker oil is likely to cause, especially in light of its quality; potentially high clean-up costs incurred by this type of pollution were an additional factor. Bunker spills are not confined to minor spills occurring during bunkering operations; they may also result from accidents. It is noteworthy that disposal of the oil recovered during clean-up operations may also be a problem. Relatively recent casualties reported to involve bunker fuel oil include the *Rena* (2011) off the coast of New Zealand, the *Marathassa* (2015) in English Bay, Vancouver, Canada, the *Aframax River* (2016) on Houston Ship Channel, USA, etc.

The Bunkers Convention is structured over strict liability with limited exceptions from liability, obligatory insurance, and limitation of liability through reference to other instruments. These features will be explained below.

The Convention covers liability flowing from incidents which cause pollution damage or create a grave and imminent threat to cause pollution damage. Bunker oil is central to the meaning of pollution damage under the Convention. It means hydrocarbon mineral oil, including lubricating oil, used or intended to be used for the operation or propulsion of the ship as well as the residues from the use of such oil.[60] Within the scope of the Convention fall not only pollution damage but also preventive measures.[61] "Pollution damage" is defined by the Convention as "a loss or damage caused outside the ship by contamination resulting from the escape or discharge of bunker oil from the ship, wherever such escape or discharge may occur, provided that compensation for impairment of the environment other than loss of profit from such impairment shall be limited to costs of reasonable measures of reinstatement actually undertaken or to be undertaken". Pollution damage also means "the costs of preventive measures and further loss or damage caused by preventive measures".[62] Furthermore, pollution damage covered by the Convention must be caused in the territory, including the territorial sea, of a State Party, or in the State Party's Exclusive Economic Zone.[63]

---

60 Article 1(5) of the Bunker Convention.
61 Article 2.
62 See Article 1(9).
63 See Article 2.

Preventive measures taken to prevent or minimise pollution damage are covered "wherever taken".[64]

Ships covered by the Convention are seagoing vessels and seaborne craft "of any type whatsoever".[65] The liability regime applies to all ships but compulsory insurance[66] is required from registered owners for ships larger than 1,000 GT. This is a "strict liability" regime, not requiring proving the fault of the shipowner (or other eligible entities[67]), allowing for a direct action against the insurer.[68]

Contrary to similar instruments on limitation of liability, the Bunkers Convention does not set out any limits of liability. The approach adopted by the Convention consists to allow the shipowner or his insurer to limit liability with reference to other instruments. In this context, the instruments of reference are any applicable national or international regime, the above-mentioned LLMC on global limitation included. Consequently, limits of liability of the shipowner will be shaped in practice on the applicable regime in the State concerned, national or international in origin (e.g. LLMC 1976, as amended). The result of this approach entails the risk to have bunker pollution damage claims not being subjected to a truly uniform regime despite the existence of an international text; this is additional to the risk of exposure to unlimited liability in some national systems.

Like similar instruments, the Convention sets out the circumstances under which no liability shall attach to the shipowner[69] or when the shipowner is exonerated wholly or partially from liability;[70] furthermore, a number of exclusions from the entitlement to limit liability are set out.[71]

11.8 Limitation of liability for pollution from chemicals: the 2010 HNS Convention

Carriage of hazardous and noxious substances (HNS) by sea represents nowadays a voluminous trade and, as such, it gives rise to challenges, including the risk of chemical pollution, and the imperative to ensure compensation.[72] More than 6,000 substances have been classified at the international level as HNS. As discussed in Chapter 6, chemicals in the form of bulk cargoes or packaged goods may generate adverse effects on humans and the environment, and trigger the liability of the polluter. A number of casualties involving chemical

---

64 *Ibid.*

65 See Article 1(1).

66 See Article 7.

67 See Article 1(3).

68 See Article 7(10).

69 See Article 3(3).

70 See Article 3(4).

71 Article 4.

72 An interesting discussion of liability and compensation regime governing HNS on the international and domestic level, can be found in Transport Canada, *Maritime Transport of Hazardous and Noxious Substances: Liability and Compensation*, Discussion Paper, International Maritime Policy (October 2010).

pollution can be identified such as *The Princess of the Stars* (2008), carrying pesticides, the *Napoli* (2007), with explosives, flammables and pollutants, the *Fu Shan Hai* (2003), carrying potash, the *Bow Mariner* (2004), laden with ethanol, the *Samho Brother* (2005), involving benzene, the *Ievoli Sun* (2000), syrene, methyl-ethyl-ketone, the *Co-Op Venture* (2002), corn, the *Adamandas* (2003), deoxidized iron balls, or the *Ascania* (1999), vinyl acetate. These accidents have involved respectively the main categories of chemicals, ranging from products transported in packages and containers, to dissolvers, floater, sinkers, gases or evaporators in bulk.

The 1996 HNS Convention, amended by a protocol dating to 2010, has been the response of the international regulator to the problem. Despite attempts to simplify the regime in question, the Convention (text referred to as 2010 HNS Convention) has not entered into force up to this stage. The small number of ratifications may be partly attributed to the features of the Convention, including the duty to report the quantities of HNS received by sea in the territory concerned, or the setting up of a reporting system for packaged goods.

A substance is classed as HNS by the Convention if it is comprised in one or more lists of conventions and codes adopted by the IMO designed to ensure maritime safety and prevention of pollution. Substances covered also comprise oils and petroleum products such as gasoline, light diesel oil and kerosene, which are not grasped by the 1992 CLC/Fund Convention – oil being defined under CLC as any persistent oil.[73]

Persistent oil is of interest to CLC/Fund Conventions and the 2010 HNS Convention but in a different manner. The CLC/Fund Conventions cover pollution damage by persistent oil; the HNS Convention covers non-pollution damage (e.g. personal injury) caused by persistent oil, i.e. damage caused by fire or explosion.

The Convention aims to compensate claimants for damage arising from the international or domestic carriage of HNS by seagoing vessels. The Convention is centered on a two-tier liability regime, and on a shared liability between shipowners (first tier), who compensate in the first place, and receivers or importers of HNS cargo (second tier), who supplement, if needed. Contrary to the CLC and Fund Conventions, this tiered regime has been accommodated in a single text. Obligatory insurance of shipowners for ships registered in a State Party transporting HNS is set out. The HNS Fund, which represents the complementary tier, will require contributions made post-event, i.e. contributions due upon happening of the incident. Contributors are entities located in a ratifying State which in the preceding calendar year received a determined quantity of persistent oil, LPG, LNG or any other bulk HNS cargo (in the latter case, including oils other than persistent oil).

Depending on the place of the incident, the damage to be covered varies. Consequently, the territorial scope of the Convention is not uniform. This aspect can be seen below, where Article 3 of the HNS Convention is presented.

---

73 UNCTAD, p. 35.

ARTICLE 3 OF THE HNS CONVENTION

The Convention shall apply exclusively:

(a) to any damage caused in the territory, including the territorial sea, of a State Party;

(b) to damage by contamination of the environment caused in the Exclusive Economic Zone of a State Party, established in accordance with international law, or, if a State Party has not established such a zone, in an area beyond and adjacent to the territorial sea of that State determined by that State in accordance with international law and extending not more than 200 nautical miles from the baselines from which the breadth of its territorial sea is measured;

(c) to damage, other than damage by contamination of the environment, caused outside the territory, including the territorial sea, of any State, if this damage has been caused by a substance carried on board a ship registered in a State Party or, in the case of an unregistered ship, on board a ship entitled to fly the flag of a State Party; and

(d) to preventive measures, wherever taken, to prevent or minimize such damage as referred to in (a), (b) and (c) above.

It is noteworthy that damage from HNS on land before or after carriage by sea, as well as damage caused by radioactive material in bulk or packaged form, is not covered by the Convention.

Specific limitation ceilings have been set out by the instrument. However, the Convention has not entered into force. Consequently, relevant limits are not currently applicable at the international level. National limits are likely to be applicable, which may vary. Under the first tier, the ceilings range on the basis of the tonnage of the vessel. They range from 10 million SDR for bulk HNS and 11.5 million SDR for packaged HNS, to 100 million SDR for bulk HNS and 115 million SDR for packaged HNS. Additional coverage may stem from the HNS Fund, when claims under the first tier exceed liability. The additional protection provided by the second tier would reach 250 million SDR, including the contribution of the shipowner.

11.9 Liability of the shipowner in the context of wreck removal: the 2007 Nairobi Convention

Not only may shipwrecks be a problem to navigation and safety, they may also be a source of marine pollution (on the definition of "wreck" see the Glossary under paragraph 11.2). With the vast majority of wrecks dating to the Second World War, there is a risk due to corrosion that dangerous substances or contents are released into the oceans.[74] Interestingly, inventories of potentially pollut-

---

74 See Council of Europe, Resolution 1869(2012) adopted on 9.3.2012, Doc. 12872, 'The Environmental Impact of Sunken Shipwrecks'.

ing wrecks drafted by various stakeholders identified more than 8,500 wrecks around the world. Wreck-removal operations are generally considered complex and highly expensive (e.g. the *Costa Concordia*). Wrecks generally give rise to a number of important legal questions involving liability and insurance. It is observed that most casualties leading to shipwrecks tend to happen in territorial waters, a sea area which is not fully covered by the international instrument intended to deal with the problem.

The Nairobi International Convention on the Removal of Wrecks 2007 was adopted by the international community on 18 May 2007 (entry into force on 14 April 2015).[75] This is the international text which provides for uniform rules on the removal of wrecks located beyond territorial waters (the Convention can be extended, however, to the territorial sea of a State; this is the case, for example, of the United Kingdom). It is noted on this point that States have their own legal regime governing wreck removals within their territorial waters. Moreover, in order to prevent and mitigate marine pollution threats that would affect States concerned, wreck removal from the exclusive economic zone (EEZ) of States is supported by other international instruments. These are the International Convention relating to Intervention on the High Seas in Cases of Oil Pollution Casualties 1969, as amended, or the Protocol relating to Intervention on the High Seas in Cases of pollution by Substances other than Oil (the Intervention Conventions).

The Nairobi Convention sets out the strict liability of the registered owner in relation to the costs of locating, marking and removing the hazard represented by a wreck, following a lawful order of a competent authority. The registered owner has limited liability on the basis of the tonnage of its ship for property claims under the 1976 LLMC, as amended. Registered owners of 300 gross tonnage and over registered in a State Party to the Convention or entering or leaving a port in the territory of a State Party are required to take out insurance or ensure other financial security in order to cover wreck-removal costs. A right of direct action of States against insurers has also been provided. Ships registered in a State Party are held to obtain certificates from that State.

It should be emphasised that the Convention on the Protection of the Underwater Cultural Heritage has a different scope than the above instrument as it applies to wrecks at least 100 years old, and not to wrecks of commercial nature.[76]

11.10 Liability stemming from maritime carriage of radioactive substances

As discussed earlier, under the 1976 LLMC, as amended, some claims are excepted from limitation of liability. Amongst others, this is the case of claims

---

75 Patrick Griggs CBE, 'Law of Wrecks', in David J. Attard (General Ed), *The IMLI Manual on International Maritime Law*, Volume II, *Shipping Law* (Oxford University Press, Oxford, 2016, pp. 502–512).

76 See J. Rogowska and J. Namiésik, 'Environmental Risk Assessment of WWII Shipwreck Pollution', in S.K. Sharma and R. Sanghi (eds), *Wastewater Reuse and Management* (Springer, 2013) p. 475 *seq.*

(subject to international or national provisions governing or prohibiting limitation of liability) for nuclear damage.[77]

Furthermore, according to the Paris Convention of 29 July 1960 on Third Party Liability in the Field of Nuclear Energy and its Additional Protocol of 28 January 1964 and the Vienna Convention of 21 May 1963 on Civil Liability for Nuclear Damage, in case of damage caused by a nuclear incident occurring in the course of maritime carriage of nuclear material covered by such Conventions, the operator of a nuclear installation is the person liable for such damage.[78] The Paris Convention, which was adopted under the auspices of the OECD Nuclear Energy Agency, and the Vienna Convention, which was adopted by the International Atomic Energy Agency, apply to liability for nuclear damage caused by a nuclear accident, or in the course of transport of nuclear material to or from a nuclear installation.

Aimed at ensuring clarity and that the operator of a nuclear installation will be exclusively liable for damage caused by a nuclear incident occurring in the course of maritime carriage of nuclear material, the Convention Relating to Civil Liability in the Field of Maritime Carriage of Nuclear Material was adopted by the IMO on 17 December 1971 (entry into force 15 July 1975) (see Article 1 below). The Convention says that any person who might be held liable for damage caused by a nuclear incident under any international or national law applicable in the field of maritime transport shall be exonerated, upon conditions, from such liability.

ARTICLE 1 (NUCLEAR)

Any person who by virtue of an international convention or national law applicable in the field of maritime transport might be held liable for damage caused by a nuclear incident shall be exonerated from such liability:

(a) if the operator of a nuclear installation is liable for such damage under either the Paris or the Vienna Convention, or

(b) if the operator of a nuclear installation is liable for such damage by virtue of a national law governing liability for such damage, provided that such law is in all respects as favourable to persons who may suffer damage as either the Paris or the Vienna Convention.

Contrary to the above, liability involving the Antarctic does not flow from an IMO convention. The related regime is, however, briefly discussed below as a subject of rising interest.[79]

---

77 See Article 3(c).

78 The Convention on Supplementary Compensation for Nuclear Damage (CSC) is also noted. It was adopted in 1997 by the International Atomic Energy Agency (entry into force 15 April 2015) together with the Protocol to Amend the Vienna Convention in order to increase the amount of compensation available in the event of a nuclear incident through.

79 On the growing interest of the protection of the Antarctic, see, amongst others, *Maritime Executive*, Plastic Pollution in the Antarctic Worse than Expected (19 June 2017).

11.11 Liability and the protection of the Antarctic

The Arctic, often referred to as an ocean surrounded by a continent, and the Antarctic, a continent surrounded by an ocean, have clearly been in the spotlight in recent years. An illustration of this is the adoption of the Polar Code (International Code of Safety for Ships Operating in Polar Waters), touched upon in previous chapters (entry into force 1 January 2017). While Arctic and Antarctic waters have a number of similarities, they are also distinguished by differences.[80] A reduction in sea-ice nowadays, harsh environmental conditions and the remoteness of operations are some of the features of Polar waters.

Against this background, a legal regime governing liability in the Antarctic was elaborated by the international community. It stems from the so-called Liability Annex (adopted in 2005, not entered into force yet), i.e. the Antarctic Treaty Environmental Protocol Liability Annex.

Technically speaking, this is Annex VI to the Protocol on Environmental Protection to the Antarctic Treaty. The Liability Annex gives for the first time a liability regime proper to the activities in Antarctica. This is despite the fact that incidents in the Antarctic waters have not been of the same dimension as major oil spills experienced in other parts of the world.[81]

That said, the Annex should be understood in the context of the Antarctic Treaty (adopted in 1959; entry into force in 1961). The Treaty set the premises for peaceful use and cooperation among the States with interests in the region. In this context, the status of territorial claims of a number of interested Parties was frozen and military activities and nuclear explosions were banned.[82]

The Protocol on Environmental Protection to the Antarctic Treaty was adopted in 1991 (entry into force in 1998); it banned all activities relating to mineral resources, including oil drilling and mineral extraction, with the exception of scientific research. Disposal of wastes was also regulated.

The Liability Annex provides for strict liability, i.e. it establishes a not fault-based liability. The Annex applies to environmental emergencies which relate to scientific research programmes, tourism and all other governmental and non-governmental activities in the Antarctic Treaty area.[83] The Annex will also apply to tourist vessels that enter the Antarctic Treaty area, and to environmental emergencies which relate to other vessels and activities as may be decided. Each operator, i.e. natural or legal person organising activities in the Antarctic Treaty area, is held to take prompt and effective response action to environmental

---

80 For example, Arctic navigation is primarily destination-driven and it largely relates to natural resource development.

81 A number of incidents involving fishing vessels, yachts, etc. are reported in ASOC (Antarctic and Southern Ocean Coalition), 'Follow-up to Vessel Incidents in Antarctic Waters', Antarctic Treaty Consultative Meeting XXXV, Hobart 2012, p. 7.

82 E.T. Bloom, 'Introductory Note to Antarctic Treaty Environmental Protocol Liability Annex' [2006] International Legal Materials 45(1), 1–4.

83 Article 1.

emergencies arising from its activities.[84] If an operator fails in that regard, it will be liable to pay the costs of the response action, if any, taken by others.[85]

The instrument sets out specified limits of liability in conjunction with tonnage.[86] Like other instruments on limitation of liability, the right to limit may be lost in specified circumstances. Interestingly, the provisions on limits of liability do not affect the right to limit liability under any applicable international limitation of liability treaty (e.g. LLMC 1976, as amended).

BIBLIOGRAPHY

Anderson, Helen (ed), *Director's Personal Liability for Corporate Fault – a Comparative Analysis* (Wolters Kluwer Law & Business, Netherlands, 2008)

Antarctic and Southern Ocean Coalition (ASOC), 'Follow-Up to Vessel Incidents in Antarctic Waters', Antarctic Treaty Consultative Meeting XXXV, Hobart 2012, p. 7

Bahamas Maritime Authority (The), *Report of the Investigation Into the Loss of the Bahamian Registered Tanker "Prestige" off the Northwest Coast of Spain on 19th November 2002* (2004)

Bloom, E.T., 'Introductory Note to Antarctic Treaty Environmental Protocol Liability Annex' [2006] International Legal Materials 45(1), 1–4.

Christodoulou-Varotsi, Iliana, 'Recent Developments in the EC Legal Framework on Ship-Source Pollution: The Ambivalence of the EC's Penal Approach' [Fall 2006] Transportation Law Journal 33(3), 371–386

Council (EU) Framework Decision 2005/667/JHA [2005] OJ L255/164

Council of Europe, Resolution 1869(2012) adopted on 9.3.2012, Doc. 12872, 'The Environmental Impact of Sunken Shipwrecks'

European Parliament and Council (EC) Directive 2009/20 on the insurance of shipowners for maritime claims (Text with EEA relevance) [2009] OJ L 131/128

EMSA, *EU States Claims Management Guidelines – Claims Arising Due to Marine Pollution Incidents* (2012) p. 16

European Parliament and Council (EC) Directive 2005/35 of 7 September 2005 on Ship-Source Pollution and on the Introduction of Penalties for Infringements [2005] OJ L 255/11

European Parliament and Council (EC) Directive 2009/123/EC amending Directive 2005/35/EC on ship-source pollution and on the introduction of penalties for infringements (Text with EEA relevance) [2009] OJ L280/52

Griggs, Patrick, CBE, 'Law of Wrecks' in David J. Attard (General Ed), *The IMLI Manual on International Maritime Law, Volume II, Shipping Law* (Oxford University Press, Oxford, 2016), pp. 502–512

Gutiérrez, Norman A Martínez, 'Limitation of Liability for Maritime Claims' in David Joseph Attard (General Ed), *The IMLI Manual on International Maritime Law*, Volume II, *Shipping Law* (Oxford University Press 2016), pp. 551–575

Hawke, Neil, 'Corporate Environmental Crime: Why Shouldn't Directors Be Liable?' [1997] The London Journal of Canadian Studies 13, 12–24.

IOPC Funds, *Claims Manual* (IOPC Funds, 2016)

---

84 Article 5.
85 Article 6.
86 Article 9.

IOPC Funds, *The International Regime for Compensation for Oil Pollution Damage, Explanatory Note* (IOPC Funds, 2017)

Juste-Ruiz, José, European Courts Go Beyond the IMO Conventions on Civil Liability for Oil Pollution Damage, Insight dating to 5 April 2013, MEPIELAN Centre E-bulletin

Mandaraka-Sheppard, Aleka, *Modern Maritime Law, Volume 2, Managing Risks and Liabilities* (3rd edition, Informa Law, Routledge, 2013)

Maritime Executive, Plastic Pollution in the Antarctic Worse than Expected (19 June 2017)

Rogowska, J., and Namiésik, J., 'Environmental Risk Assessment of WWII Shipwreck Pollution' in S.K. Sharma and R. Sanghi (eds), *Wastewater Reuse and Management* (Springer, Heidelberg, 2013)

Rue, Colin de la, and Anderson, Charles B., *Shipping and the Environment* (2nd edition, LLP, London/New York, 2009)

Transport Canada, *Maritime Transport of Hazardous and Noxious Substances: Liability and Compensation*, Discussion Paper, International Maritime Policy (October 2010)

Tsimplis, Michael, 'Marine Pollution from Shipping Activities' in Yvonne Baatz (ed), *Maritime Law* (3rd edition, Informa Law, Routledge, 2014) pp 368–427

INDEX

accidental spillage: meaning 32
air pollution 179–204; bioenergy/
   biofuels 203; contribution of shipping
   to 181–3; EU emission trading scheme
   191–2; EU level regulatory framework
   188–92; glossary 182–3; IAPPC 193;
   IEEC 193–4; IMO's fuel consumption
   data 202; inspections 192–3; key
   management issues streaming from
   EU regime 199–200; liquefied natural
   gas 202; market–based approaches
   201; MARPOL 73/78 Annex VI
   80–1 *see also* MARPOL Annex VI;
   Monitoring, Reporting and Verification
   Regulation 190–1, 199–200; nature of
   problem 180; post state control 200–1;
   recent European Union developments
   202; regulatory and non–regulatory
   approaches 184; regulatory framework
   183–92; SEEMP 194–9; surveys
   192–3; who is working on agenda 184
Amoco Cadiz 35–6
Antarctic, protection of: limitation of
   liability, and 332–3
anti–fouling systems 206–32; AFS
   convention 217–18; best management
   practices 218–20; certification 218;
   key terms/definitions 207; nature of
   problem 216–20; surveys 218
AQUAPOL 239
Arctic: EU policy for 25
atmospheric pollution: offshore oil and gas
   industry 67

ballast water 206–32; BWM convention
   213; documentation 213–5;
   international regulations 209–13;
   interphase with marine environment
   208; key management issues 213–5;
   key terms/definitions 207; MEPC. 279
   (70) 210–3; post state control 215–6;

Baltic Sea: sewage 116–7
Basel Convention: wastes 138–40
best industry practices: marine pollution
   from oil, and 49–50
bio energy 203
biofuels 203
Bunker Pollution Convention 2001 326–7

cargo record book 174
cargo residues: definition 131
carriage of chemicals by sea 156–78;
   European Union Regulation 1272/2008
   164–5; GESAMP hazard profiles
   163–4; glossary 160–1; MARPOL
   Annex II *see* MARPOL Annex II;
   MARPOL Annex III 171–2 *see also*
   MARPOL Annex III; selected systems
   of classification 161–5; Standard
   European Behaviour Classification 163;
   UN GHS 161–2
challenges for preparedness and response
   247–8
chemicals: nature of 156; offshore oil and
   gas industry, and 66
civil liability 305–6
classification societies 20–1; history of
   20; nature of 20
CLC 315–25
CLEE 1977 85
Clean Water Act: civil liability 96–8;
   financial responsibility 98–9; USA
   95–9
climate change: contribution of
   shipping to 181–3; who is working
   on agenda 184
coastal states: role 11–19; UNCLOS III,
   and 13–19
compensation 296–7
coordinated framework 234–59; glossary
   239–41; UNCLOS III 235–7
criminal law 296

335

INDEX

criminal liability 306–10
criminalisation of seafarers 286–90
customary international law: offshore oil and gas industry 69

damages loss and claims 297–305; damage–related costs 298; involvement of IOPC funds 198–300; P&I clubs 300–1; salvors, involvement of 301–2
dangerous goods: meaning 157
discharge: MARPOL 73/78 definition 76
drill cuttings: offshore oil and gas industry, and 65
drilling fluid: offshore oil and gas industry, and 64–65
dumping: definition 130–1; London Convention 1972 82–3; offshore oil and gas industry, and 67

emission control areas 185–6
EMSA 238–9
energy efficiency design index 187
environmental regulations: current position 26; future of 26–8
Erika 37
Espoo Convention 88–9
European Union 21–5; agenda on marine pollution, future of 24–5; Arctic, policy for 25; CFP 22; contribution of 21–5; IMP 22; Marine Directive 21–2; maritime safety policy 22–3; maritime transport policy 22; monitoring, reporting and verification system 24; private operators, and 23–4; regulatory framework 21–5; sewage 117–8; WFD 22
EU Directive 2005/35 as amended 309–10
EU Directive 2009/20/EC 313–4
European Union regulation 1272/2008 164–5

fatigue 285–6
flag states: role 11–19; UNCLOS III, and 13
Formal Safety Assessment: approach 4
Four Pillars of shipping legislation 5, 6
FPSO & FSU Guidelines 79
fuel oil tankers: protection 44–5
Fund Convention 1992 315–25

garbage: definition 129; options for shipboard handling and discharge 142; wastes, and 128

garbage management: definition 129
garbage management and disposal: MARPOL 73/78 Annex V 79–80
Garbage Management Plans 145
garbage record book 146–7
Geneva Conventions 1958: offshore oil and gas industry 69–70
GESAMP: offshore oil and gas industry, and 60
GESAMP hazard profiles 163–4
GHS 161–2
grey water: definition 129

harmful substances: MARPOL 73/78 definitions 78; meaning 157–8
Hazardous and Noxious Substances (HNS) 158–9
hazardous chemicals: nature of 156–7
Hebei Spirit 37
hot pursuit: right of 16
human element 261–9; identifying 262–6; ILO MLC 2006 268–74; ISM Code 279–85; key management issues 290–3; key terms/definitions 266–8; regulatory framework 268–90; STCW 2010 274–9

IAPPC 193
IEEC 193–4
ILO MLC 2006 268–74
IMSAS: sewage 121–2
industry best practice 26
international law 296
International Maritime Organisation 5–10, 237–8; adoption of conventions 7–9; amending existing instruments 8; circulars 9; codes 9; conventions 9; description 5–7; draft instruments 8; fuel consumption data 202; protocols 9; resolutions 9; role 5–10; ship certification 9; structure 5–7; typology of acts 9
IMO Guide to Good Practice for Port Reception Facility Providers and Users: sewage 115–9
international oil pollution prevention certificate 48
International Organisation for Standardisation 26
International Safety Management Code: marine pollution from oil, and 48–9
international sewage pollution prevention certificate 120–1

336

INDEX

INTERPOL 239
intervention rights on high seas 234–59; glossary 239–41; UNCLOS III 235–7
IOPC Funds 298–300
IOPPC 48
ISM Code 279–85; marine pollution from oil, and 48–9
ISO 21070; definition 130

Kiev Agreement 87

landmark accidents: impact on legal framework 234
legal aspects of marine pollution from ships 295–334
liability, types of 305–10
limitation of liability 310–333; Antarctic, protection of 332–3; Bunker Pollution Convention 2001 326–7; CLC 315–25; concept 310–1; EU Directive 2009/20/EC 313–4; Fund Convention 1992 315–25; HNS Convention 2010 327–9; LLMC 311–3; maximum limits of compensation 317; Nairobi Convention 2007 329–30; radioactive substances, carriage of 330–1; STUPIA 2006 325; Supplementary Fund Protocol 2003 315–25; TOPIA 2006 325
liquefied natural gas 202
London Convention 1972 81–3; dumping 82–3; limitations 91; offshore oil and gas industry 81–3; wastes 133–5
London Protocol 1996; wastes 135–7

managerial aspects of response 251–8; challenges 254–8
marine debris: key land and ocean–based sources 127
marine mammals: ship strikes with 226–7
marine pollutant: meaning 158
marine pollution: accidental spillage 32; *Amoco Cadiz* 35; best industry practices 49–50; causes of large oil spills 34; certification 46–8; challenges 32–41; definitions 39–41; documentation 46–50; effects 33; enforcement 52–5; *Erika* 37; *Hebei Spirit* 37; international oil pollution prevention certificate 48; implementation 52–5; International Safety Management Code 48–9; key management issues 46–50; key terms 39–41; MARPOL Annex I 38–9, 41–6

see also MARPOL Annex I; *Nakhodka* 36; national jurisdiction 52–5; oil record book 47–8; operation at time of incident for large oil spills 34; port state control 38–9; *Prestige* 37; Polar Code 51–2; reduction 33; selected cases 52–5; ship–to–ship transfer of crude oil and petroleum products 50–1; shipboard oil pollution contingency plan 47; surveys 46–8; *Torrey Canyon* 35
marine pollution control regulatory framework overview 10
marine pollution from oil 31–56
marine pollution outside scope of MARPOL 206–32
MARPOL 73/78 75–81; Annex I: regulations for preparation of pollution by oil 76–9; application 76–7; compliance 77; harmful substances 78; oil filtering equipment 77–8 *see also* MARPOL Annex I; Annex V: garbage management and disposal 79–80 *see also* MARPOL Annex V; Annex VI: air pollution 80–1; discharge, definition 76 *see also* MARPOL Annex VI; FPSO & FSU Guidelines 79; limitations 91; offshore oil and gas industry, and 75–81; ships, definition 75
MARPOL Annex I 38–9, 41–6; construction requirements 44; control of operational discharge of oil from machinery spaces 45; discharges from cargo area of oil tankers 46; key resolutions 42–4; overview of legal basis 41–2; protection of fuel oil tanks 44–5; structure 42
MARPOL Annex II 166–71; IBC Code, and 166–7; cargo record book 174; categorisation of noxious liquid substances 167–8; certificates 172–4; design and construction 168–9; discharge prohibitions 169–70; material scope of application 167; Polar Code 170–1; port reception facilities 175–6; port state control on operational requirements 174–5; procedures and arrangements manual 174; shipboard marine pollution emergency plan for noxious liquid substances 174; surveys 172–4; verification of compliance 170
MARPOL Annex III 171–2; documentation 176–7; exceptions

INDEX

172; labelling 172; marking 172; material scope of application 171–2; NLS certificate 173–4; packing 172; port state control on operational requirements 177; quantity limitations 172; stowage 172; substantial requirements 172

MARPOL Annex V 140–53; areas of special interest 151–3; communication and advance notice of wastes 149–50; considerations during MARPOL residues/wastes delivery 150; considerations prior to delivery of residues/wastes onshore 147; documentation 144–50; garbage record book 146–7; Garbage Management Plans 144–5; general prohibition 141; good practices for shipmasters, shipowners and operators 147–50; logistical and commercial arrangements 147–8; key management issues 144–50; key regulations 141; minimization and management of ship–generated residue/waste 148–9; overview 140–4; placards 145–6; port reception facilities, adequacy of 151; port state control findings 152; summary of restrictions to discharge of garbage 143

MARPOL Annex VI 184–8; control of emissions of nitrogen oxide 186; emission control areas 185–6; identifying challenges 187–8; measures involving ship energy efficiency 186–7; regulation of ozone–depleting substances 186; setting sulphur caps on content of marine fuels 185; sewage 109, 110–9, 120–1

Monitoring, Reporting and Verification Regulation 190–1

MRV Regulation 199–200

Nairobi Convention 2007 329–30
Nakhodka 36
National Contingency Plan: USA 102–3
national jurisdictions: marine pollution from oil, and 52–5
nitrogen oxides: control of emissions 186
NLS certificate 173–4
non–governmental organisations 25–6; contribution 25–6

offshore oil and gas industry 57–94; atmospheric pollution 67; chemicals 66; CLEE 1977 85; customary international law 69; deleterious ecological effects 63; domestic legal sources 68; drill cuttings 65; drilling fluid 64–5; dumping 67; Espoo Convention 88–9; future directions 92–3; Geneva Conventions 1958 69–70; GESAMP, and 60; international instruments addressing liability, clean up and compensation 83–6; international instruments addressing specific pollution sources 75–83; international law and policy 68–90; international legal framework 61–2, 68–75; international policy statements 86–9; Kiev Agreement 87; limits of international legal framework 90–2; London Convention 1972 81–3 *see also* London Convention 1972; maritime zones under coastal state jurisdiction 68; MARPOL 73/78 *see* MARPOL 73/78; Offshore Pollution Liability Agreement 1974 84–5; oil 64; OPRC 1990 85–6; OSPAR Convention 89–90; pollution created by 57–94; pollution from seabed activities 64–67; produced water 65–6; sound production 66; regional agreements 89–90; regulating pollution from 60–2; relative contribution to pollution 60; Rio Draft 60; source of pollution, as 58–9; specific sources of pollution 61, 63–7; Stockholm Declaration 1972 69; UNCED 86–7; UNCLOS III 70–75, 83–4 *see also* UNCLOS III; UNEP 87–8; vessels, pollution from 67

Offshore Pollution Liability Agreement 1974 84–5

oil: definition 32; offshore oil and gas industry, and 64

Oil Pollution Act 1990: civil liability 96–8; financial responsibility 98–9; USA 95–9

oil record book 47–8

oil spill management 251–4

oil tankers, cargo area of: discharges from 46

operational discharge of oil: machinery spaces, from 45

operational wastes: definition 130

OPOL 1974: limitations 91

OPRC 1990 85–6; limitations 91–2

OPRC Convention 242–4

338

INDEX

OPRC–HNS Protocol 244–6
ozone–depleting substances:
   regulation 186

P&I Clubs 300–1
placards: MARPOL Annex V 145–6
Polar Code: marine pollution from oil, and
   51–2; MARPOL Annex II, and 170–1;
   sewage 119; wastes, and 152–3
pollution of the marine environment:
   meaning 2; UNCLOS III definition 63
port reception facility: definition 131
port state control: air pollution 200–1;
   ballast water 215–6; marine pollution
   by oil, and 38–9; USA 101–2
port states: role 11–9; UNCLOS III,
   and 13–9
Prestige 37
private operators: EU, and 23–4;
   UNCLOS III, and 19
produced water: offshore oil and gas
   industry, and 65–6
protection of marine environment: legal
   instruments 3; priority, as 3

radioactive substances, carriage of:
   limitations of liability 330–1
regional framework 248–9
REMPEC 249–51
Rio Draft 60

salvors: damages loss and claims, and
   301–2
SEEMP 194–9
self–regulation: concept 4–5
sewage 107–23; areas of special interest
   in relation to legal framework 121–2;
   Baltic Sea 116–7; best practice
   121; certification 120–1; challenges
   for marine environment 107–10;
   control of discharges into sea 113–5;
   definition 129; discharge of 111–2;
   documentation 120–1; European
   Union 117–8; IMO guide to Good
   Practice for Port Reception Facility,
   Providers and Users 115–9; IMSAS
   121–2; international sewage pollution
   prevention certificate 120–1; key
   management issues 120–1; key terms
   and definitions 109–10; legal basis,
   overview 110–9; MARPOL Annex IV
   109, 110–9, 120–1; meaning 107–10;
   operational requirements 119; Polar

waters 119; reception facilities 115–9;
   statistics 108; summarised framework
   of prohibitions of discharge 114;
   surveys 120–1; USA 118–9
ship certification: IMO, and 9
ship energy efficiency: measures involving
   186–7
ship recycling 206–32; EU action 224–6;
   Hong Kong Convention 2009220–4;
   key terms/definitions 207; nature of
   problem 220
ship–to–ship transfer of crude oil and
   petroleum products 50–1
shipboard oil pollution contingency
   plan 47
shipping legislation: four pillars 5, 6
ships: MARPOL 73/78 definition 75
sound production: offshore oil and gas
   industry, and 66
special area: definition 131
spill notification requirements: USA 103
spill response contracts 246–7
Standard European Behaviour
   Classification: chemicals 163
standard–setting process 3–5; Formal
   Safety Assessment approach 4; nature
   of 3–5; prescriptive approach 3–4;
   self–regulation 4
state obligations to protect and preserve
   marine environment: UNCLOS III 71
state obligations to regulate dumping:
   UNCLOS III 72–4
state obligations to regulate pollution from
   activities carried out in area: UNCLOS
   III 75
state obligations to regulate pollution from
   or through atmosphere: UNCLOS II 74
state obligations to regulate pollution from
   seabed activities: UNCLOS III 72
STCW 2010 274–9
Stockholm Declaration 1972: offshore oil
   and gas industry 69
STOPIA 2006 325
sulphur caps: setting on content of marine
   fuels 185

TOPIA 2006 325
Torrey Canyon 35
transboundary movement: definition 131

UNCED 86–7
UNCLOS III 11–26, 70–5, 235–7;
   coastal states, and 13–19;

INDEX

compensation 83–4; contents 11; flag states, and 13–19; limitations 90; marine pollution enforcement powers 14; offshore oil and gas industry 70–5; part XII 12–13; pollution of the marine environment, definition 63; port states, and 13–19; private operators, and 19; state obligations to protect and preserve marine environment 71; state obligations to regulate dumping 72–4; state obligations to regulate pollution from activities carried out in area 75; sate obligations to regulate pollution from or through atmosphere 74; state obligations to regulate pollution from seabed activities 72; waste 133

underwater energy, monitoring of: EU action 229–31

underwater noise emissions 227–9

UNEP 87–8, 238

UN Recommendations on the Transport of Dangerous Goods 165–6

United States of America 95–106; Clean Water Act 95–9; civil and criminal penalties 104–5; framework for prevention and response to marine oil pollution incidents 95–106; marine oil pollution 95–106; National Contingency Plan 102–3; Oil Pollution Act 1990 95–9;penalities for failure to comply with response plan requirements 102; port state control 101–2; prevention of pollution 99–102; response 102–5; sewage 118–9; spill notification requirements 103; vessel response plans 99–101

vessels: offshore oil and gas industry 67

vessel response plans: USA 99–101

wastes 125–54; Basel Convention 138–40; definition 127–8, 130; garbage, and 128; general regulatory framework 131–40; identifying problem 125–8; Jeddah Convention 131,133; key land and ocean–based sources 127; key terms and definitions 128–31; legislative background 131–40;London Convention 1972 133–5; London Protocol 1996 135–7; management hierarchy showing priority and less preferred options 127; MARPOL Annex V *see* MARPOL Annex V; Polar Code 152–3; regulation of discharges of dumping (non exhaustive list of related instruments) 132; statistics 126; UNCLOS III 133